SCHOOLS FOR STATESMEN

Schools
for
Statesmen

The Divergent Educations of the
Constitution's Framers

ANDREW H. BROWNING

 University Press of Kansas

Published by the University Press of Kansas (Lawrence, Kansas 66045), which was organized by the Kansas Board of Regents and is operated and funded by Emporia State University, Fort Hays State University, Kansas State University, Pittsburg State University, the University of Kansas, and Wichita State University

Library of Congress Cataloging-in-Publication Data

Names: Browning, Andrew H., author.
Title: Schools for statesmen : the divergent educations of the constitution's framers / Andrew H. Browning.
Description: Lawrence : University Press of Kansas, 2022. | Includes bibliographical references and index.
Identifiers: LCCN 2021038325
  ISBN 9780700633098 (cloth)
  ISBN 9780700633104 (ebook)
Subjects: LCSH: Education—United States—History—18th century. | Education—History—18th century. | Statesmen—Education—United States—History—18th century. | Universities and colleges—United States—History—18th century. | Universities and colleges—History—18th century. | Founding Fathers of the United States—Education. | United States. Constitution.
Classification: LCC LA206 .B76 2022 | DDC 370.97309/033—dc23/eng/20211221
LC record available at https://lccn.loc.gov/2021038325.

British Library Cataloguing-in-Publication Data is available.

Printed in the United States of America

10 9 8 7 6 5 4 3 2 1

The paper used in this publication meets the minimum requirements of the American National Standard for Permanence of Paper for Printed Library Materials Z39.48-1992.

To my sons, Mark and David

CONTENTS

DELEGATES TO THE 1787 FEDERAL CONVENTION: AGE AND EDUCATION

New Hampshire

NICHOLAS GILMAN, 32 (Exeter, NH, common school)

JOHN LANGDON, 46 (Portsmouth, NH, grammar school)

Massachusetts

ELBRIDGE GERRY, 43 (tutored by John Barnard?; Harvard)

NATHANIEL GORHAM, 49 (Charleston, MA, common school)

RUFUS KING, 32 (Dummer School; Harvard)

CALEB STRONG, 42 (tutored by Samuel Moody; Harvard)

Connecticut

OLIVER ELLSWORTH, 42 (tutored by Joseph Bellamy; Yale; Princeton)

WILLIAM SAMUEL JOHNSON, 59 (tutored by his father, Samuel Johnson; Yale)

ROGER SHERMAN, 66 (self-taught)

New York

ALEXANDER HAMILTON, 32 (Elizabethtown Academy; King's College)

JOHN LANSING, 33 (Albany, NY, common school)

ROBERT YATES, 49 (New York City grammar school)

New Jersey

DAVID BREARLEY, 42 (unknown)

JONATHAN DAYTON, 26 (Elizabethtown Academy; Princeton)

WILLIAM CHURCHILL HOUSTON, 41 (Presbyterian school in North Carolina; Princeton)

WILLIAM LIVINGSTON, 63 (tutored by Henry Barclay; Yale)

WILLIAM PATERSON, 41 (Princeton)

Pennsylvania

GEORGE CLYMER, 47 (self-taught)

THOMAS FITZSIMONS, 46 (Irish hedge school?)

BENJAMIN FRANKLIN, 81 (self-taught)

JARED INGERSOLL, 37 (Hopkins School; Yale; Middle Temple)

THOMAS MIFFLIN, 43 (Friends' Public School; College of Philadelphia)
GOUVERNEUR MORRIS, 35 (Philadelphia Academy; King's College)
ROBERT MORRIS, 53 (tutored by Rev. Mr. Gordon)
JAMES WILSON, 45 (Cupar Grammar School; St. Andrews; Glasgow)

Delaware
RICHARD BASSETT, 42 (unknown)
GUNNING BEDFORD JR., 40 (Philadelphia Academy; Princeton)
JACOB BROOM, 35 (Wilmington Old Academy?)
JOHN DICKINSON, 54 (tutored by William Killen; Middle Temple)
GEORGE READ, 53 (New London Academy)

Maryland
DANIEL CARROLL, 56 (St. Omer's)
LUTHER MARTIN, 43 (Princeton)
JAMES MCHENRY, 33 (Presbyterian academy in Dublin; Newark Academy)
JOHN FRANCIS MERCER, 28 (tutored at home; William and Mary)
DANIEL OF ST. THOMAS JENIFER, 64 (tutored or King William's School?)

Virginia
JOHN BLAIR, 55 (William and Mary; Middle Temple)
JAMES MADISON, 36 (Donald Robertson's school; tutored by Thomas Martin; Princeton)
GEORGE MASON, 61 (tutored by Henry Williams; self-taught)
JAMES MCCLURG, 41 (William and Mary; Edinburgh)
EDMUND RANDOLPH, 33 (William and Mary)
GEORGE WASHINGTON, 55 (tutored by John Hobby?; self-taught)
GEORGE WYTHE, 61 (self-taught)

North Carolina
WILLIAM BLOUNT, 38 (tutored at home)
WILLIAM RICHARDSON DAVIE, 31 (Queen's Museum; Princeton)
ALEXANDER MARTIN, 47 (New London Academy; Princeton)
RICHARD DOBBS SPAIGHT, 29 (tutored in Ireland?; Glasgow)
HUGH WILLIAMSON, 51 (New London Academy; College of Philadelphia; Edinburgh)

South Carolina
PIERCE BUTLER, 42 (tutored at home in Ireland; self-taught)
CHARLES PINCKNEY, 29 (tutored by David Oliphant)

CHARLES COTESWORTH PINCKNEY, 41 (Westminster School; Oxford; Middle Temple)

JOHN RUTLEDGE, 46 (tutored by David Rhind; Middle Temple)

Georgia

ABRAHAM BALDWIN, 34 (Guilford grammar school; Yale)

WILLIAM FEW, 39 (self-taught)

WILLIAM HOUSTOUN, 32 (tutored?; Inner Temple?)

WILLIAM PIERCE, 34 (William and Mary?)

Harvard, Oxford, GEORGE WASHINGTON, and BENJAMIN FRANKLIN are familiar names today. WILLIAM FEW, JACOB BROOM, and the College of St. Omer were obscure even in 1787, but they were not likely to be mistaken for other people or institutions with the same names. However, there was often confusion in their own lifetimes between JAMES MADISON (the Framer and future president of the United States) and his cousin James Madison (the president of the College of William and Mary), and there were at least five Charles Pinckneys living in Charleston, South Carolina. Not only did eighteenth-century American families have a marked tendency toward repetition, but the popularity of the first names George, William, James, and Charles (the recent kings of England), and the limited number of last names in an almost entirely Anglo-Scottish society make one grateful for the occasional ELBRIDGE GERRY. Dr. Samuel Johnson could be either the great English poet and lexicographer or the first president of King's College, father of the Framer WILLIAM SAMUEL JOHNSON. Even scholars of the period have been known to confuse the numerous influential William Smiths. Moreover, individuals and institutions could change titles and names: the William Smith who arrived in New York in 1751 was ordained the Rev. William Smith in 1753 and became Provost William Smith of the College of Philadelphia in 1755; that college was renamed the University of the State of Pennsylvania in 1779 and then the University of Pennsylvania in 1791. James Madison (cousin of the Framer) became the Rev. Mr. Madison in 1775 and Bishop Madison in 1790, but from 1777, when he took on the presidency of the College of William and Mary, until the federal election of 1808, anyone who spoke of "President Madison" meant him and not his cousin. To minimize confusion, the names of the Framers have been set in a SMALL CAPITALS; DANIEL OF ST. THOMAS JENIFER is the delegate to the convention, but Daniel of St. Thomas Jenifer is his namesake grandfather.

Besides numerous individuals, there are also schools to keep straight. King's College became Columbia after the Revolution; the College of New Jersey was sometimes called Nassau Hall after its primary building but was already becoming known by its location as Princeton. (In 1996, Trenton State College renamed itself the College of New Jersey, complicating things further.) There have been no significant changes in the names of the Scottish or English universities, but Queen's College, Oxford, must not be confused with the Queen's College in New Jersey that became Rutgers or the Queen's College (also called Queen's Museum) in Charlotte, North Carolina, preparatory school of WILLIAM RICHARDSON DAVIE. "College" was an ambiguous term: Christ Church College was a subordinate part of the University of Oxford, but the College of William and Mary was an independent institution; neither St. Omer's College nor North Carolina's Queen's College had the authority to confer degrees, but their graduates might receive one elsewhere after only a year or two. Secondary schools were especially important at a time when few students went on to pursue college degrees. I avoid the confusing modern name of Philadelphia's William Penn Charter School, which is not a "charter school" in the popular sense, preferring Friends' Public School, the name used when THOMAS MIFFLIN was a student. The school attended by RUFUS KING near Newbury, Massachusetts, was first called the Dummer School and then for many years Governor Dummer Academy; recently it has rebranded itself as The Governor's Academy. In general, I have tried to use names that were current when the Framers were students, but I have made it my first rule to avoid confusion.

Spelling was unpredictable in a largely oral age; John Adams thought WILLIAM CHURCHILL HOUSTON's last name was "Euston," which tells us it was pronounced differently from that of Georgia's WILLIAM HOUSTON (or HOUSTOUN)—pronounced "howston" like the Manhattan street that was named for him. MADISON, who was already acquainted with both men, evidently kept them straight himself simply by pronunciation—although he is almost always careful to distinguish between the two Pinckney cousins. He spells many names inconsistently (usually Patterson but sometimes Paterson, Elseworth or Elsworth rather than Ellsworth, Rutledge or Rutlidge, Dickinson or Dickenson, and Pinkney as often as Pinckney). Most of the other Framers spelled *his* name Maddison. JAMES MCCLURG was frequently M'Clurg or McLurg, even to his old classmate Thomas Jefferson, and WILLIAM PIERCE's good friend St. George Tucker wrote to him as Pearce. Historians remain divided between Brearley and Brearly for the New Jersey Framer.

The two CHARLES PINCKNEYS and WILLIAM HOUSTONS are not the only pairs of Founders who must be kept straight. In the following pages, LUTHER MARTIN and ALEXANDER MARTIN will almost always be given their full names, as will ROBERT MORRIS and GOUVERNEUR MORRIS (whose first name received every spelling imaginable, even among those who knew him well, and was evidently pronounced "Gooveneer"). Careful distinction will be made among the William Smiths who were so important in New York and Philadelphia, and among the multiple James Madisons, John Mercers, and George Masons. Readers need not fear but may consider themselves warned.

Introduction

There is no shortage of books about the Constitution of the United States, but this book is about the individuals who created that document, and in particular about the ways their different educations yielded different assumptions about government and thus influenced their behavior at the Federal Convention in 1787. The new Constitution replaced a governing framework, the Articles of Confederation, that had only recently been adopted, and the change was opposed by a significant segment of the population. It was the work of a very mixed group who argued, sometimes bitterly, for more than three months before arriving at a final draft that none of them thought was ideal. These individuals have been hailed as an assembly of demigods, condemned both as elitists and as radicals, accused of making a pact with the devil, and praised for creating a charter of freedom.[1] Too often we speak of "what the Framers had in mind," glossing over their many disagreements. More than ever, amid the bitterly contentious politics of the twenty-first century, we need to be aware of the reasons behind the Framers' arguments over the relative power exercised by state legislatures or the voting public, over the ways of electing and removing presidents, and—most of all—over the complex system of checks and balances that JAMES MADISON and his supporters believed would prevent the tyranny of faction. But if we are ever to understand how they produced the Constitution that the states went on to ratify, we must see them as distinct individuals, and we must consider not only their positions at the Convention but the variety of formative experiences that led different Framers to find different arguments persuasive or unconvincing. To that end, we must examine an aspect

[1]

of their lives that is too often overlooked: the different educations that shaped their understanding of politics, government, and human nature.

Who were these individuals, and why had they out of all their countrymen come together in Philadelphia in the spring and summer of 1787? What had prepared the rising generation of MADISON, HAMILTON, and GOUVERNEUR MORRIS (all in their thirties) to take the lead in designing the lasting frame of government that such experienced statesmen as WASHINGTON and DICK-INSON (in their fifties) or LIVINGSTON and SHERMAN (in their sixties) seemed unable to devise? Historians have struggled to explain the Framers' decision to exceed their mandate to revise the Articles of Confederation, choosing instead to scrap a system that had been ratified only six years earlier and was still widely popular. Why did these particular individuals finally settle on the document that they adopted? Explanations have historically fallen into five broad categories: (1) the Framers' personal financial motives, (2) their republican (or else classically liberal) ideology, (3) their experience in the Revolutionary War, (4) their religious beliefs, and—most recently—(5) their "elitism." Each of these influences offers its insights, but none alone is sufficient to explain what happened.[2]

The Framers shared common concerns about both the nation's and their own financial welfare. Even those who had not taken leadership roles in the Revolution were locally prominent men, and—like their Anti-Federalist adversaries who opposed ratification—they were concerned with preserving their own influence in society. But delegates from the same regions, or of the same generations, with the same economic interests and the same wartime experience and often the same church membership, could nonetheless approach questions from fundamentally different directions, disagreeing on basic assumptions. Indeed, their disagreements threatened to derail the entire Convention until they were resolved by unexpected compromises. (The genesis of the most critical of these—the Great Compromise over the states' representation in Congress—has never been adequately explained.) Those who would rationalize the Constitution in terms of financial interests or "elitism" must account for these differences between men of similar social and economic standing. Forrest McDonald's careful analysis of individual Framers' economic interests in relation to their voting patterns at the Convention has not been superseded. He summarizes one of many examples: "The conflict over the proposal to grant to Congress exclusive power over commerce was partly one of personal interests, partly one of state and sectional interests, and partly one of opinions based on little more than abstract philosophy." What he then says about the states' ratifying conventions is just as true of the Framers themselves: "A substantial number of delegates who believed that their interests would be improved by the adoption of the Constitution voted for it," but others comparably situated did not. "A large number favored ratification on philosophical grounds, and [others] opposed it on similar grounds."[3]

What accounts for their conflicting "philosophical grounds"? The Framers themselves probably would have agreed with New Jersey's WILLIAM LIVINGSTON. A 1741 graduate of Yale, LIVINGSTON wrote:

> Whatever Principles are imbibed at a College, will run thro' a Man's future Conduct, and affect the Society of which he is a Member, in proportion to his Sphere of Activity; especially if it is considered that even after we arrive at Years of Maturity, instead of entering upon the difficult and disagreeable Work of examining the Principles we have formerly entertained, we rather exert ourselves in searching for Arguments to maintain and support them.

Gideon Mailer has recently noted, "In 1725, Francis Hutcheson suggested that 'strong affections' excited the pursuit of virtuous action and could be understood self-consciously for the first time during youth. This was an impressionable phase, which Hutcheson's student Hugh Blair later described as a stage 'when your character is now . . . of your own forming; your fate is, in some measure, put into your own hands.'" Blair, the influential Edinburgh professor of rhetoric, told his students that their school years "will form the channel in which your life is to run." It is thus essential that we know *what* principles were acquired in the Framers' own youth, *how* and *where* they were "imbibed," and *why* they differed so much. Those different principles were felt from the opening days of the Convention; they were evident in the competing proposals about what that Constitution should say, in the numerous objections that were raised, and often in the reasons why some arguments ultimately proved acceptable to some Framers who had initially resisted them. Ideas absorbed in their formative years could even make some more inclined to seek accommodation or make others less likely to compromise. Indeed, the Framers' different educations help explain why some were among the Convention's most persuasive speakers while others remained silent throughout the long summer.[4]

It is the thesis of this book that critical agreements and disagreements at the Constitutional Convention cannot be understood without examining the very different educations of the various Framers. But any discussion of their educations must first sort out numerous troubling errors and contradictions that have accumulated over time. As recently as 2015, one of the most prominent historians of the period wrote, "Twenty-nine had college degrees, and the same number had studied law"; the correct numbers, as we shall see, turn out to be nineteen and thirty-three, respectively. How could there be so many conflicting claims about of the educations of these men who created the Constitution of the United States? Was ALEXANDER HAMILTON really a graduate of Columbia (then called King's College)? Did New Jersey's DAVID BREARLEY go to Princeton? Did WILLIAM HOUSTOUN study law at the Inns of Court? Was the Scottish native JAMES WILSON a graduate of St. Andrews University? Did South Carolina's CHARLES COTESWORTH PINCKNEY earn an Oxford degree and study law under the legendary William Blackstone? Were JAMES MADISON and Aaron Burr classmates? Only the last of these assertions is true (or was until MADISON skipped a year and graduated early), but all are frequently encountered. It is apparent that some otherwise careful biographers have uncritically accepted traditional accounts of their subjects' early years, and many of the Constitution's lesser-known Framers are still waiting for a careful biographer. Too many historians repeat stories that, upon examination, conflict with existing records. Expectations and assumptions about education change over time, and there has been a tendency to inflate, embroider, or simply confuse the facts.[5]

Many details of the Framers' schooling are simply lost, but much of their experience can be reconstructed from what does remain in memoirs, letters, and school archives, and not only in America: more than a quarter of the Framers were educated partly or entirely in England, Ireland, Scotland, or France. Then, we must understand their experiences within the changing context of education in the eighteenth century. For almost half of that century there were only three colleges in the American colonies, and one of those, William and Mary, was primarily a grammar school (i.e., a school that taught Latin grammar through classical literature). At that time, in the colonies and abroad, there was a single-minded focus at all levels of schooling on classical Latin, the language of Cicero and Virgil. Authors more recent than Tacitus or Livy were rarely taught. And the older the Framers were, the less likely they were to have had much formal school at all. Outside of a few towns in New England and Scotland, there was no public education for boys or girls; parents or neighbors might teach the alphabet, but the only real alternatives for children were private tutors or distant boarding schools such as Eton and Westminster across the Atlantic. Over the decades, things gradually changed. Reforms began in Scottish universities, and Scottish teachers arrived to set up schools in the colonies.

New colleges opened, and their graduates fanned out to teach in Pennsylvania, Delaware, Maryland, Virginia, and North Carolina. FRANKLIN, the oldest of the Framers, entered school in 1714 and left a year later. RUFUS KING was the last to graduate from college in 1777, two years after the American Revolution had begun; by then another revolution was well underway in education. For many of the Framers, education had meant little more than the Greeks and Romans, as it had for centuries, but others had begun to study such living authors as David Hume and Adam Smith.

Most of all, it is necessary to understand how these differences in education influenced the Framers' ideas and actions at the Constitutional Convention. Only a few, such as ROGER SHERMAN, were entirely self-taught, but almost all pursued self-education throughout their lives, subscribing to the first American edition of Blackstone's *Commentaries*, reading Montesquieu's *Spirit of the Laws*, or lending one another copies of *The Wealth of Nations* as those books became available. What remained most significant, however, was the acquisition of lifelong values and assumptions during their adolescent years or early twenties, the years when they were forming those "channels" through which their lives indeed ran. LIVINGSTON was hardly alone in seeing his school days as the period during which he "imbibed" the principles that would "run thro' [his] future conduct." In 1814, GOUVERNEUR MORRIS looked back twenty-seven years to the Convention, and beyond to his college days: "In all probability, what I should now do would be what I then did, my sentiments and opinions having undergone no essential change in forty years."[6]

When FRANKLIN, WASHINGTON, SHERMAN, and DICKINSON were young, schools were few and far apart. By the second half of the eighteenth century, when GOUVERNEUR MORRIS attended the Philadelphia Academy and King's College, American education was encountering a wave of change, and by the 1770s the experience of JONATHAN DAYTON and his classmate WILLIAM DAVIE at Princeton had little in common with that of LIVINGSTON and WILLIAM S. JOHNSON at Yale a generation earlier. The changes extended beyond the college level: as early as the 1750s, Pennsylvania's New London Academy, where HUGH WILLIAMSON, ALEXANDER MARTIN, and GEORGE READ studied, had a far broader scope than JOHN LANGDON's Portsmouth, New Hampshire, grammar school, teaching not just Latin and basic math but contemporary moral philosophy and English composition. The schools that Presbyterian ministers opened in North Carolina offered a more ambitious program than even the best town schools of New England, preparing WILLIAM CHURCHILL HOUSTON so well that he entered Princeton as a junior. Even autodidacts found opportunities expanding: in the early 1700s, FRANKLIN's remarkable self-education would have been unimaginable outside of

Boston or Philadelphia, but by midcentury young WILLIAM FEW could find many of the same books—and new ones—on the Carolina frontier. Only private tutoring remained little changed, and it was fading out as schools became more available.

The wave of immigration by Ulster Scots (the "Scotch-Irish") was just beginning as the older Framers were entering school; the Presbyterian schoolmasters who followed it arrived too late to make much impression on the members of the First or Second Continental Congresses. The important Scottish philosopher Francis Hutcheson was familiar to only a few in those early Congresses: Jefferson (who had had been taught by the Scot William Small at William and Mary), JAMES WILSON and John Witherspoon (who had both been educated in Scotland), Benjamin Rush (who had spent two years at Edinburgh getting his MD), and three former students of New London's Francis Alison, including GEORGE READ. In 1776, the College of New Jersey (Princeton), the College of Philadelphia (now the University of Pennsylvania), and King's College (now Columbia) were still new, and only in New England were local leaders likely to have college degrees. A decade later, after the war had accelerated the careers of many young men, things were different. By then the many new schools south of New England had had a dramatic effect, and graduates of the newer colleges were exerting an influence disproportionate to their numbers.

The educational demographics of the nation's founders were changing. Fewer than half of the signers of the Declaration of Independence had spent even a year in college; eight of the twenty-five collegians had gone to Harvard, four to Yale, and three each to Cambridge University and William and Mary. Of the remaining seven, two were graduates of Princeton and two of the College of Philadelphia; one was a graduate of the University of Edinburgh, one had studied at St. Andrews and Glasgow, and one had gone to the Jesuit College of St. Omer, in France (Charles Carroll, who as a Catholic was barred from the other colleges). Eleven years later, at the 1787 Convention, Yale again had four alumni as did William and Mary; the College of Philadelphia was once more represented by two graduates, and there was again one from St. Omer's—DANIEL CARROLL this time, cousin of Charles. But now, in place of three from Cambridge there was only one from Oxford. Now there were two Framers who had been to the innovative University of Glasgow and another two who had studied medicine at Edinburgh; and there were also two from King's College in New York. Most strikingly, the proportion from Harvard and Princeton had reversed: the Constitution's Framers included nine graduates of the newer college at Princeton and only three from 150-year-old Harvard.

The geographic distribution of college alumni was also changing. In Congress in 1776, all but one of the Harvard men had represented New England states; all but one from Yale had represented either Connecticut or New York; most delegates had been born in the states that sent them. In 1787, the Harvard contingent at the Convention was even more local, all representing their native Massachusetts, and the Yale graduates were still all natives of New York or Connecticut; William and Mary remained a school for Virginians. But the nine Princeton graduates present in 1787 were born in Ireland, England, North Carolina, Virginia, Pennsylvania, and Connecticut as well as New Jersey, and they now represented six different states: North Carolina, Virginia, and Maryland in the South, the middle states of Delaware and New Jersey, and Connecticut in New England. Among them were the authors of the Virginia Plan (MADISON) and the New Jersey Plan (PATERSON), and the chief architect of the Great Compromise (ELLSWORTH).[7]

With rare exceptions such as FRANKLIN, the members of the Continental Congresses had been men of purely local experience; when Jefferson and Adams first met in Philadelphia in 1775, neither had ever been that far from home before. To South Carolina's congressmen, Massachusetts was more exotic than London; two of them had been educated in England, but none had ever been to Boston. At William and Mary one met only Virginians, at Harvard only New Englanders, and the provincial representatives in Congress had to be convinced that independence was the right thing for their particular provinces. Patrick Henry's early boast that he was not a Virginian but an American soon evaporated in the parochialism of a Congress that was often stymied by one or two states. By 1787, the Anti-Federalist Henry had apparently reversed his primary identity and chose to stay home in Virginia, but now there was a significant core of Convention delegates who had been at college with young men from distant regions of the country or—like MADISON, HOUSTON, and DAVIE—had themselves traveled far to school. They returned home more open-minded about their neighbors from other states.

Of the dozen delegates who took the lead at the 1787 Convention, half—MADISON, HAMILTON, GOUVERNEUR MORRIS, ELLSWORTH, WILLIAMSON, and DAVIE—had been educated at the three newer colleges, and JAMES WILSON, a Scot by birth, had gone to the reformed St. Andrews and Glasgow. On the other hand, of the seven delegates who rejected the new Constitution, three—GERRY, RANDOLPH, and MERCER—attended the two oldest American colleges, and only LUTHER MARTIN was a graduate of one of the newer schools. Two others, JOHN LANSING and ROBERT YATES, had been only to primary or secondary schools in their native New York, and GEORGE MASON had begun with a private tutor and then taught himself.

The older schools were resistant to change: England's ancient universities and "public schools," the older American colleges, and the grammar schools of New England were all conservative institutions, slow to relinquish the habits with which they had entered the eighteenth century. That is not to say that they were static: by RUFUS KING's graduation in 1777, Harvard had made some changes, but it would still have seemed far more familiar to GERRY (class of 1762) and STRONG (1764) than would the College of Philadelphia or Princeton of their own era. The contrast between C. C. PINCKNEY's Oxford and WILSON's Glasgow in the mid-1760s was even more marked, the former lingering indolently in the past while the latter was a hotbed of new ideas; Oxford students were still learning politics from Aristotle at a time when Glaswegians heard lectures by Adam Smith and Thomas Reid. Colleges were changing, but some more rapidly than others.

"Innovation" was a pejorative term in the eighteenth century; continuity was valued. Throughout that century, tradition held sway at Oxford and Cambridge, the bastions of classical education in England, and for most of that time at Harvard, Yale, and William and Mary, which had similarly well-established places in their respective colonies. Change began on the periphery—in the "cultural provinces" of Scotland and Ireland and in the middle colonies of British North America where there was a gradual replacement of Aristotelian deductive reasoning by a Baconian / Newtonian inductive method; at the same time, the formalistic, Ciceronian rhetoric of classical Rome was challenged by "a 'new' rhetoric defined by the plain style and experiential logic of the sciences." In England, Aristotle's logic and Cicero's rhetoric reigned at Oxford and Cambridge (where instruction still took place in Greek or Latin); the "new" logic and rhetoric were taught (in the English language) by Scots, Irishmen, and English dissenters like FRANKLIN's friend Joseph Priestly.[8]

Thomas Miller ascribes the Scottish curricular reforms to professors of moral philosophy and rhetoric who believed that "the best method for advancing knowledge was to reason inductively from the individual experience or phenomenon to the laws that governed the natural order." One of the first of those reformers was George Turnbull at Aberdeen University. He published his *Principles of Moral Philosophy* in 1740 with an epigraph quoting Francis Bacon and a dedication proposing "to account for MORAL, as the great *Newton* has taught us to explain NATURAL appearances." Cambridge, where Newton had studied and taught, paid no attention; neither did Oxford. But that same year David Hume published the final volume of his *Treatise on Human Nature*; in it he declared that "the science of man is the only foundation for the other sciences." The faculty of Aberdeen, quickly followed by the other Scottish universities, revised not only their methods—lecturing in English and replacing generalist tutors with specialized professors—but also their subject matter. At Aberdeen, the curriculum culminated with "the Philosophy of the Human Mind and the sciences that depend upon it," including "Logic, Rhetoricke, the Laws of Nature and Nations, Politicks, Oeconomicks, the fine Arts and Natural Religion." These changes would soon appear at Edinburgh and Glasgow, but not for many years in England, New England, or Virginia.[9]

The new developments at the Scottish universities reverberated at some colleges in the colonies, but at which ones, and why? John Brubacher makes a puzzling statement: "Although even Harvard was not immune to the Scottish university influence, it was at William and Mary that it was felt most directly." His reason is William and Mary's administrative structure, with a Board of Visitors that followed the Scottish method of oversight by members of the community, and he adds, "Even William and Mary's architecture reflected Scottish influence," an impression that might have surprised both Scots and Sir Christopher Wren, the college's reputed architect. But William and Mary's founder, James Blair, had left Aberdeen in the seventeenth century and was no longer alive when that college's reforms took place; the Scottish academic influence was actually felt far more significantly elsewhere, and in more important aspects than architecture. Miller suggests that "the teaching of moral philosophy and English assumed greater importance in New York, Philadelphia, and Princeton"; by 1768 the rector and vice-rector of the College of Philadelphia and the president of Princeton were themselves Scots, educated at Aberdeen, Glasgow, and Edinburgh. Theirs were the American colleges where Scottish influence was strongest.[10]

The primary academic influence in Virginia was clearly Oxford, which supplied nearly all of William and Mary's faculty up until the Revolution. The other two long-established colonial colleges effectively insulated themselves from Scottish or English academic trends: Harvard's president and faculty were all Harvard men, as were Yale's until Yale graduates became available. Though the New England colleges modernized their science curriculum and replaced the Aristotelian logic of Peter Ramus with the newer inductive textbooks of Isaac Watts, both stuck with the rhetoric of Demosthenes and Cicero and the Puritan ethics of William Ames. Late in the century, Harvard students apparently began reading the Genevan political philosopher Jean-Jacques Burlamaqui, but otherwise politics remained the realm of Aristotle.

Schools and colleges in the eighteenth century were small enough that one person could make a big difference, especially a charismatic headmaster or college president. Six of the delegates to the Constitutional Convention had been students of Francis Alison, either at the Academy and College of Philadelphia or at Alison's New London and Newark Academies; five Framers learned moral philosophy and political science from the lectures of Princeton president John Witherspoon. These two apostles of the Scottish Enlightenment represented rival wings of the Presbyterian Church in America, but they saw eye to eye on the moral and political philosophy of the Scottish moderate Francis Hutcheson; together they did more than anyone else to introduce the Scottish Enlightenment to the colonies. Provost William Smith further expanded the College of Philadelphia's curriculum, until that school and Witherspoon's Princeton were the only colleges in the colonies where students studied the political thinking of Hutcheson, David Hume, and the English Commonwealthmen James Harrington and Algernon Sidney. Lawrence Cremin has written that "Smith had advanced a generation beyond his contemporaries in New Haven and New York," and Witherspoon's biographer Jeffry Morrison does not exaggerate much when he says that the Princeton president "almost single-handedly gave a philosophy to the embryonic nation and helped transform a generation of idealists into hardheaded politicians of the first rank."[11]

Almost all the delegates who came to the 1787 Convention were seeking some alternative to the fatally flawed Articles of Confederation, but it was those "hard-headed politicians" at the Convention—Princeton's MADISON and the Glasgow-trained WILSON above all—who took charge. The rest, whose political philosophy had been shaped by the Greeks and Romans, found themselves short of new ideas. Even those with little formal education knew from experience that under the Confederation government—or in any federation of equal states—interstate and international commerce was chaotic; moreover, the Articles allowed a few small states to dictate to the rest. But what could the alternative be? The victors of the American Revolution would never go back to a monarchy, even though HAMILTON and GOUVERNEUR MORRIS were tempted. Cicero's *De officiis* (*On Duties*) and Plutarch's *Lives of the Noble Greeks and Romans* had taught the delegates that the only thing worse than a tyrant was a democracy, which must give way to tyranny anyway. Most understood from Aristotle's *Politics* that a good government divided its powers among the monarch, the aristocracy, and the people, but they struggled to apply that formula in the American Republic. Most of all they believed that the success of any republic depended on the virtue of its citizens, but they were inclined to doubt the virtue of the general public—and not just because of the shock of Shays's Rebellion the previous year. Original sin had been drummed into the many Calvinists in their infancy: "In Adam's fall, we sinned all." But two newer Adams, Ferguson and Smith, plus Hume, Lord Kames, and especially Hutcheson, pointed the way to the thoroughly mixed or blended government that MADISON proposed, one that balanced branch against branch, faction against faction to protect against despotism. This was a new and unfamiliar approach to most of the delegates, but it was based on principles that *were* familiar to those Framers who had studied at the newer schools. MADISON's vision seemed to contradict the ideals of republican virtue and strictly divided government that had been inculcated at Harvard, Yale, and the New England grammar schools or absorbed in the private libraries that were the schools of the self-taught. The "old-school" Framers struggled to accept it; most, like DICKINSON and SHERMAN, finally did, but some, including GERRY and MASON, could not. All were fearful of democratic excesses and most believed in a natural aristocracy of men of "superior wisdom" whose eloquence as speakers suggested (in the words of Aberdeen's Turnbull) their "right to lead (but not to command)"; in modern shorthand, they were elitists. All valued education, but they discovered that, as Pennsylvania Framer THOMAS MIFFLIN had earlier written in a college notebook, "Different Means of Education will always occasion differences of opinions even between good Men."[12]

Twelve states eventually sent fifty-five good men to Philadelphia. (Contrarian Rhode Island refused to participate; New York left early, before New Hampshire arrived.) Just over half had attended college, in the New World or the Old. The schooling of others was limited to reading, writing, and arithmetic. Some were self-taught, or privately tutored, or trained in Latin grammar schools. Most had been educated in ways that were thoroughly traditional, reading similar authors and doing similar lessons. A significant minority, however, had been to schools that offered a different kind of education, with a curriculum and methodology that were still uncommon in the second half of the eighteenth century, an education that had not even existed when the oldest Framers of the Constitution were students. Between the 1710s and the 1770s, most of the Framers were taught the classics (mainly Roman) and the basics of Christian theology. Those classics might be read in Greek by a few, in Latin by many, or in English translation by the rest; that theology might be Anglican in Virginia or Oxford, Calvinist in New England or Scotland, Roman Catholic for THOMAS

FITZSIMONS at an Irish hedge school or at the Jesuit College of St. Omer in Flanders, where young DANIEL CARROLL was sent. But those who led the way out of the disagreements that had already paralyzed Congress—and that now threatened to stop the 1787 Convention in its tracks—were shaped by educations that added to all this the moral and political philosophers of the Scottish Enlightenment. Unlike their elders (or their contemporaries at older schools), these students had also been taught the "common sense" philosophy of Thomas Reid rather than the idealism of Plato, George Berkeley, or Jonathan Edwards. As Mailer notes, a new generation of American teachers "saw few problems in highlighting their debt both to Hutchesonian moral philosophy and to newer strands of common sense reasoning." And whether their students were presided over by orators such as Samuel Davies, taught to write English prose by masters as demanding as Alison, or trained in college debating clubs such as the American Whig and Cliosophic societies, they were called upon early to hone their rhetorical skills in the political controversies of the times. At the newer colleges, students were increasingly given forensic debating assignments in English; at the older schools, antiquated syllogistic disputation in Latin persisted much longer. Seven Princeton Framers were members of college debating clubs; there were none of those at Harvard, Yale, or Oxford, and William and Mary's debating club was organized too late for any of the Framers but WILLIAM PIERCE to take part.[13]

In the pages that follow, the Framers are introduced in chapter 1, and chapter 2 identifies the subjects and standard authors of an eighteenth-century education, along with the newer authors whose influence was just beginning to be felt. The traditional education most common in that century becomes the focus of chapters 3 through 7. More particularly, chapter 3 looks at the experiences of those Framers of the Constitution who educated themselves and those who were privately tutored, whether as their entire education or with the expectation that they would then go to college. Chapter 4 tracks those who learned to read and write at common schools or prepared for college at traditional grammar schools. Chapters 5 and 6 examine education at America's three oldest colleges, Harvard, William and Mary, and Yale, during the years the Framers were students, and chapter 7 follows those who crossed the Atlantic to the still older Oxford or St. Omer, and those educated in Ireland. Chapter 8 describes the great variety of professional education undertaken by the many Framers who became lawyers, whether at England's Inns of Court or through apprenticeship under attorneys whose guidance ranged from the almost nonexistent to the equivalent of a college program. In all of these, two common threads will be evident: the predominance (almost to the exclusion of all else) of the Greek and Roman classics, and the imitation in America of traditional English models.

Chapters 9 through 12 turn to a newer model, beginning at its place of origin in Scotland. A chapter on the Universities of Edinburgh and Glasgow, where four of the Framers were students, is followed by a chapter on the new academies opened from Pennsylvania to North Carolina, modeled on the Presbyterian academies of the Ulster Scots in Ireland. Chapters 11 and 12 look closely at the innovative educations Framers encountered at the new College of Philadelphia, King's College, and Princeton.

Chapter 13 analyzes developments at the Convention that reveal the differences made by these different educations: not only did the content of the "new school" education suggest solutions to otherwise intractable problems, but those Framers whose educations were most traditional (or most limited) had the most trouble accepting those solutions. Moreover, the lasting influence of one early tutor (a close friend of three Princeton presidents), along with close personal connections made in college, are shown to be instrumental in achieving agreements through which the Convention avoided collapse. This chapter offers a new analysis of the Great Compromise, and it reveals the important role of education in the reception of MADISON's proposals to meet the Convention's great challenge: "You must first enable the government to control the governed; and in the next place oblige it to control itself."

At Philadelphia in 1787, "different Means of Education" did much more than "occasion Differences of Opinions." They provided the intellectual frames of reference through which the Framers understood the Constitution of the United States of America.

Part I

I

The Framers

Whatever Principles are imbibed at College will run thro' a Man's whole future Conduct, and affect the Society of which he is a Member, in Proportion to his Sphere of Activity.
WILLIAM LIVINGSTON, *Independent Reflector XVII*, March 22, 1753

In the closing days of the Constitutional Convention, the Committee of Style composed a final draft beginning, "We the People of the United States, in order to form a more perfect Union . . . " Those words announced a sharp break from the Second Continental Congress, which had produced both the Declaration of Independence and the Articles of Confederation, the frame of government that this new Constitution would replace. The Committee on Style was made up of WILLIAM SAMUEL JOHNSON, ALEXANDER HAMILTON, GOUVERNEUR MORRIS, RUFUS KING, and JAMES MADISON. Not one of them had been in Congress in 1776—JOHNSON had been elected to the First Continental Congress but declined, and the other four were then all under twenty-five. Now, in the summer of 1787, they knew the reaction their words would provoke. Patrick Henry's response was typical: "Who authorized them to speak the language of *We, the People* instead of *We, the States?*" It was a fair question.[1]

Although they had been called only to revise the Articles of Confederation, it was the *imperfect* union created by the Articles— Henry's "We, the States"—that the Framers were determined to replace entirely. When they proposed a "more perfect Union," they certainly did not mean to imply a government that was close to flawless. They understood the word "perfect" in the sense of the "perfect" tenses in grammar: "completed," from the Latin *perfectum*, past participle of *perficere*, "to accomplish, perform, complete." What they wanted (and what "particularists" like Henry opposed) was a more complete unification of the states into a government with a far more national character than the Articles' "league of friendship."

At least three-quarters of the Framers were semifluent in Latin and thus far more likely than modern Americans to hear the Latin roots in words like "perfect," "union," "federal," or "constitution," English words that were not yet so familiar as they are today. All of the Framers were painfully aware of the extent to which the union of their states was imperfect—not yet accomplished, incomplete—and they had no illusions about the compromise solution that they were offering. Well acquainted as they were with the standard classical authors, they needed no footnotes when twice that summer Convention delegates (PIERCE BUTLER and GUNNING BEDFORD JR.) invoked Plutarch on the constitution Solon had given to Athens: not the best government that could be devised, but the best that the people would accept. That was how they saw their own work. By the Convention's final day, most agreed with BENJAMIN FRANKLIN: "I confess that there are several parts of this constitution which I do not at present approve, but I am not sure I shall never approve them. . . . Thus I consent, sir, to this constitution because I expect no better, and because I am not sure, that it is not the best."[2]

Why did FRANKLIN think so, when men like Patrick Henry—appointed as a delegate by Virginia but unwilling to attend the Convention—were bitterly opposed? Why did such patriots as GEORGE MASON and ELBRIDGE GERRY ultimately refuse to join their old friends GEORGE WASHINGTON and ROGER SHERMAN in supporting the new Constitution? For that matter, why, after youthful revolutionaries EDMUND RANDOLPH and JOHN FRANCIS MERCER refused to sign the document, did the equally young, equally revolutionary ALEXANDER HAMILTON and JAMES MADISON pour their energies into ratification? A total of fifty-five delegates appeared at some point in Philadelphia. (Just as in Congress at the time, states could send as many representatives as they wished, but each state would cast a single vote.) Thirty-nine of them affixed their signatures after staying to debate for all or most of three and a half months; four walked out in protest, and three others remained to the very end but then refused to sign. Even those three, if not all four walkouts, had accepted their commissions because they feared that unless the existing union were made "more perfect," it might soon dissolve. The Articles of Confederation provided no executive officer or federal judiciary; each state had one vote in Congress, but important questions required a supermajority, and by 1787 government was grinding to a halt. Even MERCER, who stayed less than two weeks in Philadelphia and objected to nearly everything he heard, had written to JAMES MADISON in 1785: "For my part I have no hopes but in a convocation of the states." Six of the delegates had themselves signed the Articles of Confederation: GERRY, SHERMAN, GOUVER-NEUR MORRIS, ROBERT MORRIS, JOHN DICKINSON, and DANIEL CARROLL. DICKINSON and SHERMAN had served on the committee appointed to compose that document, and DICKINSON had written the original draft himself. Now, led by men a generation younger, they were back in the same room in Philadelphia, prepared at the end of all the debating to cast aside the league of states they had so recently designed and replace it with a truly national government—something they knew most Americans didn't particularly want.[3]

Twenty who had been chosen by their states declined the assignment. Their reasons include insufficient funds and ill-health, but some were darkly suspicious of the Convention's purpose. Henry is supposed to have said he "smelt a rat." Of those who accepted, two had to turn around and go home after only a week: GEORGE WYTHE received word that his wife was gravely ill, and WILLIAM CHURCHILL HOUSTON was himself too ill with tuberculosis to remain. The New Hampshire delegation did not arrive until the Convention was half over, and by that time the New York delegation had left. (HAMILTON returned at the end.) There were never more than eleven state delegations in attendance, never more than forty-eight delegates present at once, usually about forty on any given day.

Rhode Island, which seemed to exemplify everything that was wrong with the Articles of Confederation, boycotted the Convention. The last thing that contentious state wanted was a more constraining national government. Rhode Island issued its own worthless paper money, imposed its own international and interstate tariffs, refused to pay its share to support the federal government, and vetoed every attempt by the other states to strengthen the ability of Congress to govern. Under the Articles of Confederation, Congress could do nothing about any of that. New York was almost as difficult. When Gov. George Clinton grudgingly sent three delegates to Philadelphia, two of them had instructions to oppose any serious reforms.[4]

The delegates ranged in age from twenty-six (JONATHAN DAYTON) to eighty-one (FRANKLIN); HAMILTON and CHARLES PINCKNEY III both claimed to be several years younger than they really were, in an apparent effort to impress with their precocity. The greatest number were lawyers, but only a handful actually made their living at the law. A dozen were merchants on varying scales. Three, including WASHINGTON, were trained surveyors, and at one time or another several had been teachers, preachers, or physicians. Half called themselves farmers, conscious that the patrician heroes of the Roman Republic had done so. Regardless of their occupations, more than two-thirds owned at least one slave at some point during their lives—nearly all the southerners and about half the northerners, including FRANKLIN and HAMILTON, who briefly owned slaves before founding antislavery societies in Philadelphia and New York. (In 1787, Massachusetts was the only state that had ended slavery, although others had taken preliminary steps in that direction. The first census in 1790 counted 40,000 slaves north of Mason and Dixon's line.) DICKINSON, formerly Delaware's largest slaveholder, had just completed the manumission of his slaves the year before the Convention. WASHINGTON, one of Virginia's largest slaveowners, would free his slaves in his will, and the same week that the Convention adopted its fugitive slave clause and three-fifths compromise, southern delegates WILLIAM BLOUNT, WILLIAM PIERCE, and WILLIAM FEW were away in New York, voting in Congress to forbid slavery in the Northwest territories.

Over the preceding decade, 80 percent of the Framers had served in Congress and had come to know each other to some extent. JAMES WILSON and ELBRIDGE GERRY, political veterans, were already acquainted with all but a dozen of the other delegates. Others who had not been congressmen, men such as JOHN LANSING or JACOB BROOM, knew next to nobody outside their own delegations. Some knew each other from military service together during the Revolution, such as Georgia's PIERCE and New Jersey's DAYTON. GOUVERNEUR MORRIS had been the deputy to Superintendent of Finance ROBERT MORRIS (no relation), and HAMILTON had been WASHINGTON's aide-de-camp before resigning over hurt pride. JAMES MCHENRY, a physician, had also been on WASHINGTON's staff and had prescribed for HAMILTON's hangovers and indigestion. FRANKLIN had met HUGH WILLIAMSON in London and JARED INGERSOLL in Paris, had served with SHERMAN on the committee that drafted the Declaration of Independence, and had known GEORGE CLYMER since CLYMER was an infant, but in May 1787 he was meeting JAMES MADISON for the first time. MASON and MERCER were cousins; so were CHARLES PINCKNEY III and CHARLES COTESWORTH PINCKNEY, once removed. The latter PINCKNEY and BUTLER were brothers-in-law. WASHINGTON, MASON, JENIFER, and CARROLL had been neighbors along the Potomac all their lives. On the other hand, MERCER did not even arrive in Philadelphia until New York's ROBERT YATES had already left, and the two never did meet, even though both lived into the next century.

A remarkable number of the Framers had known one another in school. READ, ALEXANDER MARTIN, and WILLIAMSON had gone to the New London Academy together as young boys, and HAMILTON had met DAYTON at the Elizabethtown Academy. College acquaintances included LIVINGSTON and JOHNSON at Yale in the 1740s, GERRY and STRONG at Harvard in the 1760s, and three sets of Princetonians: ELLSWORTH and LUTHER MARTIN class of 1766, MADISON and BEDFORD class of 1771, and DAYTON and DAVIE class of 1776. ELLSWORTH, who founded a college debating society with MARTIN and PATERSON (class of 1763) had also been INGERSOLL's classmate at Yale for two years before transferring to Princeton. WILLIAM CHURCHILL HOUSTON, who left the Convention early, had been the college instructor of MADISON, BEDFORD, DAYTON, and DAVIE.

Study of the law had introduced a number of the Framers to one another. DICKINSON had entered London's Middle Temple in the same year as JOHN BLAIR JR.; before that, DICKINSON and READ had been legal apprentices together in Philadelphia in the office of John Moland. LANSING had read law under YATES, who had read law under LIVINGSTON. LUTHER MARTIN had been examined for the Virginia bar by WYTHE, and SHERMAN had first hired JOHNSON as a lawyer and then studied law with his help. PATERSON, appointed attorney general of New Jersey by Governor LIVINGSTON, regularly argued before DAVID BREARLEY, the state's chief justice from 1779 to 1789, and he had persuaded HOUSTON to give up teaching to become a lawyer.

→ main goal

For a few of the delegates, the framing of the Constitution was the penultimate step in a long campaign to create a stronger central government (but only penultimate, because the struggle for ratification still remained). At the heart of this group were WASHINGTON, HAMILTON, and MADISON. Certainly no one was more painfully familiar with the states' inability to act to together than WASHINGTON. Hundreds of messages to Congress throughout the Revolutionary War record his frustration trying to lead an army made up of independent state militias. Even before peace was concluded in 1783 he told HAMILTON that he hoped members of Congress were "aware of the great defects of their Constitution [i.e., the Articles of Confederation]," *G. Washington* adding that "it is clearly my opinion that unless Congress possess powers competent to all general purposes, that the distresses we have incurred, and the blood we have spilt in the course of an eight year war, will avail us nothing." Less than three weeks later he wrote, "My wish to see the Union of these States established upon liberal & permanent principles—& inclination to contribute my mite in pointing out the defects of the present Constitution, are equally great—All my private letters have teemed with these Sentiments, & whenever this topic has been the Subject of conversation, I have endeavoured to diffuse & enforce them."[5]

HAMILTON was, more than anyone, a creature of the Revolution: in 1774 he had been a penniless, illegitimate youth, newly come from the West

Indies, but his meteoric rise through WASHINGTON's military "family"—despite his impulsive resignation, soon forgiven—brought him an otherwise unimaginable prominence in less than a decade. HAMILTON also owed much to LIVINGSTON, who had taken the teenager into his home when he had first arrived from St. Croix, but he owed nothing to the political establishment of the state of New York, and in 1787 his boundless ambition seemed blocked by the political machine of Governor Clinton. As early as 1783 he wrote to John Jay, "Every day proves the inefficacy of the present confederation," and he drafted a proposal for a federal convention but put it aside at the time with the note, "abandoned for want of support." MADISON, the tireless student of political philosophy who appeared to have no life outside of government, became the equally tireless leader of the movement to strengthen the feeble power of the Congress. First Rhode Island and then New York and even MADISON's own Virginia had demonstrated that all attempts to alter the Articles of Confederation were doomed to founder on the rock of a single state's veto: amending the Articles of Confederation required unanimous consent. It had become clear to MADISON that the only solution was to start over.[6]

The first, cautious step toward the Philadelphia Convention was the Mt. Vernon Conference in the spring of 1785. Acknowledging Congress's inability to control interstate commerce, Virginia and Maryland were making an attempt to achieve cooperation along the Potomac River and Chesapeake Bay. MADISON had worked in the Virginia legislature to set up the meeting, and he and RANDOLPH were among the state's appointed commissioners. Although this was only a very small step in the direction of perfecting the union, Gov. Patrick Henry was determined to block it and chose not to tell MADISON or RANDOLPH when the meeting was scheduled; Virginia's MASON and Maryland's DANIEL OF ST. THOMAS JENIFER were among the few commissioners who happened upon each other in the river town of Alexandria and finally wound up conferring at WASHINGTON's home. Despite Henry's apparent attempted sabotage, the commissioners who did meet not only signed agreements but invited Pennsylvania and Delaware to join in them.[7]

Following Mt. Vernon's limited success, MADISON and his allies persuaded the Virginia Assembly to call for a second meeting in September 1786, this time of all the states at the midway point of Annapolis. Although the host state of Maryland declined to participate—along with Connecticut, South Carolina, and Georgia—all of the others voted to send representatives. For reasons that remain murky, the Annapolis Convention did not wait for all the participants to arrive. While other states' commissioners were still on the road to Annapolis, representatives of Virginia, New York, Pennsylvania,

Delaware, and New Jersey quickly met from September 11 to 14 and adjourned after preparing a powerful call for another meeting of all the states. Their report, written with some warmth by HAMILTON and toned down by MADISON, urged the states to send delegations to Philadelphia "on the second Monday of May next . . . to take into consideration the situation of the United States, to devise such further provisions as shall appear to them necessary to render the constitution of the federal government adequate to the exigencies of the Union."[8]

The chairman of the Annapolis Convention was JOHN DICKINSON. Representing Delaware with him were BASSETT and READ. Among the other commissioners were PATERSON and HOUSTON of New Jersey. Foreshadowing the problems they encountered in 1787, the underfunded New Hampshire delegation was too slow to get started. Massachusetts appointed two rounds of representatives; both sets declined at the last minute, but some of their replacements (who included ELBRIDGE GERRY) were as close as Wilmington, Delaware; and North Carolina commissioner HUGH WILLIAMSON was only a day away when the Convention abruptly adjourned—to WILLIAMSON's chagrin, when he met returning Virginians crossing the Potomac. Perhaps those already present should have waited a little longer for their tardy colleagues; almost no large conference started on time, and in 1787 the Federal Convention—called for May 14—would not begin until the more punctual delegates had been waiting in Philadelphia for eleven days. But at least one contemporary observer thought their haste was part of a plan. Louis Guillaume Otto, the French chargé d'affaires, wrote to the Comte de Vergennes the following month that the organizers "had no hope, nor even desire, to see this Assembly . . . succeed" but intended all along to find an excuse to call for a convention with a more ambitious agenda: "The Commissioners do not wish to take into consideration the grievances of Commerce, infinitely interesting to the people, without perfecting at the same time the fundamental constitution of Congress." There is some support for Otto's belief in MADISON's letter to Jefferson a month ahead of the gathering: "Many Gentlemen both within & without Congs. wish to make this Meeting subservient to a Plenipotentiary Convention for amending the Confederation. . . . [M]y wishes are in favor of such an event."[9]

Jack Rakove has observed that the final years of the Articles of Confederation "do not foreshadow the intensity, scope, and sophistication of the debates of 1787–88." Calvin Johnson flatly states, "It was MADISON's work before the Convention, at first alone, that caused the Constitutional Revolution." But when the 1787 Convention began to assemble on the second Monday of May, it included a core of delegates who had already been working to form a stronger, "more perfect" union than the Articles of Confederation allowed. They—and a few adversaries—would dominate the debates that summer. RANDOLPH, who later got cold feet, seized the initiative by introducing MADISON's Virginia Plan, based on proportional representation in a bicameral Congress. WILSON and GOUVERNEUR MORRIS energetically promoted it, while PATERSON and BEDFORD argued against it on behalf of the smaller states, countering with the New Jersey Plan for equal representation of states regardless of size. CHARLES PINCKNEY III continued the arguments he had begun making in Congress for a stronger central government. Resistance came from SHERMAN, GERRY, LUTHER MARTIN, and, in the closing days, RANDOLPH and MASON. When the debate highlighted the competing interests of North and South, MORRIS, WILSON, and KING clashed repeatedly with South Carolina's C. C. PINCKNEY, RUTLEDGE, and BUTLER. After it became clear that the opponents would not give ground, critical compromises were the work of the Connecticut and North Carolina delegations, especially ELLSWORTH, JOHNSON, DAVIE, and WILLIAMSON. And from the beginning FRANKLIN and WASHINGTON lent their all-important prestige, WASHINGTON silently but visibly as the president of the Convention and FRANKLIN through his optimistic encouragement, both on the floor and then after hours in informal gatherings at his home or the Indian Queen tavern.[10]

HAMILTON, who had worked for more than a year to bring about the Convention, was consistently outvoted in his own delegation. Before decamping for the months of July and August he made a few passionate speeches, including a daylong lecture that proposed a purely national government headed by a powerful executive elected for life—a speech that, by JOHNSON's account, was "praised by everybody . . . [but] supported by none."[11] In later years that intemperate speech (publicly reported by YATES in violation of the delegates' confidentiality oath) would lead to the persistent accusation that HAMILTON was plotting to turn the federal government into a monarchy.

The document that would be hammered out in his absence bore little resemblance to what HAMILTON had proposed. His real contributions were made before and after the Convention. He, along with WASHINGTON and MADISON, had been among the primary movers behind the campaign to revise—and in the event, to replace—the existing frame of government. And though the immediate effect cannot be measured, the *Federalist* essays of 1788 (written by HAMILTON, MADISON, and Jay) made the most widely read and admired arguments for the Constitution, even though HAMILTON had many misgivings about the plan he was promoting. In 1802 he would write to his friend and fellow King's College alumnus GOUVERNEUR MORRIS:

Mine is an odd destiny. Perhaps no man in the United States has sacri-ficed or done more for the present constitution than myself; and con-trary to all my anticipations of its fate . . . I am still labouring to prop the frail and worthless fabric, yet I have the murmurs of its friends no less than the curses of its foes as my reward. What can I do better than withdraw from the Scene? Every day proves to me more and more that this American world was not made for me.[12]

About fifteen Framers were primarily responsible for the proposals, modifications, and compromises that resulted in the Constitution, some pushing hard for substantial change, others reluctantly accepting it as the price of national survival. These were the dominant personalities of the Convention—advocating a stronger government, resisting it, or find-ing ways to make it possible. Still, we must not overlook other men who stayed out of the limelight but cast the essential votes. Eleven delegates were silent or nearly so, but some of them played important roles behind the scenes. (Without BLAIR, Virginia's final vote would have been a tie, with WASHINGTON and MADISON in favor but MASON and RANDOLPH opposed, pre-venting a unanimous endorsement by all the states present.) Only three of the delegates worked consistently to block all reform: MERCER, LANSING, and YATES. LUTHER MARTIN's opposition was sporadic and inconsistent. MA-SON, RANDOLPH, and GERRY struggled in good faith to find a solution, before concluding—at least for a while—that the new Constitution of the United States was worse than the old Articles of Confederation.

In 1913, Charles Beard, in *An Economic Interpretation of the Constitution*, made his case that the Framers and their supporters were motivated by a desire to protect their investments in Continental securities (the IOUs from Congress that had funded the Revolutionary War but were becoming worth-less without a solvent government to pay them back). The Beard thesis arose during the economic conflicts of the Progressive Era and remained popular for a generation thereafter. It had been under increasing attack for some time when Forrest McDonald's *We the People* showed in exhaustive detail that the facts would not support it. McDonald himself saw real estate specula-tion as a powerful motivation, and more recent research has used statisti-cal methods to argue that economic interest of some kind often influenced votes. But as Joseph Ellis noted in 2015, "much of [the Progressive School's] work has not aged well, chiefly its claim that the founders were driven pri-marily by economic motives." Moreover, economic interest fails to account for differences between individual Framers. Many of the Constitution's ad-vocates were indeed among the nation's largest investors, but so were some of its fiercest opponents. Two of the five largest security holders among the Framers, GERRY and MASON, refused to sign the Constitution and then led the fight against ratification in their states, where the final votes were close. Others who owned no securities (MADISON, HAMILTON, GOUVERNEUR MORRIS) were nevertheless among the Constitution's strongest supporters.[13]

Just as Beard saw the Constitution through muckraker's eyes, so historians during the Cold War began to see ideological influences on the Framers. During the 1950s and early 1960s, Douglass Adair, Caroline Robbins, J. G. A. Pocock, and Trevor Colbourn focused attention on the republican philosophy that the Revolutionary leaders had learned from the "commonwealth whigs" of England's Civil War and Glorious Revolution. With a flurry of influential articles in the *William and Mary Quarterly*, intellectual history began to eclipse economic history. Then, just as John F. Kennedy's New Frontier was ushering in a youth movement in politics, Stanley Elkins and Eric McKitrick published "The Founding Fathers: Young Men of the Revolution," in *Political Science Quarterly* (1961). MADISON, HAMILTON, and their contemporaries could be understood as a generation that came of age (as Kennedy said of his own generation) "tempered by war." Serving in uniform or struggling in the Congress against recalcitrant state legislatures, these young revolutionaries were more inclined to identify themselves with the new nation than with the old states. In the 1980s, with the advent of the "culture wars," books and essays by religious conservatives began asserting that the Framers' Christian convictions were central to the Constitution, a thesis complicated by the absence of any discussion of religion at the Convention. (Framers' assumptions about sin or predestination, as we shall see, were certainly elements of their worldview—and the theodicy of ELLSWORTH's tutor, the Rev. Joseph Bellamy, made a significant impression on his student). One of the most respected historians of evangelical Christianity, Mark Noll, identifies a developing "American Synthesis" of republicanism and religion: "The synthesis was a compound of evangelical Protestant religion, republican political ideology, and commonsense moral reasoning." His much-admired book, *America's God: From Jonathan Edwards to Abraham Lincoln* (2002), says a good deal about the influence of republicanism on American religion before the nineteenth century, but not vice versa. Noll acknowledges that "the language of the nation's founding documents—the Declaration of Independence, the Articles of Confederation, and the Constitution—while respectful of the deity in general, was hardly evangelical in any specific sense."[14]

Most recently, we hear from a new generation of neo-progressives that the Framers were launching a conservative counterrevolution to preserve control by the "elite" (a word that had not yet entered the English language in their century). Michael Klarman's 2016 *Framers' Coup* broadly declares, "Considering the common characteristics of the delegates in Philadelphia—their wealth, education, occupations, and national and military service—it does not seem surprising that they would share certain political views" or that "most of the Framers wanted the government to be administered by the 'better sort' of people—the well-educated and well-born elite." As we shall see, maybe half of the Framers would themselves have been considered particularly well-educated at the time; PIERCE, with at most a year of college, commented on the poor education of a number of his fellow delegates, and WASHINGTON was always sensitive about his own "defective" education. It is an even greater stretch to call the many sons of small farmers, tradesmen, or tavern keepers "well-born." And not only were they surprisingly diverse in their backgrounds, they disagreed among themselves constantly. As Klarman himself wisely acknowledges at the outset, "Plainly, no single motive or explanatory variable can account for the making of the Constitution."[15]

Economics, ideology, revolutionary youth, and Calvinism all elucidate the behavior of the Framers, but none is enough by itself. Each theory has its gaps or its inconsistencies. Delaware's BROOM was a purely local politician with little involvement or investment in the national war effort; he supported the Constitution. Connecticut's JOHNSON, already forty-nine in 1776, sat on the fence throughout the war, refusing election to the Continental Congress and losing his commission in the Connecticut militia, but he supported the Constitution. So did the self-educated Georgia farmer FEW, who owned neither slaves nor western lands, and the Virginia planter and war hero WASHINGTON, who owned hundreds of human chattels and was one of the nation's great real estate speculators; the young military veteran, slaveowner, speculator, and congressman MERCER opposed it. The deist FRANKLIN, the Catholic FITZSIMONS, and the evangelical Methodist BASSETT all supported it, but not the Calvinist GERRY or the Episcopalian MASON. The various popular theories all have trouble explaining the way certain delegates voted at certain times during the Convention. RANDOLPH, who owned substantial Continental securities, voted against requiring Congress to pay them back. The defeated proposal to grant Congress power to veto state laws was supported by BLAIR, whose only political experience was at the state level; it was opposed by SHERMAN and GERRY, who had been in Congress throughout the Revolution and were incensed by the laws of their neighbor, Rhode Island. And so on.

Certainly, many differences at the Convention can be explained by regional characteristics (commercial New England versus the agrarian, slaveowning South) or by small states' fears of dominance by large states and desire for western lands. WILSON and GOUVERNEUR MORRIS from populous Pennsylvania advocated a proportionally representative, national government that diminished the influence of the smaller states; their neighbors PATERSON and BEDFORD from little New Jersey and Delaware opposed them until the Great Compromise allowed states equal votes in the Senate, whereupon they happily supported a strong central government. Controversies over the future of slavery were pragmatic for some, moral for others, but ultimately a question of North versus South; as RUTLEDGE insisted, for South Carolina "religion and humanity had nothing to do with this question." Nevertheless, many other differences—from the issue of standing armies to the question of presidential impeachment—were almost entirely matters of political philosophy. Given the number of Framers whose arguments seem inconsistent with their wartime experience, financial interests, or sectional pressures, it is worth asking how and where they acquired their "abstract philosophy" and "philosophical grounds."[16]

A persuasive answer comes from the Framer WILLIAM LIVINGSTON of New Jersey: "Whatever Principles are imbibed at a College, will run thro' a Man's future Conduct, and affect the Society of which he is a Member, in proportion to his Sphere of Activity." Of course, the schools in which the Framers imbibed their principles were by no means all colleges. The educational backgrounds of the Framers were remarkably varied, encompassing just about every alternative then available: some graduated from the colonies' oldest colleges and some from the newest, but most were not college graduates at all. Half a dozen were educated abroad; a like number, including WASHINGTON and FRANKLIN, were essentially self-taught; and though some studied the classics with private tutors, others had no schooling beyond reading, writing, and ciphering. Three were alumni of the already venerable Harvard College, and one had gone to the even more ancient Oxford University. Four were Yale graduates, and four or five had spent a year or two at William and Mary, but none graduated. Most of the texts they read were many centuries old—Aristotle, Cicero, Plutarch—but a few teachers, such as John Witherspoon at Princeton, were beginning to assign such contemporary thinkers as Francis Hutcheson, David Hume, and Adam Smith. Out of nearly 4 million Americans in 1787, a few hundred had graduated from the small college at Princeton, but nine of the Framers were educated there and five of those, including MADISON, heard Witherspoon's lectures.

Another six delegates were at some point taught by another exponent of the Scottish Enlightenment, Francis Alison. GOUVERNEUR MORRIS, who had spent three early years under Alison at the Philadelphia Academy, graduated from King's College in New York, where HAMILTON was also a student for perhaps two years; there they too were assigned the works of Scottish philosophers.

In the Old World or in the New, the future Framers were shaped by surprisingly different educations. One of them, Pennsylvania's THOMAS MIFFLIN, wrote in a college notebook, "Different Abilities & different Means of Education will always occasion Difference of Opinions even between good Men." In the creation of the new Constitution—that most critical "Sphere of Activity"—the Framers' "different Means of Education" sometimes explain their behavior when more familiar influences fail to. We must, therefore, now turn to the task of identifying the central texts and the various "Means of Education" available to eighteenth-century Americans, beginning with the inescapable Greek and Roman classics.[17]

2

Educating Demigods

> What can be expected from uninformed and ignorant minds? . . . Zeal they
> may have in great abundance, but it is zeal without knowledge, which is
> dangerous equally in political and religious life. Without mental and moral
> improvement, neither order nor civil liberty can long be preserved.
>
> WILLIAM PATERSON, address before the Cliosophic Society, circa 1787

Two well-educated Americans, Thomas Jefferson and John Adams, were
serving as ambassadors to France and England when the Federal Convention met in 1787. From their distance, they envied the men in Philadelphia
whose activities they could only guess at. When Jefferson wrote to Adams,
"It is really an assembly of demigods," he was not expressing any veneration of MERCER or SPAIGHT, whom he knew all too well from Congress, or
of BASSETT or BROOM, whom he had never heard of. Much as he did respect
such elder statesmen as WASHINGTON, FRANKLIN, and WYTHE, he was not expressing his particular admiration for them, either. But Jefferson was speaking words which he knew John Adams would understand.[1]

For Jefferson, "the three greatest men who have ever lived, without any
exception" were Francis Bacon, John Locke, and Isaac Newton. In his letter
to Adams, Jefferson was alluding to Bacon's statement, in *The Advancement
of Learning,* that in ancient times "founders of states, lawgivers, extirpers
of tyrants, fathers of the people, and other eminent persons in civil merit
were honored . . . with the titles of heroes or demigods, such as Hercules,
Theseus, Minos, Romulus, etc." This was the enviable role in which Jefferson saw the Framers and in which they self-consciously must have seen
themselves. Jack Rakove writes in *Original Meanings: Politics and Ideas in the
Making of the Constitution,* "As a culture hero, the legislator provided the
Enlightenment's answer to the Christian saint or the Renaissance prince.
Half-mythical, half-historical, the figure of the legislator who shapes and
unifies his society dominates the political and historical writings of the *phi-
losophes.*"[2]

Adams himself had called his fellow signers of the Declaration of Independence modern-day Lycurguses and Solons. Just as Adams had gloried in his opportunity to join the "half-historical, half-mythical" company of great lawgivers in 1776, the Framers were keenly aware that the 1787 Convention was their opportunity to win undying fame—to become contemporary demigods. They had been taught by Plutarch, the most widely read of classical authors, that fame was the ultimate prize, and to the generation of the Framers, Plutarch's noble Greeks and Romans were the great exemplars. To achieve lasting fame was to become one of them, a modern Cato or Aristides.[3]

While Jefferson was in Paris, he visited the studio of Jean-Antoine Houdon, who would shortly carve his portrait bust in marble. Garry Wills calls Houdon's studio a "hero factory," where visitors could see images of contemporary figures such as Voltaire reimagined as noble Romans, offering inspiration to the next generation. At the time of the Convention, Houdon was beginning work on his statue of WASHINGTON as Cincinnatus, supported by a farmer's plow and the Roman fasces. (The first Cincinnatus had been called from his fields to become dictator of Rome at a moment of national peril; as soon as the crisis was over, he returned to his farm and resumed his plowing.) Wills notes that "America had its own 'hero factory' in Charles Willson Peale's museum" in Philadelphia. Opened in 1786, the museum quickly became one of the city's leading attractions, and during breaks in the Convention many of the delegates paid visits, perhaps imagining themselves immortalized there. During free moments in the summer of 1787, WASHINGTON was sitting for the sixth of his seven portraits from life by Peale.[4]

Years earlier WASHINGTON had himself ordered from England busts of Alexander the Great and Julius Caesar. At the end of the Revolution he was widely characterized as the modern Cincinnatus when he resigned his commission to return to Mt. Vernon. WASHINGTON was especially concerned with fame, but he was far from alone. The association of former Revolutionary officers flattered themselves with the title of the Society of the Cincinnati; they too were convening in Philadelphia that summer. As Douglass Adair points out, "The tradition of fame and honor that was most significant to the American Revolution" and to the Framers of the Constitution was "classical in its origins, and educated men of the Enlightenment were drilled and educated in it at college." But the classical historians provided more than inspiration for the young men of the eighteenth century: the Revolutionary generation actually looked to them for practical guidance on matters of government. Adair continues, "They really believed that the books they studied in class furnished an absolutely essential and complete preparation for an active political career." The young Gilbert Elliot (later Lord Minto, viceroy of India) entered Christ Church College, Oxford, in 1768, four years after CHARLES COTESWORTH PINCKNEY. Dean William Markham told him that "only classical and historical knowledge could make able statesmen." WASHINGTON, always acutely aware of his own limited education, wrote to George Chapman in 1784, "The best means of forming a manly, virtuous and happy people, will be found in the right education of youth. Without *this* foundation, every other means, in my opinion, must fail." Most Americans, like WASHINGTON, never went to college; even in such an select group as the Framers of the Constitution barely half had even a year or two of higher education. And of course, "the education of youth" in WASHINGTON's day was utterly unlike anything college students encounter today.[5]

The exteriors of Princeton's Nassau Hall and William and Mary's Wren Building have changed little over 250 years; much traditional college terminology remains in use, albeit with somewhat altered meanings: matriculation and commencement, bachelor and fellow, bursar and commons. (When Oxford students were divided into nobles, gentlemen commoners, and commoners, "commoner" simply referred to the practice of dining in the student commons or dining hall.) Such surface continuities inevitably cause confusion—being granted a diploma in the eighteenth century was sometimes called "receiving the honors of the college," leading to modern assertions that one Framer or another "graduated with honors"—but they cannot mask the enormous differences between eighteenth-century colleges and modern universities. In many ways the colleges of the 1700s were much closer to the medieval universities than to their twenty-first-century avatars, and like the medieval universities, eighteenth-century colleges existed primarily to educate the clergy—although many students had other plans.

Apart from the College of Philadelphia, every American college had been founded under the auspices of a religious denomination, and the presidents of all (including Philadelphia) were themselves clergymen. When New Light revivalism challenged Connecticut orthodoxy in the 1740s, Yale took the controversial step of banning attendance at any church *except* the required New Haven chapel; Harvard relaxed its requirement of attending Congregationalist services only for communicants of the Church of England who chose Anglican services instead. In contrast, both Princeton's and Philadelphia's charters explicitly welcomed students of all denominations, and although King's College—after bitter controversy—was dominated by the Anglican establishment, it had a number of Dutch Reformed and Presbyterian trustees and imposed no religious test on its students.

The one earned degree was the Bachelor of Arts (or the MA in Scotland), but most Oxford and William and Mary students didn't bother to pursue it. In Williamsburg, Virginia's colonial capital, the degree was not the point: "The college's main function was as a provincial center where young gentlemen from the various parts of Virginia could simultaneously acquire higher accomplishments, knowledge of government affairs, and acquaintance with one another." One or two years were enough for most Virginia gentlemen to achieve those goals, and William and Mary did not award its first bachelor's degree until 1772. Northern colleges expected students to stay four years (three at Philadelphia) and earn the degree. After waiting another three years, the graduate could return to pay a fee, deliver an oration, and receive an automatic MA. A rare student might remain for further study after graduation as JAMES MADISON did, but neither the Inns of Court nor the medical program at the University of Edinburgh expected their professional students to arrive with bachelor's degrees. Harvard's president Holyoke encouraged graduates to do some reading to prepare for their master's declamations, and graduated bachelors occasionally boarded at colleges, perhaps preparing for the ministry while waiting out their three years, but actual study was nowhere required for a master's degree. Additional master's degrees could easily be arranged from cooperative colleges if one were willing to travel: young WILLIAM S. JOHNSON (Yale class of 1744) returned to New Haven in 1747 to give his address and accept an MA, and then—endorsed by Yale's president—rode up to Cambridge to collect one there, too, without previously setting foot on the Harvard campus. Doctoral degrees were purely honorary: about to assume the presidency of Yale, Ezra Stiles was impressed to learn that Philadelphia's vice-provost Francis Alison was a doctor of divinity from the University of Glasgow and asked him to send a copy of his diploma so that he could see what it looked like. He then arranged to get himself one from Edinburgh, even though he never left America.[6]

For undergraduates, the course of study was inflexible; rare electives included French lessons at Harvard, medical lectures at King's College and Philadelphia, and instruction in Hebrew for those Princeton students aiming at the ministry. Otherwise, it was classical prose and poetry, natural and moral philosophy, mathematics, logic, rhetoric, and (in England and New England) divinity. Texts were mainly in Latin (and infrequently Greek), but lectures were now usually given in English, an innovation Francis Hutcheson apparently introduced at Glasgow in the 1730s. The means of instruction were reading, recitation, lecture, and formal disputation, the latter gradually changing from Latin syllogisms to debate in English. There was some written work, but it still followed the old model of oral disputation (and was still read aloud at Oxford). Annual examinations were a Princeton novelty that slowly caught on elsewhere; previously, subjective evaluation of each student's progress had been left up to his college tutor.[7]

Perhaps it could go without saying that American college students before the Revolution were all male, Protestant—or else they went to Catholic colleges abroad—and white, with the exceptions of very occasional Native Americans at Harvard or William and Mary (both of which had Indian Schools endowed by the English chemist, William Boyle) and two African American students admitted to Princeton by President Witherspoon, who tutored them privately. The early eighteenth century's students were younger than today's collegians, but by the 1760s the median age of Harvard freshmen had risen to seventeen and Yale matriculants were only slightly younger. A few Princeton students even matriculated in their twenties, after hearing a late call to become Presbyterian ministers. Children of wealthier families tended to start earlier, thanks to better preparation. GOUVERNEUR MORRIS entered King's College at the age of twelve and WILLIAM S. JOHNSON entered Yale at thirteen; ALEXANDER HAMILTON, who liked to be considered a prodigy, was embarrassed to be already eighteen when he prepared to enroll at King's College and subtracted two years from his age from that point on. MADISON was also eighteen when he arrived at Princeton, but he immediately took the freshman exams and skipped to the sophomore class.[8]

College students in general were likely to come from privileged backgrounds, but this too was gradually changing. Historians of education seem to be of two minds about the relationship of colonial colleges and social status, tending toward broad brushstrokes in either direction. John Thelin, in his *History of Higher Education*, is emphatic: "Clearly, the main purpose of the colleges was to identify and ratify a colonial elite." Matthew Hartley and Elizabeth J. Hollander, in "The Elusive Ideal: Civic Learning and Higher Education," agree: "The colonial colleges of the 1700s trained the children of the elite in order to perpetuate the religious and civic leadership of their communities," but they then acknowledge that there was already "a higher purpose for higher education—to foster citizenship and to serve a democratic society." Thelin acknowledges a need "to look beneath the pejorative modern connotation of elitism. In other words, the remarkable feature of the colonial colleges was not their elite character. Rather, it was the fact that established wealthy families and frugal colonial governments [chose] to impart to their privileged sons a sense of responsibility and public service." Thomas Miller, on the other hand, argues that in Britain's "cultural provinces," eighteenth-century colleges had begun "to assimilate broader classes of students into the dominant culture." Gordon Wood goes a step further, declaring that "a high proportion of the revolutionary leaders were first-generation gentlemen. That is to say, many were the first in their families to attend college, to acquire a liberal arts education, and to display the marks of an enlightened eighteenth-century gentleman."[9]

If we test these generalizations with the limited sample of the Framers, we see that fifteen or sixteen who could be described as members of the "elite" by birth did go on to college, while another ten or twelve whose families were also the "better sort" (to use the contemporary phrase) did not, although several had private tutors; a dozen of the "middling sort" managed to attend college; and, finally, another dozen from relatively humble origins had nevertheless risen to enough prominence without a college education to be chosen by their states to represent them in Philadelphia.[10]

How visible was elitism on the college campuses? Thelin says that in 1769, with the exception of the College of Rhode Island, "Harvard and the other colleges continued to list graduates by social rank," but he is mistaken. Harvard and Yale reflected social status in class rank, but William and Mary, Princeton, Philadelphia, and King's never did; Yale had already given it up in 1766 and Harvard abandoned the practice in 1769. Thelin imagines other forms of social distinction that do not seem to have actually existed in colonial colleges. He says that, "following Oxford tradition, academic robes identified socioeconomic position": full-tuition-paying students "wore long robes, as distinguished from the short academic robes of servitors, scholarship students who waited on tables." There is no record of such distinction in regalia anywhere in the colonies, and the doubtful existence of student "servitors" at meals depends on an inference from a single ambiguous passage in Harvard's 1650 laws; they would have been unimaginable at William and Mary (where all servants were Black) or where students were as generally wealthy and few in number as at King's College; there is simply no record of them at any colonial college in the eighteenth century. Scholarships certainly existed at Harvard and at William and Mary, but at least at the latter they were competitive, not based on need; the aristocratic EDMUND RANDOLPH was proud to have won a scholarship. The cost of four years' tuition was substantial, about the equivalent of a clapboard house or twice a laborer's wages for a year. A 1720 bursar's letter dunning a wealthy grandmother informed her that her grandson's tuition for four years at Harvard came to £100, where it remained for much of the century. Records for 1650–1660, when nearly all Harvard students came from well-to-do families, show only ten boys receiving financial aid, but a hundred years later, when GERRY and STRONG were students, almost half their classmates were recipients of scholarship funds. Yale, being newer and less richly endowed, could not be so generous, and Ezra Stiles recorded more than once that a student was "dismissed for indigence."[11]

Students themselves ensured that seniority was respected by underclassmen, and freshmen were expected to follow the orders of older students to a degree that would be outlawed as hazing today. At eighteenth-century Harvard, according to Josiah Quincy, "The freshman class were servitors to the whole College out of study hours, to go on errands." Along with the gowns worn by students and faculty alike, the "mortarboard" hat was part of the student uniform. (William and Mary's mysteriously named "F.H.C." society was jokingly known as the Flat Hat Club.) Morison says that at Harvard gowns were only permitted once students were sophomores, "after treating the upperclassmen to drinks," and could be of any bright color, with no distinction of social rank—he cites a 1766 student's comment on "a new Gown one side of which is red Russell and the other Plad." In 1773, for a classmate's funeral in Boston, freshmen were permitted to put on "Black Gowns and Square Hats," puzzling the local people "as they walked about the Town with their black Gowns on, the Inhabitants not knowing what it meant or who they were." When Myles Cooper became president of King's College, he required students to wear gowns off campus so that townspeople *would* know who they were and could thus report misbehavior. Judging from a student essay by WILLIAM PATERSON, Princeton students also chose colorful attire: "Gowns seem to be as essential to Nassau-Students as black coats and grey wigs to divines. . . . how often do we behold a shameless collegiate of a round, unthinking face, his hair frizzled and powdered to the tip of the mode, amble along, with now and then a hitch in his gait, in a party-colored nightgown or undress?"[12]

Without exception, eighteenth-century American colleges were small. Today's Columbia varsity football roster is twice the size of the entire student body when HAMILTON was there. William and Mary's enrollment rarely exceeded sixty before the Revolution, and that was counting its grammar school boys, who for years made up the majority of the students; Harvard and Yale normally had between 100 and 150 students and Princeton had 70 or 80 by the 1770s. (Glasgow, in contrast, enrolled 300 when WILSON was there, but many were part-time students—a category that did not yet exist at American colleges.) After two or three years as a student, it would have been impossible not to know all of one's classmates. In almost every college the students lived and ate together in one or two buildings, supervised by teachers who enforced curfews and rules of behavior with varying degrees of success. Colleges sponsored no extracurricular activities, but students enjoyed forming secret societies with names that, as at William and Mary, members were forbidden to speak in public. Students created clubs for a variety of purposes. As early as 1747, Edmund Burke and friends created their own Academy of Belles Lettres (known simply as "the Club") at Trinity College, Dublin, for the purpose of social conversation; like the six-member F.H.C. it was small (initially fewer than eight members), but by 1780 its successor, the College Historical Society, numbered its members in the hundreds. In Britain, actual debating societies were discouraged or even suppressed; Glasgow had a debating society in the 1760s, but it was admonished to avoid political topics when it became too interested in colonial controversies, and Dublin's College Historical Society was shut down by university authorities in 1780. Oxford forbade debating clubs until the nineteenth century.[13]

In the American colonies, Yale's president Thomas Clap discouraged any sign of contention, but he tolerated social clubs such as the Linonians, who organized a private library for members (as did other clubs at William and Mary and Princeton). Princeton's American Whig and Cliosophic Societies were the first true debating societies in the colonies, followed soon after by Phi Beta Kappa at William and Mary, the successor to the F.H.C. Since the Middle Ages, universities had required students to present arguments in an Aristotelian method, linking together syllogisms to deduce particulars from preceding generalizations. Princeton's president Samuel Davies had begun the shift from Latin syllogistic disputations to forensic debating in English during the 1750s, but not until 1766 did Harvard assign a tutor to teach "Elocution, composition in English, Rhetoric and other parts of the Belles Lettres," and syllogistic disputations continued there in Latin. "Belle-lettristic" influences were pronounced at colleges like Harvard that had not been strongly influenced by Scottish universities, while schools that had been, including Princeton and the College of Philadelphia, became more focused on persuasive, political rhetoric in both clubs and curriculum. Students, as usual, were ahead of their administrators; David Shields, in *Civil Tongues and Polite Letters in America*, recounts the appearance of a number of Harvard clubs in the early eighteenth century to promote "conversation, politeness, and joviality," on the one hand, or—appealing to different students—"mutual aid in cultivating holiness," on the other. None were debating societies; the "jovial" Philomusarians encouraged "Conversation, which is the Basis of Friendship," while the "holy" Society of Young Students were so far from being debaters that they announced their intent to avoid "all manner of Disagreeing." Similar clubs came and went through the century before the Speaking Club was founded in 1770 to promote oratory (though not debate). MADISON, PATERSON, and the other verbally combative Whigs and Clios at Princeton would have been puzzled.[14]

In their structures, both formal and informal, the eighteenth-century colleges attended by the Framers were all similar, but they fell into two distinct categories. Oxford, William and Mary, Yale, and Harvard broadly followed one pattern: religiously, geographically, and socially homogeneous, suspicious of innovation, and in the first two cases at least as much social as academic institutions. Glasgow, Princeton, Philadelphia, and King's were different in significant ways: they were quicker to embrace more modern methods of instruction, less religiously exclusive, and, except for King's, less narrowly local in their student bodies. (Oxford University's overall population was as geographically diverse as Glasgow's, but its many individual colleges tended to draw from particular regions of Great Britain.) Even more important, when it came to inculcating principles of political philosophy, the colleges' curricula fell into the same dichotomy: the older schools did not teach modern philosophers, while the newer schools began introducing newer authors with newer ideas—especially those of the Scottish Enlightenment. Even so, there was much common ground; MADISON or HAMILTON may have been introduced to the new philosophy of Hutcheson or Hume, but they also read the same classics that others read.

At colleges in the eighteenth century, the ability to read Latin and Greek was the sole criterion for admission. Even before Harvard opened its doors in 1636, the Massachusetts Bay Colony had created Boston Latin School to prepare boys for the anticipated college. For the next century and a half throughout the colonies, the necessary instruction in "the languages" was provided by grammar schools, clergymen, and private tutors. Many of their students were well enough served by that grounding in the classics that they felt no need to go on to college—among them such older Framers as MASON and DICKINSON, whose early preparation led them to a lifetime of reading. Out of a population of 1.5 million in 1750, fewer than one hundred students began college each year. That number slowly rose, and what they learned there changed just as slowly.

According to Thomas Miller, "The traditional liberal arts curriculum that older American universities had adopted from the English universities" meant students "studied the classics intensively, not extensively, in order to master the stylistic forms of the educated language." He also says, "Despite the reigning classicism, civic humanists like Isocrates, Cicero, and Quintilian were rarely studied in the seventeenth and eighteenth centuries" at

American colleges. But Harvard freshmen read Isocrates, by 1763 Quintilian was taught to sophomores and juniors at King's college and Isocrates to seniors, and Cicero was inescapable at preparatory schools and at colleges. Indeed, Robson, in *Educating Republicans*, says that Cicero was the most widely read Latin author, even ahead of Virgil; Mark Kalthoff suspects that Cicero's *De officiis* "may be the most copied and widely praised pagan text in the history of the Christian West," and Miller himself notes that "Witherspoon's interest in Cicero [at Princeton] is not surprising because he remained one of the best known authorities in moral philosophy until the Scots became predominant late in the century." *De officiis*, Cicero's advice to his son on the subject of morality, was at the heart of every eighteenth-century gentleman's education.[15]

College freshmen were drilled in Latin grammar, but the core curriculum was classical history. In addition to Sallust's *Jugurthine War* (chronicling the degeneration of the Republic), many colleges assigned Tacitus and Livy, whose histories extended to the early Empire. These authors, along with Aristotle, Plutarch, and Cicero, were the political authorities most often cited in the second half of the century. Plutarch's *Lives of the Noble Greeks and Romans* is missing from college reading lists simply because almost all college students were already familiar with it. Again and again, even the Framers who had no college education mention the influence Plutarch had on them. And there can be no question that these Romans were read as "civic humanists." Plutarch and the other classical poets, orators, and historians all warned against tyranny; they praised just governments and blamed their eventual downfall on the corruption of republican virtue. Nearly all of the favored classical authors wrote at times when either Greece or Rome was losing republican government to aristocracies and dictators, and both Englishmen and Americans took their warnings to heart.[16]

Aristotle taught obedience to the laws of nature and Cato the necessity of republican virtue; Sallust showed that historical crises were tests of character; Plutarch warned of the threat of tyranny, Cicero the danger of arbitrary government, and Tacitus the inevitability of corruption in an empire. When the wealthy CHARLES PINCKNEY III claimed at the Convention that there was no great economic divide in America, MADISON answered him with Aristotle: "The most palpable, and also the most specific difference [among men] is the distinction of riches and poverty; wherefore all governments have been divided into oligarchies and democracies, as the winds are divided into north and south."[17]

The Framers had been taught to look at the Greeks before Alexander, or the Romans before Caesar, and to see themselves. When DICKINSON told the

Convention, "Experience alone must be our guide," he made clear that he had in mind the "long experience" of history. When HAMILTON proposed in *Federalist*, no. 6, that "experience, the least fallible guide for human opinion, be appealed to for an answer to these inquiries," experience again meant (as it nearly always did for HAMILTON) the lessons of history. Classical history was read as a mirror of the modern world. Theology had dominated the seventeenth century, in England as in New England, but the eighteenth gave its greatest attention to history. Trevor Colbourn notes that more books of history were available than on any other subject: "This was as true of the college library as of the subscription library, of the personal collection of a Jefferson or a DICKINSON as of the advertised stocks of a Bell or a Knox [booksellers at Williamsburg and Philadelphia, respectively]." In *Proposals Relating to the Education of Youth* (published during his campaign to found the Academy of Philadelphia), BEN FRANKLIN observed, "As nothing *teaches*, so nothing *delights* more than HISTORY"; it was, he continued, a source of "almost all Kinds of useful knowledge."[18]

David Ramsay—teacher, physician, congressman, and son-in-law of John Witherspoon—was the first serious historian of the Revolution. He was sure that education, especially in history, had contributed to the success of independence. Without it, "the United States would probably have fallen in their unequal contest with Great Britain. Union, which was essential to the success of their resistance, could scarcely have taken place in the measures adopted by an ignorant multitude. Much less could wisdom in council, unity in system, or perseverance in the prosecution of a long and self-denying war, be expected from an uninformed people." Ramsay's avowed subject was the war for independence, but when his book was published in 1789, "wisdom in council" and "unity in system" also suggested the newly ratified Constitution.[19]

WILLIAM LIVINGSTON, a generation before Ramsay, reminded New Yorkers of the patriotic value of a college education for their sons: "'Tis to improve their Hearts and Understanding, to infuse a public Spirit of Love of their Country; to inspire them with the Principles of Honour and Probity; with the fervent Zeal for Liberty, and a diffusive Benevolence for Mankind; and in a Word, to make them the more extensively serviceable to the Commonwealth." Education was less a matter of acquiring knowledge than of building character, and the classical historians and poets provided memorable examples of good and bad behavior to follow or to avoid.[20]

Modern authors did their best to assume the style and character of the classics. John Trenchard and Thomas Gordon, "commonwealth whigs" who criticized the corruption they found in the British government and advocated republican reform, were best known for adopting the persona of the moral hero of Republican Rome in their series of essays, *Cato's Letters*. Bernard Bailyn calls *Cato's Letters*, "in the run-up to the Revolution, the most important sources or models for criticism"; according to Clinton Rossiter, "No one can spend any time on the newspapers, library inventories, and pamphlets of colonial America without realizing that *Cato's Letters* rather than Locke's [*Two Treatises on*] *Civil Government* was the most popular, quotable, esteemed source for political ideas in the colonial period." Indeed, FRANKLIN specified that at his academy, "Cato's Letters &c. should be Classicks."[21]

The figure of Cato of Utica, who committed suicide rather than submit to the tyranny of Caesar, had a special significance to Englishmen in America. His name was familiar from Plutarch and Sallust and from Trenchard and Gordon, but it was even better known from Joseph Addison's play, *Cato, a Tragedy*. Written in 1713, *Cato* would prove more popular in America over the coming century than any other serious drama. It was performed in 1736 by students at the College of William and Mary, it opened the first professional theater in Philadelphia in 1749, and Nathaniel Ames reported seeing it twice in one week while he was a student at Harvard in 1758. The play had no greater admirer than WASHINGTON, who ordered it performed at Valley Forge and quoted from it constantly throughout his life.[22]

Even more familiar than *Cato* were Addison's *Spectator* essays. MADISON, in his autobiography, says that the first important incident of his life was his discovery of *The Spectator* when he was eleven years old. No library was without a set; Provost William Smith listed *The Spectator* first among titles assigned to Philadelphia freshmen to be read in their "private hours." FRANKLIN, WASHINGTON, MASON, and FEW are among the Framers who lacked formal education but read *The Spectator* as boys. The prose of Addison (and his collaborator, Richard Steele) was so admired that students at the Philadelphia and New London academies were assigned *Spectator* essays as models for composition. But *The Spectator* also popularized a "spectatorial" social code: Addison, says Garry Wills, "made 'the man within the breast' the audience to whom one must play, the internalized disinterested spectator. . . . The man of public virtue solicits the good opinion of others, who become his imitators by virtue of their admiration." This, according to Alexander Pope's prologue to Addison's *Cato*, was also the aim of that play: "To make mankind in conscious virtue bold, / Live o'er each scene, and be what they behold." Newton's *Opticks* had made the lens and mirror popular eighteenth-century metaphors, and mirrors reflected two ways: those who emulated the heroes of antiquity likewise thirsted for the fame that would in turn make them models for posterity.[23]

The same concern with the "spectatorial" influence on morality appears in Adam Smith's 1759 *Theory of Moral Sentiments* (familiar to a number of the Framers): "Were it possible that a human creature could grow up to manhood in some solitary place, without any communication with his own species, he could no more think of his own character, of the propriety or demerit of his own sentiments and conduct . . . than of the beauty or deformity of his own face." Smith followed Hutcheson in the chair of moral philosophy at Glasgow. "Philosophy" was a broad term, often defined as it was by John Witherspoon: "an inquiry . . . by reason, as distinct from revelation." Natural philosophy was the usual term for what we would call science; it addressed the question of what *is*, what exists beyond human responsibility. Moral philosophy addressed the question of what *should be*, that for which humans are by definition responsible. It thus encompassed both ethics and politics, the question of what individuals should do and the question of what societies should do. Moral philosophy was obviously crucial to the framing of the Constitution, but the subject of natural philosophy also proved relevant; usually taught at school in the form of physical science and astronomy (with occasional lectures in chemistry), by the 1720s natural philosophy was almost always Newtonian.[24]

Newton joined Bacon and Locke in Jefferson's triumvirate of the greatest men who ever lived. Newton's influence on the Framers at Philadelphia was indirect, but they were not unconscious of it; in arguing for an executive "negative" (veto) during the Convention, MADISON found a metaphor in "the planetary system" as described by Newton. As he explained, "This prerogative of the General Govt. is the great pervading principle that must control the centrifugal tendency of the states; which, without it, will continually fly out of their proper orbits and destroy the order & harmony of the political system." HAMILTON had written to WASHINGTON at the time of the threatened Newburgh mutiny, "To borrow a figure from mechanics, the centrifugal is much stronger than the centripetal force in these states—the seeds of disunion much more numerous than those of union." In 1787, many of the Framers were reading John Adams's *Defence of the Constitutions of the United States*, serialized in the *Pennsylvania Mercury* even as the Convention was meeting; in its Letter 25, "Opinions of Philosophers," Adams (who learned physics from the renowned John Winthrop at Harvard) invokes "one of Sir Isaac Newton's laws of motion, viz. 'that re-action must always be equal and contrary to action' or there can never be any rest"; he therefore prefers, by analogy, a mixed government with "checks and balances" to a single legislature "without any counterpoise, balance or equilibrium."[25]

Many delegates would have recognized the persuasive Newtonian metaphors from their courses in natural philosophy at Harvard, Philadelphia, or Christ Church, C. C. PINCKNEY's college at Oxford. They also would have recognized the idea of counterpoise from the poetry of Alexander Pope. Pope was the most popular English poet of the age, and the "Essay on Man" was his most familiar poem. With his announced project to "vindicate the ways of God to man," Pope begins his "Essay" by pointing out the seeming paradox by which strife creates order in nature, and he goes on to postulate the same resolution of conflict through dynamic balance in society:

> On Life's vast ocean diversely we sail,
> Reason's the card, but Passion is the gale.
>   . . . Passion, like elements, tho' born to fight,
> Yet mix'd and soften'd, in [God's] work unite:
>   . . . Each individual seeks a sev'ral goal,
> But Heav'ns great view is one, and that the whole.
> That, counterworks each folly and caprice,
> That, disappoints th'effect of every vice.
>   (Epistle II, 107–108, 111–112, 235–238)

A similar argument for making order out of conflict, but one less orthodox than Pope's, was made in Bernard de Mandeville's 1714 *Fable of the Bees*. Mandeville anticipated Adam Smith's "invisible hand" by pointing out, in the words of his subtitle, that "Private Vices [Create] Public Benefits," since a prosperous society is ultimately built on individual selfishness. Pope was admired and celebrated, but Mandeville's poem was considered scandalous in its cynicism. It was, nevertheless, widely read. FRANKLIN revealed its influence in his first published work, *A Dissertation on Liberty and Necessity*, written at the age of nineteen, and he was excited to actually meet Mandeville in London that same year; WILLIAM SAMUEL JOHNSON's 1747 MA address at Yale (recycled at Harvard) rebutted Mandeville's argument.

Poetry could thus echo natural philosophy; both in turn prepared students for the political ideas they might encounter in moral philosophy courses. Montesquieu wrote in *The Spirit of the Laws* that individual ambition "moves all parts of the body politic; it unites them by its own action, and the result is that each individual serves the public interest while he believes that he is serving his own." That much would have been familiar from Pope or Mandeville, but Montesquieu continues in explicitly Newtonian language: "You might say that it is like the system of the universe, in which there is a force which incessantly moves all bodies away from the center and a force of gravity which brings them back to it." Newton spoke of the necessity of "counterpoise" or "overpoise" in the "balance" of physical forces, action along with equal and opposite reaction; Witherspoon employed the same terms in his *Lectures on Moral Philosophy* to argue that "every good form of government must be complex, so that one principal may check the other. . . . They must be so balanced that when every one draws to his own interest or inclination, there may be an overpoise upon the whole." MADISON, in *Federalist*, no. 51, would observe that "the policy of supplying, by opposite and rival interests, the defects of better motives might be traced through the whole system of human affairs, private as well as public."[26]

All this was "natural" philosophy. For a strict Calvinist like William Ames, whose works were assigned at Yale throughout the eighteenth century, moral questions were answered only by the Bible; "philosophy" could add nothing. But since the rise of Renaissance humanism, educated men such as the Framers had also been taught to seek moral truth in the *Ethics* of Aristotle and in the lessons of classical history. That was the message of Plutarch, of Cicero, of Tacitus. The Enlightenment suspected that in moral philosophy as in natural philosophy there were natural laws that could be discovered through empirical methods. The devoutly Calvinist, classically educated Witherspoon concludes his *Lectures on Moral Philosophy* with the same hope that Aberdeen's Turnbull had expressed in his dedication to *Principles of Moral Philosophy:* "Perhaps a time may come when men, treating moral philosophy as Newton and his successors have done natural, may arrive at greater precision"—in Hume's words, a time when "politics may be reduced to a science."[27]

Moral philosophy courses were typically taught to seniors, often by the college president. Not one of the Framers stayed at William and Mary for even a junior year, but the moral philosophy course there would have offered them little beyond the Greeks and Romans until the Rev. James Madison (cousin of the Framer) modernized the curriculum in the 1790s. President Clap lectured to his Yale seniors, but their only text on politics was Clap's own *Nature and Foundation of Moral Virtue and Obligation*, which, like both Ames and Cicero, presented moral philosophy in terms of individual duties rather than rights. At Harvard, Jean-Jacques Burlamaqui's *Principles of Natural and Political Law* may have been assigned during the Revolutionary War to RUFUS KING; the Rev. John Clarke (class of 1774) recalled in 1796 that Burlamaqui had "during many years been studied at the university," conceivably even as early as GERRY's and STRONG's time. If so, it would have been their sole modern text in political theory.[28]

Burlamaqui was one of a small group of modern political philosophers whose Calvinism rendered them acceptable in New England. Two of them, Hugo Grotius and Samuel Pufendorf, had the added appeal of having played a part (through their influence on John Locke) in the Glorious Revolution, England's rejection of the absolutist Stuart dynasty, an event that was, in Michael Barone's words, "a glowing example for the American Founders." However, as Adams bitterly complained, these philosophers were not taught at Harvard. In contrast to Grotius and Pufendorf, Burlamaqui was noted for the clarity of his prose and the orderliness of his arguments, qualities that help explain his wide readership. Burlamaqui, himself a Genevan, agreed with Calvin's belief that because absolute monarchy was likely to result in tyranny, it was "safer or more bearable for a number to exercise government." Thomas Jefferson, among others, was struck by his assertion that by natural right all men were equal, and equally entitled to pursue *le bonheur*, often translated as "happiness."[29]

Grotius and Pufendorf, the founding philosophers of natural rights, were with Burlamaqui required reading at King's College and Philadelphia, as was Francis Hutcheson. Grotius had declared, "What God hath shown to be His Will, that is law," but he had also laid the foundations for the idea of purely natural rights, declaring that "the mother of natural law is human nature itself." He maintained that "Natural Right is the Rule and Dictate of Right Reason, shewing the Moral Deformity or Moral Necessity there is in any Act, according to its Suitableness or Unsuitableness to a reasonable Nature, and consequently, that such an Act is either forbid or commanded by GOD, the Author of Nature." Pufendorf, building on Grotius, developed a political philosophy of social contract that would be expanded by Locke, and his ideas about the rights of man would influence both Burlamaqui and Hutcheson. He suggested that large nations were better suited to be governed as monarchies, believing republics more successful if they were compact and relatively homogeneous.[30]

Pufendorf and Burlamaqui were sometimes assigned to students at Christ Church College, Oxford, but there everything depended on the choices of the individual's tutor. Christ Church graduate John Locke's *Essay on Human Understanding* was widely read in American colleges, usually under the heading of metaphysics, but his *Two Treatises on Government* were on the reading list only at Princeton and Philadelphia until William and Mary added them in 1801. Because Locke was English—and also associated with the constitutionalism of the Glorious Revolution—he was especially influential in the colonies. Gordon Wood believes that what is "extraordinary about the views of late-eighteenth century Americans is the extent to which most educated men shared the premises of Lockean sensationalism [i.e., the *Essay on Human Understanding*] that all men were born equal and had only the environment working on their senses that made them different." One important variable element of that environment, of course, was their "different means of education."[31]

An article of faith that most delegates brought with them to the Convention was the necessity of the separation of powers. This idea, originating in Polybius's *Histories* in the second century BCE, was popularly identified with Montesquieu's *Spirit of the Laws*, where it actually plays a small part. College students in the 1760s and 1770s would have been more likely to encounter the idea of "balanced" government in Hutcheson's *System of Moral Philosophy*, but only at schools where it was assigned (or available in club libraries). At Princeton and Philadelphia students might read Montesquieu, but not yet at other colleges. Ezra Stiles introduced *The Spirit of the Laws* at Yale in 1789, commenting that it had been in use at Princeton; Joseph C. Cabell lists it as a text at William and Mary, but not until 1798. Although no college seems to have assigned Polybius, MADISON and others read him on their own.[32]

Locke, Bacon, and Montesquieu are well-known names; less familiar today are the "Commonwealthmen" or "Real Whigs," the late seventeenth- and early eighteenth-century English political writers such as Trenchard and Gordon who were well known to the Framers. Caroline Robbins, whose *Eighteenth-Century Commonwealthman* brought them to the attention of American historians in 1959, writes that "the American Constitution employs many of the devices which the Real Whigs vainly besought Englishmen to adopt and in it must be found their most abiding memorial." Among those "devices" are the ideas of rotation in office, a supreme court, and separation of church and state. Pre-Revolutionary Americans were finding these writers' warnings about concentrated power and political corruption increasingly relevant, even as they were falling out of fashion in the England of George III.[33]

In his 1776 "Thoughts on Government," Adams acknowledged that the Commonwealth writers were considered passé by the British: "A man must be indifferent to the sneers of modern Englishmen to mention in their company the names of Sidney, Harrington, Locke, Milton, Nedham, Neville, Burnet, and Hoadly. No small fortitude is necessary to confess that one has read them." Adams himself read these authors only after he left Harvard, and, as he implies, they would not be found in the curriculum at Oxford or Cambridge either—and certainly not at Catholic St. Omer's, where they were viewed as traitors to the martyred Stuarts. Sidney was endorsed in FRANKLIN's *Proposals*, and James Harrington, the influential author of *Oceana*, was listed in William Smith's 1756 plan for the College of Philadelphia along with two other Commonwealthmen, Richard Cumberland and John Selden. All four were also recommended to John Witherspoon's students at Princeton, along with Edward Montagu. Montagu's *Rise and Fall of the Antient Republics* was one of several books that MADISON would return to in preparation for the Convention.[34]

MADISON's reading under Witherspoon went well beyond the required texts. His biographer Ralph Ketcham believes that by graduation or shortly thereafter (he stayed an additional six months) he had read the natural rights philosophers Grotius, Pufendorf, Locke, Barbeyrac, Cumberland, Selden, and Burlamaqui, in addition to Hobbes, Machiavelli, Harrington, Sidney, Montesquieu, Ferguson, Kames, and Hume—all recommended in Witherspoon's lectures. Less than three years after leaving Princeton, MADISON was writing to his college friend William Bradford in Philadelphia, grateful to hear from him that the delegates to the Continental Congress were making "great and constant use" of the collection of the Library Company there, especially Vattel (a disciple of Grotius), Burlamaqui, Locke, and Montesquieu—all familiar names to these young Princeton graduates. By 1782, five years before the Federal Convention, MADISON was himself in Congress and was put in charge of a committee to draw up "a list of books to be imported for the use of the United States in Congress Assembled." When he submitted his list in January 1783 it was filled with modern authors, especially Scots. The section headed "Politics" included "Hume's political essays," "Smith on the Wealth of Nations," "Ferguson's History of Civil Society," and "Millar on the distinction of Ranks in Society." The first three were authors recommended by Witherspoon; John Millar's book—a pioneering work in sociology—was published the year MADISON graduated.[35]

Hume's religious skepticism barred him from teaching at the Scottish universities, but Adam Ferguson taught at the University of Edinburgh and Adam Smith at Glasgow, where Millar's legal lectures could have been heard by the Framers WILSON and SPAIGHT. The Scottish Enlightenment philosophers were not part of the curriculum at the older colleges. It is true that books by Francis Hutcheson, Adam Ferguson, and Lord Kames could be found in the Harvard library by 1773, along with those of the Commonwealthmen Harrington, Sidney, Burnet, Montagu and Hoadly—all donated by the English radicals Thomas Hollis and Richard Baron. But neither Harvard nor Yale encouraged students to use the library; Yale's president Clap actually made it off limits to all students except seniors. There is no sign that any of these volumes was ever an assigned text.[36]

The modern philosopher most widely assigned to college students was

Francis Hutcheson. Hutcheson, the earliest of the influential Scots, was a standard author at the College of Philadelphia, where the published 1756 curriculum includes his *Metaphysicae Synopsis* for freshman and both his *Short Introduction to Moral Philosophy* and *System of Moral Philosophy* for seniors. From THOMAS MIFFLIN's Philadelphia college notebook, it is clear that Hutcheson was central to the moral philosophy course there; MIFFLIN's teacher, Francis Alison, had probably been a student of Hutcheson's in Dublin or Glasgow. In 1763, the program of studies for King's College listed "Hutch. Mor. Phil." for seniors, and GOUVERNEUR MORRIS (class of 1768) clearly read his *Inquiry into the Original of the Ideas of Beauty and Virtue.* In that early work Hutcheson lays out his theory that an inclination to benevolence is a response to the sight of good deeds by others, a form of the argument that virtuous behavior derives from the emulation of noble examples—the spur of fame. Witherspoon disagreed with Hutcheson on matters of theology, but his Princeton *Lectures on Moral Philosophy* closely follow Hutcheson's *System of Moral Philosophy.*[37]

Hutcheson evolved a broad theory of moral sense, but he was also part of the tradition of political Calvinism that extended back to Pufendorf and Grotius, promoting natural rights, government by consent of the governed, popular sovereignty, and the right of resistance. He emphasized the concept of balancing the several branches of government as checks against each other; both Alison and Witherspoon repeated that emphasis in their lectures. (At the Convention Alison's former student GOUVERNEUR MORRIS would argue that with two houses of Congress, "One interest must be opposed to another interest. . . . The two forces will then control each other.") Hutcheson advocated a bicameral legislature consisting of a popular assembly and a senate that had a third or a quarter of its members replaced at each election, which became part of MADISON's Virginia Plan. The executive branch might be an individual monarch—or it might be a small council elected by the senate, one of the models seriously considered at the 1787 Convention. Hutcheson, like many of the Framers, also saw property as the essential qualification for participation in society; to him as to them, "the people" would have meant what it did to Thomas Gordon: "all who have property without the privilege of nobility."[38]

A second strain of the Scottish Enlightenment derives from Thomas Reid. Reid rejected both George Berkeley's idealism—the idea that only "sense perceptions" could be known to exist—and Hume's radical skepticism of any certain knowledge. He proposed instead that a literally common sense—a capacity for empirical observation shared by all humans—made a degree of practical certainty available to any intelligent observer.

CHAPTER TWO

Reid extended Hutcheson's moral sense to include the ability to distinguish between truth and falsehood. Benjamin Rush, who graduated from Princeton before Witherspoon began teaching the theory there, nevertheless discovered the Scottish philosophers while studying medicine at Edinburgh in the mid-1760s. WILLIAMSON and MCCLURG may have done the same there, at the same time as Rush. Reid, who had close friends on the medical faculty at Edinburgh, had just published his *Inquiry into the Human Mind on the Principles of Common Sense* in 1764, the year he succeeded Adam Smith as professor of moral philosophy at Glasgow. JAMES WILSON was taking classes and attending lectures at Glasgow that year and very likely heard Reid lecture. When he later gave his own lectures on law at the University of Pennsylvania, he praised Reid's theories, asserting that "common sense" alone kept humans from being (in Hume's words) nothing but "a bundle or collection of different perceptions, which succeed one another with inconceivable rapidity . . . in a perpetual flux of movements."[39]

Reid was careful not to challenge orthodoxy; Hume, however, was notorious for many reasons, including his devastating critique of cause and effect, which may serve as a reminder that we cannot be sure that any one element in the Framers' educations is the *cause* of any of their actions or beliefs. Nevertheless, it is hard to disagree with the way Douglass Adair's essay "That Politics May Be Reduced to a Science" shows MADISON's *Federalist*, no. 10, drawing on Hume to refute the popular belief that only small republics could succeed. Contradicting the conventional wisdom embodied in Montesquieu's *Spirit of the Laws*, MADISON makes the case that to "extend the sphere" by enlarging the republic is to ensure that multiple, dispersed factions will always prevent each other from seizing power. This was also part of GOUVERNEUR MORRIS's rationale for popular election of the president: "An election by the people at large throughout so great an extent of country could not be influenced, by those little combinations and those momentary lies which often decide popular elections within a narrow sphere." (He did not foresee talk radio, cable television, the internet, or Twitter.) Moreover, Hume had written in "Politics as a Science" that "a constitution is only so far good, as it provides a remedy for maladministration." This became a central belief for MADISON; in *Federalist*, no. 51, he memorably declared, "If men were angels, no government would be necessary. If angels were to govern men, neither external nor internal controls on government would be necessary. In framing a government which is to be administered by men over men, the great difficulty lies in this: you must first enable the government to control the governed; and in the next place oblige it to control itself."[40]

Jack Rakove acknowledges that MADISON "found some inspiration for his new position [on large republics] in the writings of David Hume. . . . But if there was a Humean dimension to MADISON's thought, it lay less in the foundation of a specific hypothesis about the optimal size of republics than in the way in which MADISON sought to derive general rules of politics from the experience of history." The experience of history—at least classical history—was the heart of an eighteenth-century student's education. Added to that, an acquaintance with Newton's laws of physical forces encouraged him to find comparable natural laws in moral philosophy, where one interest checked or balanced another. And for students at the newer colleges, moral philosophy included the natural rights of the seventeenth-century liberal philosophers, the republican virtue of the Commonwealthmen, and the empirical reasoning of the Scottish Enlightenment.[41]

A college student's first opportunity to display his education in public came at the college commencement exercises. The published topics of many of the speeches and disputations suggest the extent to which degree candidates in the Framers' classes began to direct their learning less to the traditional religious topics and more and more to contemporary political issues. In 1765, following the Sugar Act, ELBRIDGE GERRY posed this timely question in his MA address: "Can the new prohibitory duties, which make it useless for the people to engage in commerce, be evaded by them as faithful subjects?" In 1770 at Princeton, a commencement speaker maintained that "subjects are bound and obliged by the law of nature to resist the king whenever he inflicts intolerable cruelties on them or overthrows the rights of the state; and they must defend their liberties." Sometimes the speakers debated questions that would be directly addressed at the 1787 Convention; in 1781, this apt question, central to the Convention six years later, was debated at Harvard: "Is public virtue the best security of republican liberty?"[42]

Clearly, graduates of American colleges were turning their attention to the political crises unfolding from the 1760s through the 1780s. Equally clearly, their education in moral philosophy provided their conceptual framework for responding to those crises. Cicero and Plutarch or Sidney and Addison might inculcate republican virtue, passion for virtue might spark a revolution, but by 1787 the men who met in Philadelphia would have told the Harvard commencement speaker that "public virtue" was not the answer. They were, as Daniel Walker Howe says, "fed up with the Articles of Confederation and their reliance on uncoerced popular virtue." MADISON privately wrote in April of that year, in notes he titled "Vices of the Political System of the United States," that the Confederation was failing because of "a mistaken confidence that the justice, the good faith, the honor, the sound policy of the several legislative assemblies" could ensure a successful republic. MADISON's title clearly indicates his focus for the upcoming Convention: not reinforcing the people's virtues but fixing the *system's* vices.[43]

As Adair reminds us, eighteenth-century college students "really believed" practical political suggestions that they could follow might be found in the moral philosophers they studied. But what about the majority of the Framers, who took no college courses in moral philosophy? Even those leaders of the revolutionary generation who had been to college had, with few exceptions, encountered no modern political philosophers there until the late 1760s—and many had hardly been inside a school, let alone a college. When they came to Philadelphia in 1787 to deal with the failures of the Articles of Confederation, what intellectual preparation were they depending on? The following chapters examine the differences between the older and newer colleges' curricula, along with the widely varying understandings acquired by young men whose education was obtained in what we would call primary or secondary schools. Some had private tutors to prepare them for higher education; for others, a few years with a trusted clergyman or a young tutor fresh out of college were all the formal education they would have. But we begin with a remarkable group whose education was obtained largely on their own.[44]

Part II

3

The Self-Taught and the Tutored

RICHARD BASSETT, WILLIAM BLOUNT, DANIEL CARROLL, GEORGE CLYMER, JOHN DICKINSON, OLIVER ELLSWORTH, WILLIAM FEW, BENJAMIN FRANKLIN, ELBRIDGE GERRY, ALEXANDER HAMILTON, WILLIAM SAMUEL JOHNSON, WILLIAM LIVINGSTON, JAMES MADISON, GEORGE MASON, JOHN FRANCIS MERCER, ROBERT MORRIS, CHARLES PINCKNEY III, JOHN RUTLEDGE, ROGER SHERMAN, CALEB STRONG, GEORGE WASHINGTON, GEORGE WYTHE

Preceptors lay the cornerstone, but the edifice can be finished only by the pupil himself.
EDMUND RANDOLPH, *History of Virginia*

In the eighteenth century the lack of a college education was no obstacle to leadership—social, political, or intellectual. FRANKLIN, WASHINGTON, DICKINSON, ROBERT MORRIS, and MASON were among the most influential men in America; all five have colleges named for them, but not one ever set foot in a college classroom. Like many eighteenth-century boys, some received a few years of private instruction and were then on their own. Others spent their youth with a tutor and went on to professional education—for RUTLEDGE and DICKINSON, at the Inns of Court. Wealthy families might hire a tutor to prepare their sons for college. For the less privileged, like the young FRANKLIN, SHERMAN, and FEW, there was the possibility of self-education, easier in Boston or Philadelphia but possible even in small-town New England or on the Carolina frontier. Whereas their privately tutored contemporaries pursued time-honored training in the classical languages, reading Cicero, Virgil, and Sallust, the young autodidacts sought a more modern education in English literature, history, and mathematics. SHERMAN and WASHINGTON mastered the geometry and trigonometry of surveying, while FRANKLIN and FEW—one in the city and the other on the frontier—found the humanities far more congenial, reading *The Spectator*, Plutarch, Smollett, and the French historian Rollin; both FRANKLIN and WASHINGTON, like so many in their era, were drawn to the republican ideals of Addison's *Cato*. A rare tutor, like Joseph Bellamy, might plant seeds that would bear fruit at the Convention, but political theory would come later—if at all.

BENJAMIN FRANKLIN was already the most famously self-educated American, even though his *Autobiography* had not yet been published when the Convention met. His study began early and seems to have continued all his life. By his own account, he was sent at the age of eight to Boston Latin School with the goal of a career in the ministry; Cotton Mather's son Sammy was a schoolmate. But after only a year, in a blow that BEN never really got over, Josiah Franklin changed his mind, and his son's dream of a scholarly life was over. Young FRANKLIN was briefly enrolled in "a school for Writing and Arithmetic" run by George Brownell, where he "acquired fair Writing pretty soon," but not so much arithmetic. That was enough to satisfy his father, and FRANKLIN's short time with Brownell was the last schooling he would know. He was apprenticed first to an uncle with a cutlery shop and then, in a fateful stroke of fortune, to his brother James, a printer. In James Franklin's print shop young BEN's self-education began.[1]

The printer's apprentice seems to have spent every free hour reading. He began with his father's meager library, which did include the ubiquitous Plutarch's *Lives of the Noble Greeks and Romans*, Cotton Mather's *Bonifacius: An Essay upon Good*, and Daniel Defoe's *Essay on Projects*. Plutarch's *Lives* was the great historical treasure house of good and bad characters; it probably meant more to FRANKLIN to read it in English for its substance than it would have to plow through it at school for its classical grammar. He remembered Defoe and Mather, saying they "perhaps gave me a Turn of Thinking that had an Influence on some of the future Events of my Life." Indeed, the *Autobiography* itself could have been subtitled "an essay on projects."[2]

Young FRANKLIN was not reading for amusement; he was already on a mission of self-improvement. He made friends with a bookseller's apprentice who let him take home books, "which I was careful to return soon & clean." Sometimes he read all night in order to return books by morning. "And after some time an ingenius [sic] Tradesman who had a pretty collection of Books and who frequented our Printing-House, took Notice of me, invited me to his Library, and very Kindly lent me such Books as I chose to read." FRANKLIN was discovering how gratifying it was when people "took Notice" of him; he loved to be the center of attention and hated being in anyone's shadow. He and his friend John Collins were in the habit of debating a great variety of questions; FRANKLIN couldn't bear losing, and so he developed the habit of writing out his arguments ahead of time. This competitive streak, coupled with his hunger to be noticed, led him to pay attention to writing along with reading. Had he stayed in grammar school he would have been "making Latin": writing compositions modeled on Roman authors. Instead, he went to work in English:

> About this time [he was 14 or 15] I met with an odd Volume of the *Spectator*. It was the third. I had never seen any of them. I bought it, read it over and over, and was much delighted with it. I thought the Writing excellent, and wished, if possible, to imitate it. With that View, I took some of the Pages, and making short Hints of the Sentiments in each Sentence, laid them by a few Days, and without looking at the Book tried to complete the papers again, by expressing each limited Sentiment at length, and as fully as it had been expressed before, in any suitable Words that should come to hand.

Years later, FRANKLIN would recommend this same method for the instruction of students at his Philadelphia Academy.[3]

FRANKLIN began slipping compositions under the print shop door at night; they professed to be the work of a matron named Silence Dogood. FRANKLIN must have been torn between the gratification of hearing his satires praised by his elders and the frustration of being unable to claim the credit. (The authorship of the Silence Dogood letters in James Franklin's *New-England Courant* would remain secret for decades.) The fourth of the letters, written in 1722, is evidence that being pulled from the grammar school and denied the prospect of Harvard still rankled. FRANKLIN's resentment took the form of sour grapes: the letter mocked Harvard students' pretensions and dismissed the study of Latin as superficial and irrelevant. For the rest of his life, he would champion instruction in English and take every opportunity to challenge the place of Latin at the heart of the curriculum. When, at twenty-six, he decided to teach himself languages, he learned French, Italian, and Spanish before Latin.[4]

In 1724, a chance encounter with Pennsylvania's lieutenant governor William Keith resulted in the offer of support for a trip to London. Once there, FRANKLIN discovered that Keith's promises of financial help were empty, but he found work in London printing shops: "I spent but little upon my self except in seeing Plays & in Books." On March 6, 1725, Addison's *Cato* was performed at Drury Lane; this was a play FRANKLIN knew well. Three years later he quoted from it in his *Articles of Belief*, and he would quote from it much later when he wrote the *Autobiography*. In London, his ego was gratified when he was introduced to Bernard de Mandeville, author of the notorious *Fable of the Bees*. The introduction was occasioned by FRANKLIN's brash publication of *A Dissertation on Liberty and Necessity, Pleasure and Pain*, his reaction against William Wollaston's *Religion of Nature Delineated*, the third edition of which he had just been hired to set in type. (Wollaston, who describes a natural world that follows the plan of a benevolent God, was required reading at Yale and would be for years to come.) In his anonymous pamphlet, the young skeptic challenged the idea that humans were motivated by anything more than the pursuit of pleasure and the avoidance of pain. The *Dissertation* showed the teenage FRANKLIN's acquaintance with Lucretius's *De rerum natura*, along with Locke, Addison and Steele, Bacon, Hobbes—and Mandeville.[5]

FRANKLIN's thirst for learning remained unslaked. After his return to Philadelphia, even as he was scrambling to establish himself as a printer, he organized the Junto, "a Club, for mutual Improvement" that would last forty years with a continually evolving membership. "The rules that I drew up required that every member, in his turn, should produce one or more queries on any point of Morals, Politics, or Natural Philosophy, to be discussed by the company; and once in three months produce an essay of his own writing, on any subject he pleased." The Junto performed for FRANKLIN and his friends the same function that the American Whig Society would at Princeton or Phi Beta Kappa at William and Mary, and it anticipated those organizations by forty years. Looking back, FRANKLIN declared it "the best school of Philosophy, Morality, and Politics that then existed in the Province." With the creation of the Philadelphia Subscription Library that same year, he put in place the final formal element of his lifelong program of self-improvement.[6]

FRANKLIN did not read the Scottish philosophers during his formative years; indeed, he was already thirty-five by the time Hume's *Essays Moral and Political* appeared, and Hutcheson's *System of Moral Philosophy* was published when he was forty-nine. The Scots, however, certainly became aware of him. He became "Doctor FRANKLIN" with the honorary degree awarded by St. Andrews University in 1759. In Edinburgh that year he met Lord Kames, Adam Ferguson, William Robertson, and Adam Smith, and in 1771 he actually lived for a time in the home of David Hume. But when he completed his *Autobiography*, in his eighties, he could not close without a wistful recollection of his earliest disappointment: "The Library afforded me the means of Improvement by constant Study, for which I set apart an

Hour or two each Day; and thus repair'd in some Degree the Loss of the Learned Education my Father once intended for me."[7]

There was only one BEN FRANKLIN, but he was not the only Framer who could boast that he had essentially educated himself. None left an autobiography like his, but WILLIAM FEW, delegate from Georgia, did write a brief memoir summarizing his self-education. After a single term with an itinerant schoolmaster, FEW's education was entirely his own work; he read *The Spectator* during rest breaks while plowing his father's fields. In the town of Hillsborough, on the North Carolina frontier, "I obtained access to a gentleman's library that contained a small collection of well-chosen books, which gave me the highest satisfaction. Here I first saw Rollin's work [probably *Ancient History*], Plutarch and Smollett, etc., which I seized with delight and read with pleasure. . . . I indulged the most insatiable propensity for reading, and if I could not get such books as I wanted, I would read what I could get." He evidently read a good deal; the French chargé d'affaires, Louis-Guillaume Otto, observed at the time of the Convention that FEW "has more knowledge than his name and his exterior would appear to indicate." He eventually taught himself law and wound up president of the City Bank of New York, today's Citibank.[8]

WILLIAM PIERCE, in the sketches he wrote of his fellow Framers, had this to say about his Georgia colleague: "Mr. FEW possesses a strong natural Genius, and from application has acquired some knowledge of legal matters." He had a much harder time summing up another self-made man, ROGER SHERMAN of Connecticut:

> Mr. SHERMAN exhibits the oddest shaped character I ever remember to have met with. He is awkward, unmeaning, and unaccountably strange in his manner. But in his train of thinking there is something regular, deep, and comprehensive; yet the oddity of his address, the vulgarisms that accompany his public speaking, and that strange New England cant that runs through his public as well as his private speaking make everything that is connected with him grotesque and laughable;—and yet he deserves infinite praise,—no Man has a better Heart or clearer Head. If he cannot embellish he can furnish thoughts that are wise and useful.[9]

Wisdom and usefulness counted for more than embellishment at the Convention. Like FRANKLIN, SHERMAN became an important agent for compromise. And also like FRANKLIN—the only Framer who was older—at Philadelphia he had difficulty giving up old assumptions. SHERMAN was raised in Stoughton, Massachusetts, before that township opened its first school. There is a long-standing tradition (but no evidence) that the town's young minister, recently an usher at Boston Latin School, took an interest in the boy. Whether in his parents' home or in the parsonage of the Rev. Samuel Dunbar, SHERMAN learned to read, write, and cipher. How much more is unknown, but there is a tantalizing hint in one of his memorandum books. It contains a biblical quotation, in his handwriting, in which the word "prototokos" (firstborn) is written in Greek characters.[10]

Benjamin Rush came to know SHERMAN in the Continental Congress and described him as "a plain man of slender education [who] taught himself mathematics, and afterwards acquired some property and a good deal of reputation by making almanacs." To the readers of his *Boston Almanac* of 1750, SHERMAN introduced himself thus: "I have for several years past for my own Amusement spent some Hours in the study of *Mathematicks*." Having risen to some prominence as a self-taught lawyer and justice of the peace in Connecticut, he served as treasurer of Yale College for eleven years, receiving an honorary MA in 1768, but there is no evidence that he ever entered a schoolroom. SHERMAN, like FRANKLIN and FEW, was a true autodidact, but no doubt one of more limited reading.[11]

GEORGE WYTHE also educated himself to become a lawyer who was trusted and admired by his neighbors, but his life could not have been more different. WYTHE was Virginia's preeminent legal scholar, mentor of Thomas Jefferson, John Marshall, and Henry Clay. He was famous for his classical erudition. Jefferson, who idolized WYTHE, wrote, "It is said, that while reading the Greek Testament, his mother held an English one, to aid him in rendering the Greek text conformably with that." Some accounts give Margaret Wythe a larger role. US attorney general William Wirt wrote, eleven years after WYTHE's death, "There is a story circulated, as upon his own authority, that he was initiated by his mother in the Latin classics." EDMUND RANDOLPH, his fellow delegate to Philadelphia, acknowledged the popular account but doubted it:

> GEORGE WYTHE is said to have been indebted to his mother for the literary distinction which he attained. But it is more probable, that she was by chance capable of assisting him in the rudiments of the Latin tongue, and that he became a scholar by the indispensable progress of his own industry in his closet. Preceptors lay the cornerstone, but the edifice can be finished only by the pupil himself, under the auspices of good taste.[12]

WYTHE departed the Federal Convention after only a week, called home by his wife's fatal illness. He had been appointed during that opening week to chair the Convention's first committee, charged with laying out its rules. One can only speculate about what he might have contributed had he remained.

Two of the most respected Virginians of WYTHE's generation are also often described as self-educated. GEORGE WASHINGTON and GEORGE MASON went to the Convention as friends and allies but left as adversaries who never reconciled. WASHINGTON was the unanimous choice to preside over the debates; MASON spent most of the summer working tirelessly to ensure the success of the Convention, only to turn against its final draft in the closing weeks. With five members of the state's all-important delegation present for the ultimate vote, it was probably MASON's influence that led RANDOLPH to withhold his signature and WASHINGTON's that persuaded BLAIR to add his, leaving MADISON, appropriately, to decide the outcome. Both WASHINGTON and MASON had educations that were essentially their own doing, one meager and the other extensive. Like WYTHE, both lost fathers at an early age and were raised by determined mothers who, never remarrying, made careers of raising their children while managing plantations. Dependable records of their childhoods are scarce, but it seems fair to characterize both boys as recipients of early tutoring who went on to educate themselves through their own reading.

Mason Weems (creator of the cherry tree fable) asserted in 1800 that WASHINGTON's first teacher was John Hobby, an indentured servant. Weems's credibility is shaky, but there actually is evidence to support this claim. Hobby was transported to Virginia in 1736 for stealing silver spoons, and his indenture was purchased by Augustine Washington, GEORGE's father. Two years later when the family moved to Ferry Farm, near Fredericksburg, Hobby went with them; WASHINGTON was then six years old. Later on, Hobby kept a school a mile south of Ferry Farm. Even before Weems, a similar assertion was made by Jonathan Boucher, the tutor of John Parke Custis, WASHINGTON's stepson. Boucher, a loyalist who returned to England when the Revolution began, wrote that WASHINGTON, "like most people thereabouts at that time, had no other education than reading, writing, and accounts, which he was taught by a convict servant whom his father bought for a schoolmaster."[13]

The practice was common in Maryland and Virginia; in 1746 Edward Kimber published "Itinerant Observations" of his American tour in *The London Magazine*, explaining that when the gentry "can't afford to send their Children to the better schools. . . . Often a clever Servant or Convict, that can write and read tolerably, and is of no handicraft Business, is indented to some Planter, who has a number of children, as a School-Master." "The better schools" that Kimber had in mind were those in England, where WASHINGTON's two older half brothers had been sent to attend Appleby School, their father's alma mater. The death of Gus Washington in 1743 evidently prevented GEORGE's following them, as Mary Ball Washington seemed determined to keep her son close at hand.[14]

After his father's death, WASHINGTON went to live for a while with his brother Austin, whose Pope's Creek plantation was just down the Potomac from the Mason plantation at Chopawamsic. Not yet twelve, the boy could have been briefly taught by Henry Williams, who was then at nearby Mattox Creek and had tutored the Mason children from 1736 to 1740. David Humphreys wrote in WASHINGTON's authorized 1786 biography that he had been "primarily educated by a private tutor." WASHINGTON read Humphreys's draft and made a number of changes, but he left that statement untouched. Both Hobby and Williams could have been so described. WASHINGTON was always sensitive about his deficiencies in the liberal arts; he declined invitations to visit France because he could not speak French and rejected Humphreys's suggestion that he write an autobiography: "I am conscious of a defective education, & want of capacity to fit me for such undertaking." As a boy, he gave most attention to mathematics. A surviving copybook is filled with geometric demonstrations, and WASHINGTON evidently taught himself trigonometry and logarithms. Sometime before 1747 he learned surveying—his father had left him his surveying instruments—and he was paid two pounds, three shillings for a surveying job when he was not yet sixteen years old. His copybook, which contains forty-seven pages of surveying exercises, is initially dated August 13, 1745, and was probably finished by 1748. The following year he was licensed as a surveyor by the College of William and Mary, his only official connection with the college until he was named its chancellor forty years later.[15]

Surveying was WASHINGTON's practical focus as a teenager, but he was no less interested in learning to be a gentleman. The first volume of his copybooks is a penmanship exercise and manual of genteel behavior entitled "Rules of Civility and Decent Behaviour in Company and Conversation." Besides copying such advice as "Shift not yourself in the Sight of others nor Gnaw your nails," WASHINGTON made some effort to acquire the gentleman's sine qua non: an acquaintance with the classical authors. His biographer Paul Leicester Ford asserts that he made at least a stab at learning Latin, revealed on the flyleaf of a 1742 Latin translation of Homer, "in a schoolboy hand":

Hunc mihi quaeso (bone Vir) Libellum
Redde, si forsan tenues repertum
Ut Scias qui sum sine fraude Scriptum
Est mihi nomen
Georgio Washington
GEORGE WASHINGTON
Fredericksburg,
Virginia.

I pray you, good man, return this little book if you find it, slim as it is. Written so that you may know that, in truth, my name is GEORGE WASHINGTON.[16]

The Latin didn't stick, and WASHINGTON's other volumes of classical literature were translations. By the 1750s he had read (in English) Caesar's *Commentaries on the Gallic Wars,* and he owned *An Abstract of Seneca's Morals,* inscribed with his youthful signature. Other early acquisitions that remained in WASHINGTON's library at his death include James Greenwood's *Royall English Grammar* and two volumes of Richard Steele's *Guardian,* along with Smollett's *Adventures of Peregrine Pickle* and Fielding's *Tom Jones.* But the strongest, most lasting impression was made by Addison's neoclassical tragedy, *Cato.*[17]

There is no way of knowing when WASHINGTON first encountered *Cato,* but the play's influence lasted his entire life; quotations from it in his writings are second only to the Bible in frequency. As a young man he was not above flirting with his (married) neighbor Sally Fairfax by proposing them for the roles of the play's star-crossed lovers: "I should think our time more agreeably spent, believe me, in playing a part in Cato, with the company you mention, and myself doubly happy in being Juba to such a Marcia, as you must make."[18]

Twenty years later, in very different circumstances, WASHINGTON had *Cato* performed before his officers at Valley Forge, defying a congressional ban on theatrical productions. Capt. JOHN FRANCIS MERCER may have been in the audience, alongside Col. DAVID BREARLEY, Lt. Col. ALEXANDER HAMILTON, and JAMES MCHENRY, who had just joined WASHINGTON's staff without a commission. By this time the play was so familiar to him that he often quoted it; on various occasions during the war he paraphrased act 1, scene 2, reminding the French admiral DeGrasse, Gov. William Greene of Rhode Island, and the as-yet loyal Gen. Benedict Arnold, "'Tis not in mortals to command success, but we'll do more . . . we'll deserve it." (This was the play's most popular line; John Adams also quoted it in a letter to his wife from the Continental Congress). WASHINGTON again borrowed from the play in his Newburgh address in March 1783 to army officers who had threatened, like Cato's soldiers, to mutiny, and in his letter informing HAMILTON of his decision to retire from office in 1796, a "determination to seek the post of honor in a private station." The public came to see him as the American Cincinnatus, but he clearly saw himself as the self-sacrificing Cato. His belief in a strong national government was the consequence of his wartime experiences, and *Cato* helped him conceptualize his powerful sense of patriotic duty.[19]

Cato is a special case, but throughout his life WASHINGTON tried to strengthen his "defective" education through reading more than many of his friends realized. When he married Martha Custis, he acquired her late husband's English-language copies of Suetonius's *Lives of the Twelve Caesars* and Cicero's *On Duties* (*De officiis*), two of the centerpieces of eighteenth-century education. Later on, filling in what contemporary college students would have read, he purchased (again in English translation) Pufendorf's *Laws of Nature and Nations* and Grotius's *Rights of War and Peace*. Although he eventually accumulated a library of more than nine hundred volumes, he never seemed to shake the conviction that his education, in his formative years, had been inadequate.[20]

Libraries the size of WASHINGTON's were uncommon but by no means unknown in Virginia; the collections of William Byrd II and Robert Carter of Nomini Hall were even larger. GEORGE MASON had access as a youth to John Mercer's library of more than 1,500 volumes. MASON's early tutoring in Latin gave him the academic start that WASHINGTON lacked; Mercer's library likewise gave him an advantage in pursuing his self-education. GEORGE MASON IV was ten when his father drowned while crossing the Potomac between his Maryland and Virginia plantations. His mother, the redoubtable Ann Mason, and his uncle, the prominent lawyer John Mercer, became his legal guardians. In the following years, the Prince William County orphans' guardians' account lists four annual payments of 1,000 pounds of tobacco to Henry Williams for teaching the boy. A "Master Wylie" also received 845 pounds of tobacco for instruction and books in 1738–39. In addition, Ann Mason's accounts record that the Rev. Alexander Scott selected books for GEORGE's use and ordered them from England. Scott, a Glasgow MA, was one of the Scottish clergymen who were playing an increasing role in educating young Virginians.[21]

Although the wintery Potomac had been fatal to George Mason III, crossing it was a part of life for planters on both banks. Ann Mason continued to farm plantations on both sides, and when their tutor relocated to

Maryland in 1737, GEORGE and his brother Thomson followed him, boarding with a Mrs. Simpson in Charles County. The brothers had friends in Maryland, including the future Framers DANIEL OF ST. THOMAS JENIFER and DANIEL CARROLL. JENIFER was named "DANIEL OF ST. THOMAS" after his grandfather, and no more explanation for the name has been discovered. He had a younger brother whose name was simply Daniel. Their early education is unknown, but it is tempting to imagine the Mason boys meeting the Jenifers in Williams's Maryland schoolroom. In 1773, Thomson Mason addressed a lighthearted letter to JENIFER, urging him to marry: "And now my old friend, how have you been this long time? Words cannot express how glad I should be to see you." JENIFER remained a lifelong bachelor, but when GEORGE MASON married in 1750, his bride was a neighbor of JENIFER's from Charles County.[22]

There is no record that GEORGE MASON had a teacher after 1740; any expenditure for tuition would have been entered in the orphans' guardians' records until 1746, when he turned twenty-one. But John Mercer's library was open to him. Mercer had married Catherine Mason, sister of GEORGE's father, and their nephew was a frequent visitor at Marlborough, Mercer's Stafford County plantation, until 1750 when Catherine died and Mercer remarried. That year GEORGE MASON also married, and soon he was building his own manor house, Gunston Hall.　 1,500 volumes

Mercer was famous for his vast library. He kept careful records of purchases—in 1726 early acquisitions included Plutarch's *Lives*, Locke's *Essays*, and "Tilly's" [i.e., Cicero's] *Orations*—but the ledgers from the years of GEORGE MASON's youth are missing. At some point before 1746 Mercer prepared a catalogue of the library, which gives an indication of what MASON might have found there: Machiavelli's *History of Florence*, eight volumes of *The Spectator*, four of Addison's other works, Newton's *Opticks*, eight volumes of Shakespeare and nine of Pope, various histories of England, Scotland, and Europe. None of the Commonwealth political authors is listed; the sole representative of the Scottish Enlightenment is "Hutchinson on Virtue"—Francis Hutcheson's early *Inquiry Concerning the Original of Our Ideas of Beauty and Virtue*, published in 1725 (five years after Mercer left Dublin for Virginia).[23]

In 1747, when MASON was no longer a minor in the orphans' guardians' records, Mercer listed books he bought for an account identified only by the initials "GM." (He kept seventeen such accounts identified by pairs of initials; only three of these have been identified as Mercer's neighbors.) MASON's biographers differ in their assumptions about the initials GM. Helen Hill Miller calls them GEORGE MASON's initials, but Patricia Copeland assumes that in Mercer's library catalogue "he recorded the initials JM and

GM for all the volumes ordered for his sons, James and George." The latter conclusion is doubtful, since the books marked JM consist of medical texts, and James Mercer was then ten years old. The GM books include Schrevelli's Latin lexicon and a Greek grammar and New Testament, possible schoolbooks for the fourteen-year-old George Mercer, who was preparing for William and Mary, but almost all of the rest are English translations of Ovid, Lucretius, Homer, Martial, Virgil, Terence, Sallust, Plutarch, Horace, and Lucian, among whom can be found the first exponents of republican virtue. (Earlier entries in the catalogue marked GM include *The Spectator*, *The Guardian*, and Addison's *Works*.) Whether or not any books in Mercer's library were purchased with MASON in mind, they were there if he chose to read them, and MASON grew to be a well-read man, with an extensive library of his own at Gunston Hall that contained many of the titles marked GM in Mercer's accounts. At the Convention, despite his early determination to replace the Articles of Confederation, his political philosophy remained conservative, reflecting the dominance of the classics in his early reading and the absence of anything truly new.[24]

Mercer's library remained at Marlborough after his death a decade later for the use of his two young sons by his second wife: Roy and JOHN FRANCIS MERCER. The latter would later join his cousin GEORGE MASON at the Convention. MERCER followed his elder brothers to William and Mary; he was tutored well enough in Latin and Greek to be admitted in 1774, but he stayed only one year. MERCER shared his father's notoriously quick temper; he was indignant when his close friend James Monroe was passed over by Virginia after lobbying hard to be a delegate to the federal Convention in 1787. (Monroe considered this a personal slight and thereafter opposed ratification.) MERCER stayed less than two weeks in Philadelphia, walking out well before MASON changed his mind and decided not to sign. Jefferson, who knew him well, summed him up: "One of those afflicted with a morbid rage of debate, of an ardent mind, prompt imagination, and copious flow of words, he heard with impatience any logic that was not his own."[25]

When MASON's brother Thomson later studied law in London at the Middle Temple, he made the acquaintance of another young man from the Chesapeake, JOHN DICKINSON. On the Eastern Shore, a boy's choices before midcentury were to stay home with a tutor, board in a city such as Philadelphia, or make the journey to England. Samuel Dickinson, master of Croisador plantation in Maryland's Talbot County and Poplar Hall in Kent County, Delaware, sent his first three sons to school in England, where all three contracted smallpox and died. That scourge was far less common in the colonies, so Samuel kept JOHN at home.

JOHN DICKINSON was born in 1732, the same year as WASHINGTON. He would have been too young to benefit if, as tradition has it, the young Ulster Scot Francis Alison tutored the older Dickinson children before founding his academy in New London, Pennsylvania. James Orr, another Presbyterian from Ireland, definitely tutored the Dickinson children and those of several neighbors. But it was a third Ulsterman, William Killen, who became not only the tutor but the lifelong friend of JOHN DICKINSON. Only ten years older than his pupil, Killen had come to Delaware with a sound classical education acquired in the north of Ireland. Killen read law under Samuel Dickinson, who was judge of the county Court of Common Pleas; in return, he taught JOHN DICKINSON Latin beginning about 1745. Perhaps he started with Caesar's *Commentaries*; the young DICKINSON entertained himself by building a model of the bridge over the Rhine that Caesar describes. Killen became chancellor of the state of Delaware; DICKINSON gained a lasting love of the classics and a neoclassical prose style that served him well as the "Penman of the Revolution." There is no indication that his studies in history or philosophy went beyond the Romans.[26]

In New England, such youthful scholarship would lead to Harvard or Yale, but Delaware was not New England—and as a Quaker, DICKINSON would have found those doors closed to him. The Inns of Court presented a much more attractive alternative. After persuading his parents to let him risk going to England, he continued to read Latin authors for pleasure, bringing crates of books back with him. His *Letters of a Farmer in Pennsylvania*, written in the following decade, offer reminders of the importance of the Roman Republic to the arguments of American patriots, and his later letters in support of the Constitution, published under the classical pseudonym of Fabius, are also stocked with citations of Roman Republican authors.

The Latin curriculum Killen followed for DICKINSON was conventional in all the colonies and throughout the century. A later tutor at Nomini Hall in Virginia, Philip Vickers Fithian, recorded in his diary, "The eldest Son [of Robert Carter] is reading Salust: Grammatical Exercises and Latin Grammer." Sallust was nearly as universal as Cicero; he gave DICKINSON a favorite phrase that he quoted in a 1764 speech to the Pennsylvania Assembly and again four years later in the *Letters of a Farmer*: "I will assuredly contend for that glorious plan of *Liberty* handed down to us from our ancestors." Like Cicero and Plutarch, Sallust was a touchstone of the civic virtue that DICKINSON would depend upon even after he was disillusioned by the failure of the Articles of Confederation. At the Convention he worked for compromise, unsure about the new ideas he was hearing from MADISON and

WILSON. Like MASON, his worldview was that of Republican Rome, not the Scottish Enlightenment.[27]

Planters of the upper Chesapeake could always send their sons to William and Mary; most, like the Dickinsons, never considered it. In the Deep South, American colleges were even less often appealing options. Some boys, such as South Carolina's Middleton and Pinckney brothers, might be sent to Oxford or Cambridge—or much less often, if there were family connections, to Scotland or Ireland, as in the cases of C. C. PINCKNEY's Charleston friend Alexander Garden and the North Carolina Framer RICHARD DOBBS SPAIGHT. Most families settled for tutors who were themselves products of British universities. The more isolated the plantations, the harder tutors were to find: WILLIAM BLOUNT, born in Bertie County, North Carolina, was fifteen before any "settled teacher" appeared who might teach him or his two brothers; his biographers agree that "the boys' training was necessarily carried out by their parents." We know nothing about the education of WILLIAM HOUSTOUN in Savannah, Georgia, but HOUSTOUN's older brother John was educated "under an eminent gentleman in Charleston, S.C.," according to John Adams, who met him at Congress. Perhaps WILLIAM was, too.[28]

Good teachers were certainly available in sophisticated Charleston, where JOHN RUTLEDGE and CHARLES PINCKNEY III were educated entirely by tutors. The Rutledges employed Dr. David Rhind, a Scotsman who had tutored the neighbors' children. According to David Ramsay, the physician and historian who served in Congress with RUTLEDGE, Rhind was "an excellent classical scholar, and one of the most successful of the early educators of youth in South Carolina"; he may have been the "eminent gentleman" who taught John Houstoun. Although Ramsay says RUTLEDGE "made considerable progress in the Latin and Greek classics," there were dissenting opinions. Like WASHINGTON and SHERMAN, RUTLEDGE was more interested in mathematics than Latin; one of his later law students, John Pringle, doubted in 1774 whether RUTLEDGE possessed the "extensive Education and Reading" to be truly eloquent, and Adams, who came to admire him later, grumbled during the First Continental Congress that "RUTLEDGE don't exceed in Learning or oratory, though he is a rapid Speaker." A tough negotiator, he spent most of his energies at the Convention defending the interests of the Deep South—especially slavery. He made no original suggestions about government.[29]

Two decades after RUTLEDGE, CHARLES PINCKNEY III was tutored by another Scottish physician. Dr. David Oliphant had been a schoolmate of John Witherspoon at the University of Edinburgh in the 1730s. A Jacobite, he left Scotland after Bonnie Prince Charlie's defeat at Culloden in 1747, the year after Hutcheson died and six years after Hume published *Essays Political and Moral*. He surely knew Hutcheson and Hume by reputation and could certainly have read their early works. In 1773, he was serving in the colonial assembly along with PINCKNEY's father. Perhaps he took the boy on as a favor to the family. PINCKNEY was sixteen and had received previous tutoring in Latin; the three years he spent with Oliphant were essentially higher education. Unlike RUTLEDGE, he really was an avid student. PIERCE found him "in possession of a very great variety of knowledge. Government, Law, History and Phylosophy are his favorite studies, but he is intimately acquainted with every species of polite learning, and has a spirit of application and industry beyond most men." In Congress, PINCKNEY demonstrated that he was very well read indeed, and at the Convention he seemed comfortable with the new Scottish political thought, whether thanks to his Scottish tutor or his own investigations. After Congress made Oliphant director general of hospitals in the Southern Department in 1776, PINCKNEY traveled to Philadelphia to be inoculated for smallpox; Dr. Ramsay then testified to the soundness of his education too, writing a letter of introduction to his Princeton classmate and medical mentor, Benjamin Rush.[30]

Most eighteenth-century education began at home; it was often completed there, as DICKENSON and PINCKNEY demonstrate, but for other youths, tutoring was preparation for college. There is no better example than WILLIAM SAMUEL JOHNSON, chosen ahead of SHERMAN to represent Connecticut at the Convention. JOHNSON had the advantage of being the son of the Rev. Samuel Johnson, who turned down FRANKLIN's offer to head the College of Philadelphia in order to become the president of King's College in New York. Raised Calvinist, the elder Johnson had been part of the shocking conversion of Yale faculty to Anglicanism in 1722, "the Great Apostasy." In 1724, Johnson began training Yale graduates in his home for the Anglican ministry, more than sixty of them by his death in 1774. He also began taking in the sons of New York families to prepare them for Yale, along with his own boys, WILLIAM SAMUEL and Samuel William (called Billy). He did not dispute the quality of the Connecticut grammar schools that had taught him Latin and Greek, but he was determined to avoid their Calvinism. He taught his students the Episcopal catechism along with mathematics, logic, and "the languages." WILLIAM SAMUEL JOHNSON was judged ready for Yale when he turned thirteen.[31]

The thorough classical instruction JOHNSON received contrasts strikingly with the meager preparation of his Yale schoolmate, WILLIAM LIVINGSTON.

The Livingstons were lords of a 250-square-mile domain in upstate New York, but WILLIAM's boyhood was spent on the frontier in Albany. Although the town was a century old, it retained its wooden palisade, blockhouses, and nightly watch. Albany's school was conducted by the sexton of the Dutch Reformed Church, and the instruction was rudimentary. LIVINGSTON's older brothers Robert and Henry were sent 150 miles away to the New Rochelle school of a respected Huguenot teacher and went from there to Yale.[32]

WILLIAM, however, was the favorite of his grandmother, Sarah Cuyler Van Brugh. Like WASHINGTON and DICKINSON, the youngest son stayed home rather than following older half brothers away to school. His grandmother took charge of his instruction, and his family attributed his "impatience and irritability of temper" to "her excessive fondness and undiscriminating indulgence." It must have been understood that even a Livingston could not count on "undiscriminating indulgence" by the Yale examiners, but a tutor was available to provide the necessary cramming. Henry Barclay, son of an Albany neighbor, had gone to Yale with the older Livingston boys. In 1734, the *Journal of the Society for the Propagation of the Gospel* (SPG) announced: "Young Mr. Barclay has spent 4 years & taken his degree at Newhaven College, but not yet being of age for priest's orders would willingly be employed as a catechist or schoolmaster among [the Mohawk Indians], learn their language & be thus more able to instruct them."[33]

Rather than miss a rare opportunity, at thirteen LIVINGSTON was sent along with Barclay. As he later recalled, "I spent a year among the Mohawks (the chief of the Six Nations) with a missionary for the Society for Propagating the Gospel, under whom I then studied their language, and had an opportunity to learn the genius and the manner of the nation." Barclay also drilled him in Latin and Greek sufficiently to satisfy Yale. In light of LIVINGSTON's later hostility to the Church of England, he was evidently immune to the SPG tutor's missionary efforts.[34]

The Johnsons had turned away from Connecticut's pubic grammar schools; Massachusetts was the colony where public grammar schools had first been ordained by law, but none of the four Massachusetts delegates in 1787 went to them. GORHAM's education stopped with common school, but GERRY, STRONG, and KING all went to Harvard. GERRY was probably tutored in his home town; STRONG and KING were both prepared by the respected Samuel Moody, the former privately in the district of Maine (although his family lived in Massachusetts proper) and the latter at Moody's subsequent academy in Massachusetts (although *his* family lived in Maine). In the plantation South, a tutor would often move in with his pupils' family; in New England, it was not unusual for families to send their sons to live, sometimes for years, with tutors who would prepare them for college. Often those tutors made lasting impressions.

In the 1750s, Moody's reputation drew students from some distance to his home in York, Maine, including CALEB STRONG of Northampton, Massachusetts. In 1763, three years after STRONG departed to enroll at Harvard, Moody began a thirty-two-year career as the headmaster of an academy endowed by the will of Lt. Gov. William Dummer, where RUFUS KING was to be his pupil, along with a quarter of KING's entering class at Harvard. Moody was known at Dummer for teaching the Latin classics almost to the exclusion of anything else, so it seems likely that was the kind of education STRONG also received.

ELBRIDGE GERRY's road to Harvard is harder to determine. He was a native of the seaport of Marblehead, an aptly named birthplace for the hard-headed politician who was always among the most contentious in Congress and at the Convention. (It was said that whatever GERRY had not proposed, he opposed.) Marblehead was large enough that Massachusetts law required it to support a Latin grammar school; one opened in 1698, but there was little demand and it soon closed. GERRY would have had to look elsewhere for the preparation Harvard required. His likely tutor was the Rev. John Barnard of Marblehead's First Congregational Church. A 1700 graduate of Harvard, he had been offered its presidency in 1736; he demurred, suggesting instead the minister of Marblehead's Second Church, Edward Holyoke, and the Harvard Overseers took his suggestion. He was well equipped to prepare the occasional Marblehead boy who aimed at college.[35]

Barnard doubtless did a thorough job, but GERRY showed no particular scholarly interests then or later, focusing his attention on making money, holding office, and defending the interests of Massachusetts against all comers. A tutor who had a greater influence was Joseph Bellamy, teacher of Connecticut's OLIVER ELLSWORTH. ELLSWORTH was intended by his family for a Yale education and a Congregational pulpit, but like several other Framers he would abandon that vocation for a career in law. Before that, following two unhappy years at Yale, he abandoned New Haven for Princeton. But to prepare him for both his original goals, he was sent to live and study in Bethlehem, Connecticut, with Bellamy—the Congregationalists' counterweight to the Anglican Samuel Johnson. Like Johnson, Bellamy was a complex thinker. Unlike Johnson, he had struggled at Yale, where he was ranked twenty-third out of twenty-four in his class because of his humble background. He was a classmate and friend of Aaron Burr Sr., and upon graduation he became Jonathan Edwards's first theology student. He would make a profound impression upon young ELLSWORTH.[36]

As Bellamy worked out his religious synthesis and political principles, he steered an independent course through the Great Awakening as a New Light preacher. By the end of the 1750s, he had adopted an approach not unlike John Witherspoon's in the next decade. Bellamy recommended to his parishioners some authors Witherspoon would recommend to his students—including Hutcheson and Hume—not for their theology, which both men deplored, but for their moral and political philosophy. His reading of Pufendorf and Hutcheson convinced him that governments should follow moral and natural law expressed in constitutional principles; he saw the collective good as the responsibility of politicians.[37]

While ELLSWORTH was learning Latin from Bellamy, he was also adopting his teacher's ideas about political morality. If he was already in Bethlehem by 1758, he would have been in the congregation when Bellamy delivered four sermons collectively titled *The Wisdom of God in the Permission of Sin*, subsequently printed and widely read. Bellamy maintained that the righteous ruler could compromise with the depraved politician in order to benefit society; he might even compromise on policies contrary to the public good in the assurance that God's will would prevail and the depraved politician's aims would fail. In 1777, ELLSWORTH defended the French alliance to a New Light minister by invoking Bellamy's theory of compromise; for generations Roman Catholic France had been demonized among English Protestants—especially those of New England—but ELLSWORTH used Bellamy's ideas to argue that even papists could be enlisted in support of American independence, which must be God's will. A decade after that, *The Wisdom of God in Permission of Sin* would guide ELLSWORTH at the Federal Convention in 1787.[38]

ELLSWORTH followed Bellamy's route to New Haven as he had to New Light theology, but in the final, contentious years of Thomas Clap's presidency, ELLSWORTH's conflict with Yale's conservative Old Light doctrine and rigid discipline led him to withdraw, along with his close friend Waightstill Avery. At this point, his old tutor's influence was felt again. Bellamy had been a classmate of Princeton's second president, Burr, and a student of its third president, Edwards; moreover, the college's current president was another Bellamy friend, Samuel Finley, a New Side Presbyterian who had earlier preached in Connecticut. These connections were enough to lead the two boys to Nassau Hall, where another of Bellamy's students, Jonathan Edwards Jr., was already enrolled. ELLSWORTH graduated in 1766 and returned to Windsor; his friend Avery moved to North Carolina, where he helped open the school that would prepare WILLIAM RICHARDSON DAVIE for Princeton, yet another connection that would prove fateful at the Convention. ELLSWORTH's political enemies would often accuse him of hypocrisy; in 1791, Congressman William Maclay wrote in his journal, "This man has abilities, but abilities without candor and integrity, are the characteristics of the Devil." The devout New Light Congregationalist, however, was following his tutor's teaching that compromise was possible even with sin, in the confidence that God's will would ultimately prevail.[39]

MASON, STRONG, and ELLSWORTH had to board for months or years in unfamiliar homes, and LIVINGSTON shared his tutor with the Mohawks, but neither DICKINSON nor WYTHE had to leave the confines of his family home to become classically educated. When JAMES MADISON was brought home from boarding school to study with the Rev. Thomas Martin, he shared his tutor with three younger brothers, his seven-year-old sister, and probably some children of neighbors. Martin was the brother of ALEXANDER MARTIN, who would join MADISON years later as a delegate to the 1787 Convention. He was a recent graduate of the college at Princeton, a school that had already captured the attention of James Madison Sr. Perhaps the Madisons thought his familiarity with Princeton's expectations particularly qualified him to prepare young JAMES. After the Martin brothers escorted him north to the college in 1769 (accompanied by his personal slave, Sawney, who then returned to Virginia), he took the freshman exams and entered as a sophomore. He wrote to Martin in August that he had "read over more than half Horace and made myself pretty well acquainted with Prosody, both which will be almost neglected the two succeeding years"—the classics he had been studying with Martin constituted the freshman curriculum that he was now skipping. The tutor had done his job well.[40]

In addition to these influential Framers, there were other delegates who came to Philadelphia essentially self-educated or minimally tutored. Even though some were prominent, powerful men, they made little mark at the Convention. Three had access to good libraries, including North America's first lending library. None of them took the lead on the floor of the Convention, but their votes would be crucial. Like so many of the briefly tutored or self-taught, they were more likely to read the conventional authors and to be acutely aware of the limitations of their education.

Arnold Bassett, an innkeeper at the crossroads of Bohemia Ferry, Maryland, walked out after his wife gave birth to RICHARD, the last of five or six children. The cause of his departure—and possibly the actual father of RICHARD BASSETT, future Framer from Delaware—appears to have been Peter Lawson, who had been living at the inn for several years and operated it along with BASSETT's mother for the next decade, during which he probably taught young RICHARD to read and write. Lawson's brother John was an ambitious, unscrupulous lawyer who married the heiress to the vast Bohemia Manor, a simpleminded woman who was a cousin of BASSETT's mother. Augustine Herman, founder of that estate, had accumulated a large library in the manor house before his death in 1685, and BASSETT, his great-great-grandson, now had access to its dusty collection. In 1766, when BASSETT turned twenty-one, John Lawson's widow transferred 1,000 acres to him "out of love for her cousin Judith Bassett" (Peter Lawson eventually got the remaining 3,000 acres) and BASSETT was suddenly a wealthy young man; although Peter Lawson never married Judith Bassett or adopted her son, he left the rest of Bohemia Manor and numerous slaves to BASSETT when he died in 1792; BASSETT, following his conversion to evangelical Methodism, freed them all.[41]

ROBERT MORRIS was superintendent of finance of the United States and a powerful force in both national and Pennsylvania politics. He never spoke at the Convention but consistently voted with MADISON and WILSON and exerted his influence behind the scenes; GEORGE WASHINGTON stayed in his home all that summer. MORRIS had arrived in Oxford, Maryland, as a boy of thirteen, coming from Liverpool to join his father, a successful tobacco factor. Although Robert Sr. was a man of limited education, he was nevertheless "fond of books and the converse of cultivated men." He too owned a library, large enough that in his will he invited each of a number of friends to select "any six books" from it; one friend, Henry Callister, later wrote to tell young ROBERT that his father had asked Callister to read to him from Plato's *Phaedo* as he lay dying after a freak accident: a piece of cannon wadding had struck him when a salute was fired in his honor.[42]

In the tobacco port of Oxford young MORRIS was briefly tutored by an Anglican clergyman identified only as the Rev. Mr. Gordon. In 1749, a year before his father's death, he was sent to Philadelphia in the charge of another of his father's friends, Robert Greenway. Greenway was also a friend of BENJAMIN FRANKLIN and served as the librarian of FRANKLIN's Library Company from 1746 to 1763. MORRIS proved to be less interested in books than in bookkeeping and was soon apprenticed at a shipping firm where he might learn "the Art, Trade, or Mystery of Merchandize." That was apparently the extent of his education; it was enough that he became the wealthiest merchant in America by the 1780s. MORRIS's doomed efforts to reinvent himself as an aristocratic landowner, like the heroes of Republican Rome, left him a bankrupt in debtors' prison by the 1790s.[43]

Another Philadelphia apprentice was GEORGE CLYMER. Orphaned early, he was adopted by his childless aunt and uncle, Hannah and William Coleman. Coleman was another of BENJAMIN FRANKLIN's many friends, an original member of the Junto and a cofounder of the American Philosophical Society and the Library Company. When CLYMER was ten years old, Coleman became the first clerk of the trustees of the new Philadelphia Academy and the school's first treasurer. The records of the Academy's early years are very good, and they give no indication that he ever enrolled his adopted son. Instead, the boy became a clerk in Coleman's counting house; he would inherit the business fourteen years later, along with £6,000—and Coleman's library and scientific instruments. CLYMER named his first son after Coleman, but he sent both his boys to Princeton, not the College of Philadelphia.[44]

Along with another of Coleman's apprentices, the Framer THOMAS MIFFLIN, CLYMER became one more of Philadelphia's most successful merchants. He would be a trustee of both the College of Philadelphia and Franklin College (now Franklin and Marshall), but his education took place in the home of William Coleman and through FRANKLIN's Library Company. CLYMER's biographer Jerry Grundfest observes, "His literary style, in contrast to many of his educated contemporaries, was clear and unencumbered by classical or biblical allusions, drawing instead upon Jonathan Swift or Shakespeare." Benjamin Rush recalled, "His style in writing was simple, correct, and sometimes eloquent." The Library Company's only weakness compared to college libraries was a shortage of books in Latin; if it was CLYMER's "college," that is just the style one would expect. Rush found him "well informed in history ancient and modern," and Joseph Hopkinson eulogized him as "studious, contemplative . . . ever adding something to his knowledge and endeavoring to make that knowledge useful."[45]

Hopkinson's eulogy of CLYMER could serve for all the Framers with brief or uncertain educations. All were men of substance, serving in offices of responsibility, but they rarely took the lead at the Constitutional Convention; too often, their confidence or their imagination failed them. Even those who were assertive were often uncomfortable with unfamiliar new ideas. FEW, MORRIS, CLYMER, and BASSETT were nearly silent at the Convention. SHERMAN and MASON, on the other hand, were among the most vocal of all the Framers, taking opposite sides on some issues but agreeing in their fundamental conservatism and their republican suspicion of powerful government. They and DICKINSON had the confidence that came from experience creating the Articles of Confederation or the constitution of Virginia, but they were older men, with older educations, and their traditional thinking constrained them. Others who spoke often and persuasively at the

Convention—ELLSWORTH, for instance, and MADISON—had been tutored in the classics before going on to colleges that varied greatly in their curricula. But WASHINGTON, who never spoke until the Convention's final day, was the most influential of them all simply by his presence. Self-conscious as he was about his limited education, there was no denying the dignity he brought to the Federal Convention—he was the most conspicuous man in North America, the emblem of Revolutionary liberty. Two years later, after the French republicans stormed the Bastille to launch their own revolution, they knew exactly what to do with the old prison's key: they presented it to GEORGE WASHINGTON, who had never learned to speak French.

4

Writing Schools and Grammar Schools

JACOB BROOM, NICHOLAS GILMAN, NATHANIEL GORHAM, JARED
INGERSOLL, RUFUS KING, JOHN LANGDON, JOHN LANSING,
THOMAS MIFFLIN, ROBERT YATES

*The education of children is a matter of vast importance and highly
deserving of our most serious attention. The prosperity of our country is
intimately connected with it; for without morals, there can be no order, and
without knowledge, no genuine liberty.*
    WILLIAM PATERSON, *"On Education," ca. 1763*

"The child is father to the man." So wrote William Wordsworth in
1802. When the Federal Convention was meeting in 1787, the poet
was beginning his first year at St. John's College, Cambridge. His
"gradual descent into self-satisfied indolence as a student at Cambridge" was less memorable than his earliest school days, when he
first discovered that "books and things" could "act / On infant minds
as surely as the sun / Deals with a flower" (*The Prelude*, Book 5,
351–353). Princeton made a greater impression on James MADISON
than Cambridge did on Wordsworth, but MADISON too acknowledged the profound influence of his earliest schooling. He was
only eleven when he entered Donald Robertson's school, but decades later he said, "All that I have been in life I owe largely to that
man." Our understanding of the Framers' formal education must
begin in the schools where it began.[1]
    Of the twenty-some Framers who never went to college, those
who were neither tutored nor self-taught depended on a wide
range of schools that fall into two broad categories: schools that
followed patterns set in the previous century and schools such as
Robertson's that took a new approach, often under the direction
of Scots educated at Edinburgh, Glasgow, or Aberdeen. The newer
schools are examined in chapter 10. Of the older-model schools,

all but a handful were located north of the Potomac River. None of their students later celebrated his childhood as Wordsworth did; only KING (who went on to Harvard) seems to have remembered his early schooling particularly fondly, and only KING would stand out at Philadelphia. But these early schools were working on young, impressionable minds; in most cases, as the twig was bent, so indeed grew the tree. Conventional educations in these schools helped shape the conventional views of the Framers they taught.

In 1647, the Massachusetts General Court ordered towns to create and support schools:

> It being one chief project of that old deluder, Satan, to keep men from the knowledge of the scriptures . . . every Township in this Jurisdiction, after the Lord hath increased them to the number of fifty Householders, shall then forthwith appoint one within their town to teach all such children as shall resort to him to write and read. . . .
>
> And it is further ordered, that where any town shall increase to the number of one hundred Families or Householders, they shall set upon a Grammar-School, the masters thereof being able to instruct youth so far as they may be fitted for the Universitie.[2]

NATHANIEL GORHAM spent a few years at Charlestown's common school in the 1740s before leaving to become an apprentice; it is not certain whether there were two separate schools then or whether he learned his letters alongside boys who were wrestling with Latin grammar. ROGER SHERMAN was already a teenager before the town of Stoughton took steps toward opening any school. Marblehead, home of ELBRIDGE GERRY, was a much larger town than Stoughton, with a thriving commercial economy. The town obeyed the law by providing a school, but only for reading and writing in English.[3]

In New Hampshire, a public grammar school in Portsmouth was underway by 1710. By 1747 provision was made for a grammar school in Exeter to be paid for "by the inhabitants between Captain John Gilman's on Turkaway road and the little river on Kingston road and so farther as to take in Major Ezekiel Gilman on Newmarket road," in addition to the common school already "of long standing." The Gilmans were the most prominent family in Exeter, but there is no evidence that either NICHOLAS GILMAN or his brother, the future governor of New Hampshire, had more than a few years at the common school before going into the family's shipping business.[4]

Penmanship was the most valued subject of instruction. Just as the Elizabethan pronouns "thee" and "thou" were being abandoned, so the difficult, angular "secretary hand" of the sixteenth and seventeenth centuries was giving way to the rounded, open script that makes the "engrossed" Declaration of Independence and Constitution so easy to read. In a society as devoted to the written word as colonial New England, the importance of writing a clear hand was unquestioned. But even before they could handle a pen, GORHAM and GILMAN would have first learned to read following what John Locke had described in 1693 as the "ordinary Road": the hornbook for learning the alphabet, the primer for words and sentences, and then the Psalter, the New Testament, and at last the entire Bible. The *New England Primer*—beginning, "In ADAM's fall, we sinned all"—was first published in the seventeenth century and remained in use into the nineteenth; the text remained essentially unchanged, and generations of children wore their copies out. BENJAMIN FRANKLIN and David Hall printed 37,100 copies of the *Primer* between 1749 and 1766, not one of which survives.[5]

English translations of the classics appeared in increasing numbers, a reminder that many who lacked grammar-school Latin were nonetheless interested, but eighteenth-century liberal education implied an ability to read what were simply called "the languages"—Latin and Greek. The Boston Latin School course, the model for all New England grammar schools, lasted seven years. Instruction began with Josiah Cheever's *Introduction to Latin*, followed by Lily's *Latin Grammar*, Aesop, and Eutropius's *Brief History of Rome*, with English on facing pages. Older boys read Ovid, Virgil, Caesar, and Cicero. Cicero's *De officiis* taught not only Latin prose style but moral philosophy, planting (with Plutarch) the first seeds of resistance to any government that threatened to become tyrannical.[6]

Portsmouth had the oldest grammar school in New Hampshire, but it was adapting as local needs changed. JOHN LANGDON, a student there in the late 1740s, had little reason to study Latin (he may have done so), but he and the other students were now instructed in geography, arithmetic, trigonometry, "board gauging" timber (to figure the amount of cut lumber a tree would produce), and measuring tonnage of vessels, a practical curriculum for a commercial community. ABRAHAM BALDWIN went to the public grammar school in Guilford, Connecticut, to prepare for Yale, but only a few towns in New England kept up their Latin schools through the end of the eighteenth century: privately run college preparatory schools were already replacing them. Yale's first rector, Abraham Pierson, was a 1664 alumnus of New Haven's privately endowed Hopkins School, and JARED INGERSOLL was a Hopkins student before crossing the town green to enroll at Yale. INGERSOLL evidently developed little attachment to either of his old schools, sending neither of his own sons to Hopkins or to Yale.[7]

In Massachusetts, penalties for towns that failed to provide schools were repeatedly increased, but grand juries were reluctant to enforce them. Lt. Gov. William Dummer therefore bequeathed his home and a farm of nearly 300 acres near the town of Newbury to create an independent, boarding grammar school. The first headmaster, the Rev. Samuel Moody, left no doubt that it would be just that, a school where, almost to the exclusion of anything else, Latin grammar would be taught. (Long known as the Governor Dummer Academy, the nation's oldest boarding school is now called the Governor's Academy.) First as a private tutor and later at Dummer, Moody taught two of Massachusetts's four delegates to the 1787 Convention.[8]

The parents of RUFUS KING sent their son the seventy miles from Scarborough, Maine, to enroll at Moody's Massachusetts school. Nehemiah Cleaveland, the headmaster from 1821 to 1840, reported that Massachusetts senator Jeremiah Mason heard Dummer School alumni in Congress "talk in glowing terms of their eccentric but admirable instructor. He mentioned especially RUFUS KING, with whom he had served as Senator in Washington, as one from whose lips he had repeatedly heard the praises of Master Moody . . . so esteemed and so remembered, [Moody] must have had abilities and excellence of no ordinary character."[9]

Moody's eccentricities included a reluctance to employ corporal punishment and the habit of suddenly interrupting class on warm days to let students go for a swim in the river. His goal was "to fit his boys for college" by teaching them Latin; even if a majority of Dummer students passed up higher education, he believed that "there was no other discipline of equal value." According to Cleaveland, his students took away "not, indeed, a large stock of acquired knowledge—but what was incomparably more valuable—minds so formed to the habits of independent thought and careful, exact, thorough learning as made all subsequent acquisition comparatively easy and certain." KING's own mental flexibility enabled him to shift from deep suspicion of both Congress and the other states as late as 1785 to intense support for a strong central government during and after the 1787 Convention. He remained in public office longer than any other Framer, a Federalist to the end.[10]

New England's Calvinism demanded an educated clergy; its separatist tradition required that clergy to be homegrown and locally educated. But even in New England, grammar schools were scarce; most were pedagogical compromises that sent only a minority of their students to college. The more diverse middle colonies had two large cities, but (lacking New England's homogeneous religious motivation) schools were at first even fewer and poorer there. Philadelphia already had a good grammar school by the end the seventeenth century, and so did the much smaller town of Annapolis, Maryland. But in 1752, William Smith Jr. complained that New York had "been near a whole century in the hands of a civilized and enlightened People; and yet not one Seminary of Learning planted in it."[11]

Four Framers were born in the colony of New York: GOUVERNEUR MORRIS at Morrisania in the Bronx, LIVINGSTON and LANSING in Albany, and YATES in nearby Schenectady. MORRIS's parents sent him to New Rochelle when he was only six to attend the school of Huguenot refugee Pierre Stouppe, before enrolling him at the Philadelphia Academy. Stouppe's reputation attracted students from far afield. New Rochelle was less than ten miles from Morrisania, but Philip Schuyler (Hamilton's future father-in-law) and two generations of Livingstons (though not WILLIAM) were sent there all the way from Albany, 150 miles distant—evidence that Albany itself had little to offer. In 1789, when neighboring Schenectady's Academy was preparing to become Union College, *Morse's Gazette* observed that "a competent English teacher was scarcely to be found in Albany" until that town's own Academy opened in the previous decade.[12]

The first British governor of New York had licensed a teacher for English-speaking students in Albany in 1665, but perhaps there were too few of those; five years later the second governor, Francis Lovelace, decreed that two Dutch schoolmasters would be "sufficient for that place." For the next century the local people sent their children to the single school run by the Dutch Reformed Church, conducted in the Dutch language. There JOHN TEN EYCK LANSING received all his formal education before going on to read law under ROBERT YATES. LANSING had nothing to offer at the Convention but obstruction to change; his sole speech objected that "the Scheme is itself totally novel," and at the state ratifying convention he warned against "the idea of attaining a perfection which never existed." PIERCE could only say about LANSING that "his legal knowledge I am told is not extensive, nor his education a good one." Despite those drawbacks, his loyalty to Governor Clinton was repaid with appointment to the state Supreme Court; he held the office of chancellor of New York until the night of December 12, 1829, when he walked out to mail a letter and was never seen again.[13]

The town of Schenectady lay just fifteen miles northwest, on the south bank of the Mohawk. When ROBERT YATES was born there in 1738, Schenectady had at least two *triviale schoolen* (common schools to teach reading and writing in the Dutch language), but it was 1785 before the Dutch Reformed

Church negotiated with the magistrates to open the town's first *illustre school* (Latin grammar school), Schenectady Academy, much too late for YATES. He must have learned to read and write in one of the *triviale schoolen*, but a persistent tradition has him going to New York City for a classical education. There had been a New Amsterdam Latin School in mid-1600s Manhattan, but it was long gone by the time YATES was born. Society for the Propagation of the Gospel (SPG) reports mention private Latin schools that opened and closed during the years YATES might have been in the city—one or two each year between 1747 and 1752 and then none until 1761. Perhaps YATES attended one of these when he was between nine and fourteen, but they were ephemeral and have left no further record.[14]

LANSING and YATES learned their letters and numbers in Dutch and were raised in bilingual homes. Reading law—YATES with LIVINGSTON and LANSING with YATES—may have exposed them to some political philosophy, but there is no reason to question the judgment of William Smith Jr.: "Our schools are in the lowest order—the instructors want instruction; and, through a long shameful neglect of the arts and sciences, our common speech is extremely corrupt."[15]

Elsewhere in the middle colonies, schools were scarce. In 1781, DAVID BREARLEY and eighteen others in Trenton, New Jersey, (including WILLIAM CHURCHILL HOUSTON) subscribed seven pounds, ten shillings each "for the purpose of erecting a school house in the said Town, and keeping up a Regular School for the Education of Youth, to be conducted under the firm of the Trenton School Company." There is no record of where BREARLEY himself attended school; growing up in the Trenton area, he was eleven years old when Aaron Burr Sr. moved his grammar school into the newly completed Nassau Hall in Princeton only a few miles away; it is possible that he briefly attended the grammar school, but he left no record. Claims that BREARLEY was later a student at the college at Princeton began to be published two generations after his death, but they are pure conjecture. A Wilmington, Delaware, academy opened in 1765, when JACOB BROOM was thirteen. BROOM was the son of a prosperous blacksmith; he eventually held numerous local offices in Wilmington. He may have been a student at what became known as the "Old Academy," after first being taught by Pastors Erick Unander and Andrew Borell of the Old Swedes' Church. Trained as a surveyor, he drew the map that Washington used in 1777 at the battle of Brandywine. He continued to read on his own, accumulating a library that was large enough to require a separate room in the house he built in 1795. At the Convention he was silent.[16]

As proprietor of Pennsylvania, William Penn granted a charter to a school of "arts and sciences" in 1689—two years before he chartered the city of Philadelphia. Students were required to translate Latin into Greek and Greek into Latin, practice penmanship and spelling, and read scripture three times a week. Later exercise books show that students were also proving geometric theorems and studying conic sections and spherical trigonometry, well beyond the curriculum of most grammar schools. About the time THOMAS MIFFLIN was enrolled there in the 1750s, pupils studied both Ruddiman's *Latin Rudiments* and Addison's prose; they even published their own magazine imitating *The Spectator*.[17]

There were probably no more than four hundred students enrolled at any level of classical education in 1775 in the entire province of Pennsylvania, at a time when Philadelphia was the second- or third-largest English-speaking city on earth. South of Mason and Dixon's recently surveyed line, schools were fewer still. In 1773, the Rev. Jonathan Boucher complained about the state of education in Maryland: "In a country not less than half a million souls . . . there is not a single college, and only one school with an endowment adequate to the maintenance of even a common mechanic. What is still less credible is that two-thirds of the little education we receive are derived from instructors who are either indentured servants or transplanted felons." The one adequately endowed school was King William's School, in Annapolis, opened in 1696 "to instruct youth in Arithmetick, Navigation, and all useful learning, but chiefly for the fitting of such as are disposed to study divinity, to be further educated at His Majesty's College Royal in Virginia." The records of King William's School are lost. We have no idea how many of its students ever proceeded to William and Mary; few Marylanders did. Quite possibly DANIEL OF ST. THOMAS JENIFER was a student in the 1730s or 1740s. His family's plantations were along the Potomac River, but they also had an estate at Annapolis, where JENIFER lived as an adult. When King William's School became St. John's College in 1789, he contributed £100, the second largest gift the school received, perhaps from a grateful alumnus.[18]

The great challenge in Maryland and Virginia was finding teachers; the *Virginia Gazette* ran many advertisements seeking "a sober person of good morals capable of teaching children." But there were several "free schools" in Tidewater Virginia, some teaching Latin and Greek. During the eighteenth century, at least one Elizabeth City boy traveled to Cambridge University, and more than twenty went to William and Mary, including JAMES MCCLURG. That exceeded the rate that the larger Massachusetts town of Marblehead sent boys to Harvard. MCCLURG probably started at the William and Mary grammar school, as did Williamsburg town boys JOHN BLAIR and EDMUND RANDOLPH. RANDOLPH learned to read and write in Williamsburg; he wrote a letter to his children in which he recalled that he and his wife, Elizabeth Nicholas, were born less than twelve hours apart and "in childhood we were taught the elements of reading at the same school." MCCLURG, WYTHE, and PIERCE all grew up in or around the town of Hampton, no more than thirty miles from Williamsburg. Any one of those three could have learned his letters at one of the local schools endowed by the wills of Benjamin Syms and Thomas Eaton in the mid 1600s. They could just as well have been taught at home, which has always been the accepted story of WYTHE's education. There is simply no record.[19]

The common schools made little impression on those Framers whose education stopped there, beyond the grim view of human nature early inculcated by the *New England Primer*. The autodidacts were, almost without exception, better prepared. The older grammar schools, like the older colleges, followed an older idea of what should be taught. Their graduates did not shine at the Convention. At Harvard and Yale, where the grammar schools sent so many of their students, conservatism reigned. Those two colleges graduated seven of the Framers (an eighth transferred from Yale to Princeton). One, KING, was an ally of MADISON until MADISON's unfamiliar ideas of "overpoise" and mixed federal powers made him too uneasy; another, GERRY, was a vociferous and inconsistent participant in the debate, finally refusing to sign and actively opposing ratification; and the rest were notably reticent or even silent during the Convention's arguments over the philosophy of government. To those two conservative colleges—and to college education in general—we now turn.

5

The Schools of the Prophets
Harvard and Yale

ABRAHAM BALDWIN, OLIVER ELLSWORTH, ELBRIDGE GERRY,
JARED INGERSOLL, WILLIAM SAMUEL JOHNSON, RUFUS KING,
WILLIAM LIVINGSTON, CALEB STRONG

*At Harvard College in the Massachusetts Bay, and at Yale College
in Connecticut.... When the young Gentlemen have run through the
Course of their Education, they enter into the Ministry, or some Office of
the Government, and acting in them under the Doctrines espoused in the
Morning of Life, the Spirit of the College is transferred through the Colony,
and tinctures the Genius and policy of the public Administrators, from the
Governor down to the Constable.*

WILLIAM LIVINGSTON, *Independent Reflector XVII, March 22, 1753*

In 1636, a group of Cambridge graduates (with a handful of Oxford
men) founded New College in Newetown, Massachusetts Bay Colony, in order to educate future Puritan ministers locally; two years
later the town was renamed Cambridge and the college renamed
Harvard after a generous benefactor (and Cambridge alumnus),
John Harvard. When the Constitutional Convention was called,
Harvard College was already 150 years old—hardly New College
anymore. In 1650, the Massachusetts General Court granted the
college a charter, usurping a privilege formerly exercised only by
the monarch, and graduates of Harvard went on to found Yale
in 1701. When the Rev. Thomas Shepard asked the United Colony
Commissioners to support Harvard financially in 1655, he alluded
to 1 Samuel 19:18–24, requesting "some way of comfortable maintenance for the School of the Prophets that now is." It was a habit
of the New England Puritans to see themselves as the New Israel;
it also became a habit for Yale to insist that Harvard, like Jerusalem

of old, had fallen away, and in the 1720s and 1730s Yale appropriated its claim to be the "School of the Prophets." As Harvard's orthodoxy seemed to weaken, Yale was all the more determined to be the college Harvard should have been, and for the next two centuries it would oscillate between imitation and disapproval; Harvard alternated between indifference and disdain, with brief periods of jealousy. The two colleges were very conscious of their differences, but outsiders saw them as similar to the point that the visiting Englishman Edward Kimber in 1746 lumped them together as "those excellent Universities, for I must call them so, of the *Massachusetts*"—forgetting that New Haven was in Connecticut but contrasting both with Virginia's more indolent College of William and Mary.[1]

Harvard and Yale graduates so monopolized the intellectual, social, and political leadership of New England that when the region supplied fourteen signers of the Declaration of Independence, all but two were graduates of one or the other, including such luminaries as Samuel Adams, John Adams, and John Hancock. Eleven years later, there were once again four Yale men at the Constitutional Convention; as in 1776 they were cautious supporters of the movement that had brought them to Philadelphia. The Harvard delegation in 1787 had shrunk from eight to three, all from Massachusetts, but now there were no Adamses or Hancocks from Harvard boldly taking the initiative. ELBRIDGE GERRY (class of 1762) was back, but in a less revolutionary frame of mind after sitting out two terms of Congress, upset by what he considered unjust treatment of Massachusetts rather than any fundamental problem with the Articles of Confederation. Although he was shaken by Shays's Rebellion in his home state, his desire for a stronger government on that account faded over the summer. With GERRY at Philadelphia was CALEB STRONG (class of 1764), a Federalist more interested in state than national government. He would be elected to 11 one-year terms as governor of Massachusetts, defeating GERRY in three of those elections, but he had turned down appointment to Congress in 1780 and would later resign his Senate seat midterm. Along with GERRY and STRONG was their younger colleague, RUFUS KING (class of 1777). He, too, had been leery of empowering Congress until Shays's Rebellion convinced him that unbridled democracy was a greater threat. He arrived in Philadelphia a recent convert to the doctrine of strong central government and spoke nearly as often in support of that principle as GERRY did in opposition.[2]

KING was more than a decade younger than GERRY and STRONG, and his years at Harvard during the Revolutionary turmoil were very different from theirs in the early 1760s, which had been a calmer time; before the convulsions of the Stamp Act, the most disruptive issue was the quality of student food. Yale's youngest alumnus at the Convention, ABRAHAM BALDWIN (class of 1772) was a generation younger than WILLIAM LIVINGSTON (1741) and WILLIAM SAMUEL JOHNSON (1744). The latter two took the roles of elder statesmen at the Convention, speaking little but working to find compromise. BALDWIN, recently relocated to Georgia, was himself an advocate of compromise between his native and his adopted regions. The fourth Yale man, JARED INGERSOLL (1766), served on no committees and never spoke until the Convention's final day. The traumas of the Great Awakening that would affect Yale so strongly were just beginning in LIVINGSTON's and JOHNSON's days; by the time INGERSOLL graduated, the college had been wracked by religious controversy and shut down by protests against President Thomas Clap's autocratic discipline. The campus itself was much calmer when BALDWIN enrolled, but larger political issues were by then in the air; the curriculum, however, had changed only a little in the thirty-one years since LIVINGSTON was a freshman. At both Harvard and Yale, students continued to study Greek and Roman classics, along with Calvinist theology and "natural philosophy." Both colleges—Harvard especially, thanks to Professor John Winthrop—were relatively up to date in the sciences, but both—Yale especially—were well behind the newer colleges when it came to political science, a weakness that was apparent at the Convention. There was some institutional but little curricular change during the long presidencies of Edward Holyoke and Thomas Clap. The Revolutionary War would break out during KING's time at Harvard, but there would be no revolution in education for Harvard and Yale students over the eighteenth century.

Edward Holyoke became president of Harvard College in 1736, before GERRY and STRONG were born. By the time they graduated, he was approaching the end of his thirty-three-year presidency. Under Holyoke, Harvard entered its second century. The college had been growing; the class of 1771 was the largest until 1810, with sixty-three graduates. The median age of freshmen was rising from a little over fifteen in 1741 to seventeen in 1769, but GERRY was fourteen and STRONG fifteen when they matriculated. Most students came from eastern Massachusetts or New Hampshire; between 1737 and 1790 not one student came to Harvard from New York. About every other year a student from the Carolinas or the West Indies appeared, but by and large Harvard was a homogeneous place, educating local boys.[3]

The largest number typically prepared at Boston Latin or, like KING, at Dummer, but CALEB STRONG hailed from Northampton, Massachusetts, on the Connecticut River, where the usual course for a scholar led downstream to Yale. His uncle Isaac Lyman, a Yale graduate, had succeeded Joseph Moody as pastor of the church at York, Maine, where Joseph's son Samuel was developing a reputation as an unusually gifted teacher. Phoebe Strong prevailed upon her husband to send their only son to live with her brother and study with Moody, a recent Harvard graduate and a classmate of President Holyoke's son. CALEB chose to go from there to Harvard.

ELBRIDGE GERRY of Marblehead was one of a growing number of students coming from the seaports that had "reaped the first harvests from land speculation and the West India commerce, and the rum business"; in Samuel Eliot Morison's judgment, "The new crop of young men came to be made gentlemen, not to study." As early as 1711 President Leverett had noted in his commencement address that Harvard graduates became not only clergymen but also merchants, wise merchants, he hoped, "not comparable to apes, peacocks, and parrots." GERRY's father had grown rich in the West Indies trade, and GERRY went directly from Harvard into the family business, but he also went back to collect an MA three years later. So did STRONG.[4]

Whether destined to be merchants or ministers, Harvard matriculants had to come prepared for a classical education. The college required applicants "extempore to read, construe, and parse Tully [i.e., Cicero], Virgil, or Such like common Classical Latin Authors; and to write true Latin in prose, and to be Skill'd in making Latin verse, or at least in the rules of Prosodia; and to read, construe, and parse ordinary Greek, as in the New Testament, Isocrates, or such like, and decline the paradigms of Greek Nouns and Verbs." The young John Adams of Braintree, dreading the entrance exams, came close to turning his horse around at the last minute. He was greatly relieved when he learned that he had passed, but few applicants were turned away—and Harvard made every effort to see that students, once admitted, received their degrees on schedule, even those who were (temporarily) expelled for disciplinary infractions.[5]

Because preparation was often poor, freshmen spent their first year in a review of Latin grammar. When tutor Henry Flynt gave an account of the curriculum to the Harvard Overseers, he reported that "the first year The Freshmen recite the Classic Authors Learnt at School." They reread Virgil and Homer and learned rhetoric and composition from Cicero, Demosthenes, and Isocrates, even though these authors were ostensibly part of their preparation for college. From year to year the Harvard reading list also included Hesiod, Plutarch, Plato, Xenophon, and Sallust, but not, apparently, the historians Livy and Tacitus. As Thomas Miller notes, classics at Harvard were taught "not extensively but intensively," with the emphasis on developing a classical style in Latin composition and preparing students to engage in Latin syllogistic disputations. Saturdays were devoted to the study of divinity, where the seventeenth-century English Puritan William Ames eventually gave way to Johannes Wolleb's *Abridgement of Christian Divinity*.[6]

The sophomore year brought some variety, with the modern *Logick* and *Astronomy* of Isaac Watts, along with natural philosophy and mathematics. Saturdays were still given over to divinity. The junior year emphasized mathematics, along with physics, metaphysics, and ethics. Seniors continued to read ethics, primarily Aristotle's. Ames had objected in the previous century that "Aristotle holds . . . that the judgment of prudent men is the rule for virtue," arguing instead that "there can be no other teaching of the virtues than theology which brings the whole revealed will of God to the direction of our reason, will, and life." But Thomas Shepard, who had first called Harvard the school of the prophets, had also given his opinion that "law natural is part of law moral," and in the words of Perry Miller, "On the matter of ethics, New England for the one and only time rejected the leadership of William Ames." Still, Cotton Mather complained that the "employment of so much time upon Ethicks in our Colledges" was a "vile Peece of Paganism," and Yale was slower to trade Ames for Aristotle.[7]

Some Harvard students may have been reading Francis Hutcheson's first book, *An Inquiry into the Original of Our Ideas of Beauty and Virtue*, as early as the 1730s; this early work introduced Hutcheson's doctrine of the moral sense, but it stopped short of discussing political philosophy, and there is no sign that any of Hutcheson's later, more political work was assigned during the eighteenth century. Eventually Burlamaqui's *Principles of Natural and Politic Law* was added to the curriculum, but probably after Holyoke's time, too late for GERRY or STRONG. In November 1760, when GERRY and STRONG were students, John Adams (class of 1755) complained, "There are multitudes of authors on natural law that I have never read; and indeed I have never read any part of the best authors *Puffendorf* and *Grotius*."[8]

It was taken for granted that the best preparation for future political leaders was reading the history of ancient political leaders. In 1766, Harvard graduate Jonathan Mayhew preached his sermon celebrating the repeal of the Stamp Act, entitled *The Snare Broken: A Thanksgiving Discourse*. Asserting the colonists' rights, he cited Cicero, Demosthenes, and Plato, whom he had studied in college, along with Milton, Locke, and Hoadly, whom he had read only after graduating. Twenty years later, the Marquis de Chastely, after conversing with Samuel Adams (Harvard 1740), described Adams's approach as "beginning by the Greeks and Romans to get at the whigs and tories."[9]

Sam Adams's first year at Harvard was Holyoke's first year as president. Holyoke gradually replaced older works with newer ones; his additions included Watts's *Astronomy*, Locke's *Essay on Human Understanding*, and Fordyce's survey, *Elements of Moral Philosophy*. Holyoke also allowed students (with parental permission) to take private French lessons. In 1738, the new Hollis Professor of Mathematics and Natural Philosophy, John Winthrop, began lecturing on such diverse topics as electricity, sunspots, Halley's comet, and earthquakes. Winthrop became one of the great science educators in American history.[10]

Holyoke's most important reforms came too late to affect GERRY and STRONG. Until 1767 Harvard had followed the ancient practice of making a single tutor responsible for all instruction of each entering class throughout their four years. Henry Flynt, a Harvard institution, served fifty-five years as a tutor. The four tutors were now recast as specialists: one would teach Latin, a second Greek, a third logic, metaphysics, and ethics, and a fourth natural philosophy, mathematics, and geography. All four would share responsibility for rhetoric, elocution, and composition. The Hollis Professor of Divinity took charge of theology, and Winthrop delivered "experimental lectures." Veterans such as Flynt gave way to recent graduates who came and went with regularity. The entire Harvard faculty remained inbred—with the exception of the French tutors, every single teacher in the eighteenth century was himself a Harvard graduate.[11]

Apart from Holyoke's reform of teaching assignments, there was little change in the method of instruction from 1755 until the 1820s. Students' notebooks reveal gradual changes in reading habits, but they also demonstrate the stubborn persistence of a number of enduring textbooks. Commonplace books kept by Harvard students indicate both the recurrence of certain assigned texts and the variety of books read by choice. In 1746, the young Samuel Moody copied passages from William Derham's *Physico-Theology*; twenty-three years later Derham appears again in Benjamin Wadsworth's *Abridgement of What I extracted while an Undergraduate at Harvard College*. Wadsworth was at Harvard between STRONG and KING, on his way to a career in the ministry. He recorded no highlights of his freshman year, perhaps because it was largely a review of Latin grammar, but he filled three notebooks with extracts from the next three years' reading. They give an idea of the Harvard curriculum—formal and informal—at the time two Framers were there.

In his sophomore year, Wadsworth copied out passages from a history of America, a history of the Bible, and a number of works on divinity (two by the Mathers, Increase and Cotton, that had been read at Harvard for half a century). In his junior year, his reading broadened to include Rollin's popular *Ancient History* and *Belles Lettres* (which John Adams, in his junior year, considered "worth their weight in gold"), Josephus's *Jewish Antiquities*, several oratorical manuals, and popular fiction, including *Charles Grandison*, *The Devil on Two Sticks*, *Joseph Andrews*, and *Zayde: A Spanish Romance*, racy choices for a prospective Calvinist pastor. But that year Wadsworth also was thinking about his vocation, and he copied passages from even more devotional and theological works than the year before. Like most young men of his time and place, he read *Pilgrim's Progress* and several volumes of *The Spectator*.[12]

In his senior year, Wadsworth took notes from Winthrop's "experimental lectures"; he gave equal time to Increase Mather's *Discourse Concerning Comets* and to Thomas Burnet's *Sacred Theory of the Earth*. Wadsworth returned to Rollin and to Stackhouse's *History of the Bible*, took notes from Derham's still popular *Physico-Theology*, and copied passages from works as various as Addison's *Cato*, Goldsmith's *Vicar of Wakefield*, Thomas Hutchinson's recent *History of Massachusetts*, Neal's *History of the Puritans*, and a translation of the *Koran*. David Hume makes an appearance, but with his conservative *History of England*, not any of the philosophical or political essays that MADISON was then reading at Princeton.[13]

The histories by Hume, Rollin, and Hutchinson, along with *Cato*, are the closest Wadsworth came to political philosophy in 1766–1769. For further reading in moral philosophy, the Dutch Aristotelians Burgersdijk and Heereboord may still have been assigned reading, but if so they made no impression on Wadsworth. Anna Haddow, in her study of colonial political education, concludes that "it would appear from these early courses [1636–1770] that the political branch was not cultivated at Harvard, except insofar as it was incidentally touched upon under ethics." John Adams's diary supports that conclusion. In the year following his graduation he was teaching at a village school and feeling sorry for himself. He began reading Francis Hutcheson in January 1756, and on April 24 he wrote, in a burst of self-pity, "I long to know a little of Ethicks and Moral Philosophy. But I have no Book, no Time, no Friends. I must therefore be contented to live and die an ignorant and obscure fellow."[14]

Haddow makes the observation, "Undoubtedly political education was a phase of instruction, for we know that the college library had works on government and political theory." The contents of the library, however, are for several reasons a poor guide to the students' actual education. Many of the political volumes there had not been chosen by the Harvard faculty but rather by Thomas Hollis, Harvard's English patron, whose politics were a good deal more liberal than President Holyoke's. After Harvard's library was destroyed by fire in 1764, Hollis sent boxes full of new books, writing to Mayhew, "More books, especially on government, are going to New England. Should those go safe, it is hoped no principal books on that FIRST subject will be wanting in Harvard College, from the days of Moses to these times. Men of New England, Brethren, use them for yourselves, and for others." These books and more arrived after GERRY and STRONG graduated.[15]

By 1774, the replenished library shelves held numerous volumes of Enlightenment political philosophy—nearly all gifts of Hollis and not a single one assigned in any class. There is no reason to believe that any of these books had been in the collection before the fire, which occurred during STRONG's senior year. Students—at least juniors and seniors—did use the library; RUFUS KING borrowed Robertson's *History of Scotland*, Stacey's *History of Poland*, Vertot's *Sweden*, and a volume of Bolingbroke during his junior year. As a senior contemplating military service in 1776–1777, he borrowed Vauban on fortification and Hauxley on navigation, some novels, and Beccaria's *Essay on Crime and Punishment*. Beccaria and Bolingbroke are the only borrowing he might have been likely to recall during the Convention of 1787, unless, perhaps, *Don Quixote* came to mind during the more frustrating stretches.[16]

Students were allowed some degree of religious liberty at Harvard (confirming the New Haven conviction that Yale alone was truly the School of the Prophets), and in general student behavior that had once been forbidden gradually came to be tolerated. Students were occasionally expelled for various offenses and then readmitted to graduate on time with their classes. There is some evidence that certain families refused to send their sons to Harvard because of its worsening reputation, but Holyoke remained forgiving, and students never reached the point of open warfare that drove President Clap from Yale. The Overseers made the calculated decision to let the more stiff-necked abandon Harvard, rather than crack down and risk losing the wealthy and influential parents whose sons were the worst offenders. Since the days of President Leverett, two administrations before Holyoke, there had been criticism that Harvard was willing to let standards drop in order to court the rising commercial class—families like GERRY's.[17]

More and more graduates were becoming lawyers; they were heirs to the Puritan tradition of polemical sermons and sharply reasoned lawsuits, part of a culture where all other arts were subordinated to the verbal. Each MA candidate chose his own topic in consultation with the president, and theological topics gradually were replaced by political. GERRY received his MA in 1765, a year after the passage of the Sugar Act and months after the Stamp Act. He chose the question, "Can the new Prohibitory Duties, which make it useless for the People to engage in Commerce, be evaded by them as Faithful Subjects?" Needless to say, GERRY chose the affirmative, defending a policy his family's business was already following. Two years later, with the Townsend Acts newly passed and Governor Bernard in the audience, STRONG gave an affirmative answer to the pointed question, "Does a promise that has been given bind the highest magistrate in a civil government?"[18]

Although a master's degree could still be obtained on short notice simply by paying the required fee, President Holyoke encouraged the plan of preparation set out in Thomas Johnson's *Quaestiones Philosophicae in Justi Systematis Ordinem Dispositae* (Cambridge: Wm. Thurlbourn, 1735), and a significant number of graduates chose one of Johnson's topics. A student who followed Johnson's program would pursue independent reading in theology or politics. David W. Robson points out that Sam Adams's 1743 topic, the limits of the supreme magistrate's power, should have led him (if he followed Johnson's suggestions) to read Grotius and Pufendorf on law, and Locke, Sidney, and Hoadly on the philosophy of government. GERRY and STRONG had little or no instruction in political philosophy as undergraduates, but preparation for their MA *questiones* could have helped make up for it. GERRY's and STRONG's theses, however, were taken from current controversies rather than Johnson's topics.[19]

Public speaking became an extracurricular activity in 1770, with the creation of the Speaking Club. Two competing clubs, the Mercurian Society and Clintonian Club, soon followed. These were not yet debating societies, but they did offer students the chance to recite classical orations and, occasionally, original speeches. These groups may have been inspired by contemporary public orations in protest of British policy, but their main appeal was as exclusive secret societies, like William and Mary's Flat Hat Club (F.H.C.): public mention of their names meant expulsion from the clubs, and after graduation members continued to refer to them only by their initials. Like the F.H.C. they were short-lived, but in the eventful year of 1775 the Speaking Club was "revived upon its primitive foundation." One of the revivers was RUFUS KING, who delivered an address simply entitled "A Piece of Whiggism."[20]

The war years were a desperate time for the college, which was forced to relocate briefly to Concord. In July 1777, KING was among forty-one graduates who received their degrees by general diploma; Harvard held no public commencements from 1774 to 1781. Quite a few alumni were loyalists: by Morison's count, 196 of 1,224 living graduates in 1776, or 16 percent (compared with 2 percent at Princeton). Nearly all current students favored independence, but very few left college to join the army, as JOHN FRANCIS MERCER did at William and Mary, JONATHAN DAYTON did at Princeton, and RICHARD DOBBS SPAIGHT did from across the Atlantic at Glasgow University. RUFUS KING waited a year before enlisting for General Sullivan's abortive attack on Newport, Rhode Island, and within a few weeks he was back in Newburyport, reading law. KING had come to Harvard bitter about the treatment of his father at the hands of the Sons of Liberty: when Richard King defended the Stamp Act, his house in Scarborough was ransacked just as Lt. Gov. Thomas Hutchinson's was in Boston. RUFUS KING spent four years at Harvard, entering as a loyalist and leaving substantially radicalized. He would retain a lifelong distrust of democracy, but by the time he left Harvard he had also abandoned his loyalty to Great Britain.[21]

Four Framers were graduates of Yale College, and there could have been six, if not for the denominational discord and erratic discipline that disrupted the administration of President Thomas Clap. WILLIAM LIVINGSTON and WILLIAM SAMUEL JOHNSON were among Clap's first students in the 1740s, and ABRAHAM BALDWIN arrived as the dust was settling following his forced retirement. In what turned out to be Clap's final graduating class, JARED INGERSOLL and OLIVER ELLSWORTH matriculated in 1762, but ELLSWORTH transferred to Princeton after two years, unhappy like most of his classmates with Clap's arbitrary rule and probably also with his theology. Two years later, GOUVERNEUR MORRIS enrolled at King's College instead, even though his older brothers had been given pride of place in their Yale classes. The will of Lewis Morris II had guaranteed his youngest son "the best education that is to be had," so long as he didn't seek it at Yale, "lest he should imbibe that low craft and cunning so incident to the people of that Colony." (Old Morris was irritated by Connecticut's—and Thomas Clap's—opposition to the appointment of an American Anglican bishop.) So Yale lost two men who would make signal contributions at the Convention.[22]

Harvard was barely off the ground when the leaders of Connecticut colony and New Haven colony began making their own plans. Purchases of books and proposals for a college in New Haven started as early as 1656, but they were suspended with the restoration of King Charles II. In 1701, two Harvard Overseers, Judge Samuel Sewall and Massachusetts provincial secretary Isaac Addison, agreed to write a charter for a new school, "Wherein Youth may be instructed in the Arts and Sciences [and] through the blessing of Almighty God may be fitted for Publick employment both in Church and Civil State." Yale would keep both of those career objectives for its graduates, and in that order.[23]

Although the charter was approved by the Connecticut legislature, the founders were keenly aware that it did not come from the Crown and was thus not strictly legitimate. Wisely, they flew under the radar, calling their creation a "collegiate school" rather than a college. Sewell and Addison had cautiously chosen "as low a name as we could that it might better stand the wind and weather." The school's head would be called "rector" rather than "president," following attorney John Eliot's advice: "As to the Title of the Master of the said School. . . . That which shows Least of Grandeur will be Least obnoxious." The first draft of the charter included the right to grant degrees "as is usual at Harvard," but Eliot warned that "not standing on a Royall foundation we cannot give authentick or Legal Degrees." The charter as approved nevertheless promised "licenses or degrees," without mentioning Harvard's example.[24]

When Samuel Johnson, father of WILLIAM SAMUEL JOHNSON, was among the early students, the library consisted of a few books "100 or 150 years old such as the first settlers of the country brought with them." That changed dramatically a few months after Johnson's graduation in 1714, just as he was preparing to become a tutor at the college. Jeremiah Dummer (brother of the Dummer Academy's benefactor) donated about 800 books, including Bacon's *Advancement of Learning* and more recent works of John Locke and Isaac Newton, along with Enlightenment authors as yet unknown at Yale or Harvard. Years later, Johnson remembered his reaction: "All this was like a flood of day to his low state of mind . . . he found himself like one at once emerging out of the glimmer of twilight into the full sunshine of open day." Dismissing the curriculum that he had just completed as "scholastic cobwebs," the new tutor set to work trying to modernize instruction, especially in science.[25]

In 1722, Rector Timothy Cutler and several tutors and ministers (including Johnson) shocked New Haven by publicly abandoning the Congregational Church for the Church of England; the college immediately dismissed the apostates and began looking for a new head. For four years, tutor Jonathan Edwards kept the college going, serving as acting rector. (Thirty-six years later he would become president of Princeton.) The trustees finally settled on Elisha Williams, who remained in office through 1739; one of his matriculants in 1737 was WILLIAM LIVINGSTON, the youngest son of the lord of Livingston Manor in the Hudson River valley.[26]

The thirteen-year-old LIVINGSTON (like his three brothers before him) was ranked first in his class thanks to his family's status, but coming from Albany he felt very much an outsider in New Haven. He and his classmates were all told that "every student shall consider the main end of his study to wit to know God in Jesus Christ and answerably to lead a Godly sober life." The Yale Laws required, "All students after they have Done resciting rhetoric and ethics on fridays, rescite Wolebius theology [Johann Wolleb, *Compendium Theologiae Christianae*] and on saturday morning they shall rescite Ames theology thesis in his Medulla [William Ames, *Medulla Theologiae*], and on saturday evening the [Westminster] Assemblies shorter Catechism in Lattin and on Sabath Day attend the explication of Ames Cases of Conscience [*Conscience with the Power and Cases Thereof*]." This heavy dose of Calvinism filled each weekend.[27]

Every day began with early prayers. The first classes met before breakfast; after study in chambers, students had another recitation just before their midday dinner. After that, another class, evening prayer, and supper. At 9:00 p.m. they were expected in their rooms, with candles snuffed at 11:00. Students were forbidden to go to taverns without a parent or a chaperone approved by their tutors; they were warned to "avoid profane swearing, lying, needless asseverations, foolish gratings, Chidings, strifes, railings, gesting, uncomely noise, spreading ill rumors, Divulging secrets, and all manner of troublesome and offensive behaviour."[28]

Such an exhaustive list of prohibitions naturally invited disobedience. Throughout the eighteenth century, Yale students were continually defying authority; their rebellion reached a peak in the near anarchy of the mid-1760s, but as early as 1721 Jonathan Edwards wrote to his father about "monstrous impieties and acts of immorality . . . particularly stealing hens, geese, turquoise [turkeys], piggs, meat, wood &c., unseasonable nightwalking, breaking peoples windows, playing at cards, cursing, swearing, damning, and using all manner of ill language, which never were at such a pitch in the college as they now are."[29]

Somehow the students also found time to study. Admission required an examination in Latin and Greek; LIVINGSTON's year of tutoring may not have produced the desired mastery, but, just as at Harvard, the freshman year was designed to remediate deficiencies in the classical languages. Students at both colleges were expected to speak only Latin, even (theoretically) in private conversations. They read parts of the Old Testament out of Hebrew into Greek in the morning and parts of the New Testament out of English or Latin into Greek in the evening. They also studied logic, metaphysics, mathematics, physics, rhetoric, and ethics. Ezra Stiles, Yale's most widely respected eighteenth-century president, recorded that "when my father was in coll. they recited Mori Enchiridion Ethicis." Stiles's father graduated in 1722; Henry More's *Enchiridion* continued to be read for decades.[30]

LIVINGSTON evidently appreciated his education at Yale. Upon the death of his old tutor, Chauncey Whittelsey, two months after the Convention ended in 1787, LIVINGSTON wrote to a classmate, "I have reason to venerate his memory. I loved him. He deserved it. He laid the foundations of what little knowledge I have and had I been as assiduous in rearing the superstructure as he was in laying the foundation, I might by this time have been good for something." LIVINGSTON made close friends, including the elder Jared Ingersoll (who would become a stamp tax administrator), Noah Welles (who would preach a sermon against the stamp tax), and William Peartree Smith, with whom LIVINGSTON would publish the *Independent Reflector* in the 1750s and with whom he would serve as a Princeton trustee. LIVINGSTON's father gave twenty-eight pounds to Yale in 1745 "as a small acknowledgement of the sense I have for the favor and Education my sons have had there." It was used to endow Yale's first professorship, the chair of divinity that was offered to ABRAHAM BALDWIN in 1781.[31]

In 1740, as LIVINGSTON began his senior year, young WILLIAM SAMUEL JOHNSON matriculated at Yale. His arrival coincided with that of the new rector, Thomas Clap. Ten of his thirteen new classmates came from Connecticut and three from New York. JOHNSON was ranked third in his class by Rector Clap, behind the son of a wealthy Long Island landowner and the son of a member of the legislature's upper house. Thanks to years of instruction by his father, JOHNSON was far better prepared than LIVINGSTON: he had begun reading Latin at eight and Greek at ten. Indeed, his father supposedly boasted that as freshmen both he and his brother "had so little to do, their classmates being so far behind them."[32]

Although Harvard had, during the preceding twenty years, been evolving an increasingly secular (albeit conservative) curriculum, the new rector gave every indication of continuing Yale's primary emphasis on Calvinism. Nevertheless, Clap worked closely with JOHNSON's father to reform some elements of the Yale curriculum. Mathematics, previously restricted to seniors, was now taught to freshmen; to Samuel Johnson's satisfaction, astronomy and physics once again received the modernized attention he had given them when he was a tutor. Young WILLIAM SAMUEL, however, proved more interested in Latin and Greek. College laws required attendance at New Haven's First Congregational Church, but Clap allowed JOHNSON and other Anglicans to attend services in West Haven. This was not a reflection of any weakening in the Calvinism that remained consistent through his long tenure. The greater threat now, however, was coming from the evangelicals—the New Lights.[33]

There was never any doubt that Clap believed in the necessity of spiritual regeneration. His MA question at Harvard had been, "Is it possible to secure remission of sins through natural reason?" He took the negative. But after George Whitefield's popular preaching tour in 1740, the evangelicals mounted a direct attack on the establishment: the Rev. James Davenport called the Rev. John Noyes of First Church "an unconverted man; a hypocrite; a wolf in sheep's clothing, and a devil incarnate." The gauntlet was thrown down, and Clap had to respond. At his direction, the trustees voted "that if any student at this college shall directly or indirectly say that the Rector . . . the Trustees or the tutors are hypocrites, carnal or unconverted men, he shall for the first offense be expelled." In 1742, David Brainerd, the most promising student in the junior class, was dismissed for declaring that LIVINGSTON's beloved tutor Whittelsey "had no more grace than a chair."[34]

Revivalism was sweeping through New England, but not all Yale students were sympathetic. Although LIVINGSTON found the Old Light theology arid ("rather calculated to make one a Critic or a Pedagogue, than a Good Man or a Christian"), he had no patience with the emotional excesses of the New Lights. Following his graduation, he wrote to Noah Welles that the revivalists' preaching conflicted "with sense" and would not "bear the touchstone of reason . . . I can never persuade myself that such Convulsions, Agitations, Swoons, fluctuations, trances, groanings, yellings . . . howlings, cryings, Shreekings . . . genuflections, heart-beatings, breast-pantings, headach[e]s, knee-tremblings, teeth-knashings . . . are any sign that Christianity prevails among a people."[35]

Shortly after that letter was written, Clap threw up his hands and briefly closed the college, sending the students home. The campus was briefly quieter during the junior and senior years of WILLIAM JOHNSON—many of the New Lights had left—and Clap became very attached to that serious student, awarding him at graduation the Berkeley Scholarship for excellence in ancient tongues. JOHNSON remained in New Haven for an additional year to read divinity with Clap, despite their theological differences. His reasons are obscure; he was just turning seventeen, no doubt flattered by the attention of the college rector, who was known as an opponent of the revivalists and willing to accommodate his Anglican students. Perhaps the young man was motivated by the same thirst for distinction that made him want an MA from Harvard in addition to one from Yale. Perhaps he preferred this independently earned opportunity to returning to be once more a student in his father's house. After a year, however, return he did. Maybe Clap's increasingly dictatorial manner during that year made him uncomfortable; maybe he was beginning to realize that the ministry was not his calling after all. In

1746, back home in Stratford, he finally told his father that his vocation was not the priesthood but the law.[36]

The fires of the Great Awakening were by no means out. In 1745, White-field returned to New Haven, but before that Clap had expelled John and Ebenezer Cleveland for attending a Separatist service in the town of Canterbury, and he reproved friends of the Clevelands for reading Locke's *Letter Concerning Toleration*. So far, the trustees and the assembly had backed Clap. He persuaded the assembly to recharter Yale in 1745, turning the rector, tutors, and trustees into the Yale Corporation, and retitling the rector as the president. He soon felt confident enough to pursue other reforms, including the institution of a college chapel, which all students would be required to attend—even the Anglicans. But after six months he rescinded the requirement for Anglican students, following a threat from Samuel Johnson to take the issue to London. Yale's new charter, like the old one, was only from the provincial assembly, not from the Crown, a vulnerability that must have given Clap pause.[37]

In his twenty-six years as rector and president, Clap changed the corporate structure, pedagogy, and daily routines at Yale, but his curricular reforms did not go much beyond updating the study of astronomy and physics and requiring the study of Hebrew. The College Law of 1745 had ratified the curriculum that LIVINGSTON and JOHNSON went through: "In the first Year They Shall principally study the Tongues and Logic and in Some means shall pursue the Study of Tongues the Two next Years. In the second Year they shall Recite Rhetoric, Geometry, and Geography. In the Third Year, Natural Philosophy, Astronomy, and other Parts of Mathematics. . . . In the Fourth Year, Metaphysics and Ethics." A generation later that remained the plan. Ezra Stiles (class of 1746) recalled, "When I was an undergraduate we recited Wollaston's 'Religion [of Nature] delineated.'" When he became president thirty years later, he found Wollaston still a required text.[38]

In 1743, a third tutor had been added to the faculty, so that each class had its own tutor, as at Harvard, who "Carries them thro' a Course of Studies, for three Years, and the President completes their instruction in the fourth." After the addition of the Livingston Chair of Divinity, the faculty structure remained unchanged until 1770, when Nehemiah Strong was appointed Yale's first professor of mathematics and natural philosophy. Yale would be the last American college to abandon the ancient approach of assigning one tutor to teach all subjects to a class through its underclass years.[39]

Throughout his career, Clap was driven to tighten up whatever he saw as lax. As soon as he was appointed rector, he put an end to new students' habit of casually arriving at any time during their first year. The Yale library had offered a refuge to the lonely young freshman WILLIAM LIVINGSTON; in September 1740, Clap ordered "that no Person shall have liberty to take or borrow any Book out of the Library, except the Rector, Trustees, Tutors, Masters & Bachelors residing at the College & the two Senior Classes." In his campaign to prevent any unauthorized influences from corrupting his students, it sometimes seemed that whatever was not compulsory was forbidden. Tutor Thomas Darling objected that Clap "locks up a Number of Books from the Scholars to prevent their reading them," and Ezra Stiles complained that his neighbors in Rhode Island had come to view Yale as a seat of "contracted bigotry." In 1765, Clap boasted, "We have a good Library, consisting of about 4000 Volumes, well furnished with ancient Authors, such as the Fathers, Historians, and Classics; many modern valuable books of Divinity, History, Philosophy, and Mathematicks, but not many Authors who have wrote within these 30 Years."[40]

Thomas Clap's biographer observes, "If Clap was zealously intent on overhauling Yale's government, he was satisfied merely to tinker with the curriculum. He readjusted, rearranged, but did not disassemble and reconstruct. The scholarly lectures, declamations, and disputations—forms developed in the medieval universities and later instituted at Harvard— remained the central curricular exercises." In 1765, the president described the commencement program: after one student delivered a Latin salutation, "the others give a Specimen of their learning, by disputing Syllogistically [in Latin] on the Questions, printed in their Theses; which are then distributed. The like is done in the Afternoon by Candidates for the Degree of Master of Arts." Forensic disputation—actual debating in English—was replacing the medieval syllogistic method in other colleges, but it made slow inroads at Yale. Only on Tuesdays were the upper two classes permitted to vary their disputations with the more modern forensic method in the vernacular.[41]

Clap followed the practice of every colonial college except William and Mary in putting the president in charge of instructing the senior class in moral philosophy, but Clap approached the subject from the perspective of duties rather than rights. He had little patience with the idea of natural law: "I observe that whatever Fundamental Principles any Man may fix upon, let it be what it will, he calls it by the Name of Law of Nature." At Yale, moral philosophy was limited to Christian ethics, rooted in scripture. Ames would have approved.[42]

Aside from Wollaston's *Religion of Nature Delineated* and, at times, Jonathan Edwards's *Enquiry*, Clap's printed lectures were the only moral philosophy students got; aside from Cicero and other Roman writers who were assigned primarily for grammar instruction, Clap was also the students' only source for history or politics (unless, in their last two years, they ventured into the library on their own). In characteristic fashion, he explained his approach in terms of dealing with the surplus once the needs of the church had been met:

> Yet inasmuch as more have been educated, than are necessary for the immediate Service of the Churches, and are designed for various other public and important Stations in civil Life; the President therefore frequently makes public dissertations upon every Subject necessary to be understood, to qualify young Gentlemen for those Stations and Employment; such as the Nature of civil Government, the civil Constitution of *Great Britain*, the various Kinds of Courts and Offices superior and inferior, the several Kinds of Laws by which the Kingdom is governed . . . so that every one educated here might have, at least, a general and superficial Knowledge of every important Affair of Life.[43]

"General and superficial" it must have been. With little knowledge of natural sciences, Clap followed Samuel Johnson's advice on physics and astronomy (even having an orrery built for the students), but he had no comparable guide for political science, and he was apparently unfamiliar with the Renaissance and Enlightenment authors on the subject. He would not have read any of them as a student at Harvard in the 1720s, and he revealed no interest in them after his graduation. By his own account, the more recent writers, such as Hutcheson, Kames, Hume, Smith, and Reid, were not in the Yale library.

From 1714 until 1781, Yale followed Harvard in publishing broadsides of commencement theses. In 1746, Ezra Stiles syllogistically defended the proposition, "Jus regum non est jure divino haereditarium" (The hereditary right of kings is not of divine authority). The next year, JOHNSON argued against Mandevilles's thesis from *The Fable of the Bees*: "Are private vices public goods?" For Clap, the master's degree was an early target for tightening up, in this case, as in some others, much needed. Until 1740, a Yale graduate might simply show up at commencement (after three years had gone by) and request the degree; Clap required that a candidate give at least one month's notice and participate in the exercises. As with so many of his reforms, his purpose was to take control, not to add substance. Unlike Holyoke at Harvard, Clap never suggested any manual for preparation or expected that candidates would do any further study before delivering their address. He simply imposed minimal order on a process was too casual for him to tolerate.[44]

In 1740, Yale was about one-third the size of Harvard; Clap went to work to expand the school, and by 1753 Yale's graduates actually outnumbered Harvard's. Between 1753 and 1760 Yale granted 254 diplomas to Harvard's 205, a matter of some concern to the Massachusetts college. Until 1752, Yale occupied a single three-story wooden building, housing fifty students. Since there were 120 students by 1747, most were lodging in private homes in New Haven. When Connecticut Hall, Yale's oldest surviving building, opened in 1753, it provided an additional thirty-two bedrooms and sixty-four studies, but enrollment had kept growing so that even when the new building opened, "more than fifty were obliged to live out of the College."[45]

The day-to-day lives of Yale students in the late 1740s and 1750s revealed the divide between the Old Lights—generally from the more prosperous, sophisticated families—and the New Lights, who tended to come from humbler backgrounds. Social relations within the student body suffered. WILLIAM S. JOHNSON, in 1748, wrote to his friend and fellow alumnus in New York City, William Smith Jr.:

> College is Degenerated. None [of the students] but their own clan are exempted from their most Severe, not to say Inhumane Censure. If a man appears good humored and Gay, He is . . . vain & frothy without any serious sense of Religion. If he wears a clean shirt he is a fob or a beau. Is he complaisant to the Ladies Behold a man Devoted to Trifles that spends his days in Vanity & his nights in Debauchery nor remembers that for all these things he shall give an Account.[46]

Student diaries from the 1760s suggest that otherwise the daily routine was little changed from a generation earlier, but the lives of freshmen had become more rigorous. First-year students were required to stand in doorways and wait for an upperclassman's permission to enter or exit, to stand at attention when a senior deigned to speak to them, and to remove their hats before superiors (essentially, anyone but other freshmen). With the president's approval—it contributed to the atmosphere of hierarchical order—freshmen now served seniors by hauling wood and drawing water, making the morning fires, blacking boots, and running errands. In 1765, one first-year student commented sourly, "Freshmen have attained almost to the happiness of Negroes," who were still enslaved in Connecticut.[47]

Ironically, Clap's fixation on order gradually brought the college to the brink of anarchy. The College Law of 1745, approved by the Corporation but composed by the president, specified a long list of punishments for such offenses as heresy, "profane use of names," fighting, quarreling, stealing, card playing, singing, loud talking during study periods, wearing women's clothing, and—an increasing problem—"disobedience or contumacious or refractory carriage towards superiors." Clap spent more and more time on petty violations of student discipline, and students took up the challenge to find more creative ways to subvert his efforts. The climate of disrespect demoralized the tutors. Of the ten tutors appointed in Clap's last six years, half stayed only one year, and two quit during the term, something that had never happened before. By 1762 enrollment was declining; it fell by 25 percent from 1763 to 1765 as an increase in the number of students expelled or withdrawing voluntarily was coupled with a decrease in applications.[48]

One who left was OLIVER ELLSWORTH. At the time he enrolled in 1762, a petition had already been received by the assembly calling for an investigation into the disorders at Yale: "There has been a tumult, the Desk pulled down, the Bell case broken, and the bell ringing in the night." (ELLSWORTH was later one of those who, in midwinter, inverted the bell and filled it with water, freezing the clapper in place.) Like Captain Queeg in *The Caine Mutiny*, Clap developed an obsession with finding out which students had been tampering with the college bell. Having discovered his sore spot, the students targeted it mercilessly. More alarming was the complaint of "Mr. Boardman the tutor beaten with clubs."[49]

Yale records list a series of infractions by ELLSWORTH in 1763, including the puzzling charge of gathering to "scrape and clean the college yard" in the middle of the night, along with "having a treat or entertainment last winter," and joining others after prayers "who put on their hats and run and hallooed in the College Yard in contempt of the Law of the College." For all of these offenses together he was fined one shilling. The next year he was fined four shillings for taking part in "a general treat or compotation of wine both common and spiced in and by the sophomore class." At last, on July 27, 1764, President Clap entered in his journal this note: "OLIVER ELLS-WORTH and Waightstill Avery, at the desire of their parents, were dismissed from being members of the college." Both boys enrolled the next month at Princeton. Avery would become a leading patriot in North Carolina, the state attorney general, and a founding trustee of Queen's College and the University of North Carolina. He remained a good friend of ELLSWORTH.[50]

The year 1762 also saw the matriculation of JARED INGERSOLL, despite a letter to his father from Dr. Benjamin Gale, a critic of Clap's decision to remove students from Noyes's church, calling Clap "an Assuming, Arbitrary, Designing Man; who under a cloak of Zeal for Orthodoxy, designed to govern both Church & State & Damn all who would not worship the beast." The elder Ingersoll's attentions were focused on an unsuccessful attempt to control the lucrative export of pine timber masts for the Royal Navy, an effort that took him to London in 1764. It was then that he received a commission under the new Stamp Act. Ingersoll believed the act was an unjust imposition, but FRANKLIN (in a rare political miscalculation) encouraged him to accept the appointment, convincing him that the tax would be more readily accepted if administered by trusted local officials rather than English placemen.[51]

The disaster of his father's experience as stamp commissioner must have haunted JARED INGERSOLL's senior year at Yale. In May 1765, Patrick Henry delivered his fiery speech against the Stamp Act, warning that Caesar had had his Brutus, Charles I his Cromwell, and George III should profit by their example. In August, Thomas Hutchinson's Boston townhouse was ransacked by a mob, and the Massachusetts stamp distributer Andrew Oliver was hanged in effigy. Soon effigies of Ingersoll were being strung up in several towns in Connecticut. In September, the New London *Gazette* pointed out that the initials of Jared Ingersoll were the same as those of Judas Iscariot. Later that month, a crowd of several hundred men surrounded him on the road to Hartford and forced a public resignation. In October, Ingersoll wrote to his old friend WILLIAM LIVINGSTON, "It is much if you don't by this time paint me out in imagination as a kind of fiend with a Cloven foot and fiery-forked tongue—a Court Parasite and a Lover of the Stamp Act. And yet the truth is that I love the Stamp Act about as little as you do and remonstrated to the late Members [of Parliament] against it, all in my power." When the act went into formal effect on November 1, the bells of New Haven (including Yale's, functional for the occasion) tolled as a mock funeral procession carried a copy of it in a coffin to the burial ground. There is no evidence at all that the sins of the father were visited upon the son in this case, but there were plenty of things to distract his fellow students now.[52]

By the end of 1765, Yale was falling apart. Stiles wrote in his diary that Clap's rule at Yale now verged on "absolute Despotism." As enrolment plummeted, Clap abandoned any effort to punish students for their constant provocations. In an appendix to his *Annals*, describing the current state of the college, he wrote that "inasmuch as the Incomes are now lessened by the Poverty of the Country, and the Diminution of the Number of Students, it is feared that either the Salaries, or the Number of the Officers must be diminished, either of which will be inconvenient." The officer who went turned out to be Clap himself. In March 1766, all but two or three of the students signed a petition demanding his removal, citing his arbitrary and unpredictable administration of the college. They delivered this to the Overseers and then smashed the doors and windows of Connecticut Hall, built a bonfire of floorboards ripped from the building, and threatened the tutors, who fled. No classes were held from March until May, and then only forty students appeared. At the request of the Yale Corporation, Thomas Clap resigned after twenty-six years as rector and president.[53]

It took Yale a decade to recover; the number of bachelor's degrees over the next ten years was well below the number in the previous eight. The rebuilding effort was led by Naphtali Daggett, the only faculty member remaining when Clap resigned. The Overseers kept him in the office of "president pro-tempore" for twelve years while they looked for someone with a suitable reputation to take the office permanently. Among his students was ABRAHAM BALDWIN, class of 1772.[54]

The Daggett administration began with the meeting at which the system of student ranking was abolished. BALDWIN, the blacksmith's son, would benefit in a number of ways from the change in regime; INGERSOLL, on the other hand, may have graduated in the nick of time. Clap had been uninterested in larger political questions; if an issue was not religious and posed no threat to his designs for the college, Clap was indifferent. Daggett, however, was politically conscious and had written letters under the popular Whig pseudonym of "Cato" attacking the elder Ingersoll and imputing sinister motives to the British policy. He opposed the Townshend Acts, and strenuously resisted efforts to appoint an American Anglican bishop. (The ghost of Lewis Morris II must have felt vindicated in keeping young GOUVERNEUR from Yale.)[55]

President pro tempore Daggett offered a more inspirational role model for a young patriot, but he made little change in the curriculum. In BALDWIN's senior year, the moral philosophy texts were still Wollaston and Clap's *Ethics*. Students now read Locke, but only the *Essay Concerning Human Understanding*, which reached Yale students years after it appeared at Harvard and William and Mary. BALDWIN would never be known as an incisive debater, but the future member of the Georgia legislature and US Senate must have benefited from the progressive shift in emphasis in Yale's disputations: Latin syllogistics were now limited to the first Monday of the month, while forensic disputations in English were held on the other Mondays and every Thursday. Two recent graduates, John Trumbull and Timothy Dwight, were hired as tutors. Trumbull, who had graduated the year after Clap's exit, expressed his frustration with Yale's academic standards in a mock-epic poem, *The Progress of Dulness, or the Rare Adventures of Tom Brainless*, published during Baldwin's senior year. He complained that Tom Brainless, the typical Yale student, might

> Read ancient authors o'er in vain
> Nor taste one beauty they contain.
> Four years at college doz'd away
> In sleep, and slothfulness and play.[56]

Dwight and Trumbull urged the study of history and belles lettres, but the Corporation did not act on their curricular suggestions until 1776, maybe not entirely too late for BALDWIN, who was himself a tutor by then. Alone among Yale's future Framers, he went back to teach. He stayed a year into Ezra Stiles's administration before joining the army as a chaplain, making such a strong impression that Stiles offered him the chair of divinity in 1781. BALDWIN turned it down, another rising star who left the ministry in order to study law. Stiles remained a friend and correspondent after BALDWIN moved to Georgia, and between 1785 and 1790 BALDWIN often visited him while serving in Congress in New York.

Ezra Stiles's *Literary Diary* is the main source of information about Yale's curriculum at the time he succeeded Daggett in 1778 and began to update the reading list. The changes he records are reminders that Yale remained well behind such newer colleges as Philadelphia and Princeton—or even William and Mary—in the political aspect of its moral philosophy instruction. On June 24, 1779, Stiles reports, "I put the Senior class into President Clap's Ethics or Moral Philosophy . . . thro' the Confusion of the Times the Seniors have received no Ethics for several years." On November 9, 1779: "Books recited by the several classes at my Accession to the Presidency . . . Locke Human Understanding, Wollaston's Rel. Nat. delineated & for Saturdays Wollebius, Ames Medulla, Graec. Test. [New Testament in Greek] (or Edwards on the Will [Jonathan Edwards, *Freedom of the Will*], sometime discontinued). Preside. Claps Ethics." On March 12, 1789: "This day I introduced for the first time Montesquieux Spirit of the Laws as a Classical Book into Yale College. The Senior Class began to recite the first vol. this day. It was never used here before. But it has been recited in Jersey College [Princeton] ph. 3 or 4 years." On March 6, 1793: "The Senior Class having finished Locke [*Human Understanding*] begin to recite Vattel's Law of Nature & Nations. This is the first time it was ever recited at [Yale] College."[57]

As it turned out, "the foundations of what little knowledge I have" that WIL-LIAM LIVINGSTON credited to Chauncey Whittelsey's tutelage supported a more extensive "superstructure" than LIVINGSTON modestly admitted. WIL-LIAM SAMUEL JOHNSON had the advantage of his father's teaching, and JARED INGERSOLL came well prepared in the classics by the Hopkins Grammar School, but Yale added enough to their foundations that INGERSOLL cruised through the Inns of Court and JOHNSON was launched on a trajectory that took him to the presidency of Columbia. The "other" Dr. Johnson, the great English literary lion and lexicographer, wrote to him in 1773, "Of all those whom the various accidents of life have brought within my notice, there is scarce any man whose acquaintance I have more desired to cultivate than yours." Both INGERSOLL and JOHNSON were slow to shed their loyalism (or at best neutrality), and Yale had given them no background in natural rights philosophy that might have helped get them off the fence when the Revolution came. It is impossible to say whether ELLSWORTH would have been as tardy a revolutionary as his classmate INGERSOLL had he not transferred to Princeton; his family background was utterly different, and ELLSWORTH was already challenging authority as a freshman, whereas INGERSOLL's record at Yale was one of spotless obedience. But the fact remains that one went quickly into the Patriot cause while the other moved to London in the year of the Boston Tea Party, remaining abroad until after the war's 1777 turning point at Saratoga. ELLSWORTH was already in the Continental Congress, voting to adopt the Articles of Confederation, while INGERSOLL was touring Europe on his father's advice to stay out of the country. (Ingersoll Sr. was under house arrest in Massachusetts.) WILLIAM SAMUEL JOHNSON's ingrained conservatism kept him even longer from joining the Revolution. Although he had been a delegate to the Stamp Act Congress (along with DICKINSON and RUTLEDGE) and a critic of the Townshend Acts, he refused election to the Continental Congress and resigned from the Connecticut Superior Court rather than swear allegiance to the state's revolutionary government. Stripped of his commission after twenty years in the Connecticut militia, he sat out the war at home, trying to be a neutral as long as he could.[58]

Neither Harvard nor Yale prepared its alumni especially well for the challenges of the Constitutional Convention. GERRY and KING depended on their experience in Congress to navigate the political give-and-take there. The Speaking Club may have given KING confidence as an orator; the outspoken GERRY never seems to have lacked confidence about anything. Both (along with STRONG) supported MADISON's Virginia Plan because Massachusetts was one of those large states that expected to benefit from it; MADISON's later series of complex balances and divisions of power, however, inspired by Scots such as Hutcheson and Ferguson, bothered them both—GERRY to the point that he at last refused to sign. Both were looking out not only for their state but for themselves; they were two of the four Framers that Forrest McDonald concludes were motivated by their own financial interests. Harvard gave them no early grounding in political philosophy beyond Cicero's conviction that republican government required virtuous citizens, and their years in Congress disillusioned them on that score; self-interest was what they had left. (Even KING's opposition to the notorious three-fifths compromise, continuing from 1787 through the Missouri Compromise, was based primarily on the disadvantage it created for northern states in the US House.) STRONG, without their background in Congress and lacking any new ideas to suggest, was practically silent in Philadelphia. On the other hand, the absence of a philosophical commitment to any particular program may have helped STRONG and GERRY align with the Great Compromise on representation. Overall, GERRY made a great deal of noise, KING tried to keep Massachusetts's vote in the large-state camp, but none of the three made any really original contribution.[59]

From its beginning through at least the 1770s, Yale was the most conservative of American colleges. Its alumni among the Framers were also noteworthy for their lack of education in modern political philosophy. In 1787, JOHNSON had just been named president of Columbia College, but his own training in moral philosophy (beyond the Romans) was limited to *The Religion of Nature Delineated*, the *Ethica* of his father's *Elementa Philosophica*, and Clap's "general and superficial" lectures. He made deals with the Deep South to trade protection of slavery for support of New England commerce and Connecticut's interest in western lands; the other Framers' respect put him on the Committee on Style, but he said little in debate and offered no new proposals. BALDWIN was noteworthy for his flexibility, hedging for just long enough on the small state/large state conflict to keep the Great Compromise alive. (His native Connecticut was relatively small; his adopted Georgia expected to become much larger.) In the 1760s, LIVINGSTON was an inspiration to a generation with his *American Whig* essays; during the summer of 1787 he was often away attending to duty as governor of New Jersey, but when present he never took the lead. And INGERSOLL, who assiduously avoided being noticed while at Yale, did not open his mouth at the Convention from mid-May to mid-September, despite never missing a day.

During the long administration of Thomas Clap, when all but one of Yale's Framer alumni were students, political and intellectual developments were ignored as other, newer colleges embraced them. Yale did endure rebellion in 1765, but it was a student revolt against a martinet, not a political protest against the Crown; New Haven's response to the Stamp Act was tame by New England standards. Clap's contemporary, Harvard's Edward Holyoke, was a much less stubborn man, but he declared that he had been "humbled and mortified" by the presidency of Harvard. His lesson was learned too late by President Clap, but it was not wasted on President Stiles, who took the office with some trepidation: "An hundred and fifty or 180 young Gentlemen Students, is a Bundle of Wild Fire not easily controlled & governed—and at best the Diadem of a President is a Crown of Thorns." So it had proved to be at Harvard and Yale. So, for very different reasons, it also proved to be at William and Mary.[60]

6

Their Majesties' College in Williamsburg
William and Mary

JOHN BLAIR JR., JAMES MCCLURG, JOHN FRANCIS MERCER,
WILLIAM PIERCE, EDMUND RANDOLPH

*From the best inquiries I could make while I was in and about
Williamsburg, I cannot think William and Mary a desirable place to send
Jack Custis to.*
GEORGE WASHINGTON *to Jonathan Boucher, January 17, 1773*

Before 1746, if American colonists north of the Delaware River
wanted a college education for their sons, they sent them to Harvard or Yale. Those who lived south of the Great Dismal Swamp
generally chose between Oxford and Cambridge. But for those
who lived along the Potomac and James Rivers, there was William
and Mary. Edward Kimber returned from a tour of the colonies
that year and printed an account of his travels in the *London Magazine.* Under the title of "Itinerant Observations in America," Kimber had this to say about Maryland and Virginia:

> They have some considerable Seminaries of Learning in the
> Two Colonies, but *Williamsburg* College in *Virginia* is the Resort of all the Children whose Parents can afford it; and there
> they live in an academical Manner; and, really, the Masters
> were Men of great Knowledge and Discretion at this Time;
> tho' it can't yet vie with those excellent Universities, for I
> must call them so, of the *Massachusetts;* for the youth of these
> more indulgent Settlements partake pretty much of the *Petit
> Maitre* Kind, and are pamper'd much more in Softness and
> Ease than their Neighbours more Northwards.[1]

The College of William and Mary aimed to prepare young men to enter the three professions (law, medicine, and ministry) and to become gentlemen— in Virginia effectively a fourth profession and by far the most important one. Dumas Malone, biographer of the college's most famous alumnus, acknowledges that in Thomas Jefferson's time, "the gentry had no strong desire to cultivate learning for its own sake, for their ideal was the well-rounded man. [William and Mary] was preeminently a school for statesmen and as such, on the North American continent, its product has never been excelled." Malone immediately qualifies that extravagant boast: "The extraordinary distinction of its alumni is chiefly owing to the fact that its students were by birth and station the potential leaders of the Colony, and that their college days were spent at the center of provincial life." Williamsburg was about to lose its centrality in Virginia; the capital would shortly move to Richmond, and William and Mary would soon be eclipsed by "Mr. Jefferson's University" at Charlottesville. If eighteenth-century Harvard and Yale did little to educate future statesmen in modern political philosophy, William and Mary did less—simply because so few of them stayed very long.[2]

At least four and maybe five of the Framers of the Constitution had been students at William and Mary, but the three most prominent Virginians at the 1787 Convention—WASHINGTON, MASON, and MADISON—had not. EDMUND RANDOLPH, the spokesman for MADISON's Virginia Plan (before the Constitution's innovations went too far for him) was a William and Mary man, but the college's other alumni at Philadelphia were among the most obscure of the Framers: JOHN FRANCIS MERCER (who came late and left early), JOHN BLAIR JR. (who never spoke in debates), JAMES MCCLURG (who said little and also left early), and perhaps WILLIAM PIERCE (so little known that there is still disagreement over the place and decade of his birth, let alone whether he actually attended William and Mary). The most respected William and Mary man at the convention was GEORGE WYTHE, a faculty member but not an alumnus, and he was called home after only a week.

Most William and Mary students came from Virginia and remained in Virginia. They dominated Virginia politics and society, but as Malone acknowledges, they would have done so had they never gone to college. Half of the students in the eighteenth century came from less than two dozen families that for generations never doubted their right to lead. But the Blair family had a special claim at William and Mary: without them there would have been no college. James Blair set the school in motion and governed it autocratically for half a century. A graduate of Aberdeen's Marischal College, Blair came to Virginia in 1685 and returned to London in 1691 to acquire a charter for a college to be named after the monarchs who granted it. When he died in 1743, childless, he left his library to the college and the rest of his estate to his favorite nephew, John Blair. That nephew's eleven-year-old son, JOHN BLAIR JR., was probably already enrolled in the William and Mary Grammar School.[3]

The Grammar School was the mainstay of William and Mary. Boys usually entered between ages ten and fourteen and read the standard texts—Cicero, Sallust, Ovid, and the Gospels in Greek. At the end of four years, a young scholar faced the entire faculty of the college (two masters and four professors) in an oral examination. Having passed, he entered the Philosophy School, putting on the cap and gown and assuming, for the first time, the title of Student.[4]

By 1736, William and Mary's enrollment had reached sixty (nearly all in the Grammar School); by 1753, about the time BLAIR completed his studies, students numbered more than one hundred, and President William Stith wrote to the Bishop of London, "The College is at present in a very peaceable & thriving Way, & and has now more Scholars in it, than it has ever had from its first Foundation, with a fair Prospect of its still farther increasing." Instead, just when things looked so promising, enrollment declined.[5]

As numbers at the college level had grown, so had criticism of the close association on one campus of College and Grammar School. "Academicus" wrote in the *Virginia Gazette*, "Little or no distinction is made between the boys of this school and the students of the college. Entitled to, or at least indulged with, nearly the same privileges, the former too soon forget that they are boys, and the latter too seldom perceive that they have a superior character to maintain." In truth, for the first half of the century the College of William and Mary was much more a secondary school than a college. Students stayed only a year or two beyond the Grammar School; families that wanted more then sent their sons on to English schools. Lewis Burwell and Landon Carter spent several years at William and Mary before going to England, yet in England both enrolled in secondary schools. Other Carter boys went from the College to Cambridge University.[6]

After thirty-six years, William and Mary took its first steps toward becoming something more. New 1727 school statutes, the work of James Blair, called for a master of the Grammar School and a master of the Indian School (which rarely saw students but was well endowed), and for a Philosophy School faculty of two—a professor of moral philosophy who taught rhetoric, logic, and ethics, and a professor of natural philosophy responsible for "physicks, metaphysicks, and mathematicks." There were also two professors for the Divinity School, charged with preparing young men for ordination as Anglican priests; they had few takers. Although requirements for a Bachelor of Arts were set out, the college would hold no graduation exercises until 1772, when the first two bachelor's degrees were conferred.[7]

The charter Blair had obtained followed a mix of English and Scottish precedents. It created a Scottish-style governing Board of Visitors drawn from the local community, but the faculty were nearly all English; from 1729 to 1757, eight of thirteen were Oxford men, seven of them connected in one way or another to Queen's College. Following Oxford precedent, the statutes required that professors and masters remain unmarried, and all were required to subscribe to the Thirty-Nine Articles of the Anglican Church. Conflict between Visitors and faculty was constant; it was aggravated by several masters' and professors' habit of drunken misbehavior, frequently in the company of their students from both Grammar School and Philosophy School. In the early 1750s, when JOHN BLAIR JR. was a student, John Camm was professor of divinity and William Preston and Richard Graham were professors of moral and natural philosophy; by the end of the decade, when MCCLURG was in attendance, Camm had been fired and was in London appealing his dismissal (successfully—he became president in 1771) and Preston and Graham had been sacked and replaced by Jacob Rowe and William Small. Soon Rowe was dismissed also. Among other ill effects, the constant turnover created burdens for those teachers who remained. Small, a Scot who had been teaching science and mathematics, found himself teaching everything else as well; for half of MCCLURG's and Jefferson's time at William and Mary, Small appears to have been the only regular teacher at the college. He was evidently up to the challenge—Jefferson admired him deeply—but he soon left for England and a medical career.[8]

By that time Thomas Dawson had replaced Stith in the presidency, but in 1761 the Visitors dismissed him and replaced him with William Yates, an alumnus of the Divinity School and a professor of divinity. The presidency was as much a revolving door as the professorships. Yates's health was failing, and the rapid turnover continued; when MCCLURG was "rusticated," or temporarily expelled, in 1763 for "injurious behavior . . . to a family in town" (particulars unknown), the Grammar School master James Horrocks was acting president, the school's fourth head in eight years.[9]

Whatever misbehavior led to that rustication was much more characteristic of midcentury college students in general than of MCCLURG's later life, which was impeccably respectable. Ever after known for seriousness and sobriety, he was the son of a Scottish ship's surgeon who had acquired land and social standing by marriage in Virginia. Despite his lack of political experience, MCCLURG, who earned an Edinburgh MD, would often be mentioned for important public office. MADISON suggested him to Congress as secretary for foreign affairs, and WASHINGTON apparently considered him later as a successor to Jefferson as secretary of state; his international reputation as a physician and his knowledge of several languages seem to have been his perceived qualifications. He was one of several Framers who left seemingly unified state delegations and went home early from Philadelphia, believing the work was largely done; he did not anticipate Virginia's close call when MASON and RANDOLPH made their late decision to oppose the Constitution's final draft.[10]

MCCLURG's education at William and Mary was hit or miss, as the professorial merry-go-round turned. The one constant was the Greek and Roman classics, taught by the divinity professors or the underemployed Indian School master, Emmanuel Jones. William and Mary throughout the century had difficulty maintaining any consistent approach to instruction. Students in the Philosophy School were taught, as at Oxford, whatever their individual teachers thought they should learn. The Statutes of 1727 were explicit in prescribing "progress in philosophy" beyond "the logic and physics of Aristotle, which had reigned so long alone in the schools." They left it to the "president and masters, by the advice of the chancellor, to teach what systems of logic, physics, ethics, and mathematics they think fit," but the statutes did direct the professor of natural philosophy to present modern systems of thought "such as those derived from Newton and Locke."[11]

With few students seeking theological instruction, one of the two divinity professors was employed as an instructor in "oriental languages"— Greek and Hebrew. Both were responsible for teaching the Latin authors; students typically read Virgil, Horace, Catullus, and Livy. Mathematics instruction was inconsistent and, as at the other colonial colleges, generally of less interest to students. In the 1770s, Edward Gwatkin offered the first six books of Euclid, logarithms, and algebra, but surveying, bookkeeping, and practical math were in greater demand. Gwatkin's third-year course went on to conic sections, solid geometry, and some astronomy and navigation, but very few students stayed a third year at William and Mary: MCCLURG maybe, BLAIR possibly, but certainly not RANDOLPH or MERCER.[12]

The modes of instruction specified in the Statutes were "Declamations and Themes on various Subjects" and the familiar syllogistic "Disputations." Jefferson recalled that William Small gave the first lectures ever delivered at the college in ethics, rhetoric, and belles lettres in 1761. After the college was reorganized in 1779, the Rev. James Madison (cousin of the Framer) and GEORGE WYTHE lectured on natural philosophy and law, respectively. MCCLURG, appointed professor of medicine but apparently without students, may have given guest lectures on chemistry in Madison's course.[13]

As new professors arrived through the Oxford pipeline, they continued to reinforce British academic customs. One practice copied from English universities and public schools was the division of students into those who paid their own fees and those who were supported by scholarships or, in the Oxford terminology, studentships. The latter group were required to live in the original college building, known as the Wren Building after its reputed architect, Christopher Wren. There college students roomed amid grammar school boys, supervised (very loosely) by the Grammar School master. There was a roll call at 9:00 P.M., after which both students and scholars were, in theory, locked in. Those who paid their own way could choose to board in town, and most did. A second building, called Brafferton, was erected in 1723 for the Indian School. Lacking many Indian students, it was used to house the college library. The president's home was added in 1733, and these three buildings constituted the college campus during the eighteenth century.[14]

Kimber, visiting in 1746, observed that "the young Fellows are not much burdened with Study, nor are their Manners vastly polite." Complaints about student manners were constant; when MCCLURG was punished for his "injurious bevahiour," he had plenty of company. Jefferson wrote to John Page, "Affairs at W. and M. are in the greatest confusion. Walker, M'CLURG and Wat Jones are expelled pro tempore, or, as Horrox softens it, rusticated for a month. Lewis Burwell, Warner Lewis, and one Thomson have fled to escape flagellation." There was, by common consent, too much drinking, too much gambling, and an excessive addiction to horse racing—the vices of the Virginia gentry. Landon Carter probably spoke for many in his diary: "My Grandson Landon after a 6 weeks' stay at home is set off again to the college. I believe he has only improved his talent for trifling and lounging there."[15]

When not drinking, gambling, trifling, or lounging, students produced several plays in the college hall. In 1736 and again in 1746 they performed Addison's *Cato*, ahead of the earliest productions in Philadelphia or Boston. They also organized secret societies, the oldest of which was the F.H.C. Founded in 1750, it succeeded in maintaining its secrecy at least so far as its name is concerned; we can only guess that the letters stood for Latin words, perhaps *Fraternitas, Humanitas, Cognitio* or just as likely *Felicitas, Hilaritas, Caritas*. Nonmembers called it the Flat Hat Club, after the mortarboard headgear that distinguished Philosophy School students from boys in the Grammar School. Jefferson recalled late in life, "When I was a student at

Wm. & Mary College of this state there existed a society called the F.H.C. Society, confined to a number of six students only, of which I was a member, but it had no useful object." Malone says that "it was primarily convivial and its certificates of membership were couched in humorous Latin phraseology. One of its expressed desires was that each member should be 'a great ornament and pillar of things general and particular.'" JAMES MC-CLURG was also a member.[16]

Joining the F.H.C. in the next decade was EDMUND RANDOLPH, who entered the Philosophy School in 1771. By that time the society had taken on slightly more serious purposes; it maintained a library, and the one book preserved from that collection is Hutcheson's *System of Moral Philosophy,* now in William and Mary's Swem Library. In addition, personal copies of Hutcheson (in the library's Tucker-Coleman Collections) were owned by F.H.C. members St. George Tucker and James Innes, the former a friend of WILLIAM PIERCE and the latter a friend of EDMUND RANDOLPH.[17]

RANDOLPH came to William and Mary as the college was beginning to recover from decades of conflict. Four of the six professors had been dismissed in 1756, and William and Mary's reputation had fallen so low at Oxford that replacements were hard to recruit. The college was fortunate in securing Aberdeen's Small; two new Oxonians were disasters. Garonwy Owen was an accomplished poet, but he and Jacob Rowe, both Anglican clergymen, soon fell into the habits of drunkenness and debauchery of their worst predecessors. Finally, after leading students in a fight with town boys, they too were fired. In 1764, Small returned to England, having contracted malaria in Williamsburg's notoriously unhealthy climate. It was 1770 before the faculty was again at full strength. RANDOLPH had probably been at the Grammar School for four years when the new royal governor, Lord Botetourt, arrived. Determined to raise the standards of the college, Botetourt offered gold medals for scholarship in classical and "physical or metaphysical" studies. RANDOLPH remembered that the governor "inspired the youth of William and Mary with ardor and emulation." Sadly, Botetourt too fell victim to the endemic fevers; he died in October 1770 and was buried in the college chapel. Four months earlier, "the Pres. and masters of William and Mary College resolved that . . . EDMUND RANDOLPH be removed [i.e., promoted] to the Philosophy School."[18]

Randolphs were everywhere in eighteenth-century Virginia; the family supplied three Virginia governors, and only Carters outnumber them among William and Mary alumni. It was a foregone conclusion that ED-MUND RANDOLPH would be sent to the William and Mary Grammar School, at about the age of twelve. A promising and popular youth, he was elected to one of the desirable studentships and joined the Flat Hat Club. In 1771 he was chosen to deliver the Founder's Day oration. The young orator, born and raised in Williamsburg, gave proper thanks to the college's royal benefactors and namesakes: "For as far as I can trace back the scenes of life, or recall the fleeting ideas of childhood"—he had turned eighteen five days earlier—"these walls, raised by the pious hands of William, have sheltered me in my infant studies." Those studies had only two or three more months in which to mature, for by November he had resigned his studentship and left the college to begin reading law. Like many other young Virginians, he had got what he needed from William and Mary after barely a year at the college level.[19]

Early records of William and Mary are fragmentary, thanks to three devastating fires. RANDOLPH's entry to the Philosophy School and his departure the following year are recorded in surviving faculty minutes, but evidence of JOHN BLAIR's student career is essentially conjectural, and the only formal record of MCCLURG's enrollment in the Philosophy School is his expulsion from it. If WILLIAM PIERCE, Framer from Georgia, was a student at William and Mary, it must have been after RANDOLPH and before MERCER. Evidence of his attendance is circumstantial, but it does exist. For years it was thought that he was born in Georgia in the first years of that colony's existence, but it now seems clear that PIERCE was born to Matthew and Elizabeth Pierce in York County, just outside Williamsburg, in 1753. From the evidence of his correspondence, he was classically educated; his witty, articulate letters are studded with allusions to Greek and Roman history. In 1774, he met the celebrated artist Charles Willson Peale in Williamsburg and followed him to Annapolis to study painting, an educational choice unique among the Framers. He remained there until both men joined the army in 1775.[20]

In character sketches he wrote of the Framers, PIERCE makes a point of his prior acquaintance with New Jersey's JONATHAN DAYTON, who "served with me as a Brother Aid to General Sullivan in his Western expedition of '79," although the two had maintained no contact. In contrast, he describes RANDOLPH only in respectful but distant terms as "Governor of Virginia—a young Gentleman in whom unite all the accomplishments of the scholar, and the Statesman." He then gets his age wrong by two years, underestimating it as thirty-two, even though he and RANDOLPH were born in the same year. He gives no indication that they were classmates during a time when there were no more than twenty or thirty students in William and Mary's Philosophy School.

If PIERCE did enroll at William and Mary, he probably entered just after RANDOLPH left, in 1772 or 1773. What makes those dates tempting is his close friendship with St. George Tucker. In 1772, Tucker came to William and Mary from Bermuda at the age of nineteen (he was a few months older than Pierce) and stayed only until 1774. He would later be a delegate to the Annapolis Convention, WYTHE's successor as professor of law at William and Mary, and the author of *A View of the Constitution of the United States*. Tucker joined the Virginia militia in 1776, and in 1781 he was back in Williamsburg recovering from a wound he received while serving on the staff of Gen. Nathaniel Greene. During that year and the next he received at least thirteen letters from PIERCE, who remained with Greene in the Carolinas.[21]

PIERCE had arrived to be Greene's aide-de-camp only two or three weeks before Tucker was wounded and sent home, but his letters to Tucker (and one surviving reply) reveal a close and easy relationship that suggests a much longer-standing friendship of the sort demonstrated in the letters between Princeton classmates JAMES MADISON and William Bradford, who maintained a postgraduate correspondence for years after returning to their respective homes in Virginia and Pennsylvania. PIERCE teases Tucker about his recent marriage and often asks to be remembered to their mutual friend Beverley Randolph, Tucker's William and Mary classmate. Moreover, PIERCE's letters are full of facetious classical references to plucking a "laurel from the branch of Daphne," to the muses "Thalia and Melpomene," and "scorching days of Phoebus" (i.e., hot summer weather); he poses the arch question of whether Tucker "bathe[s] in Hippocrene or Helicon" (the inspirational fountain of the Muses or the pool where Narcissus fell in love with his own reflection). In one letter PIERCE compares a recent maneuver by Greene to Scipio's drawing "the Carthaginian [Hannibal] out of Rome to the plains of Zama," described by Livy in book 30 of his *History of Rome*, a standard William and Mary text. He criticizes General Leslie's letter to General Greene because it "savors a good deal of the style of an academical exercise." All of these allusions suggest a classical education shared with Tucker. Their correspondence would continue for what remained of PIERCE's life (he died in 1789), including letters exchanged in the summer of 1787 during the Convention in Philadelphia.[22]

A similar friendship was formed under just such circumstances when JOHN FRANCIS MERCER and James Monroe arrived at William and Mary in 1774, both new to Williamsburg. MERCER and Monroe left the college within a year to join the Third Virginia Regiment, and both were sent to Congress in 1783. There, they were early advocates of a Federal convention to revise the Articles of Confederation, but both ultimately opposed ratification of the Constitution. Their friendship, formed at William and Mary, could have had something to do with that reversal. If wounded pride, indignation, and loyalty to one another led them to act rashly then, it would not have been the first time. They had left William and Mary together at the age of seventeen to answer the call to arms, and when Monroe became aide-de-camp to Gen. William Alexander (the self-styled Lord Stirling), MERCER became aide-de-camp to Gen. Charles Lee. After Lee was court-martialed for disobedience at the battle of Monmouth, MERCER angrily resigned. Monroe, in turn, warmly defended Lee, even after the general was removed from office by Congress. He wrote to Lee, "I am extremely anxious for your welfare & often sincerely lament that the temper of this continent should be such as to render it expedient for you to return to Berkeley [Lee's Virginia plantation]." A Monroe biographer asks, "Why was Monroe unconvinced as to Lee's turpitude?" His answer: "So close were the aides-de-camp that it would have been strange indeed if MERCER and Monroe had not talked themselves into accord on the subject in question." Loyalty and slighted honor took first priority. In 1787 they may have once again.[23]

Only months before the Constitutional Convention began, both still shared MADISON's belief that it was the nation's best hope. MERCER had written to MADISON late in 1784 in frustration that Congress was stymied by Articles that could not be amended if even a single state refused: "Commencement [of the new Congress] however has discovered so great a relaxation in the Confœderal springs that I doubt the machine will not be long kept in motion, unless great & effectual repairs are made. For my part I have no hopes but in a convocation of the States." In 1786 he repeated to MADISON that "the wiser part [of Congress] approve strongly of the Convention in May. My last hopes have taken refuge there. They will I beleive [sic] give almost unlimited powers." In early 1787, MERCER invited MADISON to stay with him in Annapolis on the way to Philadelphia, and later that spring he accepted Maryland's appointment.[24]

Monroe had also been a voice in Congress for strengthening the central government, but he was bitterly disappointed at being passed over when a replacement was needed for Patrick Henry in the Virginia delegation to the Convention. His resentment spilled out in a July 1787 letter to Jefferson in Paris: "The Governor [RANDOLPH] I have reason to believe is unfriendly to me and hath shown (if I am well informed) a disposition to thwart me; and MADISON, upon whose friendship I have calculated, whose views I have favored, and with whom I have had the most confidential correspondence since you left the continent, is in strict league with him and hath I have reason to believe concurred in arrangements unfavorable to me; a suspicion supported by some strong circumstances, that this is the case, hath given me uneasiness." Thereafter, Monroe would no longer favor MADISON's views; he opposed the Constitution at Virginia's ratifying convention and, a year later, ran as an Anti-Federalist against MADISON for election to the first US House of Representatives.[25]

Back in 1782, Monroe had written to MERCER, "I must here observe that political connections are but slender ties between men . . . [but] those who had been educated together have a different kind of tie and more natural claim to the good offices of each other and with but few here have you or myself connections of this kind." There are a number of instances in which college friendships may have helped advance the work of the Convention; MERCER's with Monroe may be an example of the opposite happening. Reprising his reaction to the "injustice" done to General Lee, the impulsive MERCER must have been outraged to learn of what Monroe clearly believed was a treacherous plot to "thwart" him. Loyalty to Monroe, the slighted friend of his youth, is the likeliest explanation why MERCER—who had been so enthusiastic only a few months earlier—suddenly had nothing good to say for the project.[26]

Sincere philosophical principles could have led to the abrupt reversal of MERCER's position and to Monroe's decision to oppose ratification, just as they could have been at the root of GEORGE MASON's turnaround, but resentment over injured honor cannot be overlooked in any of these cases. MASON felt that the Convention's disregard for his flurry of proposals in the final weeks was personally disrespectful, and he remained hostile to the Constitution even after the Bill of Rights incorporated most of his suggestions; he eventually reconciled with MADISON but not WASHINGTON, who thereafter referred to him as "my neighbour and quandom [sic] friend."[27]

MERCER came so late and stayed so briefly at the Convention that PIERCE never mentions him. MERCER's stay at William and Mary was also brief, and it came at a time when the college was once again descending into tumult. During the two years before his 1774 matriculation there had been increasing calls for curricular reform and elimination of the Grammar School. Nothing came of the proposals (yet), and the replacement once again of half the faculty did little to raise confidence in the college. Still, as political tensions with England grew, the alternatives of Oxford or Cambridge were becoming less attractive; besides, several Virginians educated in England had in the past returned "so inconceivably illiterate, and also corrupted and vicious," in the words of Mann Page, that Page had sworn he would never send his son there.[28]

Through 1775, revolutionary events moved rapidly at William and Mary. By summer, the only teachers who had not fled were President Camm, Indian School master Jones, and professor of divinity Dixon. The student body was melting away, and by 1777 (after the loyalist Camm had been fired) there was little left but the buildings and the scientific instruments Small had acquired.[29]

In 1779, a reorganized William and Mary reopened. Capt. WILLIAM PIERCE returned to Williamsburg on furlough from General Sullivan's command in New York, along with Capt. John Marshall of the Eleventh Virginia Regiment, the future chief justice of the United States. On May 18, 1780, Marshall was elected to William and Mary's recently organized social and debating club, Phi Beta Kappa, and two weeks later PIERCE was too. They were elected to this successor of the F.H.C. only after the society passed a resolution to allow "men of riper years" as members: "Resolved that in future admission to the society not be confined to collegians." PIERCE and Marshall did attend a number of meetings where various topics were debated; when PIERCE later left the Convention for a duel in New York, he was not deterred by memory of a 1780 Phi Beta Kappa debate on the impropriety of dueling.[30]

In 1781, the college buildings became barracks for French troops that were massing for the battle of Yorktown. On the eve of that climactic event, GEORGE WASHINGTON received a fretful letter from JOHN BLAIR JR., chairman of the Board of Visitors. BLAIR's worries about possible damage to buildings and equipment must have been a minor annoyance to WASHINGTON at that hour, but he took the time to write a coldly civil reply, pointing out that winning the war was his priority. Six years later, when the two were members of Virginia's delegation to the Convention in Philadelphia, BLAIR's letter had probably been forgiven, but, knowing WASHINGTON's sensitive feelings, not forgotten.[31]

WASHINGTON's disapproval of William and Mary was expressed as early as 1773, in a letter to his stepson's tutor, Jonathan Boucher: "From the best inquiries I could make while I was in and about Williamsburg, I cannot think William and Mary a desirable place to send Jack Custis to; the inattention of the masters, added to the number of Hollidays, is the subject of general complaint, and affords no pleasing prospect to a youth who has a good deal to attain, and but a short while to do it in." WASHINGTON liked what he had heard about John Witherspoon's Princeton, but Boucher, ordained in the Church of England, persuaded him to send the boy to King's College, an Anglican school. A generation later, having now become the legal guardian of Custis's son, WASHINGTON did send young "Wash" Custis to Princeton, but the indolent seventeen-year-old failed all his classes. WASHINGTON was again faced with the problem of finding a school for a reluctant scholar. Publicly, the general had only praise for the Virginia college. He had replied to an address from its new president, James Madison, in October 1781: "The Seat of Literature at Williamsburg, has ever in my View, been an Object of Veneration." Privately, he once again crossed William and Mary off the list, telling the boy's new stepfather, "The more I think of his entering William and Mary (unless he could be placed with the Bishop's family) the more doubtful I am of its utility, on many accounts; which had better be the subject of oral communication than by letter."[32]

Given WASHINGTON's long-standing doubts about William and Mary, it seems ironic that he agreed to become the college's chancellor; indeed, he held that office even while looking elsewhere for the younger Custis's education. He accepted the purely honorific position in 1788 only after assurances that it entailed no actual duties or even visits to Williamsburg. He remained chancellor until his death in 1799. WASHINGTON was the first American and the first layman to hold a post previously reserved for either the bishop of London or the archbishop of Canterbury. A sinecure that had been a mark of subordination to the Church of England had become an acknowledgment of Virginia's (and the nation's) greatest political figure.

Fewer details survive about curriculum at William and Mary than at any other colonial college. It was certainly heavy on the classics; Ovid, Virgil, and Livy were taught even when the Philosophy School was without a professor of moral philosophy, as happened too often. Although its most successful teacher before the Revolution was a Scotsman, the Scottish Enlightenment had no discernible influence on its formal curriculum. On the other hand, the college was quicker than Yale to replace Aristotle with Newton and Locke. Some advanced study in mathematics and physical science was offered, but not so much as at Harvard, and few if any students stayed long enough to avail themselves of it. It is true that too many of the professors were too often drunken, licentious, or simply lazy, but none was incompetent, and their own educations at Oxford, Cambridge, or Aberdeen were sound. That most of their students failed to achieve comparable learning is not entirely their teachers' fault, given the cultural challenges of Virginia society pointed out by the visiting Kimber in 1746.

The author Jack Morpurgo, who in 1936 became the first British subject to be educated at William and Mary since the Revolution, summarizes:

[William and Mary] gave those who passed through its classrooms the discipline of a conventional classical education and also the excitement of access to the thought of the Enlightenment and the Age of

Reason. It was in all this not unlike the great English public schools, for the best of them were at the very same time moving towards the same synthesis.[33]

The greatest of those public schools, Westminster, prepared South Carolina's CHARLES COTESWORTH PINCKNEY for the still greater of Oxford University, but neither introduced him to "the thought of the Enlightenment." We now follow him and Maryland's DANIEL CARROLL (College of St. Omer) across the Atlantic, to institutions that truly embodied the phrase "old school."

7

The Old World's Old Schools

England, France, and Ireland

DANIEL CARROLL, THOMAS FITZSIMONS, JAMES MCHENRY,
CHARLES COTESWORTH PINCKNEY, RICHARD DOBBS SPAIGHT

*When I visited my brother in his tent at night, I often found him reading
some Greek author, in the original—upon which I remarked to him, that the
sight of a Latin translation on the other side of the page, was always to me,
at least a very pleasant sight, and a very necessary companion.*

CHARLES COTESWORTH PINCKNEY, *quoted by Alexander Garden,* Eulogy on
Gen. Charles Cotesworth Pinckney, President-General of the Society of the
Cincinnati, *1825*

There was an alternative to Harvard, Yale, or the College of William and Mary: one of the universities of the Old World. For British colonists in America, with rare exceptions, that meant Oxford
or Cambridge. But Cambridge graduates had founded Harvard
to make English universities unnecessary; Harvard graduates
had founded Yale, and for most of the century the sons of New
England stayed home at one or the other—until first Princeton
and then King's, Dartmouth, and Rhode Island College (Brown)
siphoned off a few students. Although more than one hundred
Cambridge alumni settled in Massachusetts Bay Colony, not one
Massachusetts youth went to Cambridge for a bachelor's degree
during Harvard's first century.[1]

Only in the South was there a persistent interest in British
schools. Scotland was for medical students; all eighteen Virginians
who studied there between 1690 and 1780, including JAMES MCCLURG,
studied medicine at Edinburgh. During the same period, at least
thirteen Virginians went to Oxford. Even more went to England
from South Carolina. Looking back in 1819, CHARLES COTESWORTH

PINCKNEY remembered at least twenty Carolinian acquaintances who were in England during his school days. Some were at the Inns of Court or had come for other purposes, but PINCKNEY and his brother Thomas, along with family friends William and Charles Drayton, were pupils at Westminster School and then Oxford University in the 1760s.[2]

Ironically, Americans were most drawn to Oxford at the university's lowest point, what Lawrence Stone calls "the great depression" at Oxford. Undergraduate numbers were the lowest since the Middle Ages; in the decade of 1760–1769 a total of only 1,162 students matriculated at Oxford's twenty colleges, an average of fewer than six per college each year. Christ Church College, by far the most popular, enrolled 312 new students in that decade, fewer than Harvard but more than Yale. Rising costs and changing career prospects were eroding enrollment at both of England's ancient universities, but Oxford in particular had a reputation for indolent teachers, dissipated students, and generally low intellectual standards. Edward Gibbon, author of *The Decline and Fall of the Roman Empire*, wrote in 1791, "I spent fourteen months at Magdalen College; they proved the fourteen months the most idle and unprofitable of my whole life." At a time when the Universities of Leiden, Göttingen, Edinburgh, and Glasgow were centers of intellectual dynamism, Oxford appeared to be "sunk in port and prejudice." Henry Marchand, a College of Philadelphia graduate who had visited Edinburgh and Glasgow in 1771 with FRANKLIN, was appalled by the contrast at Oxford: "One would be led to think that very little Learning Religion or Morals were to be obtained at the University."[3]

Christ Church College, however, was the exception. Gibbon conceded that under "the late Deans" there (David Gregory and William Markham), "learning has been made a duty, a pleasure, and even a fashion, and several young gentlemen do honor to the college in which they have been educated." Beginning in the 1750s, Christ Church was once again "the nursery of the governing classes," and powerful landed families who had abandoned the university gradually returned to Oxford. For the Pinckney family, so much a part of the governing class of South Carolina, it was the obvious choice.[4]

Anyone at the Convention would have agreed that CHARLES COTESWORTH PINCKNEY had the best education England could offer. According to Pierce, "He has received the advantage of a liberal education, and possesses a very extensive degree of legal knowledge." PINCKNEY, known as C. C. to distinguish him among the half dozen Charles Pinckneys in Charleston, was taken to England as a child in April 1753. Mother, father, and sister went back to South Carolina five years later, intending to return soon. But Charles Pinckney Sr. contracted malaria and died shortly after landing in Charleston, and his two sons were left alone at school in England. JOHN RUTLEDGE, recently arrived at the Middle Temple, occasionally looked in on them. While still in London, their parents had taken charge of the children of William Drayton when Drayton preceded them back to South Carolina. The Pinckneys had put William Henry and Charles Drayton in Westminster School; in 1761, Eliza Pinckney sent CHARLES COTESWORTH to join them there.[5]

Westminster boys were known for their mastery of the classical languages, so much so that Christ Church tutors automatically assigned them more ambitious texts when they went up to Oxford. Up until the beginning of the twentieth century, Westminster masters and pupils were expected to speak only Latin during school hours. When Lord Chesterfield was preparing his son to enter Westminster, he advised him, "Pray mind your Greek particularly, for to know Greek very well is to be really learned. There is no great credit in knowing Latin, for everybody knows it, and it is only a shame not to know it." C. C. PINCKNEY spent just three years at Westminster and evidently always felt more comfortable with Latin than with Greek. His old friend Major Alexander Garden, eulogizing PINCKNEY in 1825 before the Society of the Cincinnati, recalled, "His admiration of the Greek and Latin authors was enthusiastic to the end of his life. Even in camp when a respite from military duty permitted, he was not unmindful of them.—His knowledge of Latin was perfect; but his brother, General THOMAS PINCKNEY, was his superior in Grecian literature."[6]

The classical learning of Westminster boys was attained through a demanding academic regimen. Young boys able to read and write English would enter the "Petty School" to begin several years' study of Latin with the *Grammar* of Richard Busby, the school's legendary seventeenth-century headmaster, followed by Phaedrus, Martial, and Ovid. In the Upper School boys recited Virgil, Homer, and Milton (the only modern author included) and performed a Greek play at Christmastime. "Latin and Greek and the Christian Religion are the only things avowedly taught," PINCKNEY recalled, "and it is difficult to go through the school without being a fair Latin and Greek Scholar and being able to assign a reason for the faith that is in you."[7]

After the intensity of Westminster, Oxford may have been a letdown. Some students there pursued serious academic programs, but for many Oxford was, like William and Mary, primarily a social experience. One Christ Church undergraduate remarked in 1733 that the opportunity "to make any acquaintance that might be useful in future life" was "the only reason I am sent to this College." In contrast to the colonial colleges, social class was highly visible in the different caps and gowns worn by students of different ranks and in the privileges they were accorded. Peers and sons of peers were enrolled as "noblemen," but their numbers were few even at Christ Church, and they were not always distinguished from the class of "gentlemen-commoners," sons of the privileged and wealthy. Both wore silk gowns and velvet caps, with gold tassels for the noblemen. The Drayton brothers had been entered at Balliol College as gentlemen-commoners, which entitled them to use the library and (far more important to most) to dine at High Table and access the buttery and the wine cellar. Unlike these Westminster schoolmates who advertised their status as great landowners, CHARLES COTESWORTH PINCKNEY matriculated as a commoner in 1764.[8]

Until very late in the century, noblemen and gentlemen-commoners were not expected to pursue degrees or even to do much in the way of regular reading. Most commoners, however, ostensibly pursued a degree, and about half obtained one. PINCKNEY was not among them. His mother had earlier written to him, "Though you are very young, you must know the welfare of a whole family depends in a good measure on the progress you make in moral Virtue, Religion, and learning." PINCKNEY could not help but feel that heavy burden, but he understood that progress in virtue, religion, and learning had little to do with earning a degree, which was essentially a professional certificate for clerics and academics.[9]

Americans who attended Oxford and Cambridge seldom earned degrees; careers as colonial leaders did not require them. PINCKNEY joined the Middle Temple only a week after matriculating at Oxford; in practice, neither of the two institutions demanded full-time residence. His caution money (a kind of security deposit) was returned by Christ Church College in November 1766, two years after his enrollment, indicating that the college no longer considered him a student. PINCKNEY was called to the bar in January 1769, and since that actually did require twelve terms (three years) of regular dining at the Inns of Court—in fact, the *only* requirement—he could not have spent much time at Oxford after Hilary Term began in January 1766.[10]

Dining was the focal point of the day at both Oxford and the Inns. The twenty-first century may find this emphasis odd, but dinners were much less about food than they were about ritual. Dinner in the Hall at Oxford, Cambridge, or the Inns was an opportunity to assemble all of the members of the institution and remind each one of his place there within the whole. Seating at dinner was a public display of hierarchy: tables were assigned according to status, and seating at dinner corresponded to the New England colleges' processions in which students marched according to a class rank that, until after midcentury, reflected their social status rather than their academic accomplishment. At some Oxford colleges, the High Table traditionally reserved for the faculty became one of the privileges of noblemen and gentlemen-commoners. This was not the custom at Christ Church, however; gentlemen-commoners were simply too numerous there, and a Pinckney could be satisfied to be one among equals, so long as all were gentlemen. That limited sense of republicanism would be reflected in debates at the Convention, where PINCKNEY envisioned a similar equality of the privileged in the US Senate, moving that senators serve without pay: "As this branch was meant to represent the wealth of the Country, it ought to be composed of persons of wealth; and if no allowance was to be made the wealthy alone would undertake the service."[11]

In the evening hours after dinner, students might gather in clubs whose meetings often extended into supper (a private meal). Oxford lagged behind the Scottish and colonial colleges in developing debating or speaking clubs, and when they did begin to appear the tutors and masters discouraged any attempts by students to organize to discuss political or religious questions; indeed, when George Canning, later prime minister, was an undergraduate at Christ Church in the 1780s, Dean Cyril Jackson forced him to disband a debating society he had organized because its speeches were "reckless." The Oxford Union did not come into being until 1823, and in PINCKNEY's day Oxford had nothing like Princeton's American Whig and Cliosophic Societies or even the Harvard Speaking Club.[12]

Academic life at Oxford revolved around the college tutors, selected by college deans and then paid directly by their pupils. In contrast to the American system, tutors at Oxford did not teach entire classes of students. Instead, upon matriculation, each student was assigned an individual tutor by the college dean; this was an important appointment, made after careful consideration of the pupil's background and intentions. The tutor's primary functions were to assign reading appropriate to the individual student, to explain the more difficult sections, and to examine the student on his reading. In 1737, the bishop of Oxford, Thomas Secker, skeptically described the peculiar form of examination used at Christ Church: "The young people in their first years make what are called Collections: i.e., observations on such parts of Homer, Virgil, Pearson upon the Creed etc., but these they transcribe from one another. They are also examined in these books by the Dean, Subdean, Censors, and two other persons, but perhaps 40 are examined in a morning." Although standards rose under Dean Gregory, the examinations remained perfunctory and offered little assurance that books had actually been read, since the same "collections" were often copied and submitted by one student after another. Still, the surviving Collection Books at least provide evidence of what Christ Church tutors were assigning.[13]

Henry Courtenay was PINCKNEY's tutor; with the exception of PINCKNEY, all his pupils were noblemen or gentlemen-commoners, who were not required to make collections, and in the Collection Books for 1764, 1765, and 1766 there is no sign of any collections by PINCKNEY. Theoretically, all undergraduate studies were based on the BA curriculum, but in practice noblemen and gentlemen-commoners (who rarely took degrees) had their reading specially selected for their interests. PINCKNEY matriculated as a commoner, but the facts that he enrolled simultaneously at the Middle Temple, was assigned a tutor who otherwise handled only the two higher ranks, and made no collections are all evidence that he neither intended nor was expected to earn a BA.[14]

Nevertheless, two years at Christ Church for PINCKNEY—who did not need his mother's reminder that he was there to learn—certainly meant reading beyond the Westminster curriculum. The Collection Books for the 1760s reveal a growing emphasis on the Greeks, encouraged by Dean Gregory: Sophocles, Euripides, Herodotus, Theocritus, Thucydides, Xenophon, and Aristotle (*Poetics* and *Rhetoric*, but not *Ethics* or *Politics*). Among the Romans (where PINCKNEY was more comfortable), Cicero was by far the most read, especially *De officiis*, which PINCKNEY knew well from Westminster. Sallust, Livy, Virgil, Horace, and Caesar show up regularly in collections. All of these would have been familiar to PINCKNEY in texts edited by Michael Maittaire, an undermaster at Westminster, who produced standard Oxford editions of no less than nineteen Latin authors. Euclid's first six books, Henry Aldrich's *Ars Logica* and John Wallis's *Institutio Logicae*, and John Pearson's *Exposition of the Creed* also appear in collections each year that Pinckney was there, along with Grotius's *Truth of the Christian Religion*, another work well known to Westminster students. For the scholar, Christ Church offered the most ambitious reading of any of Oxford's colleges; it was scholarship, and not the social cachet, that the poet and lexicographer Samuel Johnson had in mind when he told James Boswell in 1769, "If a man has a mind to prance, he must study at Christ Church and All Souls [Oxford's entirely postgraduate college]."[15]

Moral philosophy at Oxford, an essential subject for would-be statesmen, was just beginning to take on a more modern cast. From the late 1750s, Pufendorf's *De officio hominis et civis* and Burlemaqui's *Principles of Natural Law* were being assigned at Christ Church. John Locke, alumnus of Westminster and Christ Church, was the Whig philosopher par excellence; Christ Church, Oxford's Whig college, may have had both political and scholarly reasons for replacing Burgersdijk's *Institutiones Metaphysicae* with Locke's *Essay on Human Understanding* in 1744, but his *Two Treatises* on *Government* do not appear in collections. Christ Church, above all other Oxford colleges, saw its mission as preparing young men to play important roles in public life, the presumed future of any Pinckney in South Carolina. The classical curriculum of the college was designed with that objective. But there were also occasional innovations, even at Oxford. One of these was Blackstone's lecture series on English common law.[16]

Longacre and Herring in 1834 made the first published claim that PINCKNEY was a student of William Blackstone, the famous author of the *Commentaries on the Laws of England*. They went on to make the astonishing assertion that PINCKNEY "left behind him four large volumes of manuscript containing those celebrated lectures, which, with a diligence extraordinary in so young a man, he had written down at the time." Printers and engravers, not historians, they seem to have confused the four published volumes of Blackstone's *Commentaries* with four imagined volumes of PINCKNEY's notes on them; no such notebooks have ever been found, nor has any other evidence that PINCKNEY even attended the lectures. He certainly never made such a claim. Nevertheless, like their misidentification of Cyril Jackson as PINCKNEY's tutor, this assertion continues to be repeated.[17]

Still, Blackstone's lectures were celebrated, and PINCKNEY may have been aware that 1765–1766 would be their final season. A young man just beginning the study of law would probably attend at least some of them. Blackstone became familiar to most of the Framers through several American editions of his *Commentaries*; he was cited at the Convention more often than any other book except the Bible, but what he had to say was already familiar to the Framers and was invoked in debate as a reminder of the way things were, not for any controversial suggestions of how things should be. Apart from Blackstone, and allowing for the Anglican cast of the theology, the Westminster and Christ Church curricula were not unlike Boston Latin's and Harvard's. And in many ways—again excepting the divinity studies— they were not unlike the curriculum at the English Jesuit College at St. Omer in France, where DANIEL CARROLL had been a student twenty years earlier.[18]

PINCKNEY was one of the handful of Framers who spoke French; when he was an envoy to France in 1796 along with ELBRIDGE GERRY and John Marshall, he alone could converse with their hosts, perhaps thanks to a brief stay at the military school in Caen before returning to South Carolina. GOUVERNEUR MORRIS and HAMILTON spoke French from childhood, and FRANKLIN, INGERSOLL, and MCCLURG all improved their command of the language while living in Paris. One other Framer is known to have been completely fluent in French: DANIEL CARROLL, whose six years of formal education (conducted in Greek and Latin) all took place in French Flanders, at the Jesuit College of St. Omer's.

If PINCKNEY or MCCLURG wished to study for a while in France, that was one of many options; CARROLL went to school there because he had no other option. As a Roman Catholic in 1742, he was barred from the existing American colleges and from those in England, Scotland, and Ireland too. Catholics were forbidden to send their children away to study at "Popish" academies, but Maryland never enforced that law, and England was lax about it. As a result, English and American Catholics who wanted higher education traveled to Europe; most went to St. Omer's. The (illegal) Jesuit school at Bohemia Manor, Maryland, had not yet opened, so DANIEL CARROLL was probably taught at home by his mother, who had been educated by French nuns. When he turned twelve in the summer of 1742, he left to spend the next six years in French Flanders.[19]

St. Omer's, opened for British Catholics in the sixteenth century, was more than a grammar school but less than a university; students wanting a degree could spend one more year at a Catholic university such as Liège and obtain one, as DANIEL CARROLL's brother John did. (Archbishop John Carroll would found Georgetown University in 1789, the year that the Constitution went into effect.) The classical curriculum progressed annually from "Figures" to "Rudiments," "Grammar," "Syntax," "Poetry," and "Rhetoric," as its six levels or "schools" were named. During the eighteenth century, total enrollment was usually between 150 and 200 students, about the size of Harvard. Beginning with Greek and Latin grammar, St. Omer's students were soon expected to compose speeches in both languages, culminating at the end of the sixth year in a major public oration. In addition to such standard Latin authors as Cicero, the Greeks read were Homer, Apollonius, Hesiod, Aeschylus, Sophocles, Euripides, Aristophanes, Menander, Theocritus, Pindar, and Anacreon, an impressive list even by Westminster standards, and far beyond the ambition of American colleges. There were also lectures in English history and some instruction in science and mathematics.[20]

For a South Carolina aristocrat or wealthy Maryland Catholic, an Old World education was almost a matter of course. The Calverts and Carrolls went to St. Omer's because their colonial neighbors barred them from American schools; they immersed themselves in Greek and Latin and came back better educated than those neighbors, at a time when the phrase "classical education" was a redundancy. St. Omer's produced no Newtons, no Humes, no Hutchesons, but neither did eighteenth-century Harvard, Yale, or William and Mary. If St. Omer's was mainly a grammar school, so was

William and Mary; most St. Omer's students stayed all six years and left better educated than most Oxford or William and Mary men who had spent their year or two or so making social contacts and learning small Latin and less Greek. The advantage of a thorough classical education as training for the life of a public man was unquestioned; in 1810, the provost of Oriel College still recommended Thucydides and Xenophon as the best guides for contemporary statesmen. His reasons would have resonated at the Philadelphia Convention and with readers of the *Federalist*: "From no study can an Englishman acquire a better insight into the mechanisms and temper of civil government: from none can he draw more instructive lessons, both of the danger of turbulent factions, and of corrupt oligarchy: from none can he better learn how to play skillfully upon, and how to keep in order, that finely tuned instrument, a free people."[21]

Then there was Ireland, where 3 million subjects of the Crown, who suffered taxation without representation a century before the Stamp Act, certainly did not consider themselves a free people. In Edmund Burke's scathing sarcasm, the Penal Laws that England's civil government imposed on the Catholics of Ireland were "a machine of wise and elaborate contrivance, as well fitted for the oppression, impoverishment, and degradation of a people, and the debasement in them of human nature itself, as ever proceeded from the perverted ingenuity of man." Some freedoms, including the right to educate themselves, were denied to Ireland's Presbyterian Dissenters. Four of the Framers—PATERSON, FITZSIMONS, MCHENRY, and BUTLER—were born in Ireland, and half a dozen more were only a generation removed. Of those ten families, only the Butlers, Houstouns, and Spaights were fully enfranchised Anglicans.[22]

One effect of the Penal Laws was to drive much education underground. The 1665 Act of Uniformity required teachers to be licensed by the Church of Ireland, and in 1705 the Irish Parliament condemned "instruction and education of youth in principles contrary to the established church." A few Presbyterian schoolmasters, including James McAlpine in County Antrim and his student Francis Hutcheson in Dublin, were able to conduct schools that, though technically illegal, were tolerated. But in 1731 the Anglican bishop of Derry declared with evident satisfaction, "There are not any popish schools; sometimes a straggling schoolmaster sets up in some of ye mountainous parts of some parishes, but upon being threatened, as they constantly are, with a warrant or presentment by ye church warden, they generally think proper to withdraw."[23]

In response, the Catholic Irish created "hedge schools": strictly forbidden schools that might, as their popular name suggests, be conducted outdoors, screened from prying church wardens by hedgerows, or might be held inside private houses even within the Pale of Dublin, under the noses of the Protestant Ascendancy. Some hedge schools offered a surprising degree of classical education, but they were also intended to prepare boys for employment as clerks, storekeepers, or land stewards. For the Catholic THOMAS FITZSIMONS in the 1740s they were the only education available, and they evidently served him well. Although Catholics were excluded from the professions and the organized trade guilds, many sought careers as merchants, especially in the import and export of food and raw materials. Thus, there was a demand for instruction in mercantile arithmetic, bookkeeping, and the English and French languages. This preparation was good enough that FITZSIMONS could arrive in Philadelphia at the age of nineteen, join the firm of Robert Meade, marry the boss's daughter, and set up a successful partnership with his brother-in-law—all by the time he was twenty-two—ultimately becoming one of the richest men in Pennsylvania. Benjamin Rush, who knew him well, wrote in his commonplace book on the day FITZSIMONS died: "From an obscure mechanic he became not only one of the most enlightened and intelligent merchants in the United States, but a correct English scholar and a man of extensive reading on all subjects."[24]

JAMES MCHENRY was not Catholic, but as a Presbyterian he was also affected, to a lesser extent, by the Penal Laws. Family tradition has him educated in Dublin, at a private school operated by a Presbyterian master. Francis Hutcheson had kept his Presbyterian grammar school in Dublin, at the corner of Dominick and Dorset Streets, during a window of toleration when Lord Molesworth, Archbishop King, and others feared that too many dissenters were leaving Ireland. The influential American teacher Francis Alison may have been his student, but that school had closed in 1730 when Hutcheson left to teach at the University of Glasgow. In 1782, too late for MCHENRY, enforcement of the Penal Laws was again relaxed, and many more Presbyterian schools opened. Before 1730 and after 1780 there was no shortage of schools where a bright young Presbyterian could have received an excellent classical education; during the years when MCHENRY was actually in school, however, they were much harder to find. Still, some Irish schoolmaster inspired in JAMES MCHENRY an enthusiasm for poetry and a fondness for Milton in particular and taught him Latin well enough that he could join the senior class at the Newark Academy and have no trouble the following year with Benjamin Rush's library of medical texts. More than that is impossible to say.[25]

For the Anglican upper classes of the Protestant Ascendency, education was more a matter of acquiring the familiarity with classical literature that was expected of an eighteenth-century gentleman. That might be attained in a few years at home with a tutor, but the Anglo-Irish gentry were at least as likely as the English to send their sons to university. Almost nothing is really known about the education in Ireland of the Anglicans Pierce BUTLER and RICHARD DOBBS SPAIGHT, but it is within this context that any conjecture must be made.[26]

Sir Richard Butler, 5th Baronet of Cloughgrenan, had at least eight children to educate. As the third son, not destined to inherit, PIERCE BUTLER was in need of a career, and before he was eleven years old his father had purchased him a commission in the army. He remained at home for four more years, learning Latin and arithmetic, until his regiment was sent to Halifax, Nova Scotia, in 1758. (BUTLER later spoke of "the Military system in which I was tutored from the age of fifteen.") Terry Lipscomb, the editor of BUTLER's letters, speculates that "his political thought began to take a progressive turn during the long stretches of his youth that were spent at Canadian army posts, where except for hunting and fishing he would have found little to occupy his free time other than reading books, pamphlets, and newspapers." Lipscomb points out the "ancient and modern authors that seasoned [BUTLER's] speeches and letters," and the young officer had long winters in Halifax in which to read authors more modern than those any tutor would have assigned, before he was posted to Boston in 1769. There the idea of a standing army in peacetime was bitterly resented; when a threatening mob provoked soldiers of BUTLER's regiment to open fire, he may have been an eyewitness to the Boston Massacre. He would also have heard the name of John Adams, the lawyer who defended Capt. Thomas Preston and eight soldiers against murder charges.[27]

BUTLER and his regiment were soon removed from Boston to Newport, Rhode Island. In that already fashionable summer resort, he may have met Polly Middleton escaping the heat of South Carolina. They were married a year later. Polly was one of four grandchildren of Arthur Middleton, a family friend of the Pinckneys; the sole grandson, also named Arthur, would sign the Declaration of Independence, and of the three granddaughters, one would marry another signer of the Declaration (Edward Rutledge) and the other two would marry signers of the Constitution, C. C. PINCKNEY and PIERCE BUTLER. BUTLER sold his commission and threw in his lot with the Middletons, Rutledges, and Pinckneys. At the Convention he was more likely than anyone except WILSON and GOUVERNEUR MORRIS (who spoke far more often) to invoke "Catiline and Cromwell," the Duke of Marlborough, "the great Montesquieu," the "perfidious" Stadtholder of Holland, or the various subjects of Plutarch's *Lives*, and it was he who first reminded the delegates that Solon gave Athens "not the best Govt. he could devise; but the best they wd. receive." The Revolution put a price on his head, but when peace came he sent his son to school in England.

If PIERCE BUTLER believed that the best thing one could do for a boy was to send him to the Old Country for education, the guardian of RICHARD DOBBS SPAIGHT was of the same mind when SPAIGHT's parents died in North Carolina before he was seven, leaving him the only heir to the largest estate in Craven County. SPAIGHT's father had come from Ireland with his uncle, the royal governor, and Governor Dobbs, at seventy-five, was appointed guardian in 1764. Just two years earlier he had felt sufficiently vigorous to marry the fifteen-year-old Justina Davis, but in 1763 he had suffered a stroke from which he never fully recovered. Preparing to return to his family seat in County Antrim with Justina and young SPAIGHT, he suddenly fell ill and died. His teenaged widow, who remained in North Carolina and quickly remarried, wrote to tell his eldest son in Ireland that she had lost "one of the best and tenderest of husbands, and you a kind and most affectionate father." She signed it, "your affectionate mother," even though her stepson was more than twice her age. She did not mention SPAIGHT in the letter.[28]

For a second time the question arose: What to do with RICHARD DOBBS SPAIGHT? His mother's parents were no longer living; since the governor had planned on taking Richard home with him, Ireland had to be the answer. The little boy may have spent a year or two at the newly opened school in the colonial capital of New Bern; he needed something to do while arrangements were slowly made, and he was already seven years old, old enough to begin Latin. (SPAIGHT would later send his son to that school and serve on its board of trustees.) But by 1767 he found himself in Carrickfergus, Ireland, where he knew not a soul; there was simply nowhere else to go.[29]

Conway Richard Dobbs had remained at Castle Dobbs when his father left to become governor of Carolina, and from 1768 to 1790 he held his father's old seat in the Irish Parliament. He too had just remarried when SPAIGHT arrived from North Carolina. The son of his first marriage, another Richard, was only a little older than this new member of the household. The Dobbs and Spaight families were as full of Richards as the Masons were of Georges and the Pinckneys were of Charleses. Unlike JOHNSON or JENIFER, SPAIGHT had no brother with the same name, no flock of cousins like PINCKNEY to require distinguishing nomenclature. Why then did RICH- ARD DOBBS SPAIGHT consistently use an unnecessary middle name, even in signing the Constitution? The explanation must lie in his desire to be associated with the important family of his guardians. The vast Craven County estates he inherited far exceeded those of the Dobbses, but he was now far from North Carolina. Using his full name asserted the boy's right to be there; this American was not some foundling child.

The Craven County guardians book records no charges against the Spaight estate between 1766 and RICHARD's maturity in 1779; evidently Conway Dobbs simply absorbed all expenses. Perhaps that generosity was unsurprising; communication with North Carolina was slow and unpredictable and no doubt a tutor was already hired for his own son. What would not have been expected was that the Anglican SPAIGHT would be sent to the University of Glasgow rather than Oxford, Cambridge, or Trinity College, Dublin. Here again the Dobbs connection provides the explanation. Though they were not Presbyterians, the family had roots in Scotland, and Carrickfergus was actually closer to Glasgow than to Dublin. Conway Dobbs himself had matriculated at the University of Glasgow in 1747, seven years before Arthur Dobbs left for North Carolina. He shared his father's intellectual curiosity as well as his "Commonwealth Whig" political views; both were members of the Royal Dublin Society. Notably, he was listed as a subscriber for the three-volume *System of Moral Philosophy* of Francis Hutcheson when Hutcheson's son published it in 1755; other subscribers include Lord Kames, Adam Ferguson, and Adam Smith. Conway Dobbs had arrived at Glasgow a few months too late to study under Hutcheson in person, but his family, like Hutcheson, were part of what the historian Jane Ohlmeyer calls the "North Channel World" of "Protestant preachers, planters, and profiteers who shuttled back and forth between Antrim and Ayrshire, forming a homogeneous unit."[30]

Conway's son Richard Dobbs received a classical education befitting the son of a student of philosophy; in 1773 he matriculated as his father had at the University of Glasgow. SPAIGHT turned fifteen that year. Soon he apparently followed his cousin to Glasgow. His earliest biographer, the Rev. Thomas P. Irving, had known SPAIGHT for years when he said, in a funeral sermon, that SPAIGHT remained in Ireland "until he had finished the usual course of academic studies, when he was removed to the University of Glasgow. There he completed his education, and about the year 1778 returned home, to his native soil." His source could only have been SPAIGHT himself. The university has no record of SPAIGHT's enrollment, but it acknowledges that its records are incomplete; it has no record of WILSON's enrollment, either, but there is now clear evidence that he was a student in the preceding decade. Like many students at Glasgow, SPAIGHT may not have formally matriculated, choosing instead to attend those classes that interested him.[31]

SPAIGHT knew that his inheritance awaited in North Carolina. Growing up in northern Ireland had done nothing to diminish his sympathies with the revolutionaries; in 1775, the viceroy of Ireland wrote to the prime minister: "The Presbyterians in the North . . . in their hearts are Americans." In 1778, at the age of twenty, SPAIGHT found his way back to America, evading the Royal Navy's blockade. Once home, he immediately took a commission in the militia of his native state and launched the political career that would take him to the Constitutional Convention, the governor's mansion, and his death in a duel with a political rival in 1802. If there was a people anywhere quicker than southerners to take up arms in an affair of honor, it was the Irish.[32]

Rooted in his state and eager to return though he was, SPAIGHT had avoided the more parochial perspective that growing up in Craven County would have imposed. He watched the coming of the Revolution from an Irish and Scottish vantage point that regularly reminded him that he was himself an American. Likewise, C. C. PINCKNEY, at Oxford and the Middle Temple during the traumatic years between the Stamp Act and the Boston Massacre, also found his loyalty to his American origins reinforced. In the coming decade, INGERSOLL and HOUSTOUN would be sent to England and the Inns of Court in hopes that they might escape the Revolution, but their time abroad seems only to have confirmed their American identities, too; they returned committed to independence. DICKINSON, BLAIR, and RUTLEDGE were in London at the Inns during the 1750s, when war with France encouraged English patriotism; still, even though they gained respect for the English common law, they seem to have returned with increased appreciation of their New World homes. To their education in the law—and the diverse educations of the student lawyers who never left the colonies—we now turn.

8

The Inns of Court and Legal Apprenticeship

ABRAHAM BALDWIN, RICHARD BASSETT, GUNNING BEDFORD JR.,
JOHN BLAIR JR., DAVID BREARLEY, WILLIAM RICHARDSON DAVIE,
JONATHAN DAYTON, JOHN DICKINSON, OLIVER ELLSWORTH,
WILLIAM FEW, ALEXANDER HAMILTON, WILLIAM CHURCHILL
HOUSTON, WILLIAM HOUSTOUN, JARED INGERSOLL, WILLIAM
SAMUEL JOHNSON, RUFUS KING, JOHN LANSING, WILLIAM
LIVINGSTON, ALEXANDER MARTIN, LUTHER MARTIN, JOHN
FRANCIS MERCER, GOUVERNEUR MORRIS, WILLIAM PATERSON,
CHARLES PINCKNEY III, CHARLES COTESWORTH PINCKNEY,
EDMUND RANDOLPH, GEORGE READ, JOHN RUTLEDGE, ROGER
SHERMAN, CALEB STRONG, JAMES WILSON, GEORGE WYTHE,
ROBERT YATES

You should not confine yourself to the securing of men's properties, without regard for their liberties and lives. Don't confound these branches of study, for they are distinct.

JOHN RUTLEDGE, letter to Edward Rutledge, July 30, 1769

On March 22, 1775, Edmund Burke lectured Parliament on the several "capital sources" of the fierce love of liberty in the American colonies. High on his list was education—especially in the law. According to Burke, himself a member of the Middle Temple, "In no other country perhaps in the world is the law so general a study. The profession itself is numerous and powerful and in most provinces it takes the lead. The greater number of the deputies sent to the congress were lawyers. But all who read, and most do read, endeavor to obtain some smattering of that science."[1]

Of the fifty-six signers of the Declaration of Independence, twenty-four were lawyers. When the Federal Convention assembled in 1787, thirty-three out of fifty-five Framers had training in the law. As Burke noted, not all who studied law were practicing attorneys, but three-fifths of the authors of the Constitution were members of the bar in their home states. Most of the strongest advocates of change were lawyers, but so were five of the seven who refused to sign. In 1775, Burke had concluded his words about Americans and the law with an observation that applies to these Anti-Federalists: "In other countries, the people, more simple, and of a less mercurial cast, judge of an ill principle of government only by an actual grievance; here they anticipate the grievance by the badness of the principle. They augur misgovernment at a distance; and snuff the approach of tyranny in every tainted breeze."[2]

In England, then as now, lawyers were divided into two categories. The solicitors, who prepared legal documents and gave advice in litigation, were more numerous, but the barristers, who argued cases in court, enjoyed greater prestige. That distinction never took root in the American colonies, where a lawyer was simply a lawyer. Most colonial lawyers, like the British solicitors, trained by "reading law" with an established attorney, a hit-or-miss process that sometimes succeeded brilliantly, sometimes failed miserably, and usually fell somewhere in between. More than two dozen of the Framers went through such an apprenticeship. But the Inns of Court, where all English barristers prepared, dated to the Middle Ages, and in the Tudor era they had earned fame as England's "third university." By now, like the actual universities of Oxford and Cambridge, they were in decline. Nevertheless, as many as 150 American lawyers during the colonial period pursued their legal education at Gray's Inn, Lincoln's Inn, the Inner Temple, or the Middle Temple.

A lawyer who had prepared at one of the Inns could practice law in any of the colonies; in the years following 1750, even though the reputation of the Inns had dimmed in England, more and more ambitious young Americans were determined to join that legal elite. The Middle Temple was by far the most popular choice of Americans, and for Irishmen such as Burke, perhaps because it had become "a hotbed of whiggery." There were years in the 1750s when its American and Irish students together outnumbered its English students. Eight of the future Framers were admitted to membership in the Inns of Court, but not all actually went to England. Seven of the eight were members of the Middle Temple, and a visitor to the Middle Temple Library today will find a copy of the Constitution hanging there.[3]

The first of the Framers to be admitted to the Inns of Court never went. WILLIAM LIVINGSTON was accepted by the Middle Temple in 1742, a year after his graduation from Yale at the age of nineteen. His father, who was investing heavily in building an iron works, concluded that the added expense of several hundred pounds per year was an extravagance for a lawyer in New York, where even a college education was exceptional. The son's disappointment and pride in admission may both be judged by the fact that the bookplate he used for the rest of his life read, "WILLIAM LIVINGSTON of the Middle Temple."[4]

Philadelphia's leading lawyers for half a century were members of the Inns of Court. After he read law with one of them, John Moland of the Inner Temple, JOHN DICKINSON was eager to go to London. He itemized the benefits in a letter to his father:

> As to the particular advantages in my profession, they are so many & so great that it would be needless to recount them. If the adding practize to study will be likely to fix the law strongly and clearly in the memory, if the seeing and hearing the finest speakers at the bar can contribute anything to improving & polishing one's address, & if frequent conversation on your studies with numbers engag'd in the same will instruct one in controversy, then those advantages are to be acquired here.[5]

Philadelphia, the largest city in the colonies, attracted lawyers. The only New Englander among the Framers to study at the Inns, JARED INGERSOLL, had already relocated to Philadelphia and had begun a legal practice there after reading law with Joseph Reed, himself a Middle Templar. Ingersoll stayed at the Middle Temple only two years, but while there he managed to meet William Pitt the elder, Chief Justice Lord Mansfield, William Blackstone, and the famous tragedian David Garrick; his son recorded that these acquaintances "were objects of his constant attention, and of his correspondence, and ever after among the pleasures of his memory." Such opportunities were a large part of the appeal of the Inns of Court. After independence was declared, INGERSOLL left the Middle Temple to tour Europe, meeting his fellow Philadelphian BENJAMIN FRANKLIN in Paris. He finally came home in 1778, after Reed, then in Congress, had written to the elder Ingersoll, his "ancient and valued friend," urging the son's return.[6]

Far more Americans at the Inns—especially in the later years of the century—came from the South. EDMUND RANDOLPH had hoped to follow his father and his uncle Peyton Randolph to the Middle Temple; the Revolutionary War and estrangement from his loyalist father prevented his application. At least twenty-seven Virginians made the sea voyage and were actually in residence there between 1690 and 1780; more were admitted but may not have gone. One who did go was JOHN BLAIR JR., a student at the Middle Temple at the same time as JOHN DICKINSON, 1754 to 1757.[7]

Had Carolina's JOHN RUTLEDGE not delayed his departure until 1757, he would have been the third future Framer there during those same years; he was admitted on October 11, 1754, at the age of fifteen, but spent the next three years reading law with James Parsons, who may have then advanced him the money for his expenses in England—like many southern aristocrats, the Rutledges were chronically short of cash. South Carolina sent even more students to the Inns than Virginia, and in addition to three more Rutledges, five Pinckneys were admitted. CHARLES COTESWORTH PINCKNEY was one of them. A letter from his mother, written shortly before he was called to the bar and returned home in 1769, suggests that he was a serious student: "I am alarmed, my dear child, by an account of your being extremely thin, it is said owing to intense study. . . . Let me beg of you, my dear CHARLES, for my sake as well as your own, and that of your near connexions, to take care of yourself and consider how small will be the advantage of learning, where health is wanting."[8]

Even as Eliza Pinckney was writing, C. C. PINCKNEY was arranging for his nearest "connexion"—his brother Thomas—to be admitted to the Middle Temple on December 16, 1768. In the following months he was made a barrister, traveled the circuit of English courts, and visited the Continent. Given all that PINCKNEY was doing during his last year in England, it is no wonder he was looking thin; given the "galaxy of South Carolina planters who were living as absentees in London," it is no wonder that his mother heard about it. There was a Carolina Walk at the Royal Exchange and a Carolina Coffee House at 49 Birchin Lane, "a favored lodging . . . of the many standard-bearers of prominent South Carolina families entered in the nearby Inns of Court"—more than a dozen of them between PINCKNEY's admission and his departure.[9]

CHARLES PINCKNEY III, second cousin of C. C. , was admitted to the Middle Temple on January 4, 1773, six months ahead of JARED INGERSOLL; for reasons that are unknown he never went. His biographer Marty D. Matthews blames "the events transpiring between the colonies and England," but fifteen more South Carolinians were admitted to the Middle Temple after that date, and WILLIAM HOUSTOUN had no trouble sailing to England three years later. PINCKNEY was not yet sixteen and probably, like his cousin and RUTLEDGE, had enrolled several years ahead of his planned entrance. Maybe money was short—the reason LIVINGSTON had stayed home thirty-two years earlier.[10]

HOUSTOUN was admitted to the Inner Temple on January 7, 1776. PIERCE, in his character sketches of the Framers, says this of his fellow Georgian: "As to his legal or political knowledge, he has very little to boast of." HOUSTOUN is one of the least-known Framers; the youngest son of an Irish baronet on the colony's Governor's Council, he was only five years old when his father died. His brother Patrick succeeded to the baronetcy; a barrister from the Inner Temple, Patrick probably made the arrangements for William, who was the only one of the Framers to choose that Inn. Although a middle brother, John, was a Georgia patriot sent to the First Continental Congress, the new baronet was a loyalist, and HOUSTOUN apparently went to England in 1776. The South Carolinian John Laurens, already at the Middle Temple, wrote to his father on July 1, 1776, that "a vessel from Georgia a day or two ago brought 25 passengers from that province, one of whom Mr. HOUSTOUN . . . says that he saw you in good health at your Altamaha [Georgia] plantation." That ship had sailed just before the Royal Navy began its blockade of Savannah. Sometime after 1778, when the blockade was lifted, HOUSTOUN returned. He read law with his patriot brother, now the state's governor in exile, and was admitted to the bar on August 3, 1782, three weeks after the British army departed; two years later he was sent to Congress. James Monroe remarked in a letter to Jefferson that the new representative "has been to Europe to leave behind him what little wit he had." Since current usage did not usually speak of England as "Europe," it is probable that HOUSTOUN, like INGERSOLL, had visited the Continent on a wartime grand tour of sorts and may never have pursued legal studies at the Inner Temple. The Temple has no record of his ever lodging or dining there.[11]

Of the more than two dozen South Carolinians who went to the Inns in the eighteenth century, the Rutledge brothers were among the minority who actually made the law a career. But even for them the chief benefit of three years at the Middle Temple was not preparation for the daily occupation of a lawyer in Charleston. Entering London society, reading both ancient and modern texts, and attending the sessions of Parliament overshadowed any practical training in jurisprudence—and in fact the Inns actually offered surprisingly little of that. The Inns of Court had a noble reputation, but by the eighteenth century it was no longer deserved. Between 1660 and the accession of George III a century later, enrollment had decreased along with the commitment to education. The years between 1740 and 1765, when American interest was growing, saw the lowest enrollment between 1600 and 1800. But before England's Civil War, the Inns had offered not only professional education but a rich intellectual and cultural environment attracting such figures as Sir Thomas More and Sir Walter Raleigh. Shakespeare's *Comedy of Errors* premiered at Gray's Inn in 1594, and *Twelfth Night* was written for the Middle Temple's Christmas revels of 1602, with Queen Elizabeth in the audience. In 1616, in his dedication to *Every Man Out of His Humor*, Ben Jonson called the Inns "the noblest nurseries of humanity and liberty in the kingdom."

In their early years, the Inns had developed an elaborate hierarchical structure and their own arcane terminology. Prominent members of the bar might become "benchers" at the Inns, governing them like the fellows of a university college. Second-year students or "outer barristers" took part in mock trials called "moots" and "bolts" that were judged by the benchers. During court sessions, both apprentices and practicing lawyers lived in chambers at the Inns. When trials were held at Whitehall, all of the students would attend; lawyers appearing at court held practice trials at their Inns, with students helping to research precedents and copy out pleadings. Judges, litigators, and students would all join in discussions afterwards. When courts were not in session, the most senior students gave lectures on a wide variety of topics. To be one of these "readers" was a highly sought-after honor, a necessary step to becoming a bencher.[12]

With the English Civil War, the life of the Inns came to an abrupt halt. Readings were no longer given. Despite efforts made following the Restoration, the Inns never recovered. In 1714, the Middle Temple benchers deplored "the neglect in performing Mootes & Exercises in the Hall to the decay of learning within this society" but did nothing about it. Roger North, a Middle Templar of the time, regretted that educational "exercises" were "shrunk into mere form, and that preserved only for conformity to rules, that gentlemen by appearance in exercises, rather than any sort of performance, might be entitled to be called to the bar." The call to the bar—the ceremony that conferred the right to appear in an English court—was all that remained of the Inns' original function.[13]

In a spiraling cycle of cause and effect, the decline of the traditional oral teaching methods of readings and moots led to a greater demand for the printed word; increased availability of printed law books and court reports in turn made the oral methods less important. Students at the Inns who were seriously interested in a legal career were turning to the practice of "pupiling"—the same kind of apprenticeship that was the usual route in the colonies. In the absence of moots, the chief justice set aside a section of the court at Westminster for students, and he began explaining the reasoning behind his decisions and citing the cases that informed them. The Inns themselves acknowledged the changing times by gradually expanding access to their libraries. In 1750, the benchers agreed to keep the library open in the evening during legal terms, "as otherwise the Library is of no use or advantage to the Gentlemen of the society who attend Westminster Hall." For Americans with few law books and fewer court records available at home, the libraries were a large part of the Inns' appeal.[14]

The Inns remained the only entry to a career in the English courts, but as enrollment dropped off, they needed to attract more members. In 1762, noting the popularity of Blackstone's lectures on civil law at Oxford, they determined to attract "gentlemen from the Universities" to become barristers. Like retailers raising prices before announcing discounts, they first set a five-year term between admission and call to the bar and then reduced it to three years for those who had been to Oxford and Cambridge. This requirement came too late to affect the first three Framers, and it didn't matter that C. C. PINCKNEY had not earned a degree, but the five-year requirement may have influenced INGERSOLL and HOUSTOUN to skip the call to the bar.[15]

That was the extent of the Inns' reforms. Andrew Rutledge, uncle of the Framer, observed in 1750, "There is nothing like an Academical strictness in a Temple life." In the 1790s, Daniel O'Connell, preparing to enroll at Lincoln's Inn, wrote to his uncle, "There are no public lessons given in it. No professors of it. . . . The study depends on the will only of each individual who may reside and act where and how he pleases (provided he attends the terms) for the rest of the year." O'Connell was misinformed about attendance at the courts—there was no such actual requirement. The prospective lawyer had only to wait out the three or five years, dine in the hall six times each term, and pay the fees. He might never read a book or enter a courtroom.[16]

William Blackstone painted a picture of the student newly arrived at the Inns of Court:

> A raw and inexperienced youth, in the most dangerous season of life, is transplanted on a sudden into the middle of allurements to pleasure, without any restraint or check, but what his own prudence can suggest, with no public direction in what course to pursue Ms. inquiries, no private assistance to remove distresses and difficulties which will always embarrass a beginner. In this situation he is expected to sequester himself from the world, and by a tedious lonely process to extract a theory of the law from a mass of undigested learning; or else by assiduous attendance at the court to pick up theory and practice together, sufficient to qualify him for the ordinary run of business.[17]

RUTLEDGE was barely eighteen and DICKINSON twenty-one; those "raw and inexperienced young men" were well aware of the "allurements" of London—a large part of their reason for being there—but were determined both to get their hands on the "undigested mass" of books and to make their "assiduous attendance at the court." They came expecting no systematic training, but they came to read, to immerse themselves in the legal and political world of Westminster, and to absorb English culture in London as they could not in Philadelphia, Charleston, or Williamsburg. Their reading went well beyond law books. Nine years after his own call to the bar, JOHN RUTLEDGE sent his younger brother, Edward, to follow in his footsteps. He had, in the interval, acquired a copy of Lord Chesterfield's *Letters to His Son* and felt obliged to write a long Chesterfieldian letter of advice to Edward upon his setting out: "You must not neglect the classics; but rather go through them from beginning to end. I think you had better get a private tutor, who will point out their beauties to you. . . . Read Latin authors, and the best, frequently." In particular, he recommended Horace, Juvenal, and Virgil, along with "the purest English authors, to acquire an elegant style and expression." In addition to classical and modern literature, "the history of England should be read with great care and attention. . . . It will be necessary, for your own use, to make a compendium of this history, which no man can carry in his own head."[18]

RUTLEDGE gives the impression that he is instructing his younger brother to do what he wished he had done himself; there is no record of what Edward thought of his advice, or whether he followed it. John Adams met both Rutledges at the Continental Congress. According to Adams's diary, September 3, 1774, "Young Rutledge told me he studied three years at the Temple. He thinks this a great distinction. Says he took a volume of notes." Adams, always sensitive about the advantages he lacked, made a point of being unimpressed. About the elder RUTLEDGE he added, "His brother still maintains the air of reserve, design, and cunning." That would also characterize him at the Convention, eleven years later.[19]

DICKINSON needed no admonition to study. In the spring of 1754, a few months after arriving in London, his dedication shone through in a letter to his father:

I tread the walks frequented by the ancient sages of the law; perhaps I study in the chambers where a Coke or Plowden has meditated. I am struck with veneration when I read their works. I almost seem to converse with them. . . . Why do I loiter? I quicken at their glory, I turn from their sight, and fly to books, to retirement, to labor, and every moment is an age until I am immersed in study.[20]

Besides lawbooks, DICKINSON read Cicero and Sallust, Gordon's edition of Tacitus, and Trenchard and Gordon's *Cato's Letters*, which he would cite in his 1765 pamphlet, *The Late Regulations Respecting the British Colonies*. He also kept up with London and Pennsylvania newspapers. Later that summer he wrote to his mother, "I rise constantly at five, & read eight hours every day, which is as much as I can or ought to do, for greater application would not only hurt me but would be of no service, as it would fatigue me too much," and the following January he added, "I am glad you were able to form some idea of my situation, & to trace me to my elbow chair, enveloped in Littleton and Plowden."[21]

The dry tomes that DICKINSON found fatiguing drove many apprentice lawyers to distraction: Littleton's *Tenures* and Plowden's *Commentaries*, in which he was "enveloped," Coke's *Institutes* (including the notorious "Coke upon Littleton"), and all the Year Books that published decisions of the English courts. RUTLEDGE told his brother, "Coke's Institutes seem to be almost the foundation of our law" and recommended reading all of the statutes of England, along with "all the cases reported since the [Glorious] Revolution, when the Constitution seems to have been reestablished upon its true and proper principles." More suggestions followed. He finally acknowledged, "I believe you will think I have cut out work enough for you."[22]

DICKINSON did not spend eight hours reading every day—not when the courts were in session. "Here we are not always plodding over books," he told his father. "Westminster Hall is a school of law where we not only hear what we have read repeated, but disputed & sifted in the most curious & learned manner." Like DICKINSON, RUTLEDGE considered the courts essential education. He learned shorthand in order to take notes there and encouraged his brother to do the same: "Remember what I hinted to you of attending alternately in the different courts by agreement between you and some of your intimate fellow students, and then of comparing and exchanging notes every evening." Evidently Edward followed this part of his advice faithfully, producing the volume of notes that caused Adams to raise his eyebrows.[23]

The courts—and Parliament—had an added appeal for a young man whose future lay as much in politics as in the law: they were schools of oratory. DICKINSON was in awe of Lord Mansfield both as a speaker and as a jurist: "His language is not only easy and flowing to captivate the ear, but so refined as to delight the mind, and his arguments so nervous as to force the assent of the judgment." ("Nervous" in the 1700s meant "strong and energetic," not "anxious.") RUTLEDGE saw oratory as more than mere elocution: he told Edward, "I have not so high an opinion of logic as to think no man can speak well without being a good logician; yet I think it will be of great service." He advised his brother to study Thomas Sheridan's popular *Course of Lectures on Elocution,* but he reminded him, "Reading lectures upon oratory will never make you an orator. This must be obtained by hearing and observation of those who are allowed to be good speakers: not of every conceited chap who may pretend to be so."[24]

There were plenty of bad examples. DICKINSON thought Serjeant-at-Law David Poole was very knowledgeable but "the most wretched speaker." When Tench Francis, the Pennsylvania attorney general, was in London on behalf of the province's anti-Penn faction, DICKINSON sized him up: "Francis seems to me to be a man who has read too much. His notions are extremely confused, by perpetual altercation he has got a knack rather than a method of arguing, he has such an important way of hesitating & travelling round a thing that if he spoke less he would speak better, but if he spoke better he would not appear so wise to common people as he does." Ironically, PIERCE had a similar criticism of DICKINSON thirty years later: "I had often heard that he was a great Orator, but I found him an indifferent Speaker. With an affected air of wisdom he labors to produce a trifle."[25]

The neighborhood surrounding the Inns was not one of the best in London. Inmates in the Fleet prison solicited alms from passersby through the barred windows. In *A Tale of Two Cities,* Charles Dickens describes the severed heads of traitors, mounted on spikes and "exposed on Temple Bar with an insensate brutality and ferocity." Writing to his mother, the South Carolinian Peter Manigault tactfully concentrated on the cloistered aspect of the Inns themselves:

> I fancy you would be pleased to know what sort of place it is that I am to live in: the Temple is situate remote from noise, and all paved with flat stones, so that no carriage can come into it. . . . At the landing place of each pair of stairs, there are two doors, each of which lead into apartments, where people of the best fashion live. These apartments, or according to the common phrase "chambers," consist of different numbers of rooms, from six to two, according to the size of the building. Mine have three rooms, besides a large light passage and a small place for a servant to lie in.[26]

Young Americans were usually impressed; DICKINSON certainly found life agreeable:

> A laundress attends by seven in the morning, lights our fire, brings the bread, milk, and butter and puts on our teakettle. We wait on ourselves at breakfast, which is no manner of trouble, and after, she

returns, makes our beds, and sweeps the rooms. We then follow our studies till three or four o'clock, which in winter is just dark; then we go to a chop house and dine, after which we step into a coffee house, and in a little time return to our chambers for the evening.[27]

For Americans, London was itself an education. Samuel Dickinson had done just fine without ever leaving America and had sent his elder sons to London only to have them die of smallpox; still, JOHN enthused to him, "It would be impossible to enumerate all the benefits to be acquired in London, but it cannot be disputed that more is learned of mankind here in a month than can be learned in any other part of the world. . . . Here a man learns from the example of others what in another place nothing but his own sufferings and expense could teach him." DICKINSON was one step ahead of Blackstone's concern about "raw and inexperienced youth," assuring his father that "London takes off the rawness, the prejudices of youth and ignorance."[28]

In London it was possible to rub elbows with the famous. Remarkable men were just around every corner. Besides Boswell and Johnson, literary residents of the Inns at the time included Henry Fielding and Oliver Goldsmith. Among the legal lights currently living at the Middle Temple were Matthew Bacon, whose *Abridgment of the Law* was the most widely used lawbook in America, and William Blackstone, whose *Commentaries* soon supplanted it. Edward Rutledge dined in the Temple Hall with Blackstone during Michaelmas Term of 1769; whether they conversed is unknown. If they did, Rutledge doubtless took notes; his brother had only recently written to him, "I have often thought, if I were to begin the world again, I would do what I am sure one would often find of use: make a book, and in it write down the remarkable expressions and sayings of wise and great men, whenever I met with them . . . to embellish your arguments or writings."[29]

DICKINSON reassured his mother that his close companions were "two or three Americans, & as many Englishmen, all young fellows of good parts & remarkable industry, and as we are all engaged in the same studies, we find great benefit from an acquaintance." He was a serious student, but he enjoyed the world beyond his studies. He admired David Garrick but was otherwise lukewarm about the charms of dramatic entertainment: "You must not think that I have been a stranger to the play houses, but I have found nothing so striking as report feigns." RUTLEDGE seemed to agree with DICKINSON's judgment: "Garrick is inimitable; the other actors are not worth seeing after him in the same character." He also recommended the performances to be seen in Parliament, telling Edward to "attend the House of

Commons constantly, or at least whenever anything of consequence is to come on." DICKINSON, too, paid close attention to Parliament, but he found English politics even less to his taste than the theater. In April 1754 he describes a scene out of Hogarth:

> The Westminster elections are now polling. . . . It is astounding to think what impudence and villainy are practiced on this occasion. If a man cannot be brought to vote as he is desired, he is made dead drunk & kept in that state, never heard of by his family or friends till all is over & he can do no harm. The oath of their not being bribed is as strict & solemn as language can form it, but is so little regarded that few people can refrain from laughing while they take it.[30]

References to England's easily bribed voters often came up during the debates at the Convention in 1787; in August when MADISON and GORHAM argued about the particulars of corruption in English elections, DICKINSON advised restricting the franchise to landowners as "a necessary defense agst. the dangerous influence of those multitudes without property & without principle." Britain's unelected upper house was also a recurring topic, in the context of the Senate. In June, DICKINSON announced that "he wished the Senate to consist of the most distinguished characters, distinguished for their rank in life and their weight of property, and bearing as strong a likeness to the British house of Lords as possible." He must have forgotten his first impression of that body, back in 1754: "This noble assembly has not the awfulness I expected. They meet in a room much inferior to that appointed for the representatives of Pennsylvania. . . . The nobility in general are the most ordinary men I have ever faced, and if there is any judging by the heaviness & foppery of their looks & behaviour, many of them are more indebted to fortune than their worth for a seat in that august place."[31]

For half a century young Americans flocked to the Inns of Court for many different reasons. We do not know whether HOUSTOUN ever appeared at the Inns, but we know a great deal of what DICKINSON did and thought while he was there, and we have a fair idea of what RUTLEDGE's experience was like. Still, it is hard to say how the Inns influenced their ideas. In the two years before and after DICKINSON's, BLAIR's, and RUTLEDGE's admission, the Middle Temple admitted fourteen students from New Jersey, Pennsylvania, Maryland, Virginia, and South Carolina. Only three stayed to be called to the bar. The rest spent a few terms—and their parents' money—and departed, leaving little trace in history. We can imagine the serious DICKINSON, BLAIR, and RUTLEDGE shaking their heads and getting back to work.

Of the Templars among the Framers, only two—BLAIR and C. C. PINCKNEY—went to the Inns without previous legal preparation. Four of the Framers—HAMILTON, ELLSWORTH, BALDWIN, and FEW—were entirely self-taught in law. DAVIE and ALEXANDER MARTIN had informal help from practicing attorneys. But two dozen, including most who went on to the Inns, learned their profession by apprenticeship, "reading law" with an already established lawyer. LIVINGSTON and WYTHE chafed under a servitude in which they performed menial tasks in a law office while receiving little instruction in return; others, including GOUVERNEUR MORRIS (under William Smith Jr.), MERCER (under Thomas Jefferson), and KING (under Theophilus Parsons) had mentors who were famous for prescribing broad programs of study in history and philosophy, in addition to the particulars of the law.[32]

The process of becoming a lawyer varied tremendously through the thirteen colonies and over the thirty-six years between LIVINGSTON's admission to the New York bar in 1748 and FEW's licensure by Georgia in 1784. Early on, some provinces had detailed, strict requirements: New York, at midcentury, briefly required a bachelor's degree, five years of clerking in an office, passage of an examination, and the recommendations of six attorneys. (When LIVINGSTON graduated from Yale, there were only six college-educated lawyers in New York—and three of them were his older brothers.) New Jersey also required a lengthy apprenticeship. At the other extreme, the colony of Connecticut in 1708 required only that a would-be lawyer register with the court and swear an oath. Lawyers were so uncommon and unpopular in Connecticut that a law passed in 1730 limited the number allowed to eleven; it was repealed the next year. Georgia required a separate act of the legislature to license each new attorney.[33]

In a legal apprenticeship the pupil was required to perform duties as set forth by the attorney, which might range from lighting the morning fire (the humble task performed by DICKINSON's laundress) to the drudgery of copying legal papers to occasionally assisting in court. In return, the mentor was expected to open his library and provide advice and guidance in a program of reading. Often the apprentice was directed to create a commonplace book, with an alphabetized abridgment of his reading. John Marshall's book survives through the letter L; the remainder may have been lost, or Marshall may simply have gotten bored with the task. The doodles in the margins support that suspicion.[34]

The quality of the education was entirely dependent on the capacity and interest of the master; Theophilus Parsons was so popular a teacher that he inspired a regulation in Massachusetts limiting the number of pupils a lawyer could take at one time. In 1788, Parsons directed John Quincy Adams to read William Robertson's *Charles V*, Vattel's *Laws of Nature and Nations*, Hume's *History of England*, and Gibbon's *Decline and Fall of the Roman Empire*, along with the standard legal authorities. RUFUS KING had spent two years with Parsons a decade earlier; presumably his assignments were similar. In marked contrast, WILLIAM LIVINGSTON was dismissed by his first mentor, James Alexander, after publicly criticizing Alexander's poor standard of teaching. He had complained in the *New York Post-Boy*:

If [lawyers] deserve the imputation of injustice and dishonesty, it is in no instance more visible and notorious, than in their conduct towards their apprentices. That a young fellow should be bound to an attorney for 4, 6, or 7 years, to serve him part of the time for the consideration that his master shall instruct him in the mystery of the law the remainder of the term; and that notwithstanding their solemn contract (which is binding on either side, is reciprocally obligatory) the attorney shall either employ him in writing the whole term of his apprenticeship, or, if he allows him a small portion of the time for reading, shall leave him to pore on a book without any instruction to smooth and facilitate the progress of his study, or the least examination of what proficiency he makes in that perplexed science; is an outrage upon common honesty, a conduct scandalous, horrid, base, and infamous to the last degree!

LIVINGSTON wondered that so many attorneys should "have no manner of concern for their clerk's future welfare," and called it "a monstrous absurdity to suppose, that the law is to be learnt by a perpetual copying of precedents."[35]

Absurdity it may have been, but it was the norm. After graduating from Princeton in 1763, PATERSON read law with Richard Stockton, who was fast becoming New Jersey's most prominent lawyer. (DAVID BREARLEY, who also read law in Princeton and was admitted to the bar the year before PATERSON, may have been his fellow apprentice; BREARLEY and Stockton were distant cousins by marriage, and both were members of the Masonic lodge that opened in Princeton in 1765.) Like so many apprentices, PATERSON often found clerking to be dreary work. He wrote regularly to his college friend John MacPherson, who was clerking for DICKINSON in Philadelphia. In 1767 he complained, "To be a complete lawyer is to be versed in the feudal system, and to say the truth, I am not fond of being entangled in the cobwebs of antiquity . . . in the clutches of that pedantic, rambling, helter-skelter Master Coke," whose *Institutes* were "breathed through" with "eternal egotism and dictatorial pomp." MacPherson in return complained that DICKINSON, now building his reputation as the "penman of the Revolution" through his *Farmer's Letters*, employed him in copying that work—"the whole once & some parts twice"—with no payment for his labor; DICKINSON apparently considered it part of an apprentice's duties.[36]

LIVINGSTON in New York and PATERSON in New Jersey had to endure lengthy apprenticeships because those colonies spelled out very particular requirements for would-be lawyers. But in the immediate aftermath of the Revolution, ALEXANDER HAMILTON took advantage of a loophole to qualify, on his own, in record time. At the close of the war, HAMILTON found himself at loose ends. He decided to take advantage of the New York bar's brief suspension of the apprenticeship requirement for veterans, an opening lasting only from January through April of 1782. As it turned out, he had five months to study for the examination (he was granted an extension) with no previous training in the law. As the deadline of his bar exam approached in 1782, he organized his thoughts by writing out an account of New York's legal practices and procedures. It reached 177 pages and became *Practical Proceedings of the Supreme Court of the State of New York*, the first published treatise on practices and procedures in the state. In July, after another extension, he was admitted as an attorney. HAMILTON was not the only Framer to take advantage of wartime exigencies to accelerate his preparation. JONATHAN DAYTON was admitted to the New Jersey bar after brief study, probably with Elias Boudinot, a close family friend. DAVID BREARLEY had been New Jersey's chief justice only two years when he hired a newly licensed lawyer, WILLIAM CHURCHILL HOUSTON, as clerk of the state Supreme Court. Between 1779 and 1782, HOUSTON was simultaneously Princeton's professor of mathematics and a member of Congress alongside the college president, John Witherspoon. Somehow, he also found time to prepare for a new career in the law. He was admitted to the bar in April 1781 and appointed by BREARLEY in September. Congress had also appointed him controller of the treasury in 1781, but enough was enough, and he declined. HOUSTON made a career of burning the candle at both ends, and his life was snuffed out early by tuberculosis, shortly after New Jersey ratified the Constitution. He was the first Framer to die.[37]

Any would-be lawyer faced a daunting reality: there were no American reprints of English law reports, no American editions of Coke's *Institutes* or any other of the standard legal writers, until Robert Bell's Philadelphia edition of Blackstone in 1771. Such law books and reports as existed were in the private libraries of wealthier lawyers and prominent clergymen. John Putnam, Adams's legal mentor, had a legal library of only fifteen volumes, which still made it one of the largest in Massachusetts in the 1750s. A decade later ELLSWORTH, in Windsor, Connecticut, had only Bacon's *Abridgment* and Jacob's *Law-Dictionary* from which to learn law on his own; then again, had he had access to the daunting Coke, he might have given up the attempt. Bacon and Jacob, along with Wood's *Institutes*, were standard texts in England and the colonies, but the most important text was Sir Edward Coke's *Institutes of the Laws of England*, through which DICKINSON had slogged at the Middle Temple. MADISON, who read nearly everything with interest, gave up any idea of becoming a lawyer because he found Coke's *Institutes* intolerably boring, and Joseph Story, who would serve on the Supreme Court with John Marshall, recorded his own frustration with Coke while reading law in 1798: "I took it up, and after trying it day after day with very little success I sat myself down and wept bitterly. My tears dropped upon the book, and stained its pages."[38]

But if the reader got past part 1 of Coke, part 2 laid out an important analysis of constitutionalism. Coke's views were reiterated during his years in the House of Commons in opposition to James I and the doctrine of absolute monarchy. His resistance to the single powerful leader and his glorification of Parliament as the "handmaid" of common law strengthened the belief of many lawyers among the Framers that all authority flowed from the legislature, not the executive. As a law student, Jefferson had complained, "I never was so tired of an old dull scoundrel in my life," but this "whig" element of Coke later made him forgive the dullness: "You will recollect that before the Revolution Coke Littleton was the universal elementary book of law students; and a sounder whig never wrote, nor of profounder learning in the orthodox doctrines of the British constitution, or in what were called English liberties."[39]

There were several reasons why Framers wanted to place ultimate power in the hands of the legislature, but the lawyers among them were certainly predisposed in that direction by their education—by the towering authority of Coke. But when BREARLEY pioneered the doctrine of judicial review in his *Holmes v. Walton* decision, he too was probably following Coke, who ruled in *Dr. Bonham's Case* that "in many cases, the common law will controul Acts of Parliament, and sometimes adjudge them to be utterly void: for when an Act of Parliament is against common right and reason, or repugnant, or impossible to be performed, the common law will controul it, and adjudge such Act to be void"—an early instance of checks and balances and the emerging philosophy of "common sense."[40]

Coke remained the premier authority, but some fortunate legal apprentices benefited from much broader reading. When WILLIAM S. JOHNSON returned home from college to study law on his own, he wrote to his college friend William Smith Jr., who sent him a copy of his father's manuscript notes for the instruction of young lawyers. Following the senior Smith's suggestion, JOHNSON bought a volume of Grotius and set to work filling in the gaps left by Yale's narrow curriculum. Smith Jr. built on his father's reading list and after 1760 he offered his own clerks (including GOUVERNEUR MORRIS) one of the most practical and yet wide-ranging of programs. Before any legal texts, Smith began with the moral philosophy of Grotius and Pufendorf. In addition, he followed his father's belief that among "the Sciences necessary for a lawyer" were not only "the Languages," but geometry, geography, history, logic, rhetoric, and what we would call political science, and these were also part of his curriculum. The Smiths' pupils, along with those of Theophilus Parsons, were among the best-educated lawyers in America, and four delegates to the 1787 Convention—LIVINGSTON, JOHNSON, GOUVERNEUR MORRIS, and KING—had followed their courses.[41]

Alone among the Framers, JAMES WILSON began his legal preparation in Scotland. It has only recently been discovered that he was apprenticed to a lawyer in the town of Cupar, where he had gone to grammar school. Cupar town records for 1762–1764 show him working as an apprentice on three separate cases, during the years between his studies at St. Andrews University and at the University of Glasgow. While WILSON was at Glasgow, John Millar was making that institution a magnet for legal studies. Millar had been a student of Adam Smith and was a friend of Lord Kames and a defender of the skeptic David Hume; it is unknown whether the Cupar apprentice attended his lectures, but it is hard to imagine his passing up the opportunity.[42]

After WILSON came to America, he began reading English common law, a very different thing from Scotland's legal code that was based on Roman civil law and gave greater independence to the judiciary. He clerked for DICKINSON at the same time as PATERSON's friend McPherson; DICKINSON's path and WILSON's would cross repeatedly over the next thirty years. WILSON's notebooks from this period show that he read deeply in other political philosophers in addition to those he might have heard while at Glasgow: Hume, Montesquieu, Sidney, Ferguson, and the founders of the natural law tradition. After only a year in DICKINSON's office he was ready for the bar in 1767. A leader at the Convention—only GOUVERNEUR MORRIS spoke more often—WILSON with his Scots law background was determined to keep the federal courts free of "whig" legislative control; the Constitution's Article III, as it stands in contrast to RANDOLPH's first draft, reflects his work on the Committee of Detail. He and MADISON, who was so unimpressed by Coke, gradually persuaded the reluctant Framers to move from the Confederation model, in which nearly all power was given to Congress, to a complex balance among the three branches of the new federal government.[43]

Each colony before independence—and each state afterwards—had its own rules for licensing lawyers, and the South tended to allow the legal profession more discretion in the admission of its members. Virginia statutes required that candidates be examined by practicing attorneys approved by the General Court; they could choose their own examiners. Patrick Henry, after quickly looking over a few law books, chose Robert Nicholas, John and Peyton Randolph, and GEORGE WYTHE. Each would quiz him separately, and the approval of two was sufficient. After a few basic questions, WYTHE refused to approve. Nicholas agreed only after Henry solemnly promised to study more law. That left the Randolph brothers, and John finally agreed, calling Henry a "young man of genius, very ignorant of law." Peyton was off the hook.[44]

Both of Maryland's lawyer-Framers had first joined the bar in Virginia. In the midst of the Revolution, MERCER had read law in Williamsburg under Jefferson, who like Parsons and the Smiths prescribed extensive reading in the liberal arts. Jefferson was not impressed with his pupil. In a letter to MADISON in 1784, he characterized his former student: "Vanity and ambition seem to be the ruling passion of this young man and as his objects are impure, so are his means. Intrigu[e] is a principal one on particular occasions or party attachment in the general. . . . His fondness for Machiavel is genuine & founded on a true harmony of principle." (Ironically, Jefferson himself probably assigned Machiavelli's *History of Florence* to his law clerk.)[45]

Jefferson also deprecated MERCER's "copious flow of words"; words flowed even more copiously from LUTHER MARTIN, the other lawyer representing Maryland. MARTIN was capable of many kinds of excess, but when his self-control was not lost to alcohol (a weakness he freely acknowledged), only Patrick Henry could mesmerize a jury more completely. While conducting a grammar school on Maryland's Eastern Shore, MARTIN had read law with Solomon Wright, the father of one of his students and a future judge on the Maryland Court of Appeals. He then moved down the peninsula to Virginia's Accomack County to take over the Onancock Grammar School from his Princeton friend David Ramsay, continuing to read law on his own. When he felt he was ready, he crossed the Chesapeake and presented himself to be examined by John Randolph and GEORGE WYTHE. WYTHE was evidently more impressed by MARTIN than he had been by Patrick Henry; both examiners recommended the applicant to the General Court.[46]

The three lawyers from Georgia exemplify the extremes of the Framers' differing educations. Whether he attended or not, HOUSTOUN was admitted to the Inner Temple; he did, at some point, read law in his brother's office. ABRAHAM BALDWIN, BA and MA from Yale, after turning down the Livingston Chair in Divinity and serving as an army chaplain, taught himself enough law to practice in Connecticut in 1783; the next year he was admitted to the bar in his new home of Augusta, Georgia, where he worked with Gov. Lyman Hall (another Connecticut-born Yale man) to create the University of Georgia, the nation's first public university. WILLIAM FEW was also new to the state and was the last of all the Framers to become a lawyer. When he took his first, preliminary steps in that direction, FEW was still living on the frontier of Orange County, North Carolina. His brief autobiography tells of being left there, not yet eighteen, to resolve the legal difficulties of his father who had hurriedly decamped to Georgia. But it was only after following his family to Georgia, serving in the militia under HOUSTOUN's brother, and spending a term Congress, that he decided to become a lawyer: "I had never spent one hour in the office of an attorney to prepare for the business, nor did I know anything about the practice, but I understood the general principles of law, and I had acquired a tolerable proficiency in public speaking." What followed is a reminder of the rapid entry into the legal profession made by HAMILTON in New York and DAYTON and HOUSTON in New Jersey during these tumultuous years: "I had no difficulty in getting admittance to the Bar, and at the same time commenced the study and practice of the law. I at first experienced some discouraging difficulties from the want of practical knowledge, but it rather stimulated me to greater exertions. I soon found myself progressing in the knowledge of my profession."[47]

WILLIAM FEW returned to a dysfunctional Congress in May 1786 after a two-year absence: "An evident change had taken place. The dignity and consequence of that assembly had greatly diminished. . . . After various efforts and resolves and recommendations to the States to vest Congress with more powers which were rejected by most of the States, it was resolved by

Congress to call a convention of delegates from all the States . . . to meet at Philadelphia on the second Monday of May, 1787."[48]

Over the weeks following that Monday, as the delegates at last assembled in Philadelphia, the majority were lawyers. Some made the most of their courtroom skills there. Despite his "tolerable proficiency in public speaking," FEW remained silent, listening to the eloquent speeches of GOUVERNEUR MORRIS, WILSON, and RANDOLPH, along with daylong orations by HAMILTON and LUTHER MARTIN and heated invective from BEDFORD, who excused his intemperate "warmth" as a habit of the legal profession.

Off the floor, the Convention acknowledged the negotiating skills of its lawyers. Committees that were far more important than their names suggest were chaired by experienced legal minds, often judges: WYTHE (Rules), RUTLEDGE (Detail), BREARLEY (Postponed Matters), and JOHNSON (Style). WYTHE's committee proposed the essential secrecy rule that made the Convention's free debate possible; RUTLEDGE's committee (which included RANDOLPH, ELLSWORTH, and WILSON) organized and revised the many resolutions that had been passed, creating the first draft constitution; BREARLEY's committee (including KING, SHERMAN, MORRIS, DICKINSON, and BALDWIN) sliced through the Gordian knot of choosing a president; and JOHNSON's Style Committee (with KING and MORRIS again, HAMILTON, and the nonlawyer MADISON) produced the final draft that would be ratified as the Constitution of the United States.[49]

The members of the august Inns of Court were not the leaders of the Federal Convention, although two of them—DICKINSON and RUTLEDGE—made important contributions, and C. C. PINCKNEY was always heard with respect. On the opposite end of the legal spectrum, three self-taught lawyers—HAMILTON, ELLSWORTH, and BALDWIN—played critical roles: HAMILTON in bringing about the Convention in the first place (and fighting for its ratification), ELLSWORTH and BALDWIN in achieving compromise between large and small states and between North and South. They had not had the broadening experience of traveling to London, but they had acquired a certain breadth of view by their own journeys, both geographical and intellectual: HAMILTON left the West Indies and the stigma of illegitimacy for New York City society and a rapid political ascent; ELLSWORTH left the narrow world of Thomas Clap's New Haven for Princeton's broader curriculum and broader cross section of America; and BALDWIN turned down Yale's chair of divinity to create a plan for public education in faraway Georgia. The adolescent clerk from St. Croix, the farm boy from Windsor, and the son of a Guilford blacksmith had evolved under the influence of WASHINGTON, Joseph Bellamy, and Ezra Stiles, eventually arriving at the same place: the law.

Part III

9

The New Old World
The Universities of Glasgow and Edinburgh

JAMES MCCLURG, JAMES MCHENRY, RICHARD DOBBS SPAIGHT,
HUGH WILLIAMSON, JAMES WILSON

Look around you at the nations that now exist. View, in historick retrospect,
the nations that have heretofore existed. The collected result will be, an
entire conviction of these all-interesting truths—where tyranny reigns, there
is the country of ignorance and vice—where good government prevails,
there is the country of science and virtue. Under a good government, look for
the accomplished man.

    JAMES WILSON, "Oration on July 4, 1788, to Celebrate the Adoption of
    the United States Constitution"

By 1770 as many as a third of all Americans descended from Scots,
mostly Ulster Scots who had emigrated in the previous fifty years
from the northern counties of Ireland. Many of the nation's founders were sons of Scots from one side or the other of the Northern
Channel or were themselves born in Scotland or Ireland. Four of
the Constitution's Framers studied at Scottish universities. One
was a native, two more were drawn to cross the Atlantic from
America for professional education, and the fourth had been born
in North Carolina and raised in northern Ireland. Edinburgh was
the Athens of the North, but Glasgow exerted an even greater influence on the Framers, both directly and indirectly. WILSON and
SPAIGHT were students at the University of Glasgow, where they
could have heard the lectures of Adam Smith, Thomas Reid, and
John Millar, leading lights of the Scottish Enlightenment; MCCLURG
and WILLIAMSON, in Edinburgh to study medicine, could not escape
the pervasive influences that led Declaration signer Benjamin Rush
to say, "[During] my residence in Edinburgh ... the rejection of the

political principles in which I had been educated, and the adoption of republican principles had acted like a ferment in my mind." Gibbon called his fourteen months at Oxford "idle and unprofitable time," but Rush's experience could not have been more different: "The two years I spent in Edinburgh I consider as the most important in their influence upon my character and conduct of any period in my life."[1]

"The education of our revolutionary generation," says Garry Wills, "can be symbolized by a fact: at the age of sixteen Jefferson *and* MADISON *and* HAMILTON were all being schooled by Scots who had come to America as adults." At the age of sixteen and for several years thereafter, two Framers of the Constitution, WILSON and SPAIGHT, were being schooled by Scots in Scotland. SPAIGHT was not a leader at the Convention, but his Irish and Scottish education had made him, in M. E. Bradford's judgment, "more of a nationalist than the rest of the delegation from his state" (no compliment from Bradford's perspective). A less Anti-Federalist historian, Iain McLean, argues that WILSON, together with GOUVERNEUR MORRIS and MADISON, "may fairly be regarded as the true Founding Fathers" because of their design and support for the Constitution's essential innovations; all three were powerfully influenced by Scottish teachers and Scottish political philosophers.[2]

When MADISON put together his list of books for Congress to acquire in 1783, he grouped them by categories. Under the heading of "Laws of Nations," he listed works by the Scots Hutcheson and Ferguson ahead of any English law books; under "History," he included Hume's *History of England* and under "Politics," Hume, Smith, Ferguson, Millar, James Burgh, and Sir James Steuart. Douglass Adair has demonstrated the importance of Hume for MADISON's *Federalist*, no. 10; McLean, more recently, makes the case that MADISON often followed the arguments of Adam Smith as well. He points out the close parallel between MADISON's radical endorsement of more numerous political factions in *Federalist*, no. 10, and Smith's encouragement of competing religious factions in *Wealth of Nations*, 5.1—and the even closer paraphrase of that same passage from Smith in MADISON's 1785 *Memorial and Remonstrance against Religious Assessments*. Although *Wealth of Nations*, which MADISON included by title in his 1783 list, was not published until 1776, Smith and Hume were both on President Witherspoon's list of recommended authors in MADISON's senior year. Samuel Fleischaker points out that Smith's famous "invisible hand" appears multiple times in his 1759 *Theory of Moral Sentiments*, which MADISON read as a student; he had also encountered a similar argument for balancing interests in Ferguson, whose 1767 *Essay on the History of Civil Society* was also on both his and Witherspoon's lists.[3]

GOUVERNEUR MORRIS was in childhood a student of the Glasgow graduate Francis Alison, at the Academy of Philadelphia. From there he went to
King's College, where the curriculum was influenced by the "College of
Mirania" plan of the Rev. William Smith, an Aberdeen graduate; at both
schools, Hutcheson was required reading, and MORRIS's commencement
address, "On Wit and Beauty," reveals his familiarity with Hutcheson's *On
the Original of Our Ideas of Beauty and Virtue.*[4]

But of those three "true Founding Fathers," it was WILSON, the strongest
nationalist among all the Framers, who personally followed Hutcheson and
Smith to the University of Glasgow. The great historian of the Constitutional Convention, Max Farrand, concludes that "second to MADISON and
almost on a par with him was JAMES WILSON. In some respects, he was MAD-
ISON's intellectual superior [although] in the immediate work before them
he was not as adaptable nor as practical." William Lee Miller calls WILSON
"the unsungest of the unsung heroes" of the nation's founding. WILSON,
MORRIS, and MADISON were at their most creative (and most disturbing to
conservative Framers) when they departed from the received doctrine of
the absolute separation of powers, suggesting instead a complex balance
of *shared* powers among the three branches of government—the *"nexus
imperii"* that was part of the system of Glasgow's Hutcheson, from whom
it was adopted by Princeton's Witherspoon, an Edinburgh graduate. First
at the Convention, later as a professor of law at the University of Pennsylvania, and after that on the Supreme Court, WILSON regularly cited, quoted,
or paraphrased his Scottish teachers.[5]

WILSON's education began at the Cupar Grammar School. John Knox's
First Book of Discipline had decreed a school in every parish of Scotland and
a grammar school in every considerable town, anticipating the laws of the
Massachusetts Bay Colony by nearly a century.

Cupar Grammar School was one of the best in southern Scotland.
Schoolmasters tended to stay there, several serving more than twenty
years. They were better educated, and they taught a greater variety of subjects than teachers in any other district in Fife. As at all grammar schools,
the emphasis was on the Latin language. But standard texts went further
than in New England, including not only Corderius, Cicero, Ovid, and Virgil, but also Horace, Sallust, Juvenal, and Terence, along with the sixteenth-
century humanists George Buchanan and Erasmus. Cicero, Horace, and
Sallust commended civic virtue, and Virgil praised patriotism. Erasmus was
the great proponent of religious toleration. From the age of seven, pupils
at the school were trained in grammar and composition at the same time
that they were encouraged to acquire the values of the classical authors.[6]

In Scotland, some boys moved on to the university at eleven or twelve; most (like SPAIGHT) waited until they were fifteen or sixteen. If WILSON had begun school at seven or eight, he would have been ready for the bursary trials at St. Andrews when he was fifteen, in 1757. There were nine bursarships: scholarships awarded on the basis of competition in Latin, Greek, and mathematics. According to a letter from Robert Annan to WILSON's son in 1805, WILSON was awarded one of them. (Annan was a cousin and boyhood companion who emigrated to America in 1761, five years ahead of WILSON.)[7]

WILSON's entry into the United Colleges of St. Andrews is recorded in the Senatus Minutes for 1757, and entries in the Professors and Students Receipt Books show that he was still there in 1758. The following years' books are missing, but he probably left the university in 1759, several months after seeing BENJAMIN FRANKLIN receive the honorary doctorate of civil laws. (At the Convention, the aged FRANKLIN, often too weak to stand, would depend on WILSON to read his speeches for him.) In two years at St. Andrews, WILSON studied Latin, Greek, mathematics, and logic, just as students did at Harvard or Yale. If he had stayed longer, he would have added moral philosophy in the third year, followed by natural philosophy in the fourth.[8]

Groundbreaking research by Martin Clagett has shed more light on WILSON's studies at both St. Andrews and Glasgow by examining the records of the library. As soon as WILSON matriculated, he began borrowing books, signing for them with the clear signature that appears on both the Declaration and the Constitution. Typical of the age, he first borrowed works by Joseph Addison: a collection of essays from *The Guardian* and a volume of plays that included the popular *Cato*. WILSON's often unreliable biographer Charles Page Smith maintains that he set out to study theology at the behest of his father, an evangelical Presbyterian preacher. However, Smith appears to have confused WILSON's father (actually a farmer) with a different William Wilson, a minister who died a year before JAMES was born. Bradford claims WILSON enrolled in 1762 at "St. Mary's, the theological college of the University to which he had transferred upon the completion of his B.A. the previous year," but there is no evidence of either that enrollment or the St. Andrews degree. As recently as 2016, Michael Klarman still says in *The Framers' Coup*, "WILSON was educated for the Presbyterian ministry at St. Andrews." He also imagines WILSON studying David Hume and Adam Smith at St. Andrews, which would have been outside the curriculum of his two years there and an unlikely part of any preparation for the Presbyterian clergy. It is true that JAMES WILSON did borrow the Anglican John Tillotson's *Sermons*, another unlikely choice for a would-be Presbyterian parson, but otherwise his library selections were all secular: Jonathan Swift, Hook's

Roman History, The Life of the Earl of Crawford, and the classics—Homer, Horace, Justin, and Suetonius.[9]

Rollin's popular *Ancient History* was the last book WILSON borrowed at St. Andrews. He returned volumes 6 and 7 on April 4, 1759, and the following month the seventeen-year-old was back at Cupar Grammar School, paying fees that recurred through February 1761. Annan, who was still living in Cupar, says WILSON was at this time "a tutor in a gentleman's family." The next record comes in April 1762, when his name and familiar signature appear in the Cupar Town Record Book as apprentice to a lawyer, with his participation in additional cases recorded in December 1762 and April 1764. It was probably a desire to study law that took him sixty miles down the road to the University of Glasgow.[10]

Edinburgh would certainly have been closer to home; the road from Cupar to Glasgow passes right through it. Edinburgh was already known for its medical school, but Adam Smith was lecturing on jurisprudence at Glasgow and John Millar became Regius Professor of Civil Law there in 1761; as a contemporary noted, Glasgow was becoming "as famous a school for Law as Edinburgh for Medicine." When the trustees of the College of Philadelphia awarded WILSON an honorary MA in 1766, they did so "in consideration of his merit and his having had a regular education in the Universities of Scotland." Their use of the plural reflects not only his two years at St. Andrews but the two years at Glasgow that escaped the attention of his biographers for so long.[11]

The city of Glasgow was booming in the 1760s; Edinburgh was Scotland's political center, but Glasgow was the hub of commerce and industry. Following the Act of Union in 1706, Glasgow had become the leading British tobacco port; by 1769 half the tobacco imported into Great Britain came through Glasgow, and with it came close familiarity with America. During the same period the university was growing in size and reputation. In 1700, there had been about 400 students; by 1800 there were twice that number. Between 1729 and 1780 the professors of moral philosophy were Francis Hutcheson, Adam Smith, and Thomas Reid, seminal figures in the political philosophy that shaped the Constitution. According to Caroline Robbins, "Few of the reformers and Pro-Americans of the Age of George III did not spend some of their formative years under teachers at Glasgow" or at a handful of Cambridge colleges and dissenting academies.[12]

Hutcheson had died in 1746, but Smith and Reid followed his ideas and his methods during WILSON's years at Glasgow, hewing closely the outline of his teaching even down to his preferred class hour of 7:00 a.m. Hutcheson was popular, probably the first teacher in Europe to lecture in the vernacular, and Smith adopted his technique; instead of simply reading from a text as other lecturers did, Hutcheson and Smith posed questions or propositions and then elicited student responses. Hutcheson built on Grotius's and Pufendorf's political Calvinism and the associated ideas of natural rights, government by contract and popular consent, and the right of resistance. His reputation and influence quickly spread to England and America; his *Introduction to Moral Philosophy* was the first text used in American or British colleges that dealt with man as a person, as a member of a family, and as a citizen, emphasizing both rights and obligations in contrast to the exclusively "duty" analysis of its predecessors. Of particular significance to the Framers, Hutcheson urged a balance or "equipoise" among the branches of government—a Newtonian force and counterforce, check and countercheck, contrasting with the more familiar static separation prescribed by Montesquieu in his *Spirit of the Laws*. Francis Alison and John Witherspoon followed him here as in other aspects of his teaching.[13]

Smith had been Hutcheson's student in the 1730s. He began his own lectures in moral philosophy in 1751; the organization of his course followed the same topics, in the same sequence that Hutcheson had set out. Smith's lectures dealing with ethics would be developed into *The Theory of Moral Sentiments* in 1759; those on politics and economics would be the basis for *The Wealth of Nations* in 1776. When Smith left Glasgow at the end of 1763, Thomas Reid came from Aberdeen to take the chair of moral philosophy. Reid was already becoming famous for his "common sense" philosophy; his *Inquiry into the Human Mind on the Principles of Common Sense* was in the press when he arrived in Glasgow. Like Hutcheson, he was impressed by the new empirical science, and he was eager to shore it up against not only Berkeleyan idealism but also the skepticism of Hume. According to Sophia Rosenfeld, "Starting from Newton's *regulae philosophandi* . . . Reid set out in his inquiry to offer a theory of immediate perception that, he hoped, would do away once and for all with the notion that we can have direct knowledge only of the contents of the mind (i.e., ideas), not external objects themselves."[14]

Reid described his new post at Glasgow in a letter to an Aberdeen friend. He explained that *cives* students at the university (those who had already paid tuition for two years) could take any courses at no charge: "Many attend the Moral Philosophy class four or five years, so that I have many Preachers & Students of Divinity and Law of considerable standing, before whom I stand in awe to speak without more preparation than I have leisure for: I have a great inclination to attend some of the Professors here; several of whom are very eminent in their way, but I cannot find leisure." In addition to his teaching, he had numerous college meetings to attend, plus the Glasgow Literary Society, which met weekly.[15]

Every American college had a single, inflexible curriculum for all students, although Philadelphia and King's would soon offer elective lectures on medicine; Oxford and Cambridge permitted a narrow range from which each tutor might select assignments for a given student, and both offered occasional lecture series. But Scottish students had a rich menu of choices; Regius Professor of Civil Law John Millar explained:

> While the principal schools and universities of England, from the remains of ancient prejudices, confined their attention, in a great measure, to the teaching of what are called the learned languages, those of Scotland extended their views in proportion to the changes which took place in the state of society, and comprehended, more or less, in their plan of instruction, the principles of the different sciences which came to be of use in the world.[16]

Significantly, that meant that Scottish universities included political science in their moral philosophy courses.

Besides classes, as Reid noted, there were the literary and debating clubs. A Glasgow student wrote to a former teacher, "There are a great many Literary Societies in Town: The Professors have a meeting of that kind every Friday night." The Glasgow Literary Society was begun by Smith in 1752; members included Hume and James Watt. In addition, a student literary and debating club was formed in 1761, the first in Great Britain; its political slant can be inferred from its name, "Oceana," taken from the fictional utopia in the Whig political theorist James Harrington's book of that title. Among the topics a student might hear debated in the 1760s were the Irish penal laws and "the temper of our Northern Colonies" regarding the Stamp Act, about which Reid wrote to Skene in December 1765.[17]

JAMES WILSON, while a law clerk, spent at least the fall and winter terms from 1763 to 1765 taking classes at Glasgow. Once again, the evidence of his enrollment is his signature on the library lending lists. Thus, we can know that in November 1763 WILSON borrowed volumes of Rapin's *History of England*, and in February 1764 he borrowed Rollin's *Belles Lettres* along with Middleton's *Life of Cicero*. After returning to Cupar and his apprenticeship during the long summer court session, he was back in Glasgow in the fall, signing out Stanley's *History of Philosophy*. (Conclusive evidence of SPAIGHT's presence at the University of Glasgow between 1774 and 1778 might have hidden in the same library lending books that revealed WILSON's attendance; unfortunately, the volumes for those years are missing.)[18]

But what else was WILSON doing in Glasgow besides reading? As a *cives* student, he may have been among the crowds that Reid reports auditing the moral philosophy class. During WILSON's first fall term, Adam Smith was giving the last of the lectures that would become *The Wealth of Nations*. When Smith left for France in the spring, they were completed for him by Thomas Young, and the next fall Reid began lecturing on natural law, rights and obligations of the individual, and rights and obligations of societies. Years later, in WILSON's defense of the Bank of North America, in his own law lectures at the University of Pennsylvania, in his Supreme Court opinions, and in his drafting of Article III of the Constitution, he would often invoke the principles of Scots law and repeat both Smith and Reid almost word for word.[19]

In 1785, in his *Considerations on the Bank of North America*, WILSON quoted from *The Wealth of Nations* "in a way," says McLean, "that is consistent with WILSON's having heard Smith's lectures on jurisprudence from Smith, or Young, or from [reading] one of the student transcripts" that were circulating. In his own lectures at the University of Pennsylvania, WILSON arranged his topics on the history and sociology of the law in the identical sequence that Smith employed in his 1763–1764 lectures and that Millar subsequently followed. None of this is proof that he attended Smith's or Millar's lectures or even read the lecture notes, but McLean concludes that "the intellectual kinship is striking."[20]

That WILSON's lectures consciously followed Thomas Reid, however, there can be no doubt. Consider his lecture on the "Law of Nature," published by his son Bird Wilson in 1804. WILSON says, "Moral truths may be divided into two classes: such as are selfevident, and such as, from the self-evident ones, are derived by Reasoning. If the first be not deduced without reasoning, reasoning can never discover the last." Reid, in his *Essays on the Intellectual Power of Man*, taken from his Glasgow lectures, writes, "Moral truths, therefore, may be divided into two classes, to wit, such as are self-evident to every man whose understanding and moral faculty are ripe, and such as are deduced by reasoning from those that are self-evident. If the first be not discovered without reasoning, the last never can be, by any reasoning."[21]

William Ewald, a present-day professor of law at the University of Pennsylvania, argues, "As a general matter, although common law supplied the colonies with most of the concrete rules of legal daily life, at the level of abstract and constitutional thought, the continental tradition of the civil law was at least as important; and most of the work of conveying those ideas to the colonies was performed by the teachers of the Scottish Enlightenment." Many delegates to the Philadelphia Convention were trained in English common law, but only one was trained in Scots civil law: JAMES WILSON. In the Committee of Detail, WILSON was responsible for the final draft of Article III, creating the judicial branch. In contrast to many of the existing state judicial systems, says Ewald, Article III "follows the Scots model of hierarchical courts, not the English model of competing courts." The committee's draft of what would become the "exceptions and regulations" clause, defining the Supreme Court's appellate function and giving it the "hierarchical" last word, is in WILSON's handwriting. It revises RANDOLPH's earlier draft, which proposed that "the legislature shall organize" the Court's jurisdiction. RANDOLPH, following Coke, expected the legislature to dominate the government and freely determine the Court's sphere as it saw fit; WILSON's draft, following Scots law and the idea of an "equipoise" of powers between legislature and judiciary, spells out the Court's original jurisdiction in the Constitution and declares that it shall be the final court of appeal "both as to Law and Fact."[22]

Legal scholars debate the intent and meaning of the exceptions clause, but they agree that WILSON was following Scots law tradition in trying to narrow the power over the courts that RANDOLPH would have given to the legislature. English courts, although creatures of royal prerogative, acknowledged Parliament's power over legal institutions. Scottish courts, on the other hand, were shielded from parliamentary control or revision by a constitutional framework. Contributing a term to Article III of the United States Constitution, the Act of Union declared that the Scottish Court of Sessions would be the "Supream Court of Justice" for Scotland; the name "Supreme Court" does not appear in the Philadelphia debates before WILSON's draft.[23]

Jefferson, also following Coke, saw the legislatures as the only voice of democracy; although MADISON would uneasily come to side with him in response to the threat he later saw from HAMILTON's extreme Federalism, in 1787 he and WILSON opposed efforts to give the legislature power unbalanced by the other branches. When WILSON later condemned parliamentary sovereignty, he was being true to his position at the Convention, where he regularly spoke for the natural rights of "the people"; WILSON's draft from the Committee on Detail was also the first explicit assertion that "We the people" had the authority to create the government. Just as his *Chisolm v. Georgia* decision ruled that a state's claim of sovereignty had to yield to the sovereignty of the people of the United States, so parliamentary sovereignty had to give way before the sovereignty of the people, protected in their Constitution: "The order of things in Britain is exactly the reverse of the order of things in the United States. Here the people are the masters of the government; there the government is the master of the people."[24]

In his conviction that the people not only *should* govern but *could* govern, WILSON invoked common sense, the philosophy of Thomas Reid that he first encountered at Glasgow. Common sense, WILSON insisted, "is purely the gift of heaven . . . [I]t makes a man capable of managing his own affairs and answerable for his conduct towards others." Reid declared that the possession of common sense meant that "the learned and the unlearned, the philosopher and the day labourer, are upon a level, and will pass the same judgment . . . when they are not misled by some bias, or taught to renounce their understanding from some mistaken religious principles." Rosenfeld thinks Reid added the conditional caveat "most likely to avoid potential radical implications," and WILSON at the Convention made implications that indeed struck his traditionally educated fellow Framers as radical. From his first speech on May 31, it was WILSON's position that common sense qualified the citizenry to elect their own government, even their own executive. MADISON admitted on July 19 that of all ways of choosing the executive, "The people at large was in his opinion the fittest in itself," but he feared it would founder on the fact that "the right of suffrage was much more diffusive in the Northern than the Southern States"—neither southern Framers nor their constituents would ever support a national popular vote for president, for the same reason they demanded a three-fifths rule for apportioning representatives: a large part of the southern population was unable to vote. MADISON believed "the substitution of electors obviated this difficulty." (He could not have predicted the bitter controversy when two of the twenty-first century's first three presidents were elected with a minority of the popular vote.) Still, until the closing weeks of the Convention, the delegates continued to expect that the national legislature—and perhaps only its more exclusive house, the Senate—would choose the executive. Popular election of the president was indeed rejected out of hand, with support only from WILSON, and from GOUVERNEUR MORRIS, who eventually sat on the August 31 Committee of Postponed Matters. Although the electoral college is attacked today as undemocratic, that committee's plan for choosing presidential electors in each state, potentially by popular vote, was actually a step as far as possible in the direction of popular sovereignty, justified by "common sense." The champion of that cause, JAMES WILSON, was a child of the Scottish Enlightenment; at Cupar, St. Andrews, and Glasgow he had imbibed it at the source.[25]

Scotland was also revolutionizing medical education. Medicine may seem distant from politics, but in the eighteenth-century world of small schools and highly personal relationships, the connection is not insignificant. MC-CLURG earned his MD at the University of Edinburgh, and WILLIAMSON, who had a hard time staying in one place very long, spent a year studying at Edinburgh and another in London hospitals, before finally submitting a perfunctory thesis and receiving his MD from Utrecht. MCHENRY trained in medicine in Philadelphia under the famous physician and patriot Benjamin Rush—himself an Edinburgh MD—but he would practice for only two years. These three were not leaders at the Convention (though WILLIAMSON did speak often), but they were dependable supporters of MADISON and WILSON, prepared by a web of connections both familial and educational.

MCCLURG's father was born in Scotland, WILLIAMSON's father was an Ulster Scot, and MCHENRY was himself a native of Ballymena, just outside Belfast. WILLIAMSON and MCHENRY studied at the Newark Academy founded by the Donegal-born Francis Alison. WILLIAMSON had studied for the ministry with the Rev. Samuel Finley, who preceded John Witherspoon as president of Princeton. Finley, yet another Ulster Scot, also taught his nephew Benjamin Rush and encouraged him to become a physician; Rush went to Edinburgh and returned to be the preceptor of MCHENRY in Philadelphia while he was serving in the Continental Congress. MCCLURG's teacher at William and Mary was William Small, a Scot who returned to take his MD from Aberdeen University. As Douglas Sloan has pointed out, by the 1760s the spread of Presbyterian academies, the presence in America of Scottish-trained educators such as Alison, Witherspoon, and Small, and the rising number of American medical students traveling to Scotland were all closely interrelated.[26]

The intimate relationship of apprenticeship could still be the physician's route just as well as the attorney's. The arrangements MCHENRY made with Rush in 1773 probably replicated those between Rush and John Redman a decade earlier, before Rush decided to go to Edinburgh for his MD. Rush recalls in his *Autobiography*, "In addition to preparing and compounding medicines, visiting the sick and performing many little offices of a nurse to them, I took exclusive charge of [Redman's] books and accounts." In return, Redman offered his instruction and his library: "I read in the intervals of business and at late and early hours all the books in medicine that were put into my hands by my master, or that I could borrow from other students of medicine in that city."[27]

Over three years, MCHENRY and Rush developed a close friendship. In his early biography of MCHENRY, Frederick Brown observes that by studying with Rush "at a period when the two sessions of the Continental Congress made Philadelphia a remarkable school for other things than physic, he was exposed to all the inspiring influences of the time." Indeed, it was while MCHENRY was his apprentice, living in his home, that Rush was becoming intimately acquainted with DICKINSON, MIFFLIN, CLYMER, LIVINGSTON, and WILSON, all destined to be MCHENRY's fellow Framers. In 1774, Rush met John and Sam Adams, and Patrick Henry came to Philadelphia to be inoculated by him for smallpox. At MIFFLIN's home he dined with WASHINGTON, and soon after the Second Continental Congress assembled, he renewed his friendship with FRANKLIN, whom he had met in London, and was introduced to Jefferson, WILSON, and LANGDON.[28]

Rush said he had become a republican while at Edinburgh in the 1760s; the seeds planted there were now germinating in Philadelphia. In 1775, Thomas Paine was working on an essay he was calling "Plain Truth." Rush helped edit it and suggested a new title: "Common Sense." Rush had probably been introduced to Reid's common sense philosophy (and maybe to Reid himself) by Reid's cousin John Gregory, his teacher at Edinburgh (and Small's, earlier, at Aberdeen). In 1776 he helped Paine publish the essay, which sold more than 100,000 copies. At the same time, he was publicly invoking Hume as an authority in an argument against fixing the prices of imported goods. Just as Rush had been introduced to his professors' associates and their ideas in Edinburgh, MCHENRY could not ignore the political world in which his own preceptor lived. Through Rush, MCHENRY made the contacts that would enable him to leave hospital duty at Valley Forge to join WASHINGTON's staff. From that time—just six years after arriving in America from Ireland—he was a personal and political protégé of WASHINGTON, who later made him his second secretary of war.[29]

Well before the Revolution, medical doctors were among the social and political leaders in the colonies south of New England, and more and more of them were graduates of the University of Edinburgh. Between WILLIAMSON's arrival in 1764 and MCCLURG's departure in 1770, Edinburgh awarded the MD to twenty-one Americans, and probably as many more studied there, as WILLIAMSON did, without earning a degree. Like the Americans at the Inns of Court, nearly all came from Pennsylvania, South Carolina, or Virginia. Earlier in the eighteenth century, Americans had preferred to study medicine in the hospitals of London or Paris, or at the University of Leiden, where the celebrated Herman Boerhaave held forth. Although Aberdeen and St. Andrews also awarded the MD, neither actually required coursework in medicine. In London there were brokers who could arrange Scottish medical degrees without any need to leave London; efforts to prevent this outright sale of degrees were actually opposed by Adam Smith, to whom any attempt to control distribution was an immoral restraint of trade. Oxford and Cambridge also awarded medical degrees; a widely ignored regulation actually required anyone practicing medicine in England to have a degree from one or the other, but, as in the field of common law, they offered no actual medical instruction.[30]

As early as 1749, Americans were traveling to Edinburgh to study medicine. The growing fame of Edinburgh coincided with the growing desire of Americans to go to Great Britain for education. American enrollment at the Inns of Court tripled after midcentury; only six Americans earned their MD at Edinburgh before 1760, but eight times that number did so in the next twenty years. Among them were Theodorick Bland (1763), Arthur Lee (1764), and Rush (1768), who would all serve in the Continental Congress.[31]

WILLIAMSON had already begun medical study while still teaching mathematics at Philadelphia, and in October 1763 he gave his notice to the college, sailing in the new year. What is known about WILLIAMSON's medical education derives largely from a memorial address delivered by Dr. David Hosack, who came to know him at Columbia's College of Physicians and Surgeons; he was helped in preparing his *Biographical Memoir* by WILLIAMSON's brother. According to Hosack, WILLIAMSON was often ill during his year at Edinburgh but managed to attend the courses of lectures by professors Monro, Whytte, Cullen, and Gregory. Although Monro and Whytte were semiretired by then, they and the others Hosack lists were the teachers first-year students sought out.[32]

Had WILLIAMSON continued at Edinburgh, he would have needed at least two more years to earn the MD, completing a lengthy thesis that gave many American students grief. Instead, he spent a year walking the wards of London hospitals and then traveled to the University of Utrecht, where he submitted a nine-page thesis that made superficial observations on diagnosis and treatment of conditions ranging from pleurisy to childbirth. WILLIAMSON received the MD on August 6, 1766, after passing "the usual examination." His reasons for choosing Utrecht are not hard to guess. Many students left Edinburgh after a single year, having taken what they felt were the most important courses: anatomy, chemistry, and medical practice. The cost of the full program through the MD was simply too high and the required time too long. The degree—if not the education—could be obtained more quickly and cheaply in Holland, without (as WILLIAMSON demonstrated) the long, difficult Edinburgh thesis.[33]

Edinburgh's influence extended far beyond the medical world. The city itself was becoming a European center of intellectual life. A bemused

Voltaire remarked in 1764, "Today it is from Scotland that we get rules of taste in all the arts, from epic poetry to gardening." A Prussian officer who traveled through England and Scotland in the 1780s announced that "mehr wahre Gelehrsamkeit und große literarische Talente" (more real learning and great literary talent) was to be found in Edinburgh than at Oxford and Cambridge taken together. He cited Robertson, Hume, Lord Kames, Smollett, Lord Monboddo, and Ferguson.[34]

WILLIAMSON spent 1764 at Edinburgh; in 1766, MCCLURG enrolled, earning his MD in 1770. His father had left Newton-Stewart, barely fifty miles from Edinburgh, to follow a medical career in the Royal Navy; in 1747, as surgeon's mate of HMS *Rose* on the Carolina station, he had petitioned the Admiralty as "a young man Just setting out in the World" to be allowed to set up a permanent naval hospital, something that did not yet exist in the American colonies. He was not a physician but a naval surgeon. An MD was a rarity in the navy; the 1814 Navy List, the first to be published by the Admiralty, lists 850 surgeons and 500 assistant surgeons (formerly called surgeon's mates) but only 14 physicians. The social and professional difference was considerable: at the beginning of the eighteenth century a surgeon was a skilled craftsman, but a physician was a gentleman. The younger MCCLURG had plenty of motivation to acquire the MD that his father lacked. He became a star student; according to William and Mary's president Madison, he "was a favorite pupil of the celebrated [Joseph] Black, and gained much applause by his treatise *De Calore*."[35]

MCCLURG's years at Edinburgh overlap those of Benjamin Rush, who (thanks to his preparation with Redman) needed only two years to earn his degree by 1768. MCCLURG, who came without a prior apprenticeship, took his time. He was awarded the MD in 1770, traveled to Paris and then to London, published an internationally celebrated monograph, and did not return to Virginia until 1773. A decade earlier Virginian students had been exotic characters at Edinburgh; by the 1760s they were so numerous that the Virginia Club was a popular student organization. Rush, in his *Autobiography*, lists among his American friends at Edinburgh the Virginians James Blair and Walter Jones. Blair was the younger brother of the Framer JOHN BLAIR JR.; Jones was MCCLURG's William and Mary schoolmate who had been temporarily expelled with him for obscure town and gown misbehavior.[36]

No diaries or letters home from WILLIAMSON or MCCLURG are known, but the life of an American medical student in Edinburgh can be glimpsed in the journals and letters of other students at the time. MCCLURG's friend Thomas Tucker wrote to his younger brother, St. George Tucker, who had not yet ventured to the College of William and Mary:

The building is old & irregular & too mean to merit a Description. The Students are in College only during the hours of reading [i.e., lectures], the rest of their time they employ at Home with their Tutors. . . . No Student is obliged to attend any Classes, but such as he chooses, except he is studying any Profession, and then he is expected to have studied every Branch of that Profession before he is admitted to practice it. Few take degrees here except in Physic [i.e., medicine].

Lisa Rosner has calculated that of Edinburgh medical students who did not take a degree, 70 percent stayed for one year, 20 percent for two, and only 10 percent for three or more: "The one year auditors [including WILLIAMSON] were not drop-outs who only made it through the first year of a well-defined curriculum, but instead were deliberately following the course of study . . . consisting of Anatomy and Surgery, Chemistry, and Medical Practice." These were perceived as the most important academic courses, and they were also taught by Edinburgh's "stars." Alexander Monro's lectures in anatomy were drawing nearly 300 students by the time of his death in 1767, almost half the student body of the entire university.[37]

Since it was impossible for all students to attend all lectures, they met in informal groups to pool notes, as did RUTLEDGE at the Middle Temple. There were also more formal student organizations. Thomas Parke, a Philadelphian, mentions the Chirurgo-Medical and Physico-Medical Societies (which reflected both the professional and social distinctions between surgeons and physicians); he thought the latter group contained "some sensible members." Of all the student clubs, Parke considered the Physico-Medical Society "much ye best Society of any here." It met weekly to hear papers presented by its members. It was also exclusive, but a number of Americans did become members before the Revolution, including Blair, Morgan, Lee, Rush, and Jones, the society's president in 1767. Americans admitted that year included MCCLURG.[38]

The eighteenth century was a great age of clubs and associations of all kinds. England's learned Royal Society became prominent; FRANKLIN, David Rittenhouse, and Arthur Lee were members. The 1700s saw the birth (and sometimes the entire lifespan) of societies as various as Dr. Johnson's famous Club, FRANKLIN's Junto, the Dublin Society (of which Arthur and Conway Dobbs were members), Glasgow's Oceana, William and Mary's Phi Beta Kappa and Princeton's Whig and Cliosophic Societies. WILLIAMSON, a member of FRANKLIN's American Philosophical Society, was also a founder of the New York Literary and Philosophical Society and a corresponding member of several Dutch societies.

In Edinburgh and Glasgow, it was in the many clubs that the ideas of the Scottish Enlightenment were developed and debated. An earlier Edinburgh medical society, founded by Monro, had published four influential volumes of *Medical Essays and Observations*. The fifth volume, titled *Essays and Observations, Physical and Literary*, appeared under the reorganized auspices of the Society for the Improvement of Natural Knowledge, soon known as the Philosophical Society. The preface to that volume announced the hope "that should [the medical society] turn its inquiries into more general knowledge, it would reap the advantage of preserving all its members; and needed but open its doors to gentlemen of other professions, who might enrich it with their observations and discoveries." As a sign of this intention, David Hume was made the society's secretary. The dominant force behind the reorganization was Lord Kames; the first volume of the new *Essays and Observations* included essays by him, and the next had contributions from William Cullen, Joseph Black—and BEN FRANKLIN.[39]

The faculty of the Edinburgh Medical School were intimately connected with the leading men of the Scottish Enlightenment. It was Kames who had persuaded Cullen to leave Glasgow for Edinburgh; Reid was Gregory's cousin and had helped direct his education; Cullen was Hume's personal physician and a close friend of Glasgow's Smith and Millar. The Philosophical Society had a large membership, but Edinburgh's intense intellectual life really revolved around smaller, more intimate clubs, such as the Select Society and the Poker Club, which took its name from the fireplace tool, emblematic of its mission to stir up the sparks of intellectual and political controversy. Monro and Robert Whytte, two of the founders of the medical school, belonged to the Select Society, as did Hume, Kames, Smith, and William Robertson (the historian who was also principal of the university). Robertson, Hume, and Smith were also members of the Poker Club, as was MCCLURG's mentor, Joseph Black, the chemistry professor. Smith and Black were such close friends that when Smith was dying, he sent for Black to burn manuscripts that he did not want published.[40]

Social relations between professors and their students were often close in the eighteenth century, and American students at Edinburgh were regularly introduced to their teachers' friends and colleagues. Here was another benefit of a medical education in Scotland that was simply unavailable at home. A few weeks after arriving in Edinburgh, Benjamin Rush met Hume at the home of Sir Alexander Dick, to whom he had been introduced by FRANKLIN. FRANKLIN had first come to Edinburgh in 1759, when he met Kames, Ferguson, Robertson, and Smith—and also Black, Cullen, and Monro. At Gregory's home, Rush met Robertson, and while in Scotland he also visited the Rev. John Witherspoon, whom he persuaded to accept the invitation to be president of Princeton.[41]

Although Thomas Parke was in Edinburgh barely six months, he too met Hume, when FRANKLIN was staying with him. During WILLIAMSON's year in Edinburgh and MCCLURG's three or four years, they must have heard much about the Scottish philosophers and had some opportunity to make acquaintances. A student's life was not all medicine: Parke read Duncan's *Elements of Therapeutics*, Sydenham's commentaries on Boerhaave, and James Lind on scurvy, but he also reported reading Hume's *History of England*, Locke's *Posthumous Works*, and Robertson's *Charles V*—books that MADISON was reading at Princeton. Parke wrote to tell his sister that Hume and Robertson had given him "such a relish for History, that I fear I should spend more time in the perusal of Histories, than I can spare for Medicine."[42]

It was their medical education, and the circles into which it introduced them, that gave Americans at Edinburgh the opportunity to meet Hume or Robertson and gave MCHENRY in Philadelphia an insider's view as independence was debated. Of course, the effect of the ideas in the air in the 1760s and 1770s was not equally profound for all American students. But Rush said that he first discussed Algernon Sidney at Edinburgh and first heard the authority of the king questioned there. He, WILLIAMSON, and MCCLURG were in Scotland or England when the Stamp Act storm broke. They were there when Lord Grenville's Acts were repealed and replaced by the Townshend Acts that led to the Boston Massacre and the Tea Party, which WILLIAMSON witnessed on his way back to England for a second visit in 1773. One can easily imagine these physicians-turned-statesmen concurring with Benjamin Rush: "For the first moment in my life I now [at Edinburgh] exercised my reason upon the subject of government."[43]

Rush was prepared for that moment by his time at two earlier schools in America; one was the college at Princeton, where so many of the Framers also studied. But his first school was one of many in the colonies whose teachers were Scots from either northern Ireland or Scotland. It is easy to overlook the radical nature of these Presbyterian academies and their lasting influence on their young students. Several came just short of the status of degree-granting colleges, and others did evolve into universities; most were at the cutting edge of education in the later eighteenth century.

Presbyterian Schools and Scottish Schoolmasters

GUNNING BEDFORD JR., WILLIAM RICHARDSON DAVIE, JONATHAN DAYTON, ALEXANDER HAMILTON, WILLIAM CHURCHILL HOUSTON, JAMES MADISON, ALEXANDER MARTIN, LUTHER MARTIN, JAMES MCHENRY, GOUVERNEUR MORRIS, WILLIAM PATERSON, GEORGE READ, HUGH WILLIAMSON

Donald Robertson, from Scotland, [was] a man of extensive learning, and a distinguished Teacher. . . . All that I have been in life I owe largely to that man.

JAMES MADISON to John C. Payne, 1836

JAMES MCHENRY, the medical student who traveled in the opposite direction from WILLIAMSON and MCCLURG, was born in County Antrim, Ireland. MCHENRY's family told his first biographer that he attended a grammar school in Dublin until excessive study impaired his health, and he was sent to Philadelphia in 1771 to live with William Allison, whose stepdaughter he would later marry. The Allisons (also spelled Alison and Ellison) were a large clan, among the many Ulster Scots who emigrated in the early decades of the eighteenth century; the McHenrys' choice to place their son in the care of Captain Allison suggests that the families knew each other in the old country. William Allison's brother Patrick, a prominent Presbyterian minister, was a trustee of the Newark Academy in Delaware, the school begun in the 1740s in New London by the Rev. Francis Alison, another member of that extended family who had come to America in 1734 or 1735.[1]

Encouraged by Patrick Allison, JAMES MCHENRY spent 1772 at the Newark Academy; he published verses in the *Pennsylvania Packet* that fall, including a Miltonic pastoral praising the charms of Delaware over the attractions of either regal London or scholarly Cambridge. MCHENRY's shepherd prefers "nymphs with rustic tresses" to the queen of England's "stars and garters" or "dull" Plato and his "dry" philosophy. The next year the young poet returned to Philadelphia and turned his study to medicine rather than Plato, beginning his apprenticeship with Benjamin Rush. Nothing more is heard of the nymphs.[2]

Between the Glorious Revolution of 1688 and the American Revolution of 1775, perhaps 100,000 Ulster Scots like McHenry and Alison left Ireland for the American colonies; some estimates are twice that number. Another 30,000 or 40,000 emigrated, as WILSON and Witherspoon did, directly from Scotland, mostly after 1760. Nearly all were Presbyterians, and they often brought their ministers with them or sent back to Ireland or Scotland for them, so that the Presbyterian clergy was well represented in the tide of migration. As the immigrants who spread out from the Delaware valley recognized the need to train their own ministers for the future, they followed the practice they had known in northern Ireland, setting up academies that, like Alison's, would train not only the next generation of ministers but a great many of the doctors, lawyers, and political leaders of the middle and southern colonies.[3]

Much of the formal education available south of New England took place in schools conducted by Presbyterian ministers. Between the 1727 founding of William Tennent's Neshaminy "Log College" and the end of the century, more than sixty-five academies were in operation from New York south to Georgia and west into Tennessee and Kentucky, operated by teachers who were Scots or the sons of Scots. Among their students were nearly a quarter of the Framers of the Constitution: MADISON, MORRIS, HAMILTON, WILLIAMSON, and DAVIE, who all spoke forcefully for a new and truly national form of government, and PATERSON, DAYTON, BEDFORD, READ, and LUTHER MARTIN, who vociferously defended the interests of the small states. The reticent among them, such as ALEXANDER MARTIN, were rare. WILLIAM CHURCHILL HOUSTON and MCHENRY missed much of the Convention because of illness or family emergency, but they defended the Constitution at their states' ratifying conventions. Two Framers (DAYTON and HAMILTON) were students at Francis Barber's Elizabethtown Academy; another two (PATERSON and LUTHER MARTIN) attended the Nassau Hall grammar school. WILLIAMSON and ALEXANDER MARTIN studied at West Nottingham, Maryland, with Samuel Finley; they and four others (READ, MIFFLIN, BEDFORD, and GOUVERNEUR MORRIS) were students at some point of Francis Alison. Alison, William Tennent, and Donald Robertson were graduates of the University of Edinburgh. Many other teachers were graduates or future faculty members of Princeton. Of course, the higher education pursued by some of those academies' graduates must not be overlooked: from them, nine Framers went to Princeton, two to King's College, and one to the College of Philadelphia. But outside of the three New England delegations, nearly all of the active leaders of the Convention had been taught in Presbyterian schools or by Scottish schoolmasters.[4]

Presbyterian education in America received much of its impetus from the Great Awakening, as part of a civil war among Presbyterians. Many Scottish ministers who migrated to America expected strict conformity to the Westminster Confession of Faith, but Presbyterian ministers raised in New England among Congregationalist separatists stressed individual piety and the authority of the Bible over adherence to the rules of the organized church; they were reluctant to fully acknowledge what seemed a foreign authority. Among them were Jonathan Dickinson (no relation to the Framer JOHN DICKINSON) and Aaron Burr Sr., both Yale graduates. A native Scot who agreed with them, William Tennent, was an Edinburgh graduate who had been powerfully impressed by the preaching of a Dutch Reformed revivalist, Jacob Frelinghuysen. Tennent opened a school in Neshaminy, Pennsylvania, where he began training young men for the ministry. His students, including his son Gilbert, felt no need for university degrees and were soon traveling through the region, preaching the Great Awakening throughout the middle colonies just as Jonathan Edwards was doing in Massachusetts.[5]

The Presbyterian Synod of Philadelphia reacted with alarm. In 1737, it forbade ministers from one presbytery to preach in the territory of another without its permission; the revivalist "itinerants" paid no attention. Connecticut authorities twice transported the itinerant preacher Samuel Finley from their colony, whereupon he opened his academy in West Nottingham on the Pennsylvania/Maryland border. In 1738, in an act aimed squarely at Tennent's students, the Synod required that all ministers lacking a college degree be examined by a committee of the Synod. When the committee refused to approve one Neshaminy candidate, the "New Side" Presbytery of New Brunswick licensed him anyway; the Synod expelled the Tennents' New Brunswick Presbytery, and the Schism of 1741 was under way—the "Old Side" Synod of Philadelphia versus the "New Side" Synod of New York (made up of the New Brunswick, New Castle, and Long Island Presbyteries), which would soon reach south to create a "New Side" Presbytery of Hanover in Virginia. About two dozen ministers belonged to each of the two factions.[6]

Douglas Sloan explains the proliferation of schools: "The command of educational standards and institutions offered to each side a concrete means of gaining ecclesiastical control and of propagating their own point of view." To answer accusations that they opposed education, the New Side leaders Dickinson and Burr opened the College of New Jersey, first at Newark, New Jersey, and then at its permanent home in Princeton, but the Old Side had already taken the first step. Even before Finley opened his school at West Nottingham, the Synod of Philadelphia adopted the New London, Pennsylvania, Academy of Francis Alison.[7]

Alison had been educated in an Irish Presbyterian academy, most likely that of Francis Hutcheson in Dublin. He earned an MA from Edinburgh in 1733, but since both FRANKLIN and Stiles speak of him as educated at Glasgow, he likely went on to that university to study theology for a year or two; Glasgow later awarded him a DD in 1756. Whether he actually studied with Francis Hutcheson or not, he was deeply influenced by Hutcheson's moral philosophy, which he taught first at New London and then at the College and Academy of Philadelphia. He wrote to Hutcheson for suggestions when he was seeking a collegiate charter for the Newark (Delaware) Academy. Alison, even before John Witherspoon, introduced the Scottish Enlightenment to the American colonies and was the first to teach it systematically.[8]

In 1735, the newly ordained Alison landed at New Castle, Delaware; he would divide the next forty-four years between that neighborhood and Philadelphia. He may have briefly tutored JOHN DICKINSON's older brothers, but when he was appointed minister of the Presbyterian Church of New London in 1737, he immediately began educating the children of his congregation. In 1743 the Philadelphia Synod voted to sponsor his school, paying him twenty pounds per year to conduct an academy "where all persons who please may send their children and have them instructed in the languages, philosophy, and divinity."[9]

Alison's first small class, boys seven to twelve years old, included three future signers of the Declaration of Independence (Thomas McKean, James Smith, and GEORGE READ), two Framers of the Constitution (READ and WILLIAMSON, soon joined by a third, ALEXANDER MARTIN), and the secretary of the Continental Congress (Charles Thomson). In addition to "the languages," Alison taught them English grammar by comparing it to Latin. His student Matthew Wilson later recalled, "We received the greatest advantage from his critical examination every morning of our themes, English and Latin, epistles, English and Latin, descriptions in verse, and especially our abstracts or abridgments of a paper from the Spectator or Guardian (the best standards of our language) substantially contracted into one of our exercises"—the latter technique also practiced by FRANKLIN as a youth. McKean remembered studying Greek and Latin, rhetoric, logic, moral philosophy (including ethics and political economy, based on Hutcheson), and the practical branches of mathematics. The New London Academy was, he said, the most celebrated school in Pennsylvania.[10]

The instruction Alison offered in the classics at New London was probably as good as any available at the three existing colonial colleges—Harvard, Yale, and William and Mary. Stiles called Alison "the greatest Classical Scholar in America, especially in Greek. Not great in Math. & Phil. [natural science] & Astronomy—but in Ethics, History, & general Reading is a great Literary Character. I have had long & intimate acquaintance with him." All that Alison lacked was a charter authorizing him to confer degrees, so it must have been particularly galling for him when, in 1746, the New Side's Dickinson and Burr were granted a charter for the College of New Jersey. Disappointed, the Old Side Synod of Philadelphia asked that Alison's graduates be permitted to continue at Yale and receive a degree in as little as one year. They acknowledged some weakness in science and mathematics but hoped to use the same texts that were assigned at Yale. President Clap, no supporter of the revivalists, was willing, but there is no record that any student took advantage of the opportunity.[11]

Alison would never give up his dream of turning his academy into a degree-granting college. He had just written to Francis Hutcheson about his hopes, seeking advice on books and curriculum, when Hutcheson died in 1746. Alison had promised to send Stiles a copy of Hutcheson's reply, which never came. What did come a few years later was an offer from BENJAMIN FRANKLIN's new Academy of Philadelphia, after its first rector died in 1751. The salary was two hundred pounds—ten times what the Synod of Philadelphia had initially granted him in 1742. Alison agreed to head the Latin school but declined the post of rector.[12]

Alison spent the rest of his life at the Philadelphia Academy and the College of Philadelphia that soon joined it. Over time, Alison began to worry about the direction the College of Philadelphia was taking under its provost William Smith, an Anglican. Alison had an Ulster Scot's deep-seated suspicion of the established church; he condemned the Test Act (disenfranchising all Dissenters) as a "notorious infringement on the rights of private judgment." In 1768, he published a series of essays under the pseudonym "Centinel," attacking the recent proposal to appoint a bishop for the colonies (a position that Smith was in fact angling to fill): "Every attempt upon American liberty has always been accompanied with endeavors to settle bishops among us." The Anglican New York Morrises had sent Gouverneur to the Philadelphia Academy because of Smith, not Alison; in 1764 young MORRIS had left to matriculate at King's, but he surely read the controversial essays of his former teacher, as did Alison's older Philadelphia students WIL-LIAMSON and MIFFLIN—and a newer one, GUNNING BEDFORD JR.[13]

In one of his "Centinel" essays, Alison argued that the autocratic authority of a bishop went against the principle of political balance, or "overpoise"—a principle that he had learned from Francis Hutcheson. This argument was central to his opposition to both bishops and established churches: "The passions and prejudices of men are constantly leading them into one mistake or another; and the remonstrances of reason and duty alone, are but feeble restraints. In order therefore to curb the licentiousness of leading men, it hath been found expedient to distribute the power of government among the different sorts and orders of which the community is composed, so as to excite and employ those of one rank and interest, to correct the irregularities of another." (Alison's language—particularly applicable to Pennsylvania's infighting among Quakers, Presbyterians, and Anglicans—recalls the "infidel" Hume's pragmatic argument for religious toleration.) BEDFORD, who had just left the Philadelphia Academy to enroll at Princeton, would soon hear John Witherspoon make a similarly Hutchesonian argument in his lectures on moral philosophy: "It is folly to expect that a state should be upheld by integrity of all who have a share in managing it. They must be so balanced that when one draws to his own interest or inclination, there may be some overpoise upon the whole." Familiarity (or lack of it) with that principle would be critically important to the reception of MADISON's proposals for checks and balances at the Convention in 1787.[14]

Samuel Finley had meanwhile left his West Nottingham academy for the presidency of Princeton; after his death, the "New Side" trustees of Princeton evaded an "Old Side" campaign to make Alison the college's next president, electing Witherspoon instead. With Princeton remaining in Evangelical hands and the College of Philadelphia increasingly under the control of the Anglican Smith, Alison turned his attention back to his original Academy, now relocated to Newark, Delaware; he still had hopes of making it a degree-granting college. But Proprietor Thomas Penn was supporting Smith's plans at the College of Philadelphia, and he dashed the Newark trustees' hopes of a college charter. Alison remained vice-provost at Philadelphia and president of the Newark trustees.

ALEXANDER MARTIN, son of Ulster immigrants, stayed at New London Academy until at least 1749, but he left after Alison went to Philadelphia and appears to have finished his preparation at Finley's West Nottingham school before enrolling at the College of New Jersey in 1753. Having moved to North Carolina and served a term as governor, MARTIN, a lukewarm Federalist, contributed little to the Convention in 1787. His colleague HUGH WILLIAMSON, another transplant to North Carolina and a much more energetic nationalist, wryly wrote to James Iredell about his old schoolmate: "I am inclined to think that the great exertions of political wisdom in our late Governor, while he sat at the helm of our State, have so exhausted his fund that time must be required to enable him to again exert his abilities to the advantage of the nation."[15]

GEORGE READ was another of Alison's students at New London. Read, too, was the son of an immigrant Ulster Scot, but like MARTIN he abandoned the contentious Presbyterians to join the established Church of England. After leaving Alison's Academy he clerked along with DICKINSON for Philadelphia's leading lawyer, John Moland; DICKINSON went on to the Middle Temple, but Read saw no need for that, just as he had seen no reason to go on to the College of Philadelphia. He rose rapidly in the Delaware bar to become attorney general of the province by the time he was thirty, and he was elected president (governor) of the state after independence. He was an ally of DICKINSON in the Second Continental Congress and his fellow commissioner at the Annapolis Convention.

READ was a stubborn defender of the small states—none present was smaller than Delaware—and disingenuously apologized that his delegation's instructions unfortunately forbade them from considering proportional representation; he neglected to mention that he was himself the author of those instructions. Once the Great Compromise was achieved, his genuinely national outlook could be revealed; he seems to have been sincere in offering to do away with states entirely if they could not be equal, an alternative that only Hamilton was willing to consider.[16]

READ made his entire career along the Philadelphia–Wilmington axis, but WILLIAMSON was restless. His parents (also from Ireland) were neighbors of Samuel Finley at West Nottingham. If Finley had opened his school a few years earlier, WILLIAMSON might have studied there rather than with Alison, and the Newark Academy might have lost its most energetic booster. Instead he went to New London and moved with the school to Newark when Alison left for Philadelphia, returning home to study mathematics (never Alison's strength) on his own. According to Hosack, "The father now proposed to send his son to Europe to finish his education that had been so successfully begun; but as a charter had been obtained for the academy at Philadelphia, about the time he was to have sailed, it was concluded that he would immediately proceed to that city." Accordingly, he entered the College of Philadelphia.[17]

WILLIAMSON graduated in 1757; while still an undergraduate he had begun teaching in the Academy's English and Latin schools. Then, like MARTIN, he left to study with Alison's New Side rival, his neighbor Samuel Finley. WILLIAMSON had felt a sudden calling to the ministry and briefly followed in Finley's footsteps, preaching as an itinerant in Connecticut before returning to Pennsylvania. Evidently his religious vocation was shaken by the residual hostilities of the Presbyterians' schism. Says Hosack, "The memorable controversy, too, which took place about that period in the Presbyterian church . . . proved to him a source of great disgust," and he was never ordained.[18]

Soon WILLIAMSON was back in Philadelphia, where he joined his old teacher on the college faculty as professor of mathematics until his chronic restlessness led him abroad to study medicine. Despite his time with Finley, his personal loyalty to Alison remained constant: he was Alison's student in the 1740s and 1750s, his teaching colleague in the 1760s, and his fellow trustee of the Newark Academy in the 1770s. His success as a fundraiser—he "procured a handsome subscription" in Jamaica—inspired a more ambitious expedition the following year. He and his New London classmate John Ewing sailed separately for England; just before departing from Boston at the end of 1773, WILLIAMSON witnessed the Boston Tea Party, and it was he who broke the news of it to the Privy Council when he reached London. The broadening consequences of the event he described would eventually torpedo the fundraising mission, but neither he nor Ewing could foresee that future. WILLIAMSON traveled in Europe after Ewing returned home in 1775, visiting first the Netherlands and then, after the news of independence, Paris. He may have carried dispatches from BENJAMIN FRANKLIN when he returned. Unlike such other loyal students as Ewing and Matthew Wilson, he did not share Alison's intense Old Side partisanship, but he was inspired by Alison's teaching to become a teacher himself, and like Thomson, READ, MARTIN, and McKean, he was well prepared by Alison's instruction for a career in politics. He served in the North Carolina legislature, the Confederation Congress, and the House of Representatives. To his chagrin, he arrived one day too late to take part in the Annapolis Convention.[19]

At the College and Academy of Philadelphia, Alison taught GOUVERNEUR MORRIS, BEDFORD, and MIFFLIN. An Anglican, a Presbyterian, and a Quaker, they too were much less interested in denominational controversy than in acquiring a strong preparation in the classics and—as MIFFLIN's surviving notebook reveals—in moral philosophy. Six of the Framers thus studied under Alison, whom Hosack called "the Busby of the Western Hemisphere," after the famous Westminster headmaster who had taught Christopher Wren, John Dryden, and John Locke.

Witherspoon and Finley are reminders that, for all the Old Side accusations of anti-intellectualism, the New Side Presbyterians could be just as interested in classical education and philosophy. The Old Side's Alison was not much interested himself in science; after Philadelphia Academy instructor Theophilus Grew got him up at 3 a.m. on a raw morning to look for a comet ("I nearly lost my health by it"), he announced that "as I hope with more certainty, & less trouble, to acquire this kind of knowledge in my next stage of existence, if it be necessary, I have determined to give myself no further trouble till I be allowed to converse with Newton [and] Halley . . . in heaven." But when the evangelical Witherspoon came to Princeton in 1768, one of his first successes as president was the acquisition of David Rittenhouse's celebrated Philadelphia orrery from under the noses of Alison and Provost Smith.[20]

Most of the academies of the New Side were strong in the classical trivium of grammar, rhetoric, and logic: Samuel Blair's academy at Fagg's Manor gave Samuel Davies, a future Princeton president, all his formal education, and Davies's sermons regularly quoted Horace, Plato, Tacitus, and Cicero, along with Addison and Pope. Fagg's Manor actually opened a year or two earlier than Alison's New London Academy, and Finley's West Nottingham Academy opened a year or so later. Finley had been educated entirely at the "Log College" so derided by the Old Side, but in 1763 he was made a doctor of divinity by the University of Glasgow, the same degree that Glasgow had awarded Alison in 1756. Finley's curriculum included the usual Greek and Roman authors, logic, arithmetic, geography, geometry, "Part of Ontology, and Natural Philosophy, in a more cursory manner, as far as Opticks." Rush later said that Finley's "mode of teaching inspired me with a love of knowledge," but he admitted that he was not a dedicated student, being too easily distracted by the pleasures of the outdoors. (He was barely twelve when he left for Princeton.) Rush and the other students lived in the Finley home and were looked after by Mrs. Finley, on the Pennsylvania side of the border; they attended classes in a separate building just across the invisible line in Maryland.[21]

Samuel Finley's course of study in the higher subjects, though adapted to younger students, was much like that introduced by Aaron Burr Sr. when Burr became the second president of Princeton. (Burr's Princeton students were as young as MARTIN, who entered at the age of twelve, and as old as Martin's classmate Isaac Livermore, who was already twenty when he matriculated upon experiencing a call to the ministry. None was better prepared than those who came from Finley's school.) When Finley later took over the college presidency after the brief intervening tenures of Edwards and Davies, he also took over personal direction of the Nassau Hall grammar school, where two of his earliest students were WILLIAM PATERSON and LUTHER MARTIN.[22]

Alison, Blair, and Finley saw their teaching as a vocation in itself, training the next generation of clergymen and community leaders; for many young college graduates, however, teaching at a grammar school or tutoring in a gentleman's home was a temporary expedient on the way to a career that might just as likely be in medicine or law. The master of Princeton's grammar school was usually a new graduate of the college who held the post for only a year. OLIVER ELLSWORTH's (and later WILLIAM DAVIE's) friend Waightstill Avery was one of them, as was Tapping Reeve, who next went to Elizabethtown, where he taught for a few years at the academy that Jonathan Dickinson had opened in 1740. (He taught Aaron Burr Jr., and he later married Burr's sister.) When Reeve left Elizabethtown for a career practicing and teaching law, his successor was Francis Barber. Barber eventually left to fight in the Revolutionary War; he would not live to return. Among Barber's students was JONATHAN DAYTON, who was preparing to enter Princeton himself in 1773. And just as DAYTON was leaving, ALEXANDER HAMILTON arrived. The lives of Burr, Barber, DAYTON, and HAMILTON would remain tangled together as Barber served under his former student HAMILTON in the army, Burr and HAMILTON developed the intense rivalry that climaxed with their fatal duel, and DAYTON's land speculations embroiled him in the western filibustering scheme that led to Burr's trial for treason.[23]

The youthful HAMILTON had been discovered in the West Indies by the Rev. Hugh Knox, who sent him in 1772 to two Princeton trustees, Elias Boudinot and WILLIAM LIVINGSTON, both residents of Elizabethtown. The house where HAMILTON lived as a boy on the island of St. Croix apparently contained thirty-four books, including Pope's poetry, the inescapable Plutarch, Machiavelli's *Prince*, and a collection of sermons. (His mother's possessions were catalogued in a legal dispute that followed her death.) HAMILTON's son published a biography informed by recollections of his father's conversations about his youth: "Among the books to which he had access, he preferred those which treat of some branch of ethics. His favorite authors were Pope and Plutarch, on the latter of which there remain some curious observations from his youthful pen." Unfortunately, those "curious observations" on Plutarch are now lost.[24]

It is doubtful that HAMILTON ever attended a school in the West Indies; abandoned by his father, after his mother's death he was encouraged in his studies by Knox, a Princeton graduate who was the minister at the Christiansted Presbyterian Church. When the citizens of St. Croix took up a collection to send the bright boy to the mainland for higher education, Knox wrote letters recommending HAMILTON to his friends in New Jersey and New York, who included two Princeton trustees, Elias Boudinot and WILLIAM LIVINGSTON.

Boudinot and LIVINGSTON welcomed the orphaned West Indian into their homes. Among the first entries in HAMILTON's *Papers* is a moving elegiac poem that he wrote on the death of Boudinot's daughter. The only earlier entries in the *Papers* are notes that he took during 1773 at the Elizabethtown Academy on the books of Genesis and Revelations, some translations from the *Iliad*, and an ambitious reading list put together during the few months that he was there. HAMILTON was painfully aware of the gaps in his preparation, especially in Greek and Latin; filling such gaps was Barber's specialty, and HAMILTON was quickly enrolled. Elizabethtown Academy occupied a two-story building described as "commodious." An advertisement stated that the academy would instruct youth in the several branches of mathematics, both theoretical and practical, "without detriment" to the primary function of teaching Latin and Greek. Academy students also had the opportunity to study geography and English literature, along with elocution and "Epistolary Composition, in which they are duly instructed, particularly as to Orthography, Punctuation, & c., Acquirements in which too many grown scholars are notoriously deficient." HAMILTON would later employ his skills in "epistolary composition" in keeping up correspondence with both Knox and his classmate DAYTON; right now he had to concentrate on getting his Latin and Greek up to college standards. He had been the *wunderkind* of St. Croix, and it must have been a shock to discover that DAYTON was about to enroll in at Princeton at thirteen when HAMILTON was just entering prep school at seventeen; he immediately dropped two years from his reported age.[25]

The Revolutionary War took Barber south as far as Yorktown; he died in an accident on his way home. Other Princetonians were drawn south by a different kind of mission. During the administrations of presidents Davies, Finley, and Witherspoon, more than two dozen graduates left Nassau Hall for Virginia and the Carolinas to preach, teach, and open new colleges. Among the teachers, college founders, and their students were four future Framers of the Constitution. The string is almost unbroken from the class of 1760 until the class of 1777, when war nearly closed the college. Before them, however, came native Scots and Ulstermen who became famous as teachers in the South. Thomas Jefferson spent six years at the Latin school of the Scottish Rev. William Douglas, where he recalled "mouldy pies and excellent instruction," before transferring to Rev. James Maury (born in Dublin) and then finding Aberdonian William Small, almost his only teacher at William and Mary. In King and Queen County, Virginia, JAMES MADISON began at the school of the Rev. Donald Robertson, graduate of Aberdeen and Edinburgh.[26]

Robertson left the same impression on MADISON, at an earlier age, that Small later did on Jefferson. Having Small as his teacher, Jefferson said, "fix'd the destinies of my life"; MADISON said about Robertson, "All that I have been in life I owe largely to that man." Robertson opened his Virginia school in 1758, teaching as many as forty pupils at a time. MADISON later recalled that he entered when he was eleven, and over the next four or five years he "studied the Latin and Greek languages, was taught to read but not to speak French"—Robertson's Scottish accent was too great an obstacle—"and besides Arithmetic & Geography, made some progress at Algebra & Geometry. Miscellaneous literature was also embraced by the plan of the school." He began in the English class; there he first read *The Spectator*, which he "inferred to be particularly adapted to inculcate in youthful minds, just sentiments[,] an appetite for knowledge, and a taste for the improvement of the mind and manners." Within a year he was studying Latin.[27]

While MADISON was with Robertson, he bought his own copies of Cornelius Nepos, Virgil, Horace, and Justinian, and also read Ovid, Terrence, Caesar, Eutropius, and Sallust. He learned Greek and history from Herodotus and Thucydides and began reading Plato and Plutarch. Here too he seems to have first encountered the essays of Montaigne, Locke's *Essay Concerning Human Understanding*, and Montesquieu's *Spirit of the Laws*—years ahead of his college enrollment. Robertson took his students far beyond the curriculum usual in grammar schools, and MADISON remembered him as "a man of extensive learning, and a distinguished teacher."[28]

Robertson's account books show that his school continued at least until 1773, but in 1767 MADISON was brought home at the age of sixteen to prepare for college with Thomas Martin—perhaps because Martin was being hired to tutor the younger Madison children, and it was good economy to pay only one teacher. But Martin was also a new graduate of Princeton, and Madison's father had come to know and respect Princeton president Samuel Davies when Davies was preaching in Virginia in the 1750s; he was also favorably impressed by the new President Witherspoon, who visited Virginia and, according to the *Virginia Gazette*, "preached to a crowded audience in the Capital yard (there being no house in town capable of holding such a multitude) and gave universal satisfaction." MADISON's preparation enabled him to enter Princeton in the summer of 1769 as a sophomore; he would accelerate to graduate in just two years.[29]

Davies was the best known of the Scotch-Irish Presbyterians who had been spreading south into Virginia and along the Blue Ridge into North Carolina. Patrick Henry's mother was a member of Davies's church in Hanover, where the admiring Henry often heard him preach. Around 1750 William Richardson, a Glasgow graduate, came to Virginia, lived in Davies's home, and was licensed by Virginia's Hanover Presbytery. In 1759, he became pastor to the Presbyterians in the Waxhaw District of the Carolinas, where he was joined by his sister Mary and her husband, Archibald Davie. The couple had already named their son after him: WILLIAM RICHARDSON DAVIE. The boy would eventually inherit his uncle's library and 150 acres of land, and like RICHARD DOBBS SPAIGHT he would always use his full name in his uncle's honor.[30]

As North Carolina's population grew, the Hanover Presbytery divided what had become Mecklenburg County into seven congregations. In 1766, the young Rev. Joseph Alexander was sent to the church at Sugar Creek. Alexander had been one of Finley's West Nottingham pupils; when he matriculated at Princeton, Finley warned that he considered him "somewhat rusty in ye classicks." Evidently Alexander applied himself, not only graduating in 1760, but marrying President Davies's daughter, Martha. When Davies died in 1761, Alexander followed in his footsteps as an apostle to the South. By 1767 or 1768 he had a classical school at Sugar Creek; the next year there was a school at Poplar Tent, where the new minister was Hezekiah James Balch, another recent Princeton graduate. One of the trustees who had received title to the site of that church in 1765 was Archibald Houston, father of WILLIAM CHURCHILL HOUSTON. There is some disagreement about the early education of HOUSTON. Poplar Tent, where Balch conducted a school, certainly suggests itself. Donald Come proposes Crowfield Academy, opened at Mecklenburg's Centre Church in 1760; two future classmates of HOUSTON, Ephraim Brevard and Adlai Osborne, were certainly educated there. (1768 was a particularly strong class of North Carolinians at Princeton.) But HOUSTON's biographer Thomas Glenn believes "there can be no doubt" that Joseph Alexander "personally prepared him" for Princeton at Sugar Creek. Despite Glenn's confidence, "there can be no doubt" only that HOUSTON was able to skip the first year or two of the undergraduate program, and that several good schools had opened in North Carolina just as he was preparing for college, all sponsored by Presbyterian churches.[31]

It is much easier to speak with assurance about the education of HOUS-

TON's own student and fellow Framer, WILLIAM RICHARDSON DAVIE. DAVIE entered Alexander's Sugar Creek Academy at about the age that MADISON came to Donald Robertson's school. The Academy was so successful that in 1770 North Carolina's Orange Presbytery asked Alexander to move the short distance to Charlotte, the Mecklenburg county seat, where they intended to seek a charter for a degree-granting college. DAVIE went with him. County and town were both named in honor of the new Queen Charlotte of Mecklenburg-Strelitz, the bride of King George III. The predominantly Presbyterian trustees worried (correctly, as it turned out) that the king might not grant a charter to yet another American college run by Dissenters, especially at a time when relations between the colonies and the Crown were deteriorating. Following the recent examples of the town and the county, they offered the rather transparent flattery of naming their institution The Queen's College. The trustees, a mix of clergy and laymen, included Waightstill Avery (Princeton roommate of OLIVER ELLSWORTH), the Rev. Hezekiah Balch, no less than three uncles of Joseph Alexander, and three protégés of the Rev. Samuel Davies—Henry Patillo, William Richardson, and of course Joseph Alexander. (Joel Brevard, who had just graduated from Princeton, was hired as an instructor.)[32]

Led by a younger, American-born generation, the Presbyterians of North Carolina were following the examples of Alison, Finley, Jonathan Dickinson, and Aaron Burr, creating a version of the Ulster academy that would educate both ministers and civic leaders. They too hoped to create a full-fledged college, but like Alison they would be disappointed; without the Anglican connections that the College of Philadelphia and King's College had counted on, British authorities were not inclined to grant their request. Governor Tryon, who had succeeded Arthur Dobbs in 1765, sent a cautious letter to accompany the North Carolina legislature's act of incorporation, advising King George that "though the President is to be of the established Church and licensed by the Governor, the fellows, Trustees, and Tutors I apprehend will be generally Presbyterians, the college being promoted by a respectable settlement of that persuasion." A year went by, and then the king disallowed the act on April 22, 1772.[33]

The North Carolina trustees were disappointed but by no means discouraged; a recently discovered bill for construction reveals that they spent the huge sum of £1,380 to erect a college hall that was one of the most substantial buildings between Charleston and Williamsburg. At a time when the Mecklenburg County Courthouse was a one-room log cabin, the college hall was a two-story wood-framed building on a stone foundation, measuring 116 by 40 feet; it contained twenty dormitory rooms (painted yellow with white trim), each with an attached study, and a door with a brass knob. Boasting a library of 35 books purchased by Avery and as many as 230 more contributed by other individuals, the school continued to hold classes even though it could not confer degrees, and the trustees sent a second petition to the king, this time under the name of the Queen's Museum. Again they were rebuffed. There would be no more petitions, and in May 1775 many of the original trustees were among the signers of the Mecklenburg Resolves, the so-called Mecklenburg Declaration of Independence.[34]

WILLIAM RICHARDSON DAVIE remained at Queen's Museum through the spring of 1774. With no prospect of a degree there, he rode north to Princeton that summer; two years later he graduated, came home, and like his classmate JONATHAN DAYTON, joined the army. A year later the state of North Carolina issued its own charter for the school in Charlotte; the name of Queen's College had failed to attract royal approval, and it was now patriotically abandoned in favor of "Liberty Hall Academy." Still unauthorized to grant degrees, the school gradually faded. The visiting Italian botanist Luigi Castiglione mentioned in 1786 that the school "had flourished before the war, and in it were taught the Latin and Greek languages." In 1791, President WASHINGTON spent a night in Charlotte (finding it "a very trifling place") and noted in his diary, "There is a School (called a College) in it at which, at times there has been 50 or 60 boys." The 1777 Liberty Hall trustees had included the prominent Princetonians Waightstill Avery, David Caldwell, Ephraim Brevard, Adlai Osborne, Hezekiah James Balch, and Samuel McCorkle. When the state finally chartered a degree-granting University of North Carolina in 1789, its first president would be WILLIAM RICHARDSON DAVIE.[35]

Several Presbyterian academies offered a broader curriculum than the New England grammar schools or even the great English public schools, such as Westminster. They taught science, history, and moral philosophy in addition to the classical languages and mathematics. These were much more than prep schools, as Lawrence Cremin points out: "The distinction between academies and colleges was *not* clear in the mid eighteenth century. In retrospect, some schools seemed fated to become great universities, but at the time Alison's academy or Caldwell's or Queen's Museum seemed equally promising. Princeton, Penn, Brown, and Dartmouth were all outgrowths of academies operated in the homes of clergymen." READ and MCHENRY received their entire education in the academies of Presbyterian ministers; MARTIN and WILLIAMSON in Pennsylvania, DAYTON and HAMILTON in New Jersey, MADISON in Virginia, and HOUSTON and DAVIE in North Carolina were thoroughly prepared by them and often admitted with advanced standing at the new colleges at Philadelphia, New York, and, above all, Princeton.[36]

Mirania in America

The College of Philadelphia and King's College

GUNNING BEDFORD JR., ALEXANDER HAMILTON, THOMAS
MIFFLIN, GOUVERNEUR MORRIS, HUGH WILLIAMSON

*The Idea of what is true Merit, should also be often presented to Youth,
explain'd and impress'd on their Minds, as consisting in an Inclination
joined with an Ability to serve Mankind, one's Country, Friends and
Family; which Ability is (with the Blessing of God) to be acquir'd or greatly
encreas'd by true Learning; and should indeed be the great Aim and End of
all Learning.*

BENJAMIN FRANKLIN, *Proposals Relating to the Education of Youth in
Pennsylvania*

The history of the College of Philadelphia (today's University of
Pennsylvania) begins with BENJAMIN FRANKLIN's desire to create
an English-language equivalent of the classical grammar school.
When he was in his midthirties, FRANKLIN grew concerned that
Pennsylvania had "no provisions . . . for a complete education of
youth. I therefore, in 1743, drew up a proposal for establishing an
academy; and at that time, thinking the Rev. Richard Peters, who
was out of employ, a fit person to superintend such an institution,
I communicated the project to him; but he, having more profit-
able views in the service of the Proprietor [Thomas Penn, son of
William Penn], which succeeded, declined the undertaking, and
not knowing another at that time suitable for such a trust, I let the
scheme lie awhile dormant."[1]

By 1749, FRANKLIN was ready to revive his scheme. In the summer he published *Proposals Relating to the Education of Youth in
Pennsylvania* and began soliciting contributions from Philadelphia's wealthy and influential citizens. But FRANKLIN faced a di-

lemma: the people whose support he needed had a very different kind of school in mind. FRANKLIN was determined that his academy would teach in English, but his prospective donors insisted on a classical education, in Latin. On top of that, FRANKLIN wanted his school to be nonsectarian, and Philadelphia's wealthy were mostly members of the Church of England. If he hoped to recruit the necessary support from Philadelphia's Anglican traditionalists, he would have to compromise somewhere.[2]

FRANKLIN's initial object was a school for boys age eight to sixteen; his ambitious *Proposals* called for instruction in writing, drawing, arithmetic, accounts, geometry, astronomy, English grammar, and composition. Students would also study declamation, history, geography, chronology, "antient customs," and morality. Latin and Greek, however, would be electives, on a par with agriculture and mechanics—recommended, but not required. Next FRANKLIN published the *Idea of the English School*, in which he advocated instruction in reading, spelling, composition, rhetoric, "Natural and Mechanical History" [i.e., science], mathematics, history (in particular the history of England and of the colonies), but not Latin or Greek. The method he described for teaching composition was the program he had created for himself in his youth: rewriting essays from *The Spectator* from memory or from a few "Hints of the Sentiment in each Sentence."[3]

In an awkward compromise, the Academy of Philadelphia began enrolling students in 1751 in two separate English and Latin Schools. When the trustees' first choice to head the Latin school died suddenly, FRANKLIN took the advice of Charles Thomson and turned to Francis Alison to replace him. The mostly Anglican trustees were wary of hiring an Irish Presbyterian, but Alison's reputation as a scholar and a teacher at New London Academy won them over. However, Alison was unwilling to accept the position of rector of the combined Academy. FRANKLIN was then printing the Rev. Samuel Johnson's *Elementa Philosophica*, the first American work of moral philosophy. Believing the former Yale tutor might be the ideal rector for the Academy, FRANKLIN sent Johnson a preliminary draft of his *Idea of the English School*, asking for suggestions. He told Johnson, "The Latin and Greek School has been under the care of Mr. Alison, a Dissenting minister, well skilled in those languages and long practiced in teaching. But," he pointedly added, "he refused the Rectorship, or to have anything to do with the government of the other schools. So that remains vacant." He also told Johnson, "Mr. Alison undertakes Logic and Ethics, making your work [the *Elementa*] his text to comment and lecture upon." That was highly unlikely; without exception, Alison's students describe him as a proponent of Francis Hutcheson's moral philosophy, and his Scottish realism was the antithesis of Johnson's Berkeleyan idealism. Moreover, Johnson was the best-known Anglican clergyman in the colonies, and Alison was hostile to his efforts to create an American bishop. Johnson, for his part, was reluctant to take charge of the Philadelphia school, perhaps because he knew FRANK-LIN wanted a nondenominational institution but primarily because he was waiting for a different offer. Indeed, Joseph Ellis finds "reason to believe that Johnson's negotiations with FRANKLIN over the Philadelphia job were a ploy . . . to enhance his appeal to the King's College governors." FRANKLIN kept looking for a rector.[4]

At a number of points in his *Autobiography*, FRANKLIN mentions friends who let him down or betrayed his trust; he was not always the best judge of character. In the 1750s, two conspicuous examples of his poor judgment were Richard Peters, his original choice to head the Academy, and William Smith, who did become provost of the College and Academy of Philadelphia. Peters and Smith conspired to remove FRANKLIN from the presidency of the trustees, and Smith went on to institute far-reaching departures from FRANKLIN's plan for the school. FRANKLIN may have already cooled to Peters—he did not renew his 1743 invitation when the Academy was actually ready to open—but he was blindsided by Smith. His uncritical enthusiasm when the two had barely met is hard to explain; in the words of historian Francis Jennings, "FRANKLIN became positively fatuous about young William Smith."[5]

Born in Scotland in 1727, Smith left Aberdeen's King's College without a degree and came to New York at the age of twenty-four escorting the sons of Josiah Martin, who had just been appointed to the royal governor's council. There he quickly threw himself into the controversy over the new college currently in the works, writing anonymous essays in favor of an Anglican foundation. In 1753, he composed his plan for an ideal curriculum, the *General Idea of the College of Mirania*, and presented it to Johnson. In a format imitating Harrington's *Oceana* and More's *Utopia*, Smith imagined a conversation with a visitor from the fictional land of Mirania. Boys there could attend either a "mechanical" school that Smith modeled on FRANK-LIN's *Idea of the English School* or a college that offered an unusually broad liberal arts curriculum. Johnson, who had shown FRANKLIN's essay to Smith, suggested sending a copy of *Mirania* to FRANKLIN. When he did, the response must have gratified the young author.[6]

"I know not when I have read a piece that so affected me," wrote FRANK-LIN, "—so noble and just are the sentiments, so warm and animated the language." In June 1753, FRANKLIN met Smith in New York. On June 26 he wrote to his British friend Peter Collinson, suggesting that his new acquaintance might "possibly be prevailed on" to be the rector of the Academy. Collinson did not share FRANKLIN's infatuation with Smith; having met him, he wrote to Franklin, "Mr. Smith's a Very Ingenious Man. It is a Pitty but He was more Solid and Less flighty." Collinson also shared the reservations of several trustees who feared Smith's planned ordination in the Church of England might discourage Quakers and other Dissenters from enrolling their sons. FRANKLIN brushed the concern aside: "As to his Gown, I think with you that it may not at first be proper to use it frequently in the Academy; tho' if it should prejudice the main design with some, it might perhaps advantage it as much with others." Clearly, he was still hoping to please Anglican supporters without abandoning the nonsectarian character of the school.[7]

When Smith sailed to London to be ordained, he must have seemed an ideal emissary to seek a charter for the Academy from the second-generation proprietor, Thomas Penn, who preferred to live in England and had become an Anglican in 1751. Returning the following year with charter in hand, he was now secretly on Penn's payroll, working "in an extralegal way for Penn's prerogatives" and spying on FRANKLIN for the proprietor. Nevertheless, in May 1754, endorsed by FRANKLIN and Peters, Smith was hired by the trustees "on trial" to teach logic, rhetoric, ethics, and natural philosophy; Collinson cautiously acknowledged Smith's talents and hoped that "as his years Increase, His Judgement and Understanding will grow more Mature for his Age."[8]

Smith and Peters went to work to convert the Academy to something more congenial to the proprietor's views. Smith soon arranged for Penn to replace the 1753 charter with a new charter in 1755, specifically creating a degree-granting college governed by a provost, to which office Smith was appointed at a salary of two hundred pounds (in addition to the fifty pounds Penn was secretly paying him). He was just twenty-eight years old. The new charter also required loyalty oaths of all trustees, officers, and faculty. Seeing that requirement as a direct affront, Quakers quickly lost confidence in the increasingly Anglican college. Charles Thomson resigned from the faculty rather than work under Smith.[9]

In the following year, 1756, Smith made his move to depose FRANKLIN as president of the trustees. FRANKLIN's increased political activity (especially his travel to promote the unsuccessful Albany plan of union) had resulted in numerous missed meetings of the trustees; his previous reelections had been unanimous, but this time the vote to replace him with Peters was not even close. The change now made it easier to complete the shift from FRANKLIN's idea of an English-language, practical science education to a classical curriculum. Although much of what was genuinely new in the *College of Mirania* plan that had attracted FRANKLIN was retained, the English school was quickly allowed to atrophy. And although Vice-Provost Alison and some trustees defended the nonsectarian character of the college, Smith and Peters hoped to follow the example of New York's new King's College and make theirs an Anglican institution. Smith boasted to the Rev. Philip Bearcroft of the Society for the Propagation of the Gospel (SPG) that things were changing in the College: "The Church, by soft and easy Means daily gains ground in it. Of Twenty-four Trustees fifteen or sixteen are regular Churchmen, and when our late additional charter was passed, I, who am a Minister of the Church of England . . . was voted Provost of the same by the unanimous voice of the Trustees."[10]

Perhaps because of the humiliation he suffered in losing control of his own creation, FRANKLIN speaks very little of the Philadelphia College and Academy in his *Autobiography*, summarizing the College's evolution after 1750 in just two sentences. William Smith's name is never mentioned in the *Autobiography*. For FRANKLIN, being replaced as president of the trustees was more than a personal embarrassment; he saw it as a defeat for modern, scientific education and a victory for reactionary, aristocratic values represented by Smith and Peters. For Alison, however, the struggle that really mattered was between his (and FRANKLIN's) ideal of a nondenominational college in which Dissenters (Presbyterian and Quaker) might follow a path to knowledge and virtue, and the prospect of a college dominated by a corrupt Church of England under the autocratic rule of a would-be bishop of Philadelphia, William Smith, if his lobbying paid off. Each of the three was at odds with the other two, but there was one idea on which they never disagreed—the broad philosophical curriculum of Smith's "College of Mirania." And from 1754 until its reorganization as the University of Pennsylvania, the story of the College of Philadelphia is largely the story of Provost William Smith.

It was the *Mirania* curriculum—with its nod to the *Idea of the English School*—that first brought Smith to FRANKLIN's attention and won him his appointment as professor of "Logick, Rhetorick, Ethicks, and Natural Philosophy" in 1754. Smith's emphasis on modern authors, rhetoric, and Hutcheson's moral philosophy actually aligned with Alison's own approach, both at New London and at Philadelphia, where he and Smith seem to have taken turns teaching the moral philosophy class. Smith's curriculum, no less than Alison's, was rooted in the practices of the Scottish universities. In Smith's case that meant Aberdeen; having been a student there in the 1740s, he closely followed the reforms of its Marischal College in 1753, the year he published *A General Idea of the College of Mirania*. Those reforms had included replacing the system of generalist regents (or tutors) with specialized professors; Philadelphia instructors, from the beginning, taught specific subjects. The Marischal reforms also brought a new curriculum that "progressed from particular and concrete studies to general and abstract studies"—just as in the outline of FRANKLIN's *Proposals*, which Smith had specifically praised in *Mirania*.[11]

Smith's 1759 *Account of the College, Academy, and Charitable School of Philadelphia in Pennsylvania* indicates that Hutcheson's moral philosophy continued to be taught in every year of the three-year BA program, briefly introduced in the first term through the summary in Fordyce's *Elements of Moral Philosophy* and then presented in detail through lectures in the final four of the College's nine terms. The Philadelphia curriculum included the standard Plato, Aristotle, Xenophon, and Cicero, but also Grotius, Pufendorf, Harrington, and Locke. To Hutcheson's ideas about rights, obligations, and forms of government, Burlamaqui's *Principles of Natural and Politic Law* added the reminder that men in society are obliged "to act according to their real interests and to choose the surest and best way to attain the end they are designed for, which is happiness." Cremin points out that through "his choice of textbooks alone, quite apart from whatever commentary he introduced, Smith had advanced a generation beyond his contemporaries in New Haven and New York."[12]

Of course, Smith did introduce commentary. He was briefly jailed by the assembly for a pamphlet he published following Braddock's shocking defeat at Fort Duquesne in 1755, entitled *A Brief State of the Province of Pennsylvania*. In it, Smith faulted the assembly for refusing to pass the Militia Act and suggested that legislators should be required to swear an oath of allegiance and bear arms if necessary, a clear attack on the assembly's Quaker majority. Smith was accused by the assembly of using his lectures to indoctrinate students with his political views. When the trustees investigated in June 1756, his students testified in his defense. HUGH WILLIAMSON and three classmates signed a statement identifying themselves as "such of the students of the Senior Philosophy Class as are now in town." They denied that Smith had discussed Pennsylvania politics in class and maintained that during "the whole course of Ethics, Government, and Commerce, he never advanced any other principles than what were warranted by our standard authors, Grotius, Puffendorf, Locke, and Hutcheson." They offered their lecture notes as evidence.[13]

WILLIAMSON and his classmates had been working toward their degrees since 1754, a year before the College was authorized to award any; Smith was determined to forestall competition from King's College, which opened its doors that summer. Two of his students in Philadelphia were his former charges, Tom and Harry Martin, who had followed him from Long Island in 1753. With King's now open, Josiah Martin was proposing to call his sons back to New York. Smith wrote to trustee Richard Peters, accompanying FRANKLIN at the Albany Conference, and asked him to speak with Martin. Although Philadelphia could not yet promise degrees, he suggested that Peters urge the superiority of the education the boys were already receiving at the Academy:

> What is most useful in Logic they have already acquired. Moral Philosophy we have begun, and against the vacation in October shall have completed what we intend. Greek and Latin they continue to read at proper Hours, together with two Hours every Day at Mathematics, from October till February or March we shall be employ'd in reading some ancient Compositions critically, in applying the Rules of Rhetoric and in attempting some Imitations of the most finished Models in our own language. In Spring we shall spend 5 or 6 weeks in such experiments in natural Philosophy as we shall be able to exhibit. The rest of the Summer may be usefully spent in the Elements of civil Law, the reading of History and the study of the Ends and Uses of Society, the different Forms of Government, & c. & c. All this I hope we shall be able to give our higher Class a sketch of, several of whom, particularly Mr. Martin's sons, have capacity enough for such a course of Reading.[14]

There was no grammar school in New England with such an ambitious program; indeed, Smith's nineteenth-century biographer Charles Stillé is quite right that at the time "no such comprehensive scheme of education existed in any College in the American colonies." Josiah Martin realized as much, and his boys remained at Philadelphia even as he became a trustee of King's College. In 1755, the College of Philadelphia received its charter, and its trustees approved the course that students were already following. It was essentially the *College of Mirania* adapted to a three-year program. (The curriculum was so extensive that Henry May, in *The Enlightenment in America*, mistakenly assumes it was a four-year course.) Each year was built around three daily lectures. The first began as a course in logic and metaphysics, becoming a course in moral philosophy—what WILLIAMSON and his classmates called "the Course in Ethics, Government, and Commerce." The second lecture was the course in mathematics and natural philosophy, and the third was the traditional Latin, Greek, and rhetoric.[15]

Complementing the lectures was the parallel reading. Assigned for moral philosophy were Epictetus, Cicero's *De officiis* and *Tusculan Disputations*, Xenophon's *Memorabilia*, and Plato's *Laws*. More modern political writers assigned were Grotius, Burlamaqui, and Hutcheson. In their "Private hours" students were directed to read Seneca, Hooker's *Laws of Ecclesiastical Polity*, the political philosophers Pufendorf, Cumberland, Montesquieu, Sidney, Harrington, Locke (*The Two Treatises on Government*), and still more Hutcheson.[16]

Harvard, Yale, and William and Mary offered nothing like this in the eighteenth century; not until 1763 did King's College even begin to approach such a reading list, and it would be another five years after that before Witherspoon's assignments at Princeton surpassed it. Witherspoon, Smith, and Alison were all educated at Scottish universities, and the heart of their moral philosophy courses was Glasgow's Francis Hutcheson. Although Johnson's *Elementa* still appeared on the list of outside reading, Smith's 1754 letter had pointedly reminded Peters that at King's College, "Morality and Logic are very different from ours": Johnson was a Berkeleyan "immaterialist" and thus, Smith complained, "There is no Matter by his scheme. No ground of Moral Obliga[tion]. Life is a Dream." Smith, like Alison and Witherspoon, preferred Hutcheson's moral sense philosophy and the Scottish realism of Thomas Reid.[17]

Just how closely the Philadelphia lectures followed Hutcheson's *Short Introduction to Moral Philosophy* can be seen in the notebooks of Jasper Yeates (1759) and Samuel Jones (1760) in the manuscript collection at the University of Pennsylvania, and of THOMAS MIFFLIN (1760) in the Library of Congress. MIFFLIN's notes may have been taken from lectures by Alison (as Douglas Sloan believes) or by Smith (who had taught the course to WILLIAMSON in 1756), but they are essentially Hutcheson. Moral philosophy, MIFFLIN writes in his notebook, "comprehends Ethics, the Rights of Man in a State of Natural Liberty, Politicks or the different Plans of Government, and Œconomicks." Hutcheson, in only slightly different words, defines moral philosophy as "ethics . . . and the Law of nature. This latter contains 1. the doctrine of private rights, or laws obtaining in Natural liberty 2. Economics, or the law and rights of the several members of a family; and Politics, showing the various plans of civil government."[18]

In his notebook, MIFFLIN (though raised as a Quaker) records the familiar Calvinist principle that the "necessity of civil power arises either from the imperfection or depravity of man," but he goes on to define the state as "a Society of Free Men, united under one Government for their common Interest," repeating later that the proper end of government is "the common Interest of the whole Body." Seventeen years before the Declaration of Independence, he and his classmates were taught that some rights were inalienable and that government must have the consent of the governed: "That Power alone is just, which is adapted to the public Good: other Powers tho' granted by the rash Deed of an ignorant People ha[ve] no Right. . . . There can be no Right to Power, except what is either founded upon or speedily obtained by the hearty consent of the Body of the People." And the student who would become one of Philadelphia's richest merchants also notes, following Hutcheson: "Power wherever lodged will never be stable unless it has large Property for its foundation. Wealth carries Force along with it & Men who have property will not be excluded from a Share of Power & Men in Power will exert it one way or other to obtain Property to support themselves."[19]

Perhaps that last note recurred to MIFFLIN's memory when, in 1787, he heard the former Philadelphia Academy and King's College student GOUVERNEUR MORRIS warn that "the Rich will strive to establish their dominion & enslave the rest. They always did. They always will. [But,] give them the second branch [i.e., the Senate], and you secure their weight for the public good. They become responsible for their conduct, and this lust for power will ever be checked by the democratic branch, and thus form a stability in your government." (This was Hutcheson's "overpoise.") Three days later MORRIS added, "Life and Liberty were generally said to be of more value than property. An accurate view of the matter would nevertheless prove that property was the main object of Society. The savage State . . . was only renounced for the sake of property which could only be secured by the restraints of regular Government." Property would be a matter of continual contention at the Convention.[20]

MIFFLIN's 1759 notes and the MORRIS speech that they anticipate incorporate three of Hutcheson's ideas on which the Framers would eventually agree: that property and power will reinforce each other; that competing interests (especially aristocracy and democracy) must be kept in check by a balance or "overpoise" of competing powers; and that government must be directed, in words MORRIS would contribute to WILSON's draft Preamble, to "establish justice, insure domestic tranquility . . . [and] promote the general welfare."

MIFFLIN graduated in 1760, in Philadelphia's third class. (After the intense push to grant the first degrees in 1757, there were no graduates in 1758). He had been a mediocre student at the Friends School, but he hit his stride in college. The lessons in citizenship of the moral philosophy course sank in over the next decade; he became one of the most radical members of the first Continental Congress, and John Adams described him in a letter to Abigail Adams as the "animating soul" of the revolutionary movement there. Questions about his conduct as the army's quartermaster general put an early end to his military career but did nothing to derail his political progress. He was elected president of Congress, was speaker of the Pennsylvania House at the time of the Convention, and would later be a popular governor. Although overshadowed at the 1787 Convention, MIFFLIN regularly backed the two vocal leaders of his Pennsylvania delegation: JAMES WILSON, who taught at the College of Philadelphia in 1765 and 1766, and GOUVERNEUR MORRIS, who entered the Academy the year after MIFFLIN's college graduation. With WILSON, MIFFLIN led the Pennsylvania effort to ratify the Constitution.[21]

The Philadelphia Academy admitted its first students in 1751. Ten years later its enrollment of eighty made it the foremost preparatory school in the middle colonies. Many of its students continued on to the College of Philadelphia, but others left for the colleges in New York and New Jersey. In 1761, GOUVERNEUR MORRIS began three years at the Academy before entering King's College; in 1766, GUNNING BEDFORD JR. began two years there preparing for Princeton.

At the end of his letter to Peters at Albany, Provost Smith had asked "to be remembered to Mr. Penn, Mr. Morris, and all your company." Mr. Penn was Governor John Penn, nephew of the proprietor, and Mr. Morris was Robert Hunter Morris, lieutenant governor of the province and older half brother of GOUVERNEUR MORRIS. GOUVERNEUR's half sister, Mary, was the wife of Thomas Lawrence, whose father (five times mayor of Philadelphia) was a founding trustee of the Academy. There was no shortage of Morris family connections in Pennsylvania, the state to which GOUVERNEUR would relocate in 1779 and which he would represent at the Federal Convention, walking four short blocks every morning from his house on High Street to the State House (now Independence Hall). It was Lawrence who enrolled his nine-year-old brother-in-law GOUVERNEUR MORRIS in the Academy in 1761, along with his own son. (The unrelated financier ROBERT MORRIS enrolled his son Thomas at the same time.)[22]

The College and Academy of Philadelphia struggled to live up to Smith's ambitions. Smith and especially Alison were respected scholars of philosophy and the classics, WILLIAMSON was a young but capable teacher of mathematics, and John Beveridge was certainly a competent classicist. But even with the Academy's large enrollment, the College was not big enough to support more than two administrator-teachers and two professors. Although larger than King's College, Philadelphia's student body was smaller than those of Harvard, Yale, or Princeton; its largest graduating class was only seventeen students, and in 1758, 1764, and 1774 there were no graduates at all. (The British occupation prevented commencements in 1778 and 1779.) It was embarrassing that in the city of FRANKLIN and Rittenhouse the College had chronic difficulty securing capable science tutors; Ebenezer Kinnersley, head of the English School, gave demonstrations of electrical apparatus at the same time he was responsible for teaching oratory; important as the two subjects both were in Smith's plan, science and public speaking remained weak links until the 1780s. Ironically, when Josiah Martin had considered sending his sons to King's, Smith had disdainfully asked, "Whom have they at New York for Mathematics or Nat. Philosophy, which are not the Dr's [Johnson's] province? . . . Where is their apparatus? Where a sufficient number of Students for public school acts & Disputations?" Latin disputations were the centerpieces of commencements almost everywhere, but in 1753 when the famed orator Samuel Davies attended student exercises at the Academy, he complained that they were "extremely languid and discovered Nothing of the Fire and Pathos of the Roman Soul." Thirteen years later things were no more energetic; JOHN DICKINSON's law clerk John MacPherson wrote to WILLIAM PATERSON that when the Philadelphia graduates "produced a Latin dispute . . . [t]his was ill done" because "the Latin was ill pronounced & there was no action, for they spoke from desks."[23]

Smith's students were actually speaking English much more than Latin. Despite FRANKLIN's conviction that the ideal of English language education had been betrayed, Smith constantly promoted exercises in English; while other college presidents orated in Latin or even Hebrew, and Harvard's president Samuel Locke actually addressed his first, uncomprehending commencement gathering in Chaldean, Smith delivered his first commencement address in English. In 1757, he wrote in the *Pennsylvania Gazette* that exercises in English at the new college "will contribute more to the forming of true Englishmen, and promoting Principles both of *public* and *private* Virtue, than Half the *Greek* and *Roman* Stage put together, chaste and instructive as it generally is." In his 1759 *Account of the College*, Smith promised that "attention to public speaking, which is begun here with the very rudiments of the mother tongue, is continued down to the end, and especially in the philosophy school [i.e., the College], where the youth frequently deliver exercises of their own composition at commencements, examinations, and other public occasions." In a footnote he added, "If Thomas Sheridan [the British elocutionist recommended by RUTLEDGE to his younger brother] knew of our school, he would see he was not entirely justified in complaining that no one taught proper pronunciation of English."[24]

The provost appreciated the importance of rhetorical ability in the vernacular for the governing class he was training. He understood what literary historian William Hedges points out: "Indeed, it was in part by the control of language, written and spoken, that lawyers, planters, and merchants sought to maintain the leadership which, in their view, rightly belonged in a republic to leaders like themselves." At the Convention in 1787, former Philadelphia students and faculty often dominated the debate, and they left their mark on the language of the Constitution. BEDFORD (Academy 1768) had to apologize for his flights of rhetoric in defense of the small states, pointing out "that some allowance ought to be made for the habits of his profession"—the law—"in which warmth was natural & sometimes necessary." The voluble WILLIAMSON (College 1757, faculty 1757–1758, 1761–1763) has been described as "at times almost too articulate" in his eagerness to express opinions and offer proposals. WILSON (faculty 1755–1756, 1773) spoke more often and at greater length than anyone except GOUVERNEUR MORRIS (Academy 1764)—who spoke the most despite being absent the entire month of June. (With those two and the irrepressible FRANKLIN leading the Pennsylvania delegation, it was inevitable that the other five members would be shut out.) MORRIS was so admired for his prose that he was chosen by the Committee of Style to write the final draft; as MADISON acknowledged in 1831, "The *finish* given to the style and arrangement of the Constitution fairly belongs to the pen of Mr. MORRIS."[25]

By 1757, however, FRANKLIN was no longer speaking to Smith. He told Collinson that Smith "has scribbled himself into universal dislike here . . . the Proprietary faction alone countenances him a little." Disapproving of Smith's deviousness and deception, FRANKLIN was not alone. Ezra Stiles came to know more than twenty college presidents; he called Smith "a contemptible drunken Character of tolerable academic general knowledge . . . haughty, irreligious & profane, avaricious and covetous, a consummate Hypocrite in Religion and Politics. I know him personally, tho' I am not a Witness to his Immoralities." Indeed, Smith made a career of initially charming those whose patronage he needed, only to alienate them later. Only two months after leaving New York for Philadelphia, he had sniffed, "Dr. Johnson only pretends to teach Logic and Moral Philosophy." He began a twenty-year contention with Alison through his unremitting efforts to build up the influence of the Anglican Church, what the Bridenbaughs call "a steady crescendo of religious animosity." In the 1750s, however, the beginnings of that animosity in the City of Brotherly Love were overshadowed by the bitter sectarian wrangling that attended the birth of King's College in New York.[26]

Ever since Pieter Minuit's legendary purchase of Manhattan from the Leni-Lenape, New York had been a city of sharp businessmen, with little interest in schools and none in higher education. The first Lewis Morris, grandfather of GOUVERNEUR, had suggested as early as 1704 that New York City offered an ideal location to plant a college, but Governor Cornbury gave Trinity Church the site that Morris had pointed out, and nothing came of his observation. The next sign of interest in a college came only after the news that the College of New Jersey was about to be chartered just across the Hudson in Newark, stimulating the assembly to sponsor a lottery in 1746 to raise funds for a New York college. But threats of a French and Indian attack on the Hudson valley, and an actual raid on Schenectady distracted attention. Only after peace was restored in 1748 did New Yorkers begin to think about spending the lottery's proceeds, nearly £3,500.[27]

Interest intensified with the publication of a 1749 essay entitled *Some Serious Thoughts on the Design of Erecting a College in the Province of New York*. The author was a young graduate of Yale College, WILLIAM LIVINGSTON. He was troubled when Trinity offered to donate the very spot that Morris had recommended in 1704, on the condition that the college be Anglican. When the assembly appointed ten trustees for the lottery funds, Livingston was the only Presbyterian chosen, along with seven Trinity vestrymen.[28]

In New York no more than a fifth of the population were communicants of the Church of England. They were outnumbered by both the Dutch Reformed and the increasingly numerous Presbyterians, who had thirty-five churches in the province by the 1750s. The Ministry Act of 1693 had promised support to all Protestant ministers, but royal governors had chosen to provide only for the six Anglican parishes; to Anglicans such as Samuel Johnson that meant that the Church of England was the established church of the province. An Anglican college in New York was a way to counter the "enthusiastical conceited notions" of the Congregationalists at Yale and the Presbyterians at the new College of New Jersey. Johnson considered Jonathan Dickinson and Aaron Burr Sr. "the most bitter Enemies of the Church," and predicted that their new college would "be a fountain of Nonsense."[29]

Prominent Anglican families in New York, including the De Lanceys, sent their children to be taught by Johnson at his home in Stratford. New York's leading intellectual, Cadwallader Colden, had been promoting Johnson's pedagogical abilities since the first lottery bill. In October 1752 the publisher of the New York *Gazette* printed an anonymous essay, "Some Thoughts on Education with Reasons for Erecting a College in this Province," calling for an Anglican college with an Anglican president and Anglican public prayers. As the essay was being discussed by gratified Anglicans and dismayed Presbyterians, a letter appeared in the New York *Mercury* on November 6, reprinted the next day in the *Gazette*. It proposed that a college be created by royal charter, that Johnson be named president, and that he also be made rector of Trinity Church so that he might "subsist honorably upon a less salary from the College." This letter was not anonymous; it was signed by William Smith, who was soon revealed to be the author of "Some Thoughts on Education."[30]

When Smith arrived from England in 1751, he carried a letter from the archbishop of Canterbury to Lt. Gov. James De Lancey, who had known the archbishop when both were students at Cambridge. At De Lancey's house he met Johnson. They discovered that both disapproved of the *Independent Whig*, Trenchard and Gordon's London magazine; Johnson told Smith that he objected to its authors' discourtesy to their conservative adversaries. But Smith and Johnson were not the only New Yorkers familiar with the *Independent Whig*. The next year, WILLIAM LIVINGSTON and three Yale classmates—William Smith Jr., William Peartree Smith (neither one related to Johnson's new friend), and John Morin Scott—began publishing their own magazine, which they chose to call the *Independent Reflector*. Smith Jr. was also a Yale friend of Johnson's son, WILLIAM SAMUEL JOHNSON, and the elder Johnson sent their first issue to *his* friend Smith. LIVINGSTON, the magazine's motive force, had Trenchard and Gordon clearly in mind as his models. The *Independent Reflector* would remain the colonies' only successful magazine until Philadelphia's *American Magazine* appeared in 1757, edited by the provost of Philadelphia College, William Smith.[31]

The *Reflector*'s writers had already criticized the city's Anglican leaders; beginning with their seventeenth installment, on March 29, 1753, they set their sights on the proposed college. LIVINGSTON began by reminding their readers that its graduates "will soon be visible throughout the whole Province. They will appear on the Bench, at the Bar, in the Pulpit, and in the Senate, and unavoidably affect our civil and religious principles." He held up New England's sectarian colleges, Harvard and his own alma mater, Yale, as examples to avoid:

Freedom of thought rarely penetrates those Mansions of systematical Learning. But to teach the established Notions and maintain certain

Hypotheses, *hic labor hoc opus est*. Every deviation from the beaten tract [*sic*] is a kind of literary Heresy; and if the Professor be given to Excommunication, can scarce escape an Anathema. Hence the dogmatical turn and impatience of Contradiction, so observable in the generality of Academies.[32]

LIVINGSTON declared to his readers, "The true use of education, is to qualify Men for the different Employments of Life . . . to infuse a Public Spirit and Love of their Country; to inspire them with the Principles of Honor and Probity, with a fervent Zeal for Liberty, and diffusive Benevolence for Mankind, and in a Word, to make them more extensively serviceable to the Commonwealth," and he reminded them that the beliefs absorbed by the college's students would have a pervasive influence, and "under the Influence of the Doctrines espoused in the Morning of Life, the Spirit of the College is transferred thro' the Colony, and tinctures the Genius and Policy of the Public Administrators from the Governor down to the Constable."[33]

On April 12, the *Reflector* came out explicitly for a nonsectarian college, chartered not by the king but by the assembly. Two weeks later, LIVINGSTON fired his final salvo, asking his readers:

Tamely will you submit without a Contest? Come then, and by Imagination's Aid penetrate into Futurity. Behold your Offspring trained in Superstition and bred to holy Bondage! Behold the Province over-run by Priest-craft, and every Office usurped by the ruling Party! . . . Let not the Seat of Literature, the Abode of the Muses, and the Nurse of Science be transformed into a Cloister of Bigots, an habitation of Superstition, a Nursery of ghostly Tyranny, a school of rabbinical Jargon![34]

For their part, the Anglicans charged that the *Reflector* meant to create "a most abject Republican Party, both in Politics and Religion"; they argued against any separation of church and state, rejected the very idea of natural rights as coming from "whimsical Noodles," and accused those who preached "the origin of Power in the People" of being deists at best and more likely atheists.[35]

The stigma of sectarianism marked King's College, but the reality may not have lived up to LIVINGSTON's fears—or William Smith's hopes. Smith had played both sides of the controversy. "Some Thoughts on Education" had criticized sectarian schools, but he had insisted on an Anglican president and Anglican public prayers. Church leaders in England were never closely involved in the college plans despite efforts to enlist their support. The church hierarchy was not really on top of colonial developments: in 1754 the confused bishop of London expressed his pleasure that Princeton had turned out to be an Anglican college, with Johnson as its president, and a few months later the archbishop of Canterbury congratulated Smith on being named president of King's.[36]

Once the inevitable decision was made to seek a royal charter for King's College, even that produced an ambiguous compromise. Joining the rector of Trinity on the governing board were ministers of the Dutch Reformed, Lutheran, and Presbyterian communities, and a representative of the Society of Friends. Of the college's forty-two governors, only Johnson, Henry Barclay, and the distant archbishop of Canterbury were Anglican clergymen, although eleven members of the Trinity vestry (half of the vestrymen) were appointed. An advertisement in the *Gazette* promised "Equal Liberty and Advantage of Education" to students "of any Religious Denomination," and unlike Oxford or Cambridge, King's would have no religious test. The only one of the lottery fund's trustees to vote against the charter was Livingston, but he nevertheless voted in favor of making Johnson president.[37]

In his 1754 *Gazette* advertisement, Johnson laid out an elaborate prospectus reflecting the academic innovations of the *College of Mirania*. But when he administered the admission test (as elsewhere, translating Cicero and Virgil from Latin and the Gospels from Greek), he found that his new students did so poorly that the freshman year was immediately recast as a remedial course in Latin, employing the same text used by young schoolboys at Boston Latin. Johnson always blamed the college's troubles on the absence of "a grammar school, without which as I so often inculcated, the college could never flourish, and for want of which only . . . its reputation suffered and mine with it."[38]

Through 1775, the final class before the Revolution, 155 students entered King's College but only 99 stayed to graduate, an average of 5.5 per year. The college's recent historian, Robert McCaughey, states that "its dropout rate was the highest among colonial colleges." (He overlooks William and Mary.) One of the reasons the median stay was less than two years was the cost: King's was easily the most expensive college in the colonies. For the first six years, half of the matriculants were sons or nephews of its Board of Governors, and King's never attracted the poorer scholarship students supported by Harvard and Princeton. (HAMILTON's tuition was paid by benefactors in St. Croix, through a fund managed by the brother of HAMILTON's new acquaintance, Hercules Mulligan.) Three out of four students grew up within thirty miles of the college, more than half in Manhattan. Five percent came from the West Indies, including HAMILTON and his close friend Edward Stevens. In 1772, tutor John Vardill responded to John Witherspoon's Princeton recruiting message to Jamaica by warning the sugar planters that since "Virtue and Vices" resulted "to a considerable degree" from one's "Birth, Status, and Companions," they should send their sons to King's College, where they would consort with the scions of the upper classes, rather than to Princeton, where they might be corrupted by the inferior morals of farmers' sons.[39]

King's College weathered a rocky beginning under Samuel Johnson. In 1759, he embarrassed the governors by fleeing to Westchester County during a smallpox outbreak, leaving all the teaching to his current tutor, Leonard Cutting, and in 1763 Johnson retired. Change was already in the air. In 1762, Robert Harpur, a Glasgow graduate, was hired to teach mathematics, and Myles Cooper arrived as professor of moral philosophy. Johnson had asked Archbishop Secker to find someone in England qualified to succeed him soon as president, and Secker chose Cooper, a young Oxford MA; like so many William and Mary teachers, he was a Queen's College man. Johnson at first feared that that the inexperienced Cooper would have trouble standing up to the governors of the college, "most of whom were for little else than but their gain and pleasures," but after stepping ashore in October 1762 and winning Johnson's approval, Cooper was sworn in as president six months later. Twenty-seven years old, Cooper was "extremely witty and entertaining," but "grave men were occasionally offended by the freedom and conviviality of his social habits." According to Thomas Jones, a New York loyalist who knew him well, "He loved good company and good company loved him"; Jones claimed that at Cooper's death "his library sold for £5 and the liquors in his cellar for £150." He was a striking change from Dr. Johnson.[40]

Ezra Stiles considered Cooper "a pretty neat classical Scholar, and of a good taste for the belles Lettres," but with "very slight Insight" into mathematics and science. Cooper's academic interests were made clear in the 1763 "Plan of Education" adopted by the governors. The new curriculum continued the necessary freshman remedial course in Latin, adding Grotius's *On the Truth of the Christian Religion*, currently read at Oxford. However, the second and third years were no longer given over to philosophy and mathematics: sophomores simply continued reading Ovid, Virgil, the Greek Testament, Cicero, Terence, and Xenophon, adding Quintilian, Epictetus, and—honoring local tradition—Johnson's *Elementa*. The only mention of science or mathematics was James Ferguson's *Lectures on Select Subjects in*

Mathematics; otherwise the instruction was evidently left to Professor Harpur. In the third year, the classics continued unabated, but there was a noteworthy addition: "Hutch. Met. and Ethics"—probably Hutcheson's *Synopsis of Metaphysics,* his *Original of Our Ideas of Beauty and Virtue,* and the *Short Introduction to Ethics.* The senior year called for still more of the classics: Juvenal's satires, history in Livy, Tacitus, Lucan, Herodotus, and Thucydides, rhetoric from Cicero, Longinus, Demosthenes, Dionysus of Halicarnassus, and Isocrates. But seniors also read Pufendorf or Grotius on the laws of nations, along with more Hutcheson. Samuel Clossy (Trinity College, Dublin) was hired to lecture on anatomy and help teach everything from Latin to natural philosophy.[41]

Hutcheson may seem out of place in such a conservative reading list, but Cooper told Jacky Custis's tutor, John Boucher, that the Plan of 1763 was "copied, in the most material parts, from Queen's College in Oxford" where he had been educated—and Hutcheson was, in fact, read there. Queen's College was not noted for intellectual vigor in the eighteenth century—it has been described as "the bored leading the bored"—but Queen's provost Joseph Smith had set disputation questions with assigned reading, and that reading included Hutcheson's *Beauty and Virtue* and his *Essay on the Passions and Affections,* along with Pufendorf on natural law. Christ Church College, C. C. PINCKNEY's alma mater, may have been more scholarly, but Queen's was the Oxford college quickest to embrace modern authors, including Newton and Hutcheson, and Cooper made Queen's the model for King's. He had come to New York still a novice professor of moral philosophy, and it was only natural that he proceeded to teach the subject as it had been taught to him.[42]

The population of New York City surged by 60 percent from 1756 to 1771, and King's students were beginning to come from the expanding commercial class, not just from the aristocratic families that had founded the college. With Cooper, Harpur, and Clossy on the faculty, King's was well stocked with professors, but enrollment numbers stagnated during Cooper's first decade; they were just beginning to grow when the college collapsed in the Revolution. John Jay graduated in June 1764, and the following month GOUVERNEUR MORRIS enrolled.[43]

Though only twelve years old when his widowed mother brought him home from Philadelphia, MORRIS was well prepared by his three years at the Academy and by reading in his grandfather's library; the first Lewis Morris had amassed a collection of more than 3,000 volumes, twice the size of John Mercer's library and estimated by Stiles to be second only to the library of Harvard College. Young GOUVERNEUR was a perceptive but unsystematic reader; his friend Egbert Benson recalled him at King's as "more distinguished for the quickness of his parts and facility of acquisition, than for industry, a passion for learning, or general scholarship." Another class-mate observed, "He is fond of his ease, does his best to procure it, and enjoys it as much as possible," and still another reported that the youth was all too familiar with the "demons of liberty and idleness."[44]

Liberty and idleness were demons with which every college administrator had to deal. As soon as Cooper became president of King's, the governors passed rules to which all students were required to subscribe: they had to promise to refrain from dice and cards, to remove their hats before authorities of the college, and to show respect for all their teachers. Cooper also worried about misbehavior off campus; to make students more conspicuous there and easier to identify, he required that every matriculant "shall procure, within fourteen days of his entrance, a proper academic habit in which he shall always appear (unless he have leave from the president or tutors) under penalty of two shillings for the first offense." The neighborhood surrounding the campus was notorious for its prostitutes; to contain his students, Cooper had a "board fence eight feet high with Nails at the top" built around the grounds. He also imported from Oxford the custom of stationing a porter at the front gate with instructions about when to let students pass. Cooper's "Black Book" recorded punishments for failing to do assignments or attend exams, for breaking windows, lying, sneaking over the fence (nails and all), playing card games, getting drunk, shooting guns, defying the president, stealing teacups, spitting in the cook's face, creating "Noise and Confusion," and skipping prayers and classes. In his sophomore year, GOUVERNEUR MORRIS and several equally sophomoric friends circulated a "scandalous report . . . virulently attacking the Moral Character" of Robert Harpur, the Scottish professor of mathematics. It included an obscene cartoon (drawn by Vardill, the future tutor) and contained "the most indecent language, repeatedly." The thirteen-year-old MORRIS was admonished by Cooper in front of the student body; at any other college he might have been expelled, despite his family's status.[45]

Instead, MORRIS put his indiscretions behind him (for the time being) and at the 1768 commencement he delivered an address "on the theme of Wit and Beauty." The speech was itself witty, but it also revealed its author's attention to the moral philosophers read at King's. MORRIS alluded to the social contract theories he had encountered in Grotius and Pufendorf and drew on the ideas of Hutcheson's *Beauty and Virtue*: "Philosophers who find themselves already living in society say that mankind first entered into it from a sense of their mutual wants . . . [but] the passions of barbarians must have had too great an influence on their understandings to commence this arduous task. . . . Reason unassisted by Beauty would never have smoothed away ferocity." Three years later—still a teenager—MORRIS was back to deliver an MA oration, "On Love."[46]

A year after MORRIS received his MA, ALEXANDER HAMILTON entered the Elizabethtown Academy to prepare for admission to the College of New Jersey. He was living at LIVINGSTON's Liberty Hall estate in Elizabethtown, and LIVINGSTON was no doubt chagrined when his fellow Princeton trustees turned down HAMILTON's 1773 application for special status and a waiver of the recently adopted rules of regular progress to graduation. There is no record of what the *Independent Reflector* essayist thought when HAMILTON then turned to King's College. When he entered is unclear; Robert Troup claimed that he met HAMILTON at the college in 1773, and HAMILTON's friend Hercules Mulligan remembered his first enrolling as a sophomore in 1775, but HAMILTON's name is included in Cooper's list of seventeen matriculants for 1774, and on September 20, 1774, Harpur noted in his accounts that HAMILTON "entered with me this day to study mathematics at three pounds four shillings a quarter." Apparently, King's was willing to make the concessions that Princeton would not; according to what Robert McCaughey calls "the not-always-reliable memory" of Troup, "When [HAMILTON] entered college he did it as a private student and not by annexing himself to a particular class. The professors instructed him in their leisure hours. He was studious and made rapid progress in the languages and every other branch of learning to which he applied himself." King's, always underenrolled, was happy to take a private student, and HAMILTON had the freedom to study what he pleased, when he pleased. According to Troup (who graduated in 1774 but stayed in New York to read law with Jay), HAMILTON began by auditing Clossy's lectures on anatomy; HAMILTON's biographers assume that Cooper privately tutored him in classics, theology, and moral philosophy, but the previous spring Cooper had declined to do that for WASHINGTON's stepson Jacky Custis, telling Boucher, "The young Gentleman's Guardian may rely on every Thing in my Power for his Ward's Emolument: but as to my turning private Tutor as it were—it seems to me so inconsistent with my Office (whatever others in my Situation may think fit) that I must beg to be excused." Custis was the stepson of a prominent Virginia Anglican; it seems unlikely that Cooper would make an exception a year later for a Presbyterian of no family from the Indies, especially one associated with LIVINGSTON, the college's "whipping post."[47]

An attraction for HAMILTON was the presence of his boyhood friend from St. Croix, Edward Stevens. After the death of HAMILTON's mother, he had been taken in by Edward's father; people remarked on how much the two boys looked alike, to the extent that there were persistent rumors that Thomas Stevens was HAMILTON's actual father. In HAMILTON's first months and Stevens's last, they formed an informal club with Troup and three others to practice debating, speaking, and writing, a private version of the American Whig Society at Princeton. Hercules Mulligan, another unreliable source, said that HAMILTON had initially "preferred Princeton to King's College because it was more republican." Like many of Mulligan's reminiscences, this one is open to doubt. Troup maintained that HAMILTON was "originally a Monarchist," and HAMILTON's lengthy speech at the Federal Convention confirms Troup's statement that "he was versed in the history of England and well-acquainted with the Principles of the English constitution, which he admired." HAMILTON was no democrat, but he would soon reveal that he was no loyalist either.[48]

HAMILTON's tutor Vardill, who would be a successful British spy during the Revolution, condemned Princeton's Witherspoon and his students for having "very often entered deeply into the Party Politics and Contentions of England." At King's College, Vardill declared, students were not taught "to pace in the political Trammels, of any Sect or Party." But the revolutionary spirit was spreading in New York. The unrest caught Myles Cooper by surprise. Cooper had hoped to obtain a new royal charter to convert King's into an American university, modeled on Oxford, that would administer all the existing colonial colleges except William and Mary and "diffuse a spirit of Loyalty . . . thro' His Majesty's American Dominions." In a futile effort to achieve this dream he spent much of 1771 and 1772 in England. When he returned, he found the college atmosphere changed.[49]

More than 70 percent of King's College's graduates were loyalists; of the twenty-five graduates who took up arms in the Revolutionary War, twenty-one did so on the side of the Crown, and by 1790, 20 percent of all living alumni resided in Canada, England, or the West Indies. But in the 1770s much of the student body was caught up in the incipient revolution, and the mood at King's was probably not unlike that at Columbia in the late 1960s. Respect for the president, always tenuous after Cooper took over, evaporated. Early in the 1773 term, a student rose from his seat during recitations to challenge President Cooper to a duel with pistols. The next year Cooper, showing more complacency than discretion, published *A Friendly Address to All Reasonable Americans on the Subject of our Political Confusions*, asserting that "the subjects of Great Britain are the happiest people on Earth," and of all those subjects, "those who reside in the American Colonies have been, and were they sensible of their own advantages, might still be, by far the happiest." In the wake of the Boston Tea Party he described the people of Boston as "a crooked and perverse generation" and predicted, with evident sincerity, that "it is morally certain that, in the day of trial, a large majority of Americans will heartily unite with the King's troops, in reducing America to Order." Cooper's authorship of the *Friendly Address* has been questioned, but there is no doubt that an anonymous reply to this and similar pamphlets came from the pen of his student, ALEXANDER HAMILTON.[50]

A *Friendly Address* had been joined by Samuel Seabury's *Free Thoughts on the Proceedings of the Continental Congress*, published under the pseudonym of "A Westchester Farmer"; many New Yorkers believed that both came from Cooper's hand. The month after *Free Thoughts* appeared, young HAMILTON (writing as "A Friend of America") published *A Full Vindication of the Measures of Congress* (December 16, 1774). "The Westchester Farmer" replied with a condescending *View of the Controversy*, and in February 1775 HAMILTON issued a scathing rebuttal, *The Farmer Refuted*. Cooper refused to believe that these incendiary essays were the work of one of his students, but he had little time left to worry about attributions. In April a public letter warned Cooper and four other loyalists that "the injury you have done to your country cannot admit reparation. Fly for your lives or anticipate your doom." Cooper prudently chose flight and took refuge on a British warship in New York harbor. He had just worked up the nerve to return to his office when, on May 10, 1775, a mob broke through the college gate, from which the porter had fled. Cooper barely escaped being tarred and feathered by exiting through a rear window and repairing to HMS *Kingfisher*.[51]

By April 1776, the New York Committee of Public Safety noted that few if any students remained, and the college building was taken over for use as a barracks. The college then became a hospital, with the scientific apparatus and library safely stored at City Hall. When the British army occupied the city, they too used the college as a barracks. By then HAMILTON had departed with an artillery battery, beginning a military trajectory that would introduce him to GEORGE WASHINGTON, raise him in rank to lieutenant colonel by the age of twenty-five, and launch his spectacular though brief political career. But what did he actually learn while at King's, and what effect did that education have?[52]

For GOUVERNEUR MORRIS, four years at King's had meant a steady diet of Greek and Roman poets, dramatists, historians, and orators, capped with the moral philosophy of Grotius, Pufendorf, and Hutcheson; MORRIS passed the examination for the Bachelor of Arts and returned in three years to give his MA oration. HAMILTON may have begun attending Clossy's medical lectures in the fall of 1773, and he began paying Harpur for mathematics instruction in 1774, but by the spring of 1775 the former monarchist was a full-time revolutionary, and the college was ceasing to function. HAMILTON was an idiosyncratic student for perhaps a year and a half, following his own direction.

Cooper certainly did not lead HAMILTON through the major authors on political theory as the Revolution was unfolding. In a sermon delivered after his escape to England, the president-in-exile condemned those whose minds were "filled with the ideas of Original Compacts which never existed" or who believed the authority of government "derived solely from the people" instead of being "ordained of God." There is no reason to think that in 1774 or 1775 he would have hinted to HAMILTON anything other than what he asserted in that 1776 sermon: "Health of a State requires a regular and due subordination of the Members to a governing power. . . . Let every Man then be contented with his Station, and faithfully discharge its attendant duties . . . [and not] set up their pretended Natural Rights in Opposition to the positive Laws of the State." If HAMILTON received any political indoctrination in college, that was its message. Once his formal instruction ceased, he is unlikely to have begun, as Ron Chernow imagines, "combing the superb law library at King's, steeping himself in the works of Sir William Blackstone and Sir Edward Coke." The college library was not notable for any legal holdings; it could have owned books by Coke or Blackstone, but there is no evidence that it did or that HAMILTON was yet reading them. King's did not offer legal instruction—no colonial college did. HAMILTON's crash course in law did not occur until 1782 (and Columbia's first law professor was not appointed for another decade after that). His two celebrated political essays of 1774–1775 cited Locke, Montesquieu, Hobbes, and Hume; as treasury secretary he replied to a question from WASHINGTON by citing Barbeyrac, Grotius, and Pufendorf, adding that he considered Emmerich de Vattel "the most accurate and approved of the writers on the law of nations." But were those citations signs of real familiarity, or were they simply hunted up to lend weight to arguments that were currently in the air? HAMILTON clearly had texts before him at the moment, from which he quoted, one after another.[53]

WILLIAM PIERCE, whose sketches of his fellow Framers so often betray a sense of disillusionment, was impressed by HAMILTON's learning: "He enquires into every part of his subject with the searchings of phylosophy, and when he comes forward he comes highly charged with interesting matter, there is no skimming over the surface of a subject with him, he must sink to the bottom to see what foundation it rests on." Douglass Adair quotes

PIERCE in his Yale dissertation, "The Intellectual Origins of Jeffersonian Democracy," and adds, "This thoroughness so commendable in HAMILTON is fortified by his wealth of historic examples . . . and the illustrations from Aristotle, Cicero, Montesquieu and Neckar in which HAMILTON's speech [on June 18 at the Convention] abounds bear out PIERCE's expectations." But in the same dissertation, Adair riffs on Othello's having "loved not wisely but too well": "HAMILTON had read his classical authors widely, but not too well." And within a year Adair decided that HAMILTON "was not scholarly in his approach to politics; his use of history was that of a propagandist citing examples from the past in order to make a debater's point rather than to establish historical truth. . . . HAMILTON's research [for the *Federalist*] consisted of superficially extracted bits of a speech by Demosthenes and a hasty reading of Plutarch."[54]

The language of Chernow's praise for HAMILTON's education inadvertently seconds Adair's judgment: "After King's he could rattle off classical allusions and . . . draw on a stock of lore about Greek and Roman antiquity." But rattling off allusions (as PIERCE himself loved to do in his letters) is no assurance that there is any depth of familiarity or understanding. In his introduction to Adair's posthumously published *Intellectual Origins*, Mark Yellin observes that HAMILTON somehow "regarded Hume as the most important of political thinkers" at the same time that he "insist[ed] on defending a notion of Lockean natural rights. This is significant because Hume's arguments undercut Locke's notion of the social contract and did not give much credence to the notion of abstract political rights." GOUVERNEUR MORRIS hinted at HAMILTON's habit of building his intellectual castles on shallow foundations. He presumed that HAMILTON had at some point come across Polybius's postulated progression that leads inexorably from democracy to tyranny. In an 1811 letter, MORRIS said of his late friend, "General HAMILTON hated republican government because he confounded it with democratic government, and he detested the latter because he believed it must end in despotism. . . . In short, his study of ancient history impressed on his mind a conviction that democracy ending in tyranny is, while it lasts, a cruel and oppressive domination. One marked trait of the General's character was the pertinacious adherence to opinions he had once formed"—exemplifying LIVINGSTON's belief that "after we arrive at Years of Maturity, instead of entering upon the difficult and disagreeable Work of examining the Principles we have formerly entertained, we rather exert ourselves in searching for Arguments to maintain and support them."[55]

HAMILTON certainly may have ingested a number of classical historians or even modern political theorists in a matter of months at King's, but he may not have digested them. What he and MORRIS, along with other King's students, seem to have taken to heart was "the hierarchic and antidemocratic side of the elitist political thinking" that David Humphrey considers "a matter of unusually intense conviction for Samuel Johnson, Myles Cooper, and their Anglican associates at King's College." They might have been so inclined without Cooper's reinforcement, but Jay, MORRIS, and HAMILTON all advocated what Gordon Wood calls "a hierarchical society of different gradations and a unitary authority to which deference from the lower level should be paid"—very much Myles Cooper's view in 1776.[56]

MORRIS and HAMILTON were the most frankly aristocratic of the Framers in their political views, surpassing PIERCE BUTLER and WILLIAM HOUSTOUN, whose fathers were baronets. Both admitted that they thought constitutional monarchy the ideal form of government, albeit one that would never be accepted by Americans. But their deep distrust of unchecked democracy was shared to lesser degrees by most of the Framers; that was what separated them from the Clintonians of New York, the Pennsylvania "Constitutionalists," the Virginia followers of Patrick Henry, or the North Carolina heirs of the Regulators, by whom (again in Wood's words) "every accumulation of political power, however tiny and piecemeal, was seen as frighteningly tyrannical, viewed as some sinister plot to upset the delicately maintained relationship of power and esteem." Such a view would be reason enough for the Anti-Federalists to attack the Constitution. The essays HAMILTON wrote in its defense reveal at times the antidemocratic attitude he acquired or strengthened at King's, as in *Federalist*, no. 9, where he says he cannot "read the history of the petty republics of Greece and Italy without feeling something of horror and disgust at the distortions with which they were continually agitated, and at the rapid succession of revolutions by which they were kept in perpetual vibration between extremes of tyranny and anarchy"—the fixation to which MORRIS referred in 1811. A dozen years out of college he still agreed with his former tutor Vardill, who said, "of all Tyranny I most dread that of the Multitude."[57]

After a decade-long hiatus, King's College was revived in 1787 as Columbia College, under a new charter from the state of New York. The trustees chose Samuel Johnson's son, WILLIAM SAMUEL JOHNSON, to be its president; he was on his way to the Philadelphia Convention when he got the news. GOUVERNEUR MORRIS and RUFUS KING (who moved to New York immediately after the Convention) served as Columbia trustees into the nineteenth century. As late as 1810 KING wrote to MORRIS about an issue that would not go away: whether the early gift of the campus by Trinity Church still meant that the college president must be Episcopalian. Many things had changed since the days of the *Independent Reflector*, but not everything. Meanwhile, for more than half a century, the rival college across the Hudson in New Jersey had been exerting a profound influence on the new nation.[58]

12

Princeton in the Nation's Service

The College of New Jersey

GUNNING BEDFORD JR., WILLIAM RICHARDSON DAVIE, JONATHAN
DAYTON, OLIVER ELLSWORTH, WILLIAM CHURCHILL HOUSTON,
JAMES MADISON, ALEXANDER MARTIN, LUTHER MARTIN,
WILLIAM PATERSON

*No College has turned out better Scholars, or more estimable Characters,
than Nassau.*

GEORGE WASHINGTON to George Washington Parke Custis, July 23,
1797

In May 1787, a convention meeting in Philadelphia drew up a constitution that created a federal system, based on proportional representation in a national legislature, with a single chief executive and
a limited government deriving its authority from the people. This
was not the Constitution of the United States—that would require
another fifteen weeks of contentious debate—but the Constitution
of the Presbyterian Church in the United States. The author of its
introduction, chosen to be the chief executive ("moderator") of
the Presbyterians, was John Witherspoon, president of the College
of New Jersey. He would surely have been a delegate to the Federal
Convention in 1787 if he hadn't been committed a year in advance
to the Presbyterians' convention, meeting only blocks away; he arrived in Philadelphia on May 18, and New Jersey's Framers began
arriving on May 25.

Witherspoon's influence extended far beyond the academic
world; his friend Ezra Stiles considered him a "very learned divine"
but thought he was too much engaged in politics. In the Continental Congress, Witherspoon voted for independence and signed the

Declaration. Already in 1776 he was concerned about the need for a "lasting confederacy," and in 1778 he signed the Articles of Confederation. It is a measure of the confidence Congress had in Witherspoon that in 1781 he was chosen to draft the instructions to the American peace commissioners in Paris: FRANKLIN, Adams, Jefferson, and Henry Laurens.[1]

In 1786, MADISON stopped on his way from New York to the Annapolis Convention to confer with "the old doctor." Other Framers who were not former students also sought his advice. In 1784, WASHINGTON wrote one of his longest personal letters to Witherspoon, discussing the settlement of western lands; he too stopped to see him in Princeton, on his 1789 journey from Virginia to his inauguration. Historian Fred J. Hood finds an "amazing similarity" between Witherspoon's Lectures on Moral Philosophy and HAMILTON's draft of WASHINGTON's Farewell Address, enough to make Witherspoon's influence "immediately apparent" to Hood. (In 1796, WASHINGTON had given HAMILTON MADISON's earlier draft of such an address to work from.) There is no evidence that HAMILTON ever saw a copy of Witherspoon's lectures, which were not yet in print, but Witherspoon had published An Essay on Money as a Medium of Commerce, which led HAMILTON to write to him in October 1789 seeking suggestions for "a proper provision for the public Debt" and "public Credit." The editors of HAMILTON's Papers note that his first and second Treasury Reports of 1790 contain ideas that "closely resemble the ideas advanced by John Witherspoon in his letter to the Secretary of the Treasury."[2]

One in six of the Framers was a graduate of the New Jersey college, already better known from its location simply as Princeton or, from its imposing main building, as Nassau Hall. At the school's sesquicentennial in 1896, when the name was formally changed to Princeton University, Woodrow Wilson acknowledged that "[it] would be absurd to pretend that we can distinguish Princeton's touch and method in the Revolution. . . . [But Princeton] outranked her elder rivals in the roll call of the Constitutional Convention, and seemed for a little, a seminary of statesmen rather than a quiet seat of academic learning." Witherspoon, president of the college from 1768 until 1794, is a large part of the reason, though by no means all of it.[3]

MADISON (author of the Virginia Plan) studied under Witherspoon, as did BEDFORD, DAVIE, and DAYTON. PATERSON (author of the competing New Jersey Plan) and ELLSWORTH (manager of the Great Compromise between those plans) graduated before his arrival, as did ALEXANDER MARTIN, the unrelated LUTHER MARTIN, and WILLIAM CHURCHILL HOUSTON, who taught under Witherspoon and served with him in Congress. These Framers and their Princeton classmates were a more denominationally, economically, and geographically diverse group than the graduates of other colleges. PATERSON was born in Ireland and DAVIE in England, both coming to America in early childhood. MADISON was a Virginia planter's son; DAVIE and HOUSTON were raised on modest North Carolina farms. BEDFORD was a city boy, son of a Philadelphia carpenter, and both MARTINS were sons of New Jersey farmers. The fathers of PATERSON and DAYTON were merchants in New Jersey, and ELLSWORTH was the son of a Connecticut farmer and grandson of a tavern keeper. Such backgrounds were not unusual at Princeton. Between 1769 and 1775 more than a third of the students were farmers' sons, one in six was a merchant's son, and only one in eight had a father identified as a "gentleman." At a time when virtually all William and Mary students were Virginians, when 90 percent of Harvard's students came from Massachusetts and more than 80 percent of Yale's were from Connecticut, Princeton's student body came from up and down the Atlantic Seaboard and from the West Indies.[4]

Before Witherspoon, half of the graduates became clergymen; lawyers accounted for forty-nine graduates and physicians nearly as many. Among Witherspoon's students, lawyers outnumbered ministers. The nine Princeton Framers represented Connecticut, New Jersey, Delaware, Maryland, Virginia, and North Carolina at the Convention; all except MADISON were lawyers, but HOUSTON had just left a career as a teacher, DAVIE owned plantations in the Carolinas, and DAYTON was embarking on a lifetime of land speculation. Princeton graduates were especially likely to be politically active: the two classes of 1771 and 1772 alone, with a combined thirty-three graduates, produced a president (MADISON), a vice president (Burr), a US attorney general (William Bradford), a secretary of state (MADISON again), and three members of Congress. This was not just the influence of Witherspoon: the five classes immediately before he arrived in 1768 (a total of eighty-seven graduates) yielded nine members of Congress from eight states, two justices of the US Supreme Court (PATERSON and ELLSWORTH), and judges of the supreme courts of five states. These numbers are all the more remarkable given that Princeton was barely half the size of Harvard or Yale. During the 1760s, Harvard and Yale typically graduated between thirty and forty-five students each year, Princeton fifteen to twenty. MADISON and BEDFORD were two of only eleven members of the class of 1771.[5]

Nearly half of the original trustees came from other colonies than New Jersey—a sharp contrast to the parochial makeup of the Visitors of William and Mary (all Virginians), the Harvard Overseers (all from Massachusetts), and the Trustees of Yale (all from Connecticut). Moreover, they had a breadth of vision: "Though our great Intention was to erect a seminary for educating Ministers of the Gospel, yet we hope it will be useful in other learned professions—Ornaments of the State as Well as the Church. Therefore we propose to make the plan of Education as extensive as our Circumstances will permit." When Witherspoon was offered the presidency in 1766, he was told that his students came from all the American colonies, including Canada and the West Indies.[6]

The unusually national political outlook that Princeton adopted was an intensely patriotic one. As the Revolution began, the presidents of King's College, William and Mary, and the College of Philadelphia fled or were removed as declared or suspected loyalists, but the president of Princeton was sent to the Continental Congress. Of 457 living graduates in 1776, more than one-third saw active military service in the Continental Army, and more than 130 held political office in revolutionary governments. Barely 2 percent of alumni were loyalists, in contrast to 16 percent of Harvard graduates and more than 20 percent of King's College graduates. In his study of colleges in the revolutionary era, David Robson simply states, "Princeton was the premier Patriot College."[7]

The college's first president, Jonathan Dickinson, lived just long enough to launch the first class of the College of New Jersey in his Elizabethtown parsonage, and in 1748 the school moved into Aaron Burr's home in Newark. With money scarce for the infant college—the legislature offered no state support—Burr served the first three years without salary. The college had a single tutor, a handful of students, no library or campus, and no endowment. Ten years later, at Burr's death, there were three tutors, seventy students, the largest academic building in North America, and 1,200 volumes in the library. Stiles described Burr as "a good classical scholar in the 3 learned tongues . . . well studied in Logic, Rhetoric, Natural and Moral Philosophy, the Belles Lettres, History, Divinity, and Politics. He was an excellent Divine and Preacher pious and agreeable, facetious and sociable; the eminent Christian & every way the worthy man."[8]

Dickinson and Burr based their instruction at first on the curriculum they had followed as students at Yale, gradually modified by the innovations of the Scottish universities and influenced to some degree by the dissenting academies of England. (Burr corresponded with Philip Doddridge, the principal of Northampton Academy.) As early as 1752 the college declared that it employed a Socratic method of free dialogue and discussion between professor and students—the method Hutcheson had pioneered at

Glasgow—and boasted that no teacher resorted to merely reading lectures or dogmatic discourses. The first admission requirements, however, were completely conventional: to "Render Virgil and Tully's [Cicero's] orations in English and to turn English into true & grammatical Latin & be so well acquainted with the Greek as to render any part of the Four Evangelists in that language into Latin or English &"—since applicants might know the Gospels by heart—"to give the grammatical construction of the words." In 1760, "vulgar arithmetic" was added as a requirement.[9]

In 1753, Gilbert Tennent and Samuel Davies toured England, Scotland, and Ireland to raise funds for the college; the trustees had decided to move to the town of Princeton, midway between Philadelphia and New York, and to construct a college hall there that would be the largest stone building in the colonies. Governor Jonathan Belcher had donated his 474-volume library (including Locke's *Two Treatises*, *Cato's Letters*, and Sidney's *Discourse on Government*); when the trustees asked permission to name the building for him, the governor demurred, requesting "the favor of your naming the present building Nassau Hall to honor the glorious King William III, who was a branch of the illustrious house of Nassau." Dormitory rooms, classrooms, library, offices, and assembly hall were all contained in a three-story building that measured 176 by 54 feet.[10]

In Princeton the students (who now included ALEXANDER MARTIN) were forbidden to "frequent taverns" or "keep company with persons of known scandalous lives" or play "cards or dice or any other unlawful game." All were required to room and take meals in Nassau Hall unless they had a doctor's excuse. The average age at graduation was twenty-one but ranged from fourteen to forty-seven. The youngest students were children of wealthy or better-educated parents who started school early, such as Aaron Burr Jr. and James Witherspoon, who graduated at fifteen and fourteen, respectively. The oldest students were usually candidates for the ministry who had found their calling late and had to take the time to learn "the languages" before matriculating; some were from poorer families and had to work first to raise tuition money. Two of ROGER SHERMAN's younger brothers, Nathaniel and Josiah, were at the college when MARTIN enrolled; both became ministers in Connecticut. A classmate of Josiah Sherman was Hugh Knox, recently arrived from Ireland.[11]

Burr and his successors never ranked students by social standing, the practice at Harvard and Yale. Biographer John O'Connor falls into the cliché that William Paterson must have felt out of place among classmates from "cosmopolitan Philadelphia or the sophisticated plantation society of the Old Dominion" when he "mixed with lads from wealthy colonial families" at Nassau Hall, but Princeton offered the least expensive tuition in the colonies, and "wealthy colonial families" were less represented there than at other colleges. Even so, not all of ALEXANDER MARTIN's classmates were headed for careers as teachers or clergymen. One year behind him was Stephen Sayre, who went to England after graduation, became the lover of a glamorous Drury Lane actress, and was elected high sheriff of London. Sayre befriended the notorious radical John Wilkes, and his involvement in politics led to imprisonment in the Tower of London when he was falsely accused of plotting to kidnap King George III. He was cleared, but he remained a radical—and a rake; when the Revolutionary War began, he traveled to St. Petersburg in a failed attempt to seduce Catherine the Great and bring Russia into the war on the American side.[12]

President Burr died in 1758 of a fever; he was forty-one. Esther Burr, only twenty-six, soon followed her husband. Esther's father, Jonathan Edwards, was chosen to succeed his son-in-law as president. Installed in February, he died in March. The smallpox outbreak that had driven Samuel Johnson from Manhattan had spread to New Jersey, and Edwards, wishing to set a good example for the anxious public, had himself inoculated. The process, known as variolation, was intended to confer immunity by giving a mild infection; Edwards's good intentions backfired, and the inoculation proved fatal. The dismayed trustees turned first to Samuel Finley, who declined, and then to Samuel Davies. They were unaware that the Virginia evangelist was already ill with tuberculosis and would die within two years.

Davies's tenure was brief, but southerners were drawn to Princeton by his reputation in their region. Their numbers increased significantly in the 1760s and 1770s; among them were HOUSTON, MADISON, and DAVIE. Although Davies evangelized Virginia, he had been born in Delaware in 1723 and educated at Samuel Blair's Fagg's Manor academy in Pennsylvania. He quickly became famous for his oratory; so renowned a public speaker as Patrick Henry said that he was "first taught what an orator should be" by listening to Davies preach. When calling for military volunteers in Virginia in 1758, Davies acknowledged both classical and divine inspiration for his eloquence: "Oh for the all-pervading force of Demosthenes' oratory—but I recall my wish, that I may convert it—oh for the influence of the Lord of armies, the God of battles, the author of true courage!"[13]

Oratory and patriotic public service were understood by Davies to be closely linked essentials of education. In 1753, he had been disappointed by lifeless student orations at the Academy of Philadelphia. This lack of energy and vitality he considered "one great Defect of modern Oratory; a Defect few seem sensible of, or labor to correct." As president of Princeton he would indeed labor to correct it. Davies assigned Cicero, Demosthenes, and Livy, and expected students to learn their orations by heart and recite them with conviction. Sunday afternoons, following church services, often featured original student orations, delivered before audiences of students and townspeople. Presidents Finley and Witherspoon continued his emphasis on rhetoric, both oral and written.[14]

It was an eighteenth-century commonplace that oratory was the *sine qua non* of political leadership, and Davies taught his students that politics was their duty. In 1760, he delivered a widely reprinted address to the graduating class: "Whatever, I say, be your Place, permit me my dear Youth to inculcate upon you this important instruction, IMBIBE AND CHERISH A PUBLIC SPIRIT. Serve your Generation. Live not for yourselves, but the Publick. Be the Servants of the Church; the Servants of your Country; the Servants of all." He invoked the example of King David, who rose from humble origins to deliver his oppressed people. What he did for his generation, Princeton students should do for theirs; whether at "the sacred Desk," at "the Bar," or in "the chamber of Affliction," their duty was to exert themselves strenuously to improve society.[15]

Davies's theme made a long-lasting impression. In 1896, Woodrow Wilson memorably adopted it as "Princeton in the nation's service," the college's unofficial motto through the twentieth century. But in 1760, Davies had less than six months to live; patriotism for him still meant loyalty to the king, and he did not survive to see the acts of Parliament that would drive the colonies to independence. Just five commencements later his son joined Jonathan Edwards Jr. on the platform, wearing clothes of American manufacture to protest against the Stamp Act. When the trustees met in June 1766, a committee was directed to prepare an address urging the king to repeal the Stamp Act, and at that fall's commencement, when WILLIAM PATERSON delivered a master's degree oration, "On Patriotism," the implications of that term were changing. The review of PATERSON's address in the New York *Gazette* would have pleased Davies: "Elegance in Composition and Grace and Force of Action were equally conspicuous."[16]

PATERSON's family had left Ireland when he was young; he grew up in the town of Princeton, watching the construction of Nassau Hall from his home barely a hundred yards away. He walked across the street to the grammar school in 1757 and matriculated at the college in 1759, Davies's first year as president. His diploma, four years later, was signed by President Samuel Finley. PATERSON's father had found success as a storekeeper (MADISON had an account with him during his student years), and the family had achieved a level of prosperity marked by the ownership of three household slaves. PATERSON was not yet fourteen when he entered the freshman class, and he was small for his age; his two best friends, LUTHER MARTIN and John MacPherson, were both three years behind him. PATERSON regularly surprised those who did not know him; years later, PIERCE acknowledged that PATERSON was "low in stature," but his looks were deceiving: "Mr. PAT-TERSON is one of those kind of Men whose powers break in upon you, and create wonder and astonishment. He is a Man of great modesty, with looks that bespeak talents of no great extent,—but he is a Classic, a Lawyer, and an Orator;—and of a disposition so favorable to his advancement that every one seemed ready to exalt him with their praises."[17]

In a commonplace book that runs to nearly 300 manuscript pages, PAT-ERSON recorded quotations familiar to many of the Framers—from Pope, Swift, Milton, Shakespeare, Rollin's *Ancient History*, *The Spectator*, and *The Tattler*—but also passages from Voltaire's *Universal History*, Montesquieu's *Persian Letters*, and Lord Kames's *Elements of Criticism*, which were not often encountered at Harvard, Yale, or William and Mary. He analyzes the characters of Solon, Caesar, Mark Antony, and Cicero ("possessed of real virtue, together with vast abilities, and very shining accomplishments") and also more recent historical figures, such as Martin Luther, Charles XII of Sweden, Louis XIV, and Marshall Turenne. After a fifty-page precis of English history (based on Smollett and Rapin), he offers an appreciation of Chinese culture, concluding: "What the Chinese seem to understand best, and to have most improved, is Morality and the laws. The Respect which children bear their parents is the foundation of the Chinese government."[18]

PATERSON helped found one of Princeton's first social clubs. Most of his classmates were headed for careers in the church (he and Tapping Reeve would be the only lawyers), but that didn't stop the Well Meaning Club and its rival, the Plain Dealing Club, from abusing one another in publicly declaimed burlesques that would lead to the clubs' suppression by the trustees in 1768. They reorganized in 1769, with PATERSON's help, as the Cliosophic and American Whig Societies, America's oldest student debating clubs. OL-IVER ELLSWORTH was also, like his classmate LUTHER MARTIN, a member of the Well Meaning Club. ELLSWORTH had come from Yale in 1764, fed up with the obsessive discipline of Thomas Clap. The student life at Princeton must have been a breath of fresh air for him.[19]

Like PATERSON, LUTHER MARTIN seems not to have remained close to any-one in his own graduating class; his classmate ELLSWORTH would savagely attack him during the debate over ratification. But he and the older PATER-SON hit it off. "At Princeton I early formed an acquaintance with the honor-able WILLIAM PATTERSON, of New Brunswick," he recalled. "It was there we

first formed for each other that friendship and esteem which have continued unimpaired to the present time [1801]." Indeed, MARTIN appears to have
found his closest friends in the classes ahead of him: "Among those with
whom I formed an acquaintance while at college, and who were not in the
number of my classmates I can name . . . Doctor Ramsay of South Carolina." Ramsay graduated a year ahead of Martin and then threw himself
into teaching as the master of the Onancock Grammar School on Virginia's eastern shore, ordering a long and diverse list of books for his students
from the Philadelphia bookstore of William Bradford's (1772) family. When
he left to study medicine with Rush, he handed the school over to his friend
LUTHER MARTIN.[20]

MARTIN soon left teaching for a career in the law, and in 1778 he was appointed attorney general of Maryland. His patron was the redoubtable
Samuel Chase, a recent signer of the Declaration; when the Anti-Federalist
Chase and his ally William Paca declined appointments to the Federal Convention, Maryland sent MARTIN and MERCER in their places. Once reconciled
to the Constitution, Chase was appointed to the US Supreme Court by
WASHINGTON, taking the seat vacated by JOHN BLAIR JR. When Jeffersonians
impeached him in 1805, MARTIN led his successful defense before the Senate,
as he would successfully defend his fellow Cliosophian, Aaron Burr, in his
treason trial two years later. Jefferson called him the "Federalist bulldog."

PATERSON, ELLSWORTH, and MARTIN were all students under Samuel Finley, Princeton's fifth president. Finley had emigrated from County Armagh
in 1734, a year before Francis Alison and fourteen years before his neighbors
across Lough Neagh, the Patersons; like Alison, Finley had been preparing
for the ministry in Ireland. As one of the most prominent evangelical ministers, Finley was an obvious choice to be a trustee of the new College of New
Jersey. When Edwards died suddenly in 1759, Finley declined the college presidency in favor of Davies. But with Davies's death in 1761, he had no choice but
to accept the office. Davies had recently announced that the college's mission
was to fill young minds "with useful knowledge and virtue, whereby the rude
and ignorant are civilized and rendered humane persons . . . qualified to sus-
tain with honor the offices they may be invested with, for the public service
and reverence of the deity." Finley continued Davies's emphasis on public
service, but he also went further with the modernization of instruction. In
a study of Princeton's eighteenth-century curriculum, Francis L. Broderick
notes that Finley's students "found numerous additions to the earlier curriculum, although nothing seems to have been dropped to compensate for
the additional work." On top of Burr's curriculum (Xenophon, Cicero, logic,
rhetoric, natural and moral philosophy) and the modern authors introduced

by Davies (Shakespeare, Milton, Swift, Addison), students were now reading history and "chronology." On weeknights the lower classes declaimed passages from ancients and moderns "as best adopted to display the passions and exemplify the graces of utterance and gesture," and juniors and seniors took part in both syllogistic and forensic disputation, the latter in English. They were also required to compose original orations handed in to be graded for language, spelling, punctuation, and capitalization—a reminder that the eighteenth century still thought in terms of oral communication; students' written work at Oxford was usually read aloud, and at Princeton even spelling and punctuation were taught through the texts of speeches. PATERSON, who had entered the grammar school under Burr, experienced the curriculum's gradual evolution under four presidents; for ELLSWORTH, transferring in 1764 after two years of classics and theology at Yale, the difference was sudden and dramatic.[21]

The year ELLSWORTH arrived, Samuel Blair (son of the master of Fagg's Manor and a 1760 graduate of Princeton) published his *Account of the College of New Jersey*, widely distributed to recruit students. It presented the school in the best light, but there is no reason to doubt its accuracy: rather than write his own detailed description of his academic surroundings, MADISON simply sent a copy home to his father in 1769. Blair drew attention to the low cost of education at Princeton and made sure readers understood that disciplinary fines were not the custom at Nassau Hall—unlike Yale, where they were imposed for every imaginable infraction. He also laid out the program of instruction that prevailed while PATERSON, LUTHER MARTIN, and ELLSWORTH were students and into at least the first year for MADISON and BEDFORD:

> Each class recites twice a day: and have always free access to their teachers to solve any difficulties that may occur. The bell rings for morning prayer at six o'clock, when the Senior class read off a chapter [of the Bible] from the original into English. The president then proposes a few critical questions upon it, which, after their concise answers, he illustrates more at large. The times for relaxation from study are about an hour in the morning, two at noon, and three in the evening, and in these are included the public meals.[22]

According to Blair, "the branches of literature taught" at Princeton were "the same with those which are made parts of the education in the European colleges"—at least, in the Scottish and Dutch universities. Freshmen read the classics, sophomores added science, rhetoric, geography, logic, and mathematics, juniors added history, metaphysics, and moral philosophy, and seniors reviewed it all while writing and debating. What Burr had called the "Socratic" approach of question and response continued:

> The usual method of instruction in the sciences is this. The pupils frequently and deliberately read over such a portion of the author they are studying, on a particular science, as it is judged they can be able thoroughly to impress upon their memories. When they attend their recitations, the tutor proposes questions on every particular they have been reading. After they have given, in their turns, such answers as show their general acquaintance with the subject, he explains it more at large; allows them to propose any difficulties; and takes pains to discover whether his explanations have been fully comprehended. Advantages which are seldom obtainable in the usual method of teaching by lecture.[23]

There was another marked difference from Yale: students were encouraged to read independently: "The Senior, Junior, and (towards the conclusion of this year) the Sophomore classes are allowed the use of the college library . . . especially to help them in preparing their disputations and other compositions." To emphasize the difference from the orthodoxy demanded by Clap at Yale, Blair boasted that "care is taken to cherish a spirit of liberty and free enquiry; and not only to permit but to encourage their right of private judgment, without presuming to dictate with an air of infallibility, or demanding an implicit assent to the decisions of the preceptor."[24]

Students may have been free to disagree with their teachers, but they were nevertheless held accountable for knowing their subjects. Finley instituted the practice, unique among colonial colleges, of quarterly exams for all but the senior class. In August, seniors were examined by the trustees, the college officers, "and other gentlemen of learning then present. . . . And if approved as worthy of academical honor, the President assigns them the parts they are respectively to perform at the anniversary commencement" the following month. The honor of delivering the salutation in Latin went to the top student; the valedictory address, in English, was assigned to the best orator.[25]

The surviving exercise book of Adlai Osborne (1768) illustrates the question-and-answer teaching method. It includes notes from such subjects as metaphysics, ontology, and natural theology; the section on moral philosophy alone contains 502 questions and responses. Osbourne, who would become a trustee of the University of North Carolina, came to Princeton from Mecklenburg County with his neighbor WILLIAM CHURCHILL HOUSTON.[26]

John Maclean, Princeton's president from 1854 to 1868, says that Houston, "while yet a student . . . had charge of the grammar school under the control of the President of the College." It was not unheard of for an undergraduate to teach at the grammar school—Ashbel Green, Princeton's president from 1812 to 1822, taught there while a student in the 1780s—but it was customary to place a recent graduate in charge. Those schoolmasters, who rarely stayed more than a year, included Tapping Reeve in 1765 and Waightstill Avery in 1766. By the latter year the grammar school was officially separated from the college, and Avery had full responsibility for it. Perhaps he took HOUSTON on as an assistant or handed the school over to him upon commencing legal studies in 1767; the job could have been a kind of financial aid award to a student who was far from home and far from wealthy. HOUSTON is not listed in college records as the school's master until 1768, and the following year he was hired as a college tutor, with MADISON and BEDFORD among his students. HOUSTON had arrived on campus just in time to hear PATERSON's MA oration on patriotism and see LUTHER MARTIN and ELLSWORTH graduate. In 1768, he received his own bachelor's degree, and the next year he, along with MADISON and BEDFORD, saw John Hancock and JOHN DICKINSON receive honorary degrees at the 1769 commencement. By then HOUSTON was seated among the faculty, and—after four presidents in less than ten years—Princeton had a new leader who would remain for a quarter of a century: John Witherspoon.

Old Side Presbyterians had hoped Francis Alison would succeed Samuel Finley, but they could not object to the appointment of the Rev. John Witherspoon in November 1766. However, Elizabeth Witherspoon did object. For a year she refused to leave Paisley, Scotland, for the wilds of America, and in the summer of 1767 the discouraged trustees voted to offer the presidency to Samuel Blair should Mrs. Witherspoon remain obdurate. They also appointed his uncle, John Blair, professor of divinity and moral philosophy. At the same meeting they elected HUGH WILLIAMSON to the newly created position of professor of mathematics and natural history, but WILLIAMSON, who had just launched his medical practice in Philadelphia after returning from Edinburgh and Utrecht, declined the appointment, which eventually went to HOUSTON instead. An American medical student at Edinburgh, Finley's nephew Benjamin Rush, was able to change Mrs. Witherspoon's mind that winter. After she relented, both Blairs graciously stepped aside, and President John Witherspoon took over both the presidency and the teaching of moral philosophy.[27]

Scotland had suffered its own division within the Presbyterian Church. The Moderates "avoided the finer points of religious controversy . . .

stressed ethics as the essence of religious life; and were eager to apply to preaching and theology the canons of taste and judgment being enunciated by the eighteenth-century philosophers and literati." The Evangelicals believed that the Moderates failed the test of doctrinal purity. Witherspoon was a committed Evangelical, but he did not let theological differences blind him to the worthwhile ideas of Scottish Enlightenment thinkers who happened to be Moderates (or worse yet, outright unbelievers). When at last he arrived at Nassau Hall, he brought with him more than 300 books purchased in London and the Netherlands, including the works of such Moderates as Robertson, Hutcheson, Kames, Ferguson, and Reid, and the "infidels" Adam Smith and David Hume. Witherspoon informed the trustees that "another considerable benefaction" was following close behind. One of his first presidential actions was to replace the teaching of Berkeley's "immaterialist" epistemology by tutor Jonathan Edwards Jr. with the "common sense" of Thomas Reid.[28]

Witherspoon could claim as one of his qualifications a familiarity with the methods of the Scottish universities, kept up through "constant intercourse and great intimacy with the members of the University of Glasgow," to which Reid had just come from Aberdeen as Adam Smith's successor in the chair of moral philosophy. By 1772, Princeton's course of study followed the pattern of the Aberdeen reform curriculum that had had such an influence on the College of Philadelphia through the efforts of Provost William Smith:

> In the first year [Princeton students] read Latin and Greek, with Roman and Grecian antiquities, and rhetoric. In the second, continuing a study of the languages, they learn a complete system of geography, with the use of the globes, the first principles of philosophy, and the elements of mathematical knowledge. The third, though the languages are not wholly omitted, is chiefly employed in mathematics and natural philosophy, and going through a course of moral philosophy. In addition to these, the President gives lectures to the juniors and seniors, which consequently every student hears twice over in his course.[29]

Since well-prepared students might enter Princeton as sophomores or even juniors, the final two years were especially significant. They were dominated by science, public speaking, and President Witherspoon. It was Witherspoon's lectures on moral philosophy that had the greatest influence on Princeton students over the next generation. Samuel Stanhope Smith continued them, with some modifications, into the nineteenth century. His lectures were heard (and transcribed, since each student wrote out his own copy of Witherspoon's original) by all those Witherspoon graduates who entered politics, including twelve of his fellow members of Congress.[30]

It was not unusual for the best grammar school graduates to skip the first year or even two, but the trustees were growing uncomfortable with the number entering as upperclassmen. In 1760 they decided that "every student shall be obliged to reside in College at least Two Years before his first Graduation, & therefore . . . none shall be admitted later than the beginning of the Junior Year." At the special meeting in December 1767, when Witherspoon was reappointed, they actually voted to require that all students enter as freshmen, but that vote was quickly rescinded. Aaron Burr Jr., the precocious son of the college's second president, applied for admission at the age of eleven; told that he was too young, he returned to the Elizabethtown Academy for two more years and then compromised by matriculating as a sophomore. In 1773, JONATHAN DAYTON followed his example, coming from the same school and also entering as a sophomore. ALEXANDER HAMILTON had just enrolled at Elizabethtown. When he too applied for admission—on the condition that the two-year minimum residency be waived and that he not be assigned to any particular class, proceeding instead at his own pace—the trustees, more in the mood to tighten rules than to relax them, turned him down. [31]

MADISON was given no assurance that his years at Donald Robertson's school and his tutoring by Thomas Martin would allow him to skip the freshman year of Latin and Greek; he spent a month on campus reviewing and then passed the freshman exams to begin as a sophomore. On August 16, 1769, MADISON was feeling settled in. He wrote to his tutor: "I am perfectly pleased with my present situation; and the prospect before me of three years' confinement, however terrible it may sound, has nothing in it but what will be greatly alleviated by the advantages I have to derive from it." In fact, he would graduate in only two years. He explained much later in his "Autobiography," speaking of himself in the third person: "He was joined by a fellow student Jos. Ross, in accomplishing the studies of two years within one, having obtained from the faculty a promise that in case their preparation for the usual degree, should be found unexceptionable, the honor should be conferred." It was not that MADISON was impatient to begin a career, or that the tuition was a burden to his family; in the event, he wound up staying another six months after graduation to study independently with Witherspoon. Maybe he too was uncomfortable being several years older than classmates like Burr, who would graduate at sixteen. Only many years later did he blame the increased effort for his "infirm health," but Joseph Ross, his partner in acceleration, died a year after graduating, from causes now unknown. Perhaps their experience influenced the trustee's decision to reject HAMILTON's subsequent request; no other eighteenth-century students are known to have followed their example.[32]

The youthful MADISON was already showing the characteristics that PIERCE would note during the Convention: "From a spirit of industry and application which he possesses in a most eminent degree, he always comes forward the most informed Man of any point in debate. The affairs of the United States, he perhaps, has the most correct knowledge of, of any Man in the Union." Two years later, in the House of Representatives, Fisher Ames remarked on the same qualities: "As a reasoner, he is remarkably perspicuous and methodical. He is a studious man, devoted to public business, and a thorough master of almost every public question that can arise, or he will spare no pain to become so, if he happens to be in want of information." PIERCE and Ames both worked with MADISON daily; an interested observer on the sidelines saw him the same way. Louis Otto, the French chargé d'affaires, described him as "educated, wise, moderate, tractable, studious, perhaps more profound than HAMILTON but less brilliant. . . . He is a man who must be studied a long time to form a just idea of him."[33]

Industrious, informed, studious—the characteristics that observers repeat are those that MADISON developed while in school. Douglass Adair is convinced:

> For the eighteen-year-old MADISON . . . the undergraduate years laid the foundation he was to build on all his days. At Princeton the direction of his thinking was finally set; his mind henceforward would be continually preoccupied with the analysis of society and of principles of government. The Princeton years helped also to determine the goals of his thought, and to crystalize the standards and values that were to govern his political theorizing. At Nassau Hall he was immersed in the liberalism of the enlightenment, and converted to Eighteenth-century political radicalism.[34]

Although MADISON's graduating class of 1771 had only eleven members, the college was growing under Witherspoon. At the beginning of his second year, MADISON wrote to his father: "The number of students has increased very much of late; there are almost an hundred and fifteen in the College & the Grammar School"—Nassau Hall could house 147 with three to a room—"twenty two commence [i.e., graduate] this fall, all of them in

American Cloth." The grammar school had been readopted by the trust-ees at the 1767 meeting; at the same time, they voted "that the practice of sending freshmen upon errands, or employing them as servitors in any manner whatsoever, be from henceforth totally discontinued." With none of the distinctions of social class or status that were conspicuous at Oxford, Harvard, and Yale, the school MADISON had entered was indeed a hotbed of radical egalitarianism.[35]

But, as MADISON's classmate Philip Fithian described it in 1770 to his own father, Princeton was also a school much like others:

> The bell rings at five; after which there is an Intermission of half an hour, that everyone may have time to dress, at the end of which it rings again, & prayers begin; And lest any should plead that he did not hear the Bell, the Servant who rings, goes to every Door & beats till he wakens the Boys, which leaves them without excuse. After dinner till three we have Liberty to go out at Pleasure. From three till five we study, when the Bell rings for evening Prayers. We sup at seven. At nine the Bell rings for Study; And a Tutor goes through the College, to see that every Student is in his own Room; if he finds any are ab-sent, or more in any Room than belong there, he notes them down, & the day following calls them to an account.[36]

President Witherspoon had made clear that any students "called to ac-count" for any reason faced neither corporal punishment (as at William and Mary), which he thought degrading, nor fines (as at Harvard and Yale), which punished parents rather than students. In his letter to prospective parents in Jamaica he laid out his disciplinary policy: "The collegiate cen-sures are 1. Private admonition by the president, professor, or tutor. 2. Be-fore the faculty. 3. Before the whole class to which the offender belongs. 4. The last and highest, before all the members of the College, assembled in the hall." The force of Witherspoon's personality made it rarely necessary to go beyond the first step.[37]

College life could be broadening; it was often great fun. After a year spent tutoring Robert Carter's children in Virginia, Fithian looked back nostalgically to the undergraduate years he spent with classmates including MADISON, Burr, and William Bradford. In his diary he wrote:

> Every time I reflect on that place of retirement & Study, where I spent two years which I call the most pleasant as well as the most important Period in my past life—Always when I think upon the *Studies*, the

Discipline, the *Companions*, *Neighborhood*, the *exercises* & Diversions, it gives me a secret & real Pleasure, even the Foibles which often prevail there are pleasant on recollection; such as giving each other *names* & *characters*; Meeting & Shoving in the dark entries: knocking at Doors and going off without entering; Strowing the entries in the night with greasy Feathers; freezing the Bell; Ringing it at late hours of the night.[38]

The college bell was as popular a target at Princeton as it was at Yale, but Witherspoon did not overreact to these "foibles" as Clap did. Warming to his subject as memories flood over him, Fithian goes on to reminisce about such other pastimes as setting fire to the Nassau Hall outhouse, "ogling Women with the Telescope," and lighting gunpowder squibs "in the rooms of timorous Boys & new-comers—The various methods used in natural-izing strangers . . . and trying them by Jeers & Repartee in order to make them choose their Companions & c & c—."[39]

It is easy to forget how small the colonial colleges were; there were cer-tainly "strangers" and "new-comers" at Princeton every year with students entering as sophomores or juniors, but "Companions" were chosen from schoolmates numbering only a few dozen. For MADISON, Bedford, and their friends the great choice of companionship was between the American Whig Society and the Cliosophic Society. These were in many ways like social clubs at other colleges, but they were also debating clubs several years before William and Mary's Phi Beta Kappa. Records of their first decade are almost nonexistent, but later evidence indicates that their primary ac-tivities were debating, speech-making, essay-writing—and verbally abusing the other club. Their predecessor Plain Dealing and Well Meaning Clubs seem to have been purely frivolous fraternities; a member of the latter club, the Rev. Nathaniel Perkins, class of 1770, later recalled the rivalry he found when he came to Princeton in 1766: "The object of the Well-Meaning was to collect the first young men in point of character and scholarship as its members. But the object of the Plain-Dealing was to outnumber the Well-Meaning. In the year 1768 or 1769 dissensions arose between the mem-bers of the two societies, and the tide of unpleasant feeling arose to such a height that the faculty of the College judged it expedient to abolish both."[40]

The clubs were quickly reconstituted under new names, with assurances of more serious purpose. In 1769, PATERSON (by then clerking for Richard Stockton) persuaded President Witherspoon to allow their re-formation with the promise of their reformation. He and the other Well Meaning members ELLSWORTH and MARTIN would consider themselves alumni mem-

bers of the Cliosophic Society in years to come. "Clio" was officially chartered on June 8, 1770, taking its name from PATERSON's "Cliosophic Oration"
at the 1763 commencement, and JONATHAN DAYTON joined in his junior year,
March 1775. In 1799, DAYTON summarized the club's purpose: "To promote
mutual improvement, to inspire virtuous emulation, to cultivate brotherly
affection were the primary objects of the institution." The Cliosophic Society's rival club was even quicker to reorganize, and its association with
American patriotism more explicit. On June 24, 1769, the American Whig
Society was founded. MADISON would be an early member, but despite the
claim often made by biographers and historians, he could not have been a
founder: he was just setting forth from Virginia at the end of June, and he
did not arrive in Princeton until a month after the club was chartered. The
more likely founders were a nonetheless impressive group, including Samuel Stanhope Smith (later president of Hampden-Sydney and Princeton),
William Bradford (US attorney general), and MADISON's literary friends,
Philip Freneau and Hugh Henry Brackenridge.[41]

This society's founders took its name from the series of essays then being published by WILLIAM LIVINGSTON under the pseudonym of "An American
Whig." LIVINGSTON was responding to the renewed campaign to create Anglican bishops for America. At the same time that the Stamp Act passed in
Parliament, proposals were made to bring the colonies into closer conformity
with England. To complete the homogenization, Anglican bishops would administer an established Church of England in New York and New England,
so thickly populated by Dissenters. The violent reaction to the Stamp Act was
cited as further evidence of the need for ecclesiastical oversight.

Dissenters saw a gauntlet thrown down. Francis Alison, JOHN DICKINSON,
and George Bryan published the "Centinel" essays in Philadelphia; Provost
Smith replied with "Anti-Centinel" essays, and the New York *Gazette* began
publishing essays by "An American Whig" weekly from March 1768 through
July 1769. The old *Independent Reflector* authors all contributed, but once
again the burden was largely borne by WILLIAM LIVINGSTON. In the heated
atmosphere following the recent acts of Parliament, the "American Whig"
was even more celebrated than the *Reflector* had been in the previous decade, and now the audience was much broader. At Princeton, the American
Whig Society boldly honored the essayist with its new name. In addition
to admiring LIVINGSTON's defense of religious and political liberty, the collegians admired his witty, sarcastic style, which they would do their best to
imitate in their "paper wars" with the Cliosophic Society and which may
have later made the American Whig alumnus WILLIAM RICHARDSON DAVIE
feared at the North Carolina ratifying convention.[42]

Members took pleasure "in writing witty pointed anonymous Papers, in *Songs, Confessions, Wills, Soliloquies, Proclamations, Advertisements, & c.*" during what were called paper wars between the two societies. The actual differences between the two clubs were never very clear, but Whigs liked to characterize the Clios as sanctimonious and conservative, calling them the "Tory Society"; in the paper war that broke out in 1771, Fithian (a Whig) wrote a mock will for the "dying" Cliosophic Society and signed it, "TORY CLUB." Evidently club members would take turns, before the assembled student body in the prayer hall, reading aloud their compositions. The Whigs' star satirists were the poet Philip Freneau, later recruited by Jefferson to edit the highly partisan *National Gazette*, and Hugh Henry Brackenridge, who would become one of the nation's first novelists and serve as chief justice of the Pennsylvania Supreme Court.[43]

President Witherspoon was reported to have said that he never knew the youthful MADISON "to do, or to say, any improper thing" (a line that Jefferson loved to repeat to embarrass MADISON). That disclaimer may well have been a less than candid response to some question about MADISON's verses for the Whigs, which were the most scurrilous (if least artful) of the 1771 "war." But the benefits of the two societies were much more than merely social. Princeton's later president Ashbel Green, class of 1783, went so far as to recall in his autobiography, "I used to think and say, that I derived as much benefit from the exercises of the Whig Society, while I was a member of college, as from the instruction of my teachers." The essays, orations, and debates in both clubs were certainly a valued adjunct to the formal academic program, but the only orations surviving from the 1770s are three by Aaron Burr for Clio: "Style," "On Dancing," and "On the Passions."[44]

The forensic abilities of both Whigs and Clios were put to more serious use in their commencement performances, where the clubs vied to outnumber each other on the platform. In 1770, Witherspoon's son James (an American Whig) spoke on the justice of resisting a tyrannical king. Other speakers, wearing "American cloth," praised "the Utility of American manufactures" or supported religious freedom. Ten of the eleven members of the class of 1771 took part in the ceremonies the year they graduated. The high point of the day may have been a poem by Freneau and Brackenridge, "The Rising Glory of America," which was followed by Joseph Ross's oration on the power of eloquence. The afternoon concluded with a valedictory address by GUNNING BEDFORD, on "Benevolence."[45]

The one graduate not heard from was JAMES MADISON. Sixty years later MADISON claimed that ill health, resulting from too much study, kept him from traveling home directly after graduation, but there is no contemporary evidence to support this excuse, nothing in his letter to his father on October 9, in which he asks permission to stay on in Princeton through the winter, nothing in any of his classmates' correspondence that would explain his nonparticipation. His dislike of public speaking would be sufficient to explain his desire to be excused from performing; relaxed and even voluble in small groups, MADISON was always stiff and uncomfortable before the public. Despite all his rhetorical preparation in college, his reticence was really overcome only at the Federal Convention and the ensuing Virginia ratifying convention.

MADISON stayed six more months at Nassau Hall, reading under the direction of "the Old Doctor," as he called Witherspoon, before returning to Virginia in 1772. They next met in 1780, when MADISON joined his former teacher in Congress; they were colleagues there until Witherspoon's resignation in late 1782. They would see one another again in 1783 when Congress met in Princeton, and in 1786 when MADISON traveled from New York to Philadelphia on his way to the Annapolis Convention. A year later, after the Constitutional Convention completed its work, Princeton awarded MADISON an honorary doctorate of laws.

President Witherspoon was one of the most respected educators in America. William Smith Jr. of New York (LIVINGSTON's and JOHNSON's friend, not the provost of the College of Philadelphia) credited him in 1777 with "a greater Share of Erudition than I believe any Man in this Country." He venerated the classical authors, even naming his Princeton farm Tusculum after Cicero's villa, but he also broadened the curriculum and went, in his own teaching, beyond the traditional classical and theological studies to include work in the modern languages, in rhetoric, in history, and in what we would call political science. He maintained that education was not only essential for the ministry but "of acknowledged necessity to those who do not wish to live for themselves alone, but would apply their talents to the service of the Public and the good of mankind . . . in offices of power or trust." Indeed, his students and faculty members would include a president and a vice president, fifty representatives, twenty-eight senators, three Supreme Court justices, a half dozen college presidents—and five delegates to the Constitutional Convention. Princeton provided a disproportionate share of the educational and political leadership of the new republic.[46]

Witherspoon's students seem to have admired him without exception, but it was his lectures on moral philosophy that had a lasting intellectual influence. They began with ethics and moved directly on to government and politics. As Adair says, it was in them "that MADISON encountered the ideas which were to affect his life most significantly. The syllabus of Witherspoon's lectures . . . explains the conversion of the young Virginian to the philosophy of the Enlightenment." Ashbel Green published the lectures in his 1800 edition of Witherspoon's *Works*; three student-made copies survive, dating from 1772, 1782, and 1795—two in the Princeton University Library and one in the collection of the Presbyterian Historical Society. As all copies make clear, Witherspoon's written lectures were only an outline from which the spoken lectures would expand as he asked questions, offered elucidation that varied from year to year, and responded to students' questions. Green, who heard the lectures in 1781–1782 and again in 1782–1783, remembered that they were "enlivened by anecdotes and remarks" that "were indeed often very considerable, and exceedingly interesting." But even the written versions give a clear sense of the way that he made Princeton both the American center for the Scottish Enlightenment and, during the Revolution, what loyalists called a "seminary for sedition."[47]

In 1778, Adam Ferguson, then a member of the British government's Carlyle Peace Commission, wrote to the commission's chairman, "We have 1200 miles of territory in length occupied by about 3,000,000 People of which there are about 1,500,000 with Johny Witherspoons at their head against us And the rest for us. I am not sure that the proper measures were taken but we should reduce Johny Witherspoons to the small Support of FRANKLIN Adams & two or three of the most Abandoned Villains in the world but I tremble at the thought of their Cunning and determination opposed to us." (There is no indication that Witherspoon ever knew of the letter; despite their differences, he kept Ferguson's *History of Civil Society* on his students' reading list.) To the very end of the war Witherspoon continued to be ranked by the British among their leading enemies. Ashbel Green cites a 1783 letter from a British officer to Maj. Gen. Sir Guy Carleton singling out "Dr. Witherspoon . . . the political firebrand, who perhaps had not less a share in the Revolution than WASHINGTON himself. He poisons the minds of his young students and through them the Continent."[48]

If Witherspoon was poisoning students' minds, it was with ideas that Adam Ferguson knew well: Thomas Reid's "common sense" and Francis Hutcheson's moral and political philosophy, elements of the Scottish Enlightenment that Witherspoon constantly emphasized. He had studied Locke's *Essay Concerning Human Understanding* at Edinburgh and written an MA thesis that drew on Plato and Berkeley, but his discovery of "common sense" led him to reject their idealism. From his arrival in 1768, Princeton quickly became the American center of Scottish "common sense."

Witherspoon could be scathing in his criticism of Hume's "peculiar" system of morals; he found fault with Plato, Sir Thomas More, Shaftsbury, and Mandeville, too. But it is a mark of Witherspoon's open mind that he could recognize the intellectual strengths of his Presbyterian adversaries, the Scottish Moderates, at the same time that he rejected their theology. Henry May, in his *Enlightenment in America*, is skeptical: "Witherspoon recommended to his students a catholic range of moralists, without much fear that these would be sought out and read. Most of these came from the canon of the moderate Enlightenment." But in postgraduate correspondence, Witherspoon's students MADISON, Bradford, and Freneau often referred to various works of Hume and Lord Kames—to cite only two of the recommended authors—with a familiarity that implies that those writers were indeed sought out and read, and Ralph Ketcham, after a thorough study of MADISON's education, concludes that "MADISON probably read every one of these authors either at Princeton or a few years after he left it." Above all, however, in organization, content, and development of ideas, the similarity between Witherspoon's lectures and Hutcheson's *System of Moral Philosophy* is constant and unmistakable.[49]

Following Hutcheson, Witherspoon endorsed a theory of social compact, advocated a mixed government, argued for civil liberty, and reserved the right of resistance to tyranny. Moreover, he was adamant about the continuing relevance of moral philosophy to public life. As he told prospective Princeton parents, higher education was a necessary preparation for public office. In Mark Noll's assessment, "What Witherspoon drew from Francis Hutcheson in the early 1770s was exactly what JAMES MADISON . . . would employ to construct public policy . . . in the late 1780s."[50]

Like Reid, Witherspoon begins by asserting that reason itself is underlain by first principles that are grasped intuitively by all humans through a "sense" that, like sight and hearing, is "common" to all and makes reasoning possible. Like Hutcheson, he argues that these first principles support a second faculty of moral sense, by which right and wrong are apprehended as minds reach maturity. True to the empirical approach of the Enlightenment, he declares in Lecture 1 that "the principles of duty and obligation must be drawn from [observation of] the nature of man," and in Lecture 2 he defends the trustworthiness of the external senses. Lecture 3 makes a parallel defense of "internal sensation, what Mr. Hutchinson [*sic*] calls the finer powers of perception," including beauty, harmony, proportion—and morality. The next six lectures focus on ethics. Then Lecture 10 introduces "Politics," Lecture 11 deals with "Domestic Society," 12 with "Civil Society," 13 with "Laws of Nature and Nations," and 14–16 with "Jurisprudence." After a recapitulation, he provides a list of the "chief writers" on politics and government: Aristotle, Cicero (*De officiis*), and Tacitus, and then more modern writers: Grotius, Pufendorf, Barbeyrac, Burlamaqui, Hobbes, Machiavelli, Harrington, Locke, and Sidney. But there are also authors of "some late books" who should be read: Montesquieu, Goguet, Montagu, and of course the Scots—Ferguson, Kames, Hume, Smith, Reid, and Hutcheson.[51]

Whatever one thinks Witherspoon ought to have expected, the relentless student MADISON returned to these books again and again as he prepared for the 1787 Convention, for his *Federalist* essays, and for the Virginia debate over ratification. Montagu's *Reflections on the Rise and Fall of Antient Republicks*, read at Princeton, launched his exhaustive study of the history of republican government. Ferguson's *Essay on the History of Civil Society* informs his analysis of factions. The origins of *Federalist*, no. 10, are discernible in Adam Smith and in Hume's *Essays Moral and Political*, and there is a strong affinity between MADISON's and Hume's ideas of human nature, vividly illustrated in the contrast between men and angels made in Hume's essay on "The Dignity or Meanness of Human Nature" and MADISON's *Federalist*, no. 51. Although the arguments of those essays are not Witherspoon's, all of these authors were introduced to him by Witherspoon.[52]

MADISON memorably would write: "If men were angels, no government would be necessary. If angels were to govern men, neither external nor internal controls on government would be necessary. In framing a government which is to be administered by men over men, the great difficulty lies in this: you must first enable the government to control the governed; and in the next place oblige it to control itself." Gideon Mailer finds it significant that although "MADISON's desire to check human defects in a subordinate political system reflected Hume's palliative recommendations for political confederations," Witherspoon's student nevertheless "used a religious motif" in stating his position, referring to "humans, angels, and governance" in a way Mailer finds reminiscent of Calvin's sermon on Galatians 3:19-20, "The Many Functions of God's Law." Witherspoon was certainly devoted to inculcating Christianity in his students, but he was different from Thomas Clap or Myles Cooper in an important regard: with Grotius and Hutcheson, he believed that the fundamental truths of political philosophy were not only God's will but also natural laws. What strikes Mailer as an "ironic link to Hume through MADISON's exposure to a Scottish evangelical teacher" is typical of the way in which Witherspoon succeeded in keeping his students' focus on the principles of political philosophy, whether they were Presbyterians, Anglicans, Congregationalists, or budding deists—and even when the philosophers were, like Hume, "infidels."[53]

Of course, the *Federalist* essays were not directed to the Framers in Philadelphia but to the undecided citizens of New York; still, many of MADISON's most original structural proposals also had to be explained repeatedly to more traditionally educated Framers. The initial Virginia Plan did not yet challenge the civic humanist idea that good government depended on good citizens. It was based on a moral principle—that proportional representation was the only just basis for a legislature—and it trusted a virtuous people's chosen representatives to appoint the executive and the federal courts. It was only after an entirely proportional legislature was defeated in the Great Compromise that MADISON turned to the idea of complex checks and balances that would work against the tyranny of a legislative majority—an "invisible hand" in the playing out of political power. These innovations were rooted in principles he internalized from Witherspoon's lectures, and they are based on the idea of balance. Many of MADISON's later proposals at Philadelphia contradicted the conventional belief (commonly attributed by the Framers to Montesquieu) that the legislative, executive, and judicial functions must be absolutely separate. MADISON instead advocated letting the three branches balance one another in an unconventional fashion (and check overreach on the part of any branch) by *sharing* certain powers, giving some legislative function to the executive and some judicial power to the legislative, and adopting WILSON's Scottish-style "Supream" Court that could exercise judicial review over the legislature and the executive. These all follow Witherspoon's idea of "overpoise" in Lectures 12–14, founded in Hutcheson but also echoing Newtonian principles of balanced forces in physics. In Lecture 12, Witherspoon goes beyond the Aristotelian notion that government should be *mixed* (including some elements of monarchy, aristocracy, and democracy); he states, as part of his first observation on the forms of government, that "every good form of government must be *complex*, so that one principle may check the other." Where the classical republicanism of Cicero and Plutarch presumed that good government was impossible without a virtuous citizenry, Witherspoon was pragmatic: "It is of consequence to have as much virtue among the particular members of a community as possible; but it is folly to expect that a state shall be upheld by integrity in all who have a share in managing it." (Most men were not Catos, let alone angels.) Witherspoon could condemn the morals of Mandeville and Hume, but he taught that the competing interests in the management of government "must be so balanced, that when every one draws to his own interest or inclination, there may be an overpoise upon the whole."[54]

This principle is the basis of MADISON's argument for balancing different interests and competing factions in government, the argument that has been called MADISON's most profound contribution to political thought. The complex intertwining of responsibilities among the branches puzzled those Framers whose training in political philosophy was their early study of Aristotle or more recent reading of Montesquieu. It may, however, have reminded BEDFORD, DAVIE, or DAYTON of Witherspoon's next step in his lectures: "The second observation upon the forms of government is that where there is a balance of different bodies, as in all mixed forms, there must always be some *nexus imperii*, something to make one of them necessary to the other. . . . Some of the great essential rights of rulers must be divided and distributed among the different branches of the legislature."[55] The idea of balance and even the phrase *"nexus imperii"* also appear on pages 2:244–245 of Hutcheson's *System of Moral Philosophy*, and Hutcheson's next two pages are closely paralleled in Witherspoon's Lecture 12.

Hutcheson, Smith, and Hume all proposed (in Hume's phrase) to reduce politics to a science. Witherspoon attempted to do just that in his lectures, and that goal became MADISON's goal also. At a time when Oxford, William and Mary, Harvard, and Yale still clung to the seventeenth-century pedagogy of steeping students in classical literature—with a leavening of Newtonian physics—a new philosophy of education, focused on systematic preparation for public life, was emerging at the newer colleges in Philadelphia and (especially) Princeton, where Scottish moral philosophy was first introduced by Alison and Witherspoon. It was there that the teaching of political science in America began.[56]

By the time DAYTON and DAVIE matriculated in 1774, Witherspoon was putting his teaching into practice. In New Jersey's provincial legislature he had opposed paying the duty on imported tea several months before the Boston Tea Party; in January 1774, Princeton students held their own "tea party," burning quantities of British tea in a bonfire. In 1776, just in time to cast New Jersey's vote for independence, he was sent to the Continental Congress. (Despite his growing political activity, Witherspoon kept up his college responsibilities; fortunately, Philadelphia was only a long day's ride from Princeton.) Witherspoon was becoming known as "the philosopher of Confederation." Anticipating the Framers, speaking in the same Pennsylvania statehouse in which they would gather a decade later, he insisted from the beginning on the "absolute necessity of union." Understanding that men whose first loyalty was to their native states would be wary of giving a central government the powers he believed necessary, he demanded at least a "firm confederacy." On July 30, 1776, he challenged Congress to create a constitution: "Shall we establish nothing good because we know it cannot be eternal? Shall we live without government, because every constitution has its old age, and its period? Because we know we shall die, shall we take no pains to lengthen our life? Far from it sir; it only requires the more watchful attention, to settle government upon the best principles, and in the wisest manner, that it may last as long as the nature of things will admit."[57]

With the college suspended the following year, Witherspoon—who now had a price on his head—was busy in Philadelphia, Baltimore, Lancaster, York, and then back in Philadelphia as Congress moved to avoid the British army. When classes resumed on a much-reduced scale, the day-to-day administration of the college was left to Professor WILLIAM CHURCHILL HOUSTON until he too was sent to Congress in 1779.

The Revolutionary War left Nassau Hall badly battered, shelled by artillery during the battle of Princeton and damaged further by prolonged military occupation. Between 1777 and 1781, the college struggled to remain open, graduating only five or six students each year. Witherspoon was aging. He retired from Congress in 1782, having served alongside his students HOUSTON, MADISON, and BEDFORD, and eighteen other future Framers. (When the Convention convened in 1787, only a handful there knew as many of the delegates as Witherspoon did.)

Samuel Stanhope Smith, who had gone to Virginia after graduation to become president of Hampden-Sydney College at the age of twenty-five, returned in 1779 to become professor of moral philosophy. He took over the moral philosophy lectures, joined FRANKLIN's American Philosophical Society, and was given an honorary degree by Yale. In 1794, upon Witherspoon's death, Smith became the sixth president of the College of New Jersey. In 1797, WASHINGTON enrolled his step-grandson, George Washington Parke Custis.

WASHINGTON had wanted to send the boy's father to Princeton twenty-five years earlier, but Jacky Custis's tutor, Jonathan Boucher, had just been given an honorary degree by Myles Cooper at King's College, in appreciation of his support for an Anglican bishop in America; Boucher strongly opposed the Presbyterian school and wrote to WASHINGTON on January 19, 1773, that Princeton was a college "formed on the Plans of those in Scotland, Leyden, Gottingen, Geneva: Wm & Mary & King's College resemble more those of Oxford & Cambridge. In the former, men often may become Scholars, if They will; in the latter, They must often be made so, whether they will or no." WASHINGTON doubted—correctly—that Jacky Custis could be made a scholar but knew very well that he would not become one of his own will, and Custis had a brief enrollment at King's. In the 1790s, when the new federal government moved to Philadelphia, WASHINGTON put young Washington Custis in the Academy there; disappointed in the little benefit derived from his attendance, he enrolled him in the Princeton class of 1799. "Wash" was no more a scholar than his late father had been, but WASHINGTON was determined to give him what he considered the best possible opportunity.[58]

WASHINGTON was one of a number of Framers who had not gone to college but who wanted a college education for their progeny. One of them chose Harvard, one Yale, one South Carolina College, and one the University of Pennsylvania. But perhaps because of Witherspoon's and Smith's reputations, perhaps because of the impression its alumni made at the Convention, the sons or grandsons of five of the noncollege-educated Framers went to Princeton. CLYMER, BROOM, and READ enrolled two sons each, and in 1820 William Brearley received his BA; he was the grandson of DAVID BREARLEY, who had been awarded an honorary MA by Princeton although he may never have gone to any school himself. Although college-educated Framers typically enrolled their sons in their own alma maters, not all did. Several Framers who were alumni of other colleges sent boys to Nassau Hall instead of their own schools. LIVINGSTON (Yale 1741), INGERSOLL (Yale 1766), GOUVERNEUR MORRIS (King's College 1768), and William and Mary's short-term students MERCER and PIERCE all had sons or nephews who went to Princeton. Princeton had sent the most alumni to the 1787 Convention; it likewise educated the largest share of the other Framers' children.

Most of these "young Gentlemen" came too late to study under John Witherspoon, but they still heard his moral philosophy lectures continued by Smith, whose own published lectures reveal that he made relatively few major changes. There were, however, two significant additions. Smith added the *Federalist* to Witherspoon's reading list, telling his students, "These principles of our government . . . ought to join essential objectives in the education of every American Scholar." And he ended his published *Lectures* with this instruction: "Here the federal constitution is to be committed to memory."[59]

13

At the Convention
"To Form a More Perfect Union"

All which I can now do is to ask myself what I should do were the questions stated anew; for in all probability, what I should now do would be what I then did, my sentiments and opinions having undergone no essential change in forty years.

GOUVERNEUR MORRIS to Timothy Pickering, December 22, 1814

The fifty-five men who took part in the Federal Convention of 1787 were individuals of diverse backgrounds, varied experience, and competing interests. Inevitably, many aspects of their lives influenced their thinking on the Constitution, but perhaps not so bluntly as was once thought. Charles Beard was sure that the Framers were motivated by their investments in government bonds ("personalty" investments, as distinguished from "realty"). After exhaustive investigation, Forrest McDonald concludes in *We the People* that only "four men—GERRY, KING, SHERMAN, and ELLS-WORTH—were obviously working ardently for the interests represented by their own investments. Except for these four, neither public creditors nor non-creditors evinced anything like consistent attention to the personalty interests they represented." GERRY (the largest single public creditor among the Framers) and MASON (the largest single private creditor) refused to sign the Constitution, even though it benefited creditors like them. Men of property—and especially merchants such as GERRY and ROBERT MORRIS—were more likely to support a stronger national government and thus more likely to attend the Convention in the first place, but the common factor of their wealth cannot explain the numerous conflicts in the positions they took once they got there.[1]

During the Revolutionary War, many of the Framers had become frustrated trying to prosecute a war under the very imperfect union of the thirteen states—an experience that made nationalists of soldiers such as WASHINGTON, C. C. PINCKNEY, and DAVIE and federal officials such as ROBERT MORRIS, GOUVERNEUR MORRIS, and MADISON. WASHINGTON declared, "More than half the perplexities I have experienced in the course of my command, and almost the whole of the difficulties and distresses of the army, have their origin here," that is, in the weakness of the Confederation Congress. Nevertheless, some remained more narrowly attached to their states, blaming Congress's troubles not on the limitations of the Articles of Confederation but on the selfishness they always perceived in *other* states than their own. As late as 1785, both GERRY and KING resisted the Massachusetts legislature's call for a convention to increase congressional power, arguing that their state's "republican principles" would be endangered: "Plans have been artfully laid, and vigorously pursued," they insisted, to turn "our republican Governments, into baleful Aristocracies." Shays's Rebellion changed their minds, convincing GERRY that the threat was just the opposite, namely, the "leveling spirit" that he would so often decry at the Convention. (KING, distrustful of the "mob" ever since the Sons of Liberty attacked his father's home in the 1760s, was further persuaded by his marriage to a New York heiress and by the continuing efforts of ALEXANDER HAMILTON.) By May 1787, all but four of the delegates arriving at the Convention appeared ready to approve a much more powerful national government.[2]

The four who came determined to oppose a stronger government point to still another influence on the Framers: state political factions. Samuel Chase, in Maryland, led a party that was identified with state-centered "particularism"; CARROLL and JENIFER were powerful politicians in their own right, but JOHN FRANCIS MERCER and LUTHER MARTIN were late additions to the Maryland delegation, selected by the Chase faction. As a congressman from Virginia, MERCER had said that the only hope for the government lay in a general convention of the states that would give more power to Congress; after the land-poor fifth son married a young heiress from Annapolis and moved across the Potomac, he hitched his wagon to Chase's star and now opposed that convention. The New York delegation was rendered completely dysfunctional by the appointment of JOHN LANSING and ROBERT YATES, followers of particularist Governor George Clinton who constantly outvoted the nationalist Hamilton. Almost every state had its powerful group of men whose loyalty was to their state above all, men like Virginia's Patrick Henry or North Carolina's Willie Jones, who would lead the opposition at the state ratifying conventions. Few of these particularists were present in Philadelphia, but there were a number of delegates such as New

Jersey's PATERSON and Delaware's BASSETT and BROOM whose political experience was almost entirely local, and some southerners were prepared to use their votes as bargaining chips to uphold their region's interests.[3]

Regionalism, in one form or another, was perhaps the most troublesome of the influences under which the Framers operated. It showed itself in conflicts over slavery, the regulation of commerce, and the future of the western lands. Moreover, with an intensity that seems strange today, the delegates from the "small states" of New Jersey and Delaware clung tenaciously to equal state representation in at least one house of the legislature, and on this issue the advocates of proportional representation (from the so-called large states) were equally unyielding. MADISON and WILSON were bitterly disappointed when the Convention accepted the compromise of electing one house of Congress on each principle. But in frequently acrimonious debates, running from early June through early July, even this dispute was at least argued in terms of the philosophy of government, and it was in that philosophy above all that the differences of education among the Framers stood out.

Newton's physical laws were broadly familiar by the mid-eighteenth century, and analogies to planetary motion were common at the Convention and in the *Federalist*, but during that century Newton was best known for his work in optics, and analogies from the science of vision were even more familiar. By one such analogy, education provides the lens through which the world is thereafter seen. It was just such a lens that Douglass Adair had in mind when he wrote, "The 'area' of experience that I have been most fascinated in for our eighteenth century friends is the realm of symbolic experience—their reading, their formal college training, etc.—which I feel structured and determined to a significant degree the physical world they saw with their own eyes, or didn't see."[4]

The New England Primer is one example of that "symbolic experience" in early childhood: young children in Massachusetts, New Hampshire, or Connecticut could not learn their ABC's without simultaneously learning "In ADAM'S fall we sinned all." The alphabet and original sin were absorbed together, and one could no more be forgotten than the other. Perhaps half of the Framers were raised as Calvinists, and the fundamental depravity of mankind was for them the starting point of all government. There is no question that most were orthodox members of one Christian denomination or another, intimately familiar with scripture. Daniel Walker Howe concludes that "the Framers in Philadelphia represented a variety of religious affiliations, but there was no one who could even remotely be characterized as an enthusiast." Howe forgets Delaware's RICHARD BASSETT, whom WILLIAM PIERCE actually did characterize as "a religious enthusiast, lately turned Methodist," but since BASSETT never opened his mouth in the debates, Howe's oversight may be forgivable. (OLIVER ELLSWORTH's very particular convictions about divine providence and political compromise, impressed upon him by his tutor, Joseph Bellamy, will require a closer look.) The delegates brushed aside a proposal by FRANKLIN to open each session with an "address to the Creator of the Universe"; without debate, they unanimously passed the clause barring any religious test for officeholders, and no other reference to religion appears anywhere in the document. Even the words "so help me God," added by most presidents to the prescribed inaugural oath, are not found in the Constitution. Aside from their assumptions about man's sinful nature, the Framers' religious beliefs offer limited insight into their differences on any of the matters they debated.[5]

We must also consider the powerful "symbolic experience" of the Greek and Roman classics. Latin was the second language of most of the Framers, begun as soon as the rudiments of English had been mastered, and one did not learn Latin without reading Cicero. In 1790, Noah Webster (a Yale man) observed, "The minds of youth are perpetually led to the history of Greece and Rome . . . boys are constantly repeating the declamations of Demosthenes or Cicero." JAMES WILSON read widely in the Scottish Enlightenment and studied civil law in Glasgow and Coke in Philadelphia, but his 1790 law lectures at Philadelphia cite Cicero more often than any other author; in them he calls *De officiis* "a work which does honor to human understanding and the human heart." David Hume agreed: he wrote to Francis Hutcheson, "Upon the whole, I desire to take my *Catalogue of Virtues* from Cicero's *Offices*." And the lessons of the classics were reinforced by the views of the English commonwealthmen. The influential Harvard-trained preacher Jonathan Mayhew was explicit in his sermon on the repeal of the Stamp Act: "Having been initiated in youth in the doctrines of civil liberty, as they are taught by such men as Plato, Demosthenes, Cicero, and other personages among the ancients; and such as Sidney and Milton, Locke and Hoadly, among the moderns, I liked them; they seemed rational."[6]

Understandably, the older Framers were likely to have had old-fashioned educations: tutoring in the classics or the mix of religious studies and "the languages" that in the 1740s characterized colleges as disparate as Yale and St. Omer's. At the Convention, DICKINSON and FRANKLIN worked persistently for compromise, but in debate they still held on to older political habits; even though they favored a strong national government, they had trouble shaking off the assumption that semisovereign states would continue to operate as they had in the Continental Congress. JOHNSON served capably on four committees, but like LIVINGSTON, CARROLL, JENIFER, and WASHINGTON, he had little to say in debate. SHERMAN and MASON were talkative enough— more than enough at times—but they too remained in the grip of old ways of thinking: SHERMAN's nostalgia for the New England town meeting and MASON's desire for sumptuary laws are only two of many examples. PIERCE was disappointed by a number of his fellow delegates who struck him as over-the-hill. He had heard of DICKINSON's fame as an orator but felt he "labored . . . to produce a trifle." FRANKLIN, he thought, "does not shine much in public Council,—he is no Speaker, nor does he seem to let politics engage his attention," and "there is nothing in [JOHNSON] that warrants the high reputation which he has for public speaking." The youngest Framers, conversely, may have been guilty of youthful impetuosity—CHARLES PINCK-NEY III or JOHN MERCER, for instance. PINCKNEY was well-read, but neither he nor MERCER (nor HAMILTON, for that matter) had spent much time in a classroom, and the lack of intellectual discipline sometimes showed. But the speeches of some younger Framers, such as MADISON and GOUVERNEUR MORRIS, reveal that they had had an education different in important respects from that of their elders.[7]

There was, of course, more to education than schoolwork. Those who taught themselves learned early to be self-reliant, although some (like WASHINGTON) always retained a degree of insecurity about his academic shortcomings. At Glasgow or Edinburgh, one might encounter the luminaries of the Scottish Enlightenment in a literary club or at a dinner party, while life at London's Inns of Court imparted a certain social sophistication and offered the chance of meeting John Wilkes or David Garrick—or BENJAMIN FRANKLIN. But the colleges in New England or Virginia simply introduced students to others very much like themselves, and even Philadelphia and King's offered little more variety in their student bodies. Princeton was the exception. The nine Framers who went there for college spent two, three, or four years in the company of young men from all thirteen colonies: sons of New England merchants, Pennsylvania farmers, and southern aristocrats. For them, college was indeed broadening, but elsewhere it reinforced regional outlooks. Harvard and William and Mary alumni (with such rare exceptions as MCCLURG, the Edinburgh MD) were essentially insular—John Adams remained suspicious all his life of people from other regions. BALDWIN, newly transplanted to Georgia, still kept his roots in New Haven; in the three years before the Convention he seems to have consulted most often with fellow Yale men Ezra Stiles (by letter) and Lyman Hall, the Georgia governor who had come from Connecticut only a decade ahead of BALDWIN. Americans who went abroad for education sought out companions from home, at the Carolina Coffee House in London, or in the Virginia Club at Edinburgh; at the Middle Temple, DICKINSON roomed with a childhood friend from Talbot County, and C. C. PINCKNEY went from Westminster to Oxford in company with the Drayton boys of South Carolina. Collegiate connections were not particularly strategic when all the Harvard graduates represented Massachusetts, all but one William and Mary alumnus represented Virginia, and the sole Connecticut Framer who had not attended Yale was nevertheless the college's treasurer. But PATERSON gained another state for the New Jersey Plan when his close Princeton friend LUTHER MARTIN arrived to represent Maryland, and the Princetonian Connecticut–North Carolina link between ELLSWORTH and DAVIE made the Great Compromise possible.

Indeed, Princeton offered its students the same opportunity to develop interstate social relationships that service in Congress did, at a more impressionable age and without the rivalry and suspicion that were inevitable in Congress. But the variety the college provided was more than just social. Princeton's curriculum went well beyond the familiar reading list of the older colleges. Elsewhere, Latin and Greek—along with natural philosophy and personal ethics for the college students and maybe some mathematics at grammar school—were the "old" curriculum. Although the emphasis was on the classics' Latin grammar and syntax much more than their content, boys did learn patriotism and virtue from Virgil and Cicero; history, as recounted by Plutarch or Sallust, was a means of illustrating virtue and vice in action. In those ancient authors they found their ideals of liberty and good government. They internalized the message that democracy would give way to tyranny and that power corrupted; this was the "classical republicanism" that traditional schools inculcated in future congressmen and in the Constitution's Framers.[8]

At Princeton and the College of Philadelphia—and to a lesser extent at King's College—a newer curriculum was taking shape. At those colleges and in a number of Presbyterian academies, history was given serious attention and moral philosophy took a new, Scottish turn, one which WILSON (and probably SPAIGHT) encountered directly at the University of Glasgow. In addition to Rollin's ubiquitous *Ancient History*, the modern histories of Edinburgh's Robertson and Ferguson were recommended by Witherspoon. Philadelphia's reading list included the Englishmen Sidney and Harrington and the Scot Hutcheson. Under Myles Cooper, King's College was more heavily classical than Harvard or Yale, but Cooper also assigned Hutcheson, along with Pufendorf. Witherspoon at Princeton and Alison at both New London Academy and Philadelphia gave moral philosophy lectures based on Hutcheson, continuing beyond ethics to teach politics and government.

This new curriculum still began with the classical republicanism of Cicero and his contemporaries. But then Pufendorf, Locke, and Burlamaqui introduced the idea of natural rights—fundamental to the Declaration of Independence in 1776—and the idea of *equality* of rights, a revolutionary principle for those who were framing a representative government in 1787. Framers educated in the old curriculum (including GERRY, BUTLER and CHARLES PINCKNEY III) advocated restrictions on suffrage or high property-ownership requirements for holding office, while the Princeton- or Glasgow-educated ELLSWORTH, MADISON, and WILSON argued against having different classes of citizenship; autodidacts (SHERMAN, MASON, and FRANK-LIN) were divided.[9]

The "classical republicans" and "commonwealth Whigs" depended on individual virtue and strictly separated powers in government, but those Framers who were exposed early to the Scots, as MADISON's schoolmates and WILSON were, "sought some middle ground between . . . a politics of virtue," which Cicero and Plutarch had required for a republic, and "a politics of self-interest," which had begun to look more realistic. Confidence in republican virtue had eroded among veterans of Congress, and Samuel Fleischaker notes that "[Adam] Smith did suggest a move away from the belief that people were capable of a strong concern for the well-being of the polity as a whole—of sacrificing themselves to the whole in the way that civic republican thinkers seem to have wanted people to do." Those whose formal education in political philosophy had been limited to Aristotle might have eventually encountered the idea of separation of powers (but not the complex interlinking of them) in their later independent reading of Bolingbroke or Montesquieu. "The great Montesquieu" to BUTLER, "the celebrated Montesquieu" to RANDOLPH was cited in the Convention notes taken by HAMILTON, KING, YATES, MCHENRY, and MADISON. Indeed, Montesquieu was twice invoked by MADISON himself on the danger of letting the legislature control the executive, a conservative position that he and WILSON were combatting in the latter part of the summer; they knew that his name carried weight. But MADISON was not in awe of Montesquieu; by Colleen Sheehan's accounting, "When MADISON publicly invoked the name of Montesquieu in his writings of the early 1790s, it was primarily to challenge rather than to celebrate the wisdom of the French oracle."[10]

MADISON's notes rarely mention speakers' sources—perhaps because he saw no need, or perhaps because the speakers themselves didn't acknowledge them. David Lutz notes that Montesquieu was in general the most often cited of recent writers, but he quickly points out that frequency of mention does not mean agreement. Indeed, philosophers whose ideas deeply informed a speaker's argument were more likely to go unnamed. MADISON and HAMILTON both paraphrased (and even quoted) Hume without acknowledgment. In his voluminous Convention notes, MADISON never names Smith or Hutcheson—or Witherspoon, even though half of the Framers were his personal acquaintances. But Hutcheson, who dominated the upperclass years at Philadelphia and at Princeton (through Witherspoon's lectures), spoke directly to the form of government. The Hutcheson/Witherspoon idea of balancing competing interests and blending responsibilities to produce a *nexus imperii*—an interdependence among branches of government—was a central part of MADISON's evolving plan of government, and it was strongly supported by GOUVERNEUR MORRIS and WILSON. It was a part that the old-school Framers were slow to grasp; the idea that the right structure might matter more than individual virtue simply flew in the face of what they had learned in their youth.[11]

The differences among the Framers' educational backgrounds affected six major controversies with which the Convention wrestled. During June and July, the Convention heard debates on three closely related questions: how republican government could succeed in a nation as large as the United States; how much power should be granted to the national government or reserved to the states; and whether the states would be represented equally, as in the old Congress, or proportionally according to population. The compromise that finally settled the last of these questions left the first two still undecided. In August, the Framers wrestled with popular suffrage and with the election and the powers of the executive, questions where the new "common sense" philosophy of Thomas Reid was pitted against conservative, classical suspicion of democracy. In September, with the end in sight, they struggled with the distribution of powers—strictly separated or mingled in a Hutchesonian *nexus*—among the three branches. In all six of these phases the Framers' different educations had a significant influence on their ideas and their votes. College ties played a critical role in the resolution of the bitter dispute over representation in Congress; as Monroe had earlier reminded MERCER, "political connections are but slender ties between men . . . [but] those who had been educated together have a different kind of tie and more natural claim to the good offices of each other." Finally, the differences between old school and new school preparation extended even to the decision of Harvard's GERRY, William and Mary's RANDOLPH, and the self-taught MASON to withhold their signatures from a final document that so strongly reflected the educations of Kings' College's MORRIS, St. Andrews's and Glasgow's WILSON, and Princeton's MADISON.[12]

In the opening weeks there was much talk about the failures of ancient and modern republics and confederations. Everyone acknowledged that this was MADISON's area of expertise, and he brought up the Greek confederations on at least four occasions, with WILSON and CHARLES PINCKNEY III chiming in. HAMILTON and LUTHER MARTIN delivered marathon lectures on republican government; HAMILTON's June 18 address ranged from Athens and Sparta to Venice. All day long he reviewed the republican challenges faced by Thebes, Rome, Carthage, Charlemagne, and the Hanseatic League; he cited Demosthenes, Aristotle, Cicero, Montesquieu, and Neckar, and proposed an executive who would serve, on good behavior, for life. The next day the debate resumed as if he had never spoken. (According to JOHNSON, all admired his speech, but none took it seriously.) Then on June 27, MARTIN began a two-day harangue that left the Convention exhausted. ELLSWORTH later complained that it "might have continued two months, but for those marks of fatigue and disgust" on the delegates' faces. The usually diligent MADISON made no effort to report it in detail, observing that it was delivered with much diffuseness and considerable vehemence. MARTIN demonstrated that his education in history and political philosophy was a match for HAMILTON's, as he brought up the Amphictyonic League and the Swiss and Dutch confederacies and threw in Locke, Vattel, Priestly, Rutherford, and Lord Somers. (MADISON, erratic in his spelling of even the other Framers' names, wrote "Summers" in his notes, but YATES—educated at an unknown New York City school—got it right in his.)[13]

These overwhelming displays of erudition were counterproductive; even MARTIN's allies regretted his effusions. One can imagine the Framers' dismay ten days later when GOUVERNEUR MORRIS, just returned after a month's absence, launched into his own account of those same Greek and Dutch confederacies. The privately tutored DICKINSON had an exchange with MADISON in early June on the parallels between government and the Newtonian model of the solar system; he then invoked Roman and medieval history, and the self-taught BUTLER seized opportunities to display his knowledge of Catiline's conspiracy, Solon, and "the great Montesquieu." The graduates of Oxford, William and Mary, Harvard, and Yale made no contributions to all this flurry of historical reference beyond a single mention of Magna Carta by KING. C. C. PINCKNEY, CARROLL, and the entire Yale contingent were nearly silent. Harvard's GERRY argued only from contemporary political experience. After the extravagant displays of June—and perhaps in reaction to HAMILTON's and MARTIN's excesses—the torrent of classical and medieval citations dried up, but disagreement over the possibilities of republican government continued to mark a philosophical fault line.[14]

All of the Framers, including MADISON, were influenced by the practical realities that surrounded them, but they nevertheless depended on certain habits of thought to help them interpret those realities—realities observed, inescapably, through the lens of education. PATERSON, BEDFORD, and READ had no trouble settling into the nationalist camp once the small states had secured equal representation in the Senate (whereupon proportional advocates MADISON and WILSON began looking for opportunities to restrain Congress's power). They, and most of the other strong-government nationalists, had been educated at the newer schools or in Scotland. GERRY and older or less formally educated Framers such as SHERMAN were now caught between the classical republican fear of a king-like executive and their own deep distrust of popular government: in GERRY's words in the opening debates, "The evils we experience flow from the excess of democracy." On one hand, they wanted a powerful legislative branch chosen at frequent intervals by a virtuous public, but on the other, they were determined to leave the depraved multitude out of the process, placing more trust in state legislatures to choose both a strong federal legislature and a weak (preferably plural) federal executive. As GERRY's biographer George Billias puts it, GERRY believed in the principle that the people should govern, but "only as long as they agreed with him and other local authorities." Framers educated at the newer colleges—MADISON, WILSON, HAMILTON, GOUVERNEUR MORRIS—took the opposite position: they wanted a powerful single executive, long terms of office, and direct election not only of the Congress but even (at least WILSON and MORRIS did) the executive. A balance of competing interests—the two houses of Congress against each other and both against the executive—rather than an elusive republican virtue, would be their safeguard against tyranny.[15]

In his study of ideology at the Convention, *Novus Ordo Seclorum*, Forrest McDonald uses an analogy to English politics to divide the most active Framers into "Court Party Nationalists" led by MADISON, WILSON, and MORRIS, and a "Country Party" who put more faith in the states. McDonald does not note their educations, but of the dozen or so whom he places in the first group, only Harvard's KING (a recent convert to nationalism) and William and Mary's MCCLURG (with his Edinburgh exposure) were products of the older schools. Of the second group, only two out of fifteen—Philadelphia's WILLIAMSON and Princeton's LUTHER MARTIN—were educated in the newer model. (WILLIAMSON is evidently placed in McDonald's "Country Party" simply because he thought letting congressmen hold multiple offices invited corruption, but he was otherwise strongly national-minded.) Among the nationalists he includes (again without noting their education) Alison's student GEORGE READ, Witherspoon's students MADISON and DAVIE, Glasgow's WILSON, and the two King's College alumni, HAMILTON and GOUVERNEUR MORRIS. These were the Framers most familiar with the Scottish enlightenment thinkers. This "Court Party," according to McDonald, "sought to establish a government on Humean-Mandevillian lines"—trying to make public virtues out of private vices.[16]

For Daniel Walker Howe, "Perhaps the most pervasive influence of the social thought of the Scottish Enlightenment on the American founders (and very broad one not attributable to any individual thinker) was the Scots' concern with unintended outcomes." Howe explains: "The founders wanted to create . . . a system, so that the unintended outcome of short-sightedness and selfishness would be the public good," a system by means of which, "vices could, through wise contrivance be made to do the work of virtues." He reminds us, "This was, of course, the opposite of the civic humanist reliance on public virtue" to which the "old school" Framers were initially committed, but it was just what MADISON had learned in his Princeton reading. GOUVERNEUR MORRIS explicitly invoked one such unintended outcome in his argument for allowing presidents to seek reelection: since the lust for recognition was an innate human vice, allowing reelection would give a president a "Civil road to Glory," whereas limiting him to a single term would "destroy the great incitement to merit public esteem by taking away the hope of being rewarded with a reappointment. It may give a dangerous turn to one of the strongest passions in the human breast." The alternative, he feared, would be to seek glory "by the sword."[17]

The phrase Howe employs, "civic humanist," aptly characterizes the fifteenth-century Florentines to whom it was originally applied, but like "elitist" it suffers from both anachronism and ambiguity and is not consistently helpful for eighteenth-century thinkers. J. G. A. Pocock applies it to America's older revolutionary generation, and his description of them also fits the more traditionally educated Framers with their commitment to elusive republican virtue:

> The more active a government in which they did not directly participate, the greater their sense that their independence and virtue were threatened by a force they could only call corruption, and as Machiavelli and Cato had taught them, once they mistrusted government, there was nothing they should not fear. . . . [Fear of] modern and ef-

fective government [reflected] the dread of modernity itself, of which the threat to virtue by corruption was the contemporary ideological expression.

Thomas Miller rightly points out that Hume challenged the idealistic civic humanism of much Enlightenment thought, but he and others persist in placing Francis Hutcheson and John Witherspoon squarely in an optimistic "civic humanist" tradition, even though they recommended government restrained by "overpoise" of powers in a *"nexus imperii."* Historians and political scientists can become entangled in terminology: Richard Matthews, in *If Men Were Angels*, expresses incredulity that Lance Banning and Drew McCoy call MADISON a "civic humanist" and that Banning and Martin Diamond consider him "a democrat or a representative democrat"; for Matthews, MADISON is the "cold" and pessimistic "constant liberal Prince" of a "Heartless Empire of Reason." And David Epstein, in *The Political Theory of the Federalist*, somewhat opaquely states that according to late twentieth-century scholarship, neither the Constitution nor the *Federalist* "manifest[s] an undemocratic beginning to American political democracy"; such scholarship, he says, argues that *"The Federalist* reveals the liberal beginnings of American liberal democracy, a liberalism which displaced an earlier tradition of 'republicanism' or 'civic humanism.'"* Yet Epstein thinks there is "one formidable difficulty with the view that *The Federalist* [and presumably the Constitution] rejected a classical Republican tradition in favor of Lockean liberalism. That [difficulty] is *The Federalist*'s repeated and very emphatic insistence on a 'strictly republican' or 'wholly popular' form of government," made workable by "a 'more perfect structure' than the ancient republics had."[18]

Whether the Framers were, in one sense or another, humanists, liberals, republicans, or representative democrats, it was the genius of a pragmatic younger generation—of men such as MADISON, GOUVERNEUR MORRIS, and WILSON—to combine the skepticism of Smith and Hume with the optimism of Hutcheson and Witherspoon to transcend dependence on undependable public virtue—to create a government in which, as Pocock wittily puts it, "something has been lost to virtue, but more has been gained by *virtù* [strength]." One of those hardheaded pragmatists was OLIVER ELLSWORTH.[19]

According to John Adams, ELLSWORTH had made SHERMAN his model in Congress—"praise enough for both men"—and Adams found them much alike except that ELLSWORTH "had the advantage of a liberal education and somewhat more extensive reading." The younger ELLSWORTH and the older SHERMAN rarely parted company in Congress, but at the Convention they sometimes did. Here the forty-two-year-old Princeton graduate was the more flexible; McDonald includes him in his list of "Court Party Nationalists," but he places the stubborn sixty-six-year-old autodidact in the other camp that he, tellingly, subtitles "the Ideologues." In addition to the self-taught or tutored SHERMAN, MASON, and JENIFER, McDonald lists the following (again without noting their educations) among these traditionalists who looked to republican virtue and wanted to keep power in the hands of state legislatures: Harvard's GERRY, Yale's BALDWIN, William and Mary's RANDOLPH, and Oxford's C. C. PINCKNEY: "The ideologues, taught by Bolingbroke, Montesquieu, or classical republicanism, shrank with horror at the prospect of admitting the base passions as operating principles of government." Lacking MADISON'S, BEDFORD'S, and DAVIE's early exposure to Hutcheson, Hume, Ferguson, and Adam Smith (all on Witherspoon's reading list), they resisted the idea of welcoming selfish factions in order to let them balance one another out.[20]

Predictably, the same split appears in the long-running debates over the independence of the executive and the extent of popular representation. Cicero, Tacitus, and Plutarch taught that any power, in any branch of government, is likely to be abused; Demosthenes warned against too much power concentrated in the executive, while Thucydides cautioned against too much democracy. Those combined threats left RANDOLPH, GERRY, SHERMAN, DICKINSON, and MASON—"old-school or self-taught" men—with the paradox of supporting powerful, frequently elected legislatures at the same time they distrusted the voting public. But MADISON, MORRIS, and WILSON argued that checks and balances made a forceful and energetic executive safe, while long terms of office would diminish the influence of an impulsive popular electorate. Making a *nexus imperii* out of those checks and balances became the heart of the Convention's final controversy: the distribution of powers among the branches of government.

The innovative nationalists took Hume to heart: "A constitution is only so far good, as it provides a remedy for maladministration." As MADISON soon wrote in *Federalist*, no. 51, "In framing a government which is to be administered by men over men, the great difficulty lies in this: you must first enable the government to control the governed; and in the next place oblige it to control itself." The only dependable "remedy for maladministration," he continued, was "this policy of supplying, by opposite and rival interests, the defect of better motives." It was a strategy he had discovered while still a college student, one that Hume and Ferguson had shown him "might be traced through the whole system of human affairs, private as well as public." The Convention finally adopted most of his and his allies' unconventional suggestions for balancing the different branches' "opposite and rival interests" by subdividing and distributing powers, but it did so only after lengthy debate. On July 18, MORRIS and WILSON proposed executive appointment of judges; over the next three days CHARLES PINCKNEY III, SHERMAN, RANDOLPH, and MASON argued instead for appointment by Congress, and MADISON offered the solution of presidential appointment with the approval of the Senate. He explained, "This would unite the responsibility in the Executive with the security afforded in the 2d. branch agst. any incautious or corrupt nomination by the Executive." On July 19, MORRIS suggested extending that arrangement to the power "to appoint officers & to command the forces of the Republic: to appoint 1. Ministerial officers for the administration of public affairs. 2. Officers for the dispensation of Justice." It would take time, but eventually, the majority would agree, as they would on presidential vetoes that could be overridden by two-thirds of both houses, and presidential power to call Congress into session. One of MADISON's favorites, the participation of the judiciary in the veto process, evidently went too far and was rejected; still, he and WILSON continued to argue for it up to the final weeks, sometimes with ELLSWORTH's and MORRIS's support. (LUTHER MARTIN accurately predicted that the judiciary would be able to overturn laws on its own by declaring them unconstitutional; DAVID BREARLEY, chief justice of the New Jersey Supreme Court, had already set such a precedent in his home state.) In an unsuccessful argument for judicial veto on July 21, WILSON made an important point that, over time, would sink in with most of his colleagues: "The separation of the departments does not require that they should have separate objects, but that they should act separately though on the same objects." That was the essence of the *nexus imperii*.[21]

The conservatively educated Framers did not all come around. The danger of corrupt combinations between a powerful executive and Senate was cited by GERRY, MASON, and RANDOLPH as a primary reason why those "old school" delegates refused in the end to sign the Constitution. MASON declared that he feared "the alarming dependence and connection between that branch of the legislature and the supreme Executive." He had been the primary author of Virginia's 1776 constitution, which let the General Assembly choose a governor who could himself do little without the concurrence of the Council of State; it specified that the "legislature, executive and judiciary departments shall be separate and distinct, so that neither exercise the Powers properly belonging to the other." The Princeton-educated LUTHER MARTIN, in the ratification debates in Maryland, based *his* typically lengthy arguments on his objection to proportional representation. He remained stubbornly loyal to his friend PATERSON's plan even after PATERSON abandoned it, but he was not bothered by the *nexus imperii*.[22]

Bearing in mind the nonsigners' complaints, in *Federalist*, no. 38, MADISON lists various objections by hypothetical enemies of the Constitution to the innovative blending and balancing of the branches' responsibilities. Perhaps, "In the eyes of one the junction of the Senate with the President in the responsible function of appointing to offices, instead of vesting this executive power in the Executive alone, is the vicious part of the organization." But, should that quasi-executive function be granted, "No part of the arrangement . . . is [then] more inadmissible than the trial of impeachments by the Senate, which is alternately a member both of the legislative and executive departments, when this power so evidently belonged to the judiciary department."[23]

MADISON is here reviewing for his readers controversial examples of the *nexus imperii* that he had earlier had to explain to a puzzled Convention. He is anticipating arguments that were bound to arise at the impending ratification conventions. MADISON was looking ahead, but he could not have guessed how far ahead. CHARLES PINCKNEY III had objected to MADISON's proposal that the president should be impeachable. In response, DAVIE, who had heard Witherspoon's lectures at Princeton four years after MADISON, rose to defend impeachment and removal of the president by Congress, declaring on July 12, "If he be not impeachable while in office, he will spare no efforts or means whatsoever to get himself re-elected. [Congressional impeachment is] an essential security for the good behavior of the Executive." WILSON immediately "concurred in the necessity of making the Executive impeachable whilst in office." Moments later, MADISON presciently anticipated a future president who "might pervert his administration into a scheme of peculation or oppression. He might betray his trust to foreign powers." Such a president, he believed, would deserve the impeachment that the House indeed voted in 2019 and 2021. (Later, although he never anticipated the extreme partisanship that would beset American government, MADISON would express his preference for the Supreme Court, or a tribunal that included the Court, to be responsible for trying an impeached president, instead of the Senate. Here, as in his wish to include the Court in a council of revision, he could not persuade the Convention.) MADISON's erstwhile ally, RUFUS KING—whose classical education at Harvard had not introduced him to the puzzling novelty of the *nexus imperii*—resisted the entire idea of impeachment; despite working closely with MADISON through June and the first part of July, he now demanded that the Convention "recur to the primitive axiom that the three great departments of Govts. should be separate and independent. . . . Would this be the case if the Executive should be impeachable? . . . But under no circumstances ought he to be impeachable by the Legislature." GOUVERNEUR MORRIS (who was better acquainted with Hutcheson) had begun the day opposed to the proposal, but MADISON notes that "Mr. GOVR. MORRIS's opinion had been changed by the arguments used in the discussion. He was now sensible of the necessity of impeachments." So at last were most of the others; the vote "on ye Question, Shall the executive be removable on impeachments" was eight states to two, in the affirmative. PINCKNEY's and KING's opposition prevailed only in their own South Carolina and Massachusetts delegations, which happened to be two of only four delegations present without a student of either Witherspoon or Alison.[24]

Through August to mid-September, structural checks and balances, the *nexus imperii,* and other ways of enlarging the sphere all became essential aspects of the new, complex federal government. "Old school" Framers resisted, some to the bitter end, but as Clinton Rossiter observes, "GERRY's laments over the grave of old-fashioned republicanism could no longer deflect the course of the determined and impatient majority" who had at last adopted the innovations that MADISON and his allies had synthesized from their educations under Witherspoon, Alison, and the Scots.[25]

MORRIS's reversal on impeachment is a reminder that many of the Constitution's innovations depended on the persuasion of Framers who were initially resistant. In a time before partisan lockstep, persuasive speakers could still change minds, both at the Philadelphia Convention and at the state ratifying conventions that soon followed. David Gelman has recently made a statistical study of the Framers' of participation in Convention debates. He concludes, unsurprisingly, that "ideologically extreme" delegates were more likely to participate than "ideologically moderate" delegates. This distinction, however, may be more accurately recast as one between those delegates who came to the Convention with well-assimilated philosophies of government and those who did not—or those Framers who were well prepared for debate by their education and experience and those who were not. Of course, with a sample of only fifty-five, we cannot overlook individual proclivities for gab. LUTHER MARTIN, GOUVERNEUR MORRIS, and HUGH WILLIAMSON simply liked to talk, but MADISON was one of the most frequent participants, and no one could accuse him of a penchant for volubility. In addition to frequency, Gelman also employs a metric he calls "verbosity length"—the mechanically measured (in millimeters) length of a given speech as reported in MADISON's notes. When we realize that MADISON briefly summarized such interminable speeches as MARTIN's and HAMILTON's harangues, and that he had reference copies of some prepared addresses (including notes for some of his own) but not of most, the value of that metric becomes doubtful. Finally, Gelman employs a metric he calls "college" as a control, but since he treats all colleges equally—old or new, with or without formal instruction in rhetoric (and that in English or in Latin), that metric, too, is of questionable value.[26]

It is perhaps more instructive to turn to contemporary critics. Future chief justice John Marshall was a delegate to the Virginia ratifying convention; there he heard Patrick Henry at his most histrionic, but he called MADISON "the most eloquent man I ever heard" because MADISON's calm, quiet speeches were filled with irresistible reasoning. In MADISON's Princeton graduating class, oratorical honors had gone to GUNNING BEDFORD, whose contributions at the Convention were far fewer but notably fiery. PIERCE, who described BEDFORD as a "bold and nervous" speaker, was something of a connoisseur of oratory, and his character sketches of the Framers almost always assess their speaking ability. HAMILTON, like MADISON, he found "rather a convincing Speaker than a blazing Orator," and WILSON also "draws the attention not by the charm of his eloquence, but by the force of his reasoning." Having already heard a number of the Framers in Congress, PIERCE believed the most persuasive in debate were KING, MADISON ("In the management of every great question he evidently took the lead in the Convention"), WILSON ("clear, copious, and comprehensive"), PATERSON (who "never speaks but when he understands his subject well"), and ELLSWORTH ("very happy in a reply, and choice in selecting such parts of his adversary's arguments as he finds make the strongest impressions,—in order to take off the force of them, so as to admit the power of his own"). This was one more area in which a Framer's education could make a difference. Disputation at Yale was syllogistic and in Latin, but at Philadelphia and Princeton it was forensic, in English. KING had practiced in the Harvard Speaking Club, MORRIS received early training in oratory at the Philadelphia Academy, WILSON had been at Glasgow, home of the Oceana debating society and so many others, and had experience lecturing as an instructor at Philadelphia. The other four had been Princeton debaters, two Whigs and two Clios. (DANIEL CARROLL was trained at St. Omer's to speak extemporaneously, but only in Greek or Latin; he said little at the Convention.)[27]

Rhetorical effort could go only so far. Neither of the two marathon orations made any difference, nor did most of SHERMAN's constant carping; the vehement GERRY and MASON were, in the end, unable to persuade other

Framers to reject the Constitution. Instead, through the summer, the careful reasoning of MADISON, MORRIS, and WILSON gradually won over the reluctant, although the logic of MADISON's case for proportional representation could not, to his intense frustration, move the small states' representatives. In that contest of wills, PATERSON and BEDFORD were able to draw lines that their delegations would hold, threatening to bring the Convention to an end until the first Committee of Representation negotiated the compromise that rescued the Convention. That compromise—followed by others that postponed the inescapable crisis over slavery—reveals the fateful influence of one Framer's boyhood tutor.

Henry May, in *The Enlightenment in America*, says the Constitution reflects "all the virtues of the Moderate Enlightenment, and also one of its faults: the belief that everything can be settled by compromise." The Rev. Joseph Bellamy's doctrine of compromise by the righteous ruler, internalized by OLIVER ELLSWORTH in his tutor's study, would form part of that antislavery New Englander's rationale in August for allowing the continued importation of slaves. Alone among the Connecticut Framers, neither ELLSWORTH nor his family had ever owned slaves. "If slavery was to be considered in a moral light," he said, "we ought to go further [than restricting importation] and free those already in the country." But in the end the moral light was not employed, and the Convention's support for the fugitive slave, three-fifths, and slave importation clauses was entirely pragmatic. Of the nearly 700,000 slaves counted in the 1790 census, more than 600,000 were held in Maryland, Virginia, and the two Carolinas—and in South Carolina and Georgia numbers were increasing rapidly. This geographical reality cut across the Framers' differences in education, age, religion, or experience. To Virginia's RANDOLPH, slavery was "the dilemma to which the Convention was exposed." Southern delegates WILLIAMSON and FEW found slavery repulsive enough that they eventually chose to move north, but while FEW was away at Congress in New York, voting to bar slavery from the Northwest Territory, WILLIAMSON was defending slavery as an essential interest of the state he represented. So was the Connecticut native, ABRAHAM BALDWIN, who expressed the fond hope that his adopted Georgia would, "if left to herself, probably put a stop to the evil" of the slave trade. WILLIAMSON, BALDWIN, LUTHER MARTIN, and MADISON all represented slave states on the Committee of Slave Trade that met in August. All four considered slavery immoral, as did the vocal Massachusetts member of the committee, KING. But South Carolina's C. C. PINCKNEY was adamant that any restriction of the importation of slaves would be enough to send the South Carolinians and the Georgians packing.[28]

RUTLEDGE, BUTLER, and the PINCKNEYS meant what they said; they could look ahead to ratifying conventions in the southern states that would surely reject any Constitution that took a stand against slavery. The vote to ratify would be razor-thin in Virginia as it was, with Patrick Henry condemning the Constitution as too weak in its protection of slavery from some future Congress: "May they not pronounce all your slaves free?" South Carolina's convention met ahead of Virginia's. In Philadelphia, some slaveowning Virginia Framers expressed their moral qualms: MASON lamented "the evil of having slaves," and MADISON said he "thought it wrong to admit in the Constitution that there could be property in men." Even North Carolina's DAVIE, who insisted on the three-fifths compromise, would remind his state's ratifying convention that their "unhappy" slaves were indeed "rational beings" who themselves "had a right to representation," but he also declared that "we cannot at present alter their situation." All three would nonetheless vote for all of the Constitution's various compromises protecting the institution of slavery—scrupulously avoiding naming it. We cannot know whether they, lacking ELLSWORTH's serene confidence in God's approval of the tactic of compromise, suffered pangs of conscience. But, as the legal scholar William Casto explains, "Bellamy's theodicy based on faith and optimism could easily be understood as permitting righteous rulers like ELLSWORTH to compromise their principles as long as they continued to believe that the country was moving in the right direction." ELLSWORTH reassured the delegates—and himself—that an increase in affordable hired labor must eventually "render slaves useless" and put an end to slavery (thus ensuring that the divine will would prevail); in a jarringly inaccurate prophecy, he declared that "slavery, in time, will not be a speck in our Country." Therefore, he said, he was willing to compromise with South Carolina and Georgia rather than "lose two States" and see the union "fly into a variety of shapes & directions, and most probably into several confederations and not without bloodshed." SHERMAN agreed that it was "better to let the S. States import slaves than to part with them, if they made that a sine qua non." The majority, including such antislavery northerners as GOUVERNEUR MORRIS, reluctantly agreed.[29]

The Convention could never have reached its debates over slavery if it had not first agreed to compromise on state representation in Congress. The entire project would likely have collapsed a month earlier, and the union flown into various directions then, had Bellamy's teaching about compromise and the "righteous ruler" not inspired ELLSWORTH's stage management of the Great ("Connecticut") Compromise that broke the logjam over representation. Joseph Bellamy was just becoming famous for his extended sermon *God's Wisdom in the Permission of Sin* when ELLSWORTH came to live and study with him. To quote Casto again, "In keeping with the optimism and faith of *God's Wisdom*, ELLSWORTH undoubtedly assumed that the Constitution that he helped create was part of God's plan to bring a righteous order to the chaos of the Confederation"—chaos that was threatening to break out at the end of June and derail the Convention. Just over half the states insisted on proportional representation in Congress; two or three threatened to leave unless states were given equal representation regardless of population. MADISON's notes for June 29 report ELLSWORTH's speech: "He trusted that on this middle ground a compromise would take place. He did not see that it could be on any other. And if no compromise should take place, our meeting would not only be in vain but worse than in vain." As early as June 2, JOHN DICKINSON had suggested equal representation for states in one house and proportional representation in the other; at that time almost no one had joined him. Now, after four weeks in which the small states of New Jersey and Delaware (along with the obstructionist Clintonian delegates from the larger state of New York) refused to give in to the Virginia Plan, ELLSWORTH reintroduced DICKINSON's idea, saying, "We are partly national, partly federal." The next day, his fellow Princetonian DAVIE spoke (not DAYTON as is sometimes erroneously reported). Echoing ELLSWORTH's words, he suggested that "the Govt. might in some respects operate on the states, in others on the people." Compromise was gaining support from a quarter that was completely unexpected: North Carolina had thus far voted consistently with the large states. This development was not missed by ELLSWORTH or the rest of the North Carolina delegates.[30]

Three days went by, with three busy evenings of extramural negotiations at the City Tavern or the Indian Queen following each day's adjournment. Then, over the vehement objections of MADISON and WILSON, the Convention elected a carefully chosen Grand Committee to seek a resolution, with one member from each state. The Committee was remarkable for the names that were left off: unlike the important committees of Style, Postponed Matters, and Detail, it had neither KING, nor HAMILTON, nor WILSON, nor GOUVERNEUR MORRIS, nor MADISON among its members. It consisted instead of GERRY, YATES, FRANKLIN, MASON, and RUTLEDGE (all comfortable enough with the equal representation Congress had followed since 1774), the Connecticut-raised BALDWIN rather than Georgia's only native Framer, HOUSTOUN—and five closely connected Princetonians. PATERSON, BEDFORD, and DAVIE were chosen for no other committees, but they were significant choices for this one. ELLSWORTH, PATERSON, and LUTHER MARTIN had known one another since founding the original version of the Cliosophic Society in

1765. BEDFORD had for weeks been, along with MARTIN, PATERSON's staunchest ally in promoting the New Jersey Plan. But DAVIE, the fifth selection, unexpectedly proved to be the committee's key member. The Convention at large chose him instead of North Carolina's usual leader HUGH WILLIAMSON, who served on five other committees. DAVIE had grown up just outside Charlotte, North Carolina, where leading citizens included ELLSWORTH's Princeton roommate Waightstill Avery and their classmate Hezekiah James Balch—both founding trustees of DAVIE's preparatory school, Queen's College. Avery had taken the lead in promoting public education in North Carolina, including the state university that DAVIE was currently advocating and would soon found. DAVIE had come directly to Philadelphia from serving alongside Avery in the North Carolina legislature.

Accounts of the Convention typically cast SHERMAN as the leader of the Connecticut delegation and the originator of the "Connecticut" Compromise. A veteran of the struggle for independence, he was certainly the state's most prominent political figure, even though JOHNSON was chosen first when the legislature appointed delegates. But SHERMAN was not a flexible thinker; he lacked ELLSWORTH's early acquired faith in compromise, and his ideas of government were narrowly traditional. In *The Framers' Coup*, Michael Klarman, without offering evidence of individual leadership, calls Sherman a "molder" of this and other "critical compromises" brokered by Connecticut that "ultimately enabled the Convention to succeed," but he also acknowledges that SHERMAN was consistently "one of the nationalists' main adversaries." McDonald, as we have seen, places him in the traditionalist "Country Party" but puts ELLSWORTH in the innovative "Court Party." Significantly, SHERMAN was not among the six Framers that ELLSWORTH later said the Constitution actually "was drawn by," namely, MADISON, WILSON, HAMILTON, RUTLEDGE, GORHAM (chairman of the Committee of the Whole)—and himself. A footnote that MADISON much later attached to his own notes for July 3 says that ELLSWORTH yielded his seat on the Grand Committee to SHERMAN, citing an unconvincing (and otherwise unnoticed) "indisposition." That gave the committee the added weight of SHERMAN's reputation, but it also freed ELLSWORTH to work more effectively behind the scenes.[31]

We can never know what discussions DAVIE and ELLSWORTH may have had on those humid Philadelphia evenings going into the Independence Day recess, privately or in a group of delegates. We do know that Washington's diary records a dinner at the Indian Queen on July 2, with "some members of the Convention"; among the lodgers at that inn were committee members MASON and RUTLEDGE, and also STRONG, with whom GERRY often dined. (GERRY lodged at Mrs. Daley's boarding house. ELLSWORTH and SHERMAN stayed at Mrs. Marshall's, only a block away.) In the event, despite all of DAVIE's past votes for MADISON's Virginia Plan, he cast his own vote in committee for compromise and then proceeded, on July 16, to bring North Carolina with him, starting with ALEXANDER MARTIN, the delegation's other Princetonian. Although WILLIAMSON had endorsed the idea of appointing a committee to seek a solution, on July 5 his first response had been to call the proposed compromise "the most objectionable of any kind he had yet heard." Evidently, DAVIE persuaded him to change his mind. BLOUNT had already left to represent his state at Congress in New York, and SPAIGHT, the remaining North Carolinian, was thus outvoted in the delegation three to one.[32]

Anyone who examines the Convention's process of reaching this compromise is forced to agree with Forrest McDonald on one thing: "Precisely what happened cannot be known for certain." But historians of the Convention have made game, if sometimes incoherent, efforts. McDonald himself postulates a murky deal between Connecticut (SHERMAN) and the Carolinas (RUTLEDGE and WILLIAMSON) to exchange continuation of the slave trade for southern support of Connecticut's ambitions for land in the West. Some such sectional quid pro quo would certainly explain the late August voting patterns of Connecticut and South Carolina (but *not* North Carolina); unfortunately it cannot explain the vote on July 16, when South Carolina voted against the compromise that Connecticut and North Carolina supported. If such a deal existed—and if it had anything to do with the Great Compromise, a connection that never quite seems to be made—either WILLIAMSON or RUTLEDGE (or both) reneged. (McDonald admits, in several footnotes, that his conclusions regarding this and other conspiracies are often based on "surmise," "my own surmise," "process of elimination," "inference," or even "inescapable inference.") Richard Barry, in his 1942 biography, *Mr. Rutledge of South Carolina*, imaginatively narrates a late-night meeting at the Indian Queen on June 30 between RUTLEDGE and SHERMAN. McDonald picks up the story and adds, "Late in the evening a caller appeared at the door: HUGH WILLIAMSON of North Carolina." The rest is left to surmise and inference. But a week after the supposed deal, WILLIAMSON condemned the Compromise on July 5. McDonald further infers (but offers no evidence) that DAVIE and ALEXANDER MARTIN had been for unexplained reasons crypto-supporters of the PATERSON Plan, despite North Carolina's dependably "large state" votes thus far and BLOUNT's letter to Governor Caswell, assuring him that "my Colleagues in that body were generally unanimous."[33]

A more recent historian of the Convention, Richard Beeman, is at a loss for any better explanation; he speculates that "HUGH WILLIAMSON, certainly the most distinguished member of the North Carolina delegation," had come to see that compromise was essential to prevent the Convention's collapse, and "WILLIAMSON's powers of persuasion" got DAVIE and MARTIN to follow him. But WILLIAMSON had not been chosen for the Grand Committee, he had no particular influence over those two, and he was not known for "powers of persuasion" or rhetorical skill in general—RUFUS KING said his "elocution provoked laughter in Congress"; more important, when he blasted the Committee's proposal on July 5, DAVIE was already on board with it. David O. Stewart, in his account of the Convention, makes no attempt to explain the critical change in North Carolina's vote beyond an assertion both vague and confusing that "the small-state delegates wore down their adversaries and partly overturned the WILSON-RUTLEDGE pact"— by which he seems to mean the three-fifths compromise. But the first of the "adversaries" to be "worn down," DAVIE, remained adamant on July 12 that for his state the three-fifths ratio was nonnegotiable, and WILSON's ally GOUVERNEUR MORRIS of Pennsylvania had anticipated DAVIE in backing the ratio because "he did not believe those [southern] states would ever confederate" on any other terms. Any pact for the three-fifths ratio remained fully intact—and had no discernible connection with the Compromise. RUTLEDGE may not have registered an objection to the Grand Committee's report, but he and the other South Carolinians joined WILSON and Pennsylvania in voting against the Compromise on July 16. Jeremy C. Pope and Shawn Trier have applied a statistical model of past votes and agenda items to explain the voting on the Compromise, but the result does nothing to clarify the events. They too subscribe to the theory that WILSON had made a deal with the Deep South and "achieved a marriage of the slave interest with the ideals of . . . popular republicanism," and then somehow the assurance that the three-fifths arrangement was safe encouraged the switch in North Carolina's vote. But Pope and Trier are forced to acknowledge that their model "would actually predict that Pennsylvania would have voted against proportional representation," and they admit that it also indicates that North Carolina was more likely to vote nay than aye on the Compromise. (The three-fifths rule actually *increased* the benefits of proportional representation for the South relative to the North, the reason that RUFUS KING continued to condemn it bitterly, right through the Missouri Compromise in 1820.) Moreover, Pope and Trier's purely statistical approach to voting by states masks two errors that a careful reader will note: they believe that BLOUNT was still present at the Convention and say that he and SPAIGHT switched their votes along with the rest of the delegation. Neither is true.

Finally, Michael Klarman is reduced to asserting, "The small state delegates had won a crucial victory because they were more united and intensely committed" and because on the Grand Committee "each state represented at the convention had one member." Klarman offers no rationale for North Carolina's critical switch. Since the small states (along with large New York) had lost every previous vote on representation—and each state always had one vote, eventually, on all questions—this "explanation," like the others, really explains nothing.[34]

The explanation that most closely fits the facts is that ELLSWORTH, trying to stack the deck on the Committee, had already zeroed in on DAVIE as his best chance to turn a large state vote after Davie's comments on June 30. He planned to make the Princeton connection—doubly, through their shared friendship with Avery—and then add to the Committee their three schoolmates representing New Jersey, Delaware, and Maryland. DAVIE subsequently expanded that connection to include ALEXANDER MARTIN, and it was then DAVIE's powers of persuasion that brought along WILLIAMSON, who usually had a sense of which way the wind was blowing. As recently as July 2, North Carolina had voted with four other "large states"—Massachusetts, Pennsylvania, Virginia, and South Carolina—as it always had, against such a compromise, but Maryland's vote on that day had been cast by ELLSWORTH's classmate LUTHER MARTIN alone, supporting the small states; neither CARROLL nor MERCER was in Philadelphia yet, and JENIFER, who usually voted for the Virginia Plan along with his old neighbors MASON and WASHINGTON, was strategically absent just long enough for MARTIN's solo vote to allow the debate to continue when a momentarily divided Georgia yielded a tied result, 5–5–1. BALDWIN, about to be chosen to represent Georgia on the Grand Committee, unexpectedly and temporarily followed the more senior Yale men JOHNSON and LIVINGSTON and split his state's vote with HOUSTOUN, canceling it for the moment; PIERCE and FEW were away with BLOUNT in New York, at Congress. Only after the vote had been taken did the usually punctual JENIFER stroll in. On July 16, the full Maryland delegation would vote in favor of the Compromise; MARTIN, JENIFER, and CARROLL were now present, and the Grand Committee's GEORGE MASON—who was still declaring that he would "bury his bones in this city rather than expose his Country to the Consequences of a dissolution of the Convention"— may have persuaded his boyhood friend JENIFER to go along. This time, Massachusetts was split 2–2 thanks to committee member GERRY, who evidently persuaded *his* schoolmate CALEB STRONG to join him in canceling that large state's vote. The only other divided delegation that MADISON's notes record is that of North Carolina, 3 to 1, with SPAIGHT alone voting no. (MAD-

ISON gives no indication that MASON actually voted differently than the other Virginians.) The Great Compromise passed 5–4–1 over the stunned opposition of Pennsylvania and all the southern states—except North Carolina. The Convention could continue, thanks in part to tutor Joseph Bellamy's influence on one Framer and to old school ties between several others.[35]

JAMES MADISON lost that battle, one in which what mattered was pragmatism, not philosophy. He was joined in opposition to the Compromise by WILSON and KING but abandoned this time by all of his fellow Princetonians, who took advantage of their college connections to an extent that graduates of no other, less national college could. In the weeks that followed, the "new school" students came back together to help pass MADISON's and WILSON's proposals for balancing competing interests. (Even the usually obstructionist LUTHER MARTIN moved the adoption of the supremacy clause, which Rossiter calls a "consolation prize" for MADISON.) But now the controversial proposals rooted in the Scottish philosophers were resisted by Harvard's KING and GERRY. WILLIAMSON and MIFFLIN likely recognized their Hutchesonian elements from Francis Alison's lectures at the College of Philadelphia; they and Alison's student READ were dependable votes now for MADISON's and WILSON's innovations. So was GOUVERNEUR MORRIS, who had been friendlier to the Compromise (although MADISON's tally suggests that he and even FRANKLIN ultimately joined the other Pennsylvanians in voting no). The complicated solution to the baffling problem of electing a president was ultimately the work of MORRIS and the indefatigable WILSON. MORRIS, who advocated a strong executive elected by the people, was thereafter a popular choice for committees, serving on the Second Representation Committee, the Committee of Postponed Matters, and the Committee of Style, three committees whose importance belies their modest titles. On the last of these, Yale's JOHNSON deferred to Harvard's KING, Princeton's MADISON, and the King's College duo of MORRIS and HAMILTON. The makeup of this committee, tasked with drafting the final document, contrasts dramatically with the membership of the Committee of Representation from which all five had been excluded; the Convention, having survived that threat, now acknowledged its intellectual leaders—and its future spokesmen in the ratification struggle.[36]

The "old-school" Framers did not stick together in the final weeks. Yale's four (JOHNSON, LIVINGSTON, INGERSOLL, and BALDWIN) remained nearly silent but endorsed the final draft that the Committee of Style produced. So did Oxford's C. C. PINCKNEY—quiet once slavery was protected—and St. Omer's CARROLL. But Harvard's GERRY and STRONG had split with KING over the Compromise, and at the end GERRY split with both the other two and refused to sign; as Herbert Storing says, "a rather vague residual classical republicanism played for GERRY, as well as many of the other Anti-federalists, a significant psychological as well as rhetorical role." The members of the ancient Inns of Court had nothing new to offer. William and Mary's alumni in Philadelphia were down to two at the end; MCCLURG and PIERCE had departed (their support for the Constitution clear), and the taciturn BLAIR, always willing to follow WASHINGTON, was the only one from William and Mary to sign. Two other William and Mary men were more vocal and less willing: MERCER had stormed out after ten days of nonstop objection, and RANDOLPH, who had been waffling and would waffle on through ratification, temporarily followed MASON and refused to sign. They and GERRY found the strong executive, the interdependent branches, and the many counterbalances just too strange to trust. MASON, until late August a stubborn supporter of the ongoing work, had also grown more and more uncomfortable with the new Constitution's unconventional solutions to the problems that had vexed the Confederation. Moreover, he felt the other Framers had been personally disrespectful in quickly dismissing his final flurry of proposals, including one for a bill of rights. Despite his earlier vows to produce a Constitution no matter what, he would hereafter remain intransigent in opposition, abruptly terminating a lifelong friendship with WASHINGTON.[37]

The closing hours of the Convention saw one final effort to revive a proposal that the Convention had already turned down a month earlier. On September 14, CHARLES PINCKNEY III (who had never been to college) joined JAMES MADISON (who had made more of his college studies than anyone else) in moving to grant Congress the power to create "an University, in which no preferences or distinctions should be allowed on account of religion." The older Framers had wished for a virtuous citizenry; MADISON placed his hopes on educated leaders. Men were not going to be made angels, but perhaps education could produce "a class of literati" who could be "the cultivators of the human mind . . . the teachers of the arts of life and the means of happiness." WILSON seconded the motion, but no one else spoke in favor. After three and a half months, the Convention was impatient to adjourn, and the motion failed. WASHINGTON, in the chair, was silent as usual, but in the years to come, Presidents WASHINGTON and MADISON would an-nually revive the idea of a federal university in their messages to Congress, without success. For now, however, the Framers of the Constitution, who had brought to the Convention such different educations, saw no need for Congress to charter a national school for statesmen.[38]

Conclusion

Those who would study the effects of the Framers' educations are
warned by Carl J. Richard, in *The Founders and the Classics*:

> Separating the real lessons which the founders learned from
> mere ammunition which they used to support their positions
> is virtually impossible, since there was generally an element
> of both in any given analogy or contrast. For instance, the
> fact that JAMES MADISON feared decentralization before he first
> used the Greek confederacies analogy is not evidence that he
> was only using the analogy as ammunition. . . . [T]he very
> addition of the analogy to his stock of knowledge probably
> reinforced those views.

But MADISON, it turns out, had learned the lesson of the Greek confederacies as a college student, years before he gave thought to a
designing a central government. HAMILTON, it is true, was willing to
hunt through classical sources in order to score debater's points in
his *Federalist* essays. Still, HAMILTON's "looked-up" references were
useful only if they rang a bell; they were far more likely to matter
to someone who had been trained from his youth to accept Demosthenes or Plutarch as an authority. The observation made by both
BUTLER and BEDFORD—that Solon in ancient Athens "was obliged
to establish such a government as the people would bear, not that
which he thought best"—had recently been made by John Adams
in his *Defence of the Constitutions*; Adams was quoting Plutarch, and
whether or not BUTLER and BEDFORD had read Adams's new book,
they had certainly read Plutarch. Adams assumed as much—and

he expected his readers to take the point not on his authority but on Plutarch's. They might have found the same message in Montesquieu or Adam Smith, but few had been brought up on Montesquieu and fewer still on Smith; almost every educated American knew Plutarch from his youth. (MADISON would repeat the Solon parallel, for the same reason, in *Federalist*, no. 38.)[1]

There is no denying that the Framers were men capable of growth, or that nearly every one of them continued to read and discuss political philosophy long after he left the classroom—if, indeed, he had ever been in one. By 1787 a fair number had read Montesquieu and were acquainted with Smith, at least the *Theory of Moral Sentiments*, if not *Wealth of Nations*. As the Revolution approached, newly minted lawyers and rising politicians eagerly read Blackstone's *Commentaries*, *Cato's Letters*, and Thomas Paine, and each other's published letters and essays during the critical years from 1763 to 1776. But despite all their independent reading as adults, most would have agreed with LIVINGSTON that "instead of entering upon the difficult and disagreeable Work of examining the Principles we have formerly entertained, we rather exert ourselves in searching for Arguments to maintain and support them." New ideas could certainly be adopted and some old ones abandoned—loyal subjects of the king, after all, became revolutionaries—but honesty would have compelled most to acknowledge, as GOUVERNEUR MORRIS did, that the most fundamental "sentiments and opinions" they held at the completion of their formal education had "undergone no essential change" since then. It would follow that men who had spent their formative years at Thomas Clap's Yale in the 1740s would have different assumptions from those who were taught by John Witherspoon at Princeton in the 1770s. Educated in the profoundly traditional, Anglican world of Westminster, Oxford, and the Middle Temple, C. C. PINCKNEY inevitably understood the world differently than HUGH WILLIAMSON, who was prepared by Francis Alison, shaped by William Smith's "Mirania" curriculum at the College of Philadelphia, and exposed to the intellectual ferment of Edinburgh, or JAMES WILSON, the product of Cupar Grammar School, the Universities of St. Andrews and Glasgow, and a legal apprenticeship under JOHN DICKINSON.

Over the preceding chapters, the Framers have divided themselves into eight broad categories according to their different educations: (1) those who were essentially self-taught; (2) those who were trained in the classical languages by private tutors; (3) those who had only elementary schooling; (4) those who were educated in classical grammar schools; (5) those who went to the intellectually conservative colleges of Harvard, Yale, William and Mary, Oxford, and the Jesuit College of St. Omer; (6) those educated at forward-looking Scottish universities; (7) those who were taught in the academies of Presbyterian schoolmasters; and (8) those who went to the newer colonial colleges—Philadelphia, King's, and Princeton. (In addition, more than half went on to study law, either at the Inns of Court or as clerks.) Those categories can be further boiled down to three: the first group of autodidacts, who read an unpredictable mix of classics and more recent authors, including the "civic virtue" school of Addison, Trenchard and Gordon, and the Commonwealth Whigs; groups (2) through (5) who were trained to varying degrees in traditional, almost entirely classical subject matter and were most influenced by the classical Roman republicanism of Cicero, Sallust, and Plutarch; and groups (6) through (8) who began with the classics but were then introduced to the moral and political philosophers of the Scottish Enlightenment. Law students, whatever their background, felt the additional influence of the legendary Edward Coke, who argued so forcefully for the ultimate authority of the legislature. Inevitably, individuals who were brought up from early childhood by such different methods would have absorbed, during their most impressionable years, different fundamental assumptions. In THOMAS MIFFLIN's words, "different means of education" would "always occasion difference of opinions, even between good men."

The Framers who took the lead in shaping the new frame of government (and those who rescued the Convention when it seemed to have reached a fatal impasse) had all been students at America's three newest colleges—Princeton, Philadelphia, and King's—or Scotland's venerable but recently reformed Glasgow University. When the other, educationally conservative schools of England, France, Virginia, and New England remained focused on the ancient Greeks and Romans, these four colleges (and a handful of Presbyterian academies) had taken the utterly new step of introducing their students to the ideas of modern political philosophy. They taught the "common sense" epistemology of Thomas Reid that said ordinary citizens were competent to elect wise leaders—and even to hold office themselves. Through the moral philosophy lectures and assigned reading of Alison and Witherspoon, they planted the seeds of a complex government, a *nexus imperii* of checks and balances both between and within the three branches that the Constitution would establish. And some went so far as to let slip in the radical ideas of Adam Smith, Adam Ferguson, and David Hume that suggested "enlarging the sphere" to balance competing factions in a political version of Newton's "overpoise" of physical forces. All eighteenth-century political educations began with the cultivation of individual virtue; in the more traditional educations, following the classical *De officiis* or the neoclassical *Spectator*, moral philosophy could go little further. But the new political science introduced at Glasgow or Princeton enabled the Convention's innovative leaders to find structural, not moral, responses to what MADISON recognized as the vices of systems, not individuals. Men were not angels, but effective republican government might still be possible.

Through June's debates over the question of whether any government could be at once republican and national, MADISON, WILSON, and—once he returned from an absence—GOUVERNEUR MORRIS, all educated in these new ideas, were the sources of much of the energy that moved the Convention forward; for a while they had an unexpected ally in Harvard's RUFUS KING. (The brilliant HAMILTON, who had spent his few brief terms of formal education at King's College, was absent most of the summer, frustrated by the other New Yorkers' success in rendering his vote irrelevant.) When the crisis over representation in Congress threatened to derail the entire project in July, ELLSWORTH, inspired by his old tutor Joseph Bellamy and supported by every other Princetonian except MADISON, found the way to remobilize the Convention. The self-taught SHERMAN shares the credit, but the strategic means to their common end of compromise was ELLSWORTH's design. After that—and partly motivated by a desire now to restrain the power of the Compromise's Congress—MADISON and WILSON once again took the lead, with less help from KING now but more from MORRIS. No one would shine during August's grim, frustrating debates over slavery; morality seemed as little help as political philosophy in the bitterness of sectionalism, and once again ELLSWORTH turned to his tutor's theory of compromise by the righteous ruler.

For good or for bad, old school ties proved more durable than might be expected. MERCER's close college friendship with the slighted James Monroe may have underlain his abrupt hostility toward a Convention that he had only recently endorsed; Georgia's ABRAHAM BALDWIN (faithful correspondent of Ezra Stiles) sometimes sympathized more with his fellow Yale men than his newer southern colleagues, and in the crisis over representation, alumni of both Princeton and Harvard came together even though their states' interests had previously divided them and their futures were as partisan rivals. When thirty-nine signatures were finally affixed to the Constitution, they included those of all of the "new school" Framers still in Philadelphia. The three delegates who withheld their endorsements at the last had been educated at Harvard and William and Mary and in the library of Marlborough plantation.

Aside from KING's and JOHNSON's intermittent efforts, the Harvard, Yale, William and Mary, and Oxford alumni had simply found little to say that was helpful; in the closing weeks, the erratic GERRY relapsed to an essentially reactionary posture, and the rest were silent. The prominent noncollege delegates, even the vociferous MASON, had less influence than their fellow Framers had expected. DICKINSON and FRANKLIN were conciliators, but they were only occasionally effective; their glory days were behind them. RUTLEDGE was focused almost entirely on southern interests, satisfied to strike his deals with SHERMAN and WILSON, and the powerful ROBERT MORRIS was content, like the less-known FITZSIMONS, CLYMER, BASSETT, BROOM, and FEW, simply to listen and then vote with the majority. So, in general, were New Hampshire's LANGDON and GILMAN, who arrived late but in time for debates over the slave trade and presidential election. The privately tutored CHARLES PINCKNEY III rarely let a day go by without making a proposal, some novel, some opposed to innovation, but few that gained any traction. He contributed less than he would later claim, but his speeches are a reminder that formal schooling was not the only way to acquire erudition.

Ultimately, the success of the Convention was due to its determined, inventive leaders and to the silent, pragmatic delegates who slowly came to accept their new ideas. Those whose thinking was too conventional to accept innovation could not prevail over those who arrived in Philadelphia prepared to solve old problems with new ideas. Whether molded by the deeply traditional authority of Cicero and Plutarch or the new ideas of Hutcheson, Reid, and Hume, all were shaped by their educations. At their schools, with their tutors, or in their libraries they had found the lenses through which they saw the world and had "imbibed the principles" that steered them through the Federal Convention of 1787.

Introduction

1. As recently as 2019, Nicholas Guyatt, James Oakes, and Sean Wilentz debated in print whether the Constitution was written to be a proslavery "covenant with death" or a moral assertion that there should be "no property in man"; see Wilentz and Oakes, reply by Guyatt, "'No Property in Man': An Exchange," *New York Review of Books*, June 27, 2019.

2. A thorough review of the post–Charles Beard century of historiography is given by Alan Gibson, *Interpreting the Founding*, 2nd ed. (Lawrence: University Press of Kansas, 2009). For a more recent argument that the Framers were engaged in an elitist "counter-revolution," see Michael Klarman, *The Framers' Coup* (New York: Oxford University Press, 2016).

3. Forrest McDonald, *We the People: The Economic Origins of the Constitution* (Chicago: University of Chicago Press, 1958), 104, 189.

4. WILLIAM LIVINGSTON, *The Independent Reflector*, ed. M. M. Klein (Cambridge, MA: Harvard University Press, 1963), 175; BLAIR, "On the Duties of the Young," *The Monthly Review* 56 (1777): 288, quoted in Gideon Mailer, *John Witherspoon's American Revolution* (Chapel Hill: University of North Carolina Press, 2019), 140.

5. Joseph Ellis, *The Quartet: The Orchestrating of the Second American Revolution* (New York: Random House, 2015), 140; Ellis appears to be relying on Richard Beeman, *Plain, Honest Men: The Making of the American Constitution* (New York: Random House, 2009), 56–58, and evidently assumes every Framer who enrolled in college earned a degree. As early as 1787 the Georgia Framer WILLIAM PIERCE mistakenly wrote that his colleague and neighbor ABRAHAM BALDWIN (a Yale graduate) was educated at Harvard. The errors have accumulated since then.

6. GOUVERNEUR MORRIS to Timothy Pickering, December 22, 1814, in Max Farrand, ed., *Records of the Federal Convention of 1787* (New Haven, CT: Yale University Press, 1937), 3:419.

7. The success of the Great Compromise has traditionally been credited to the leadership of Sherman; as chapter 13 will show, a better case can now be made for ELLSWORTH. On SHERMAN's possibly overstated influence, see Keith L. Dougherty and Jac C. Henckelman, "A Pivotal Voter from a Pivotal State: Roger Sherman at the Constitutional Convention," *American Political Science Review* 100 (2006): 297–302.

8. Thomas Miller, *The Formation of College English* (Pittsburgh: University of Pittsburgh Press, 1997), 3–4; see Wilbur S. Howell, *Eighteenth Century British Logic and Rhetoric* (Princeton, NJ: Princeton University Press, 1971).

9. Miller, *Formation of College English*, 158; David Hume, *Treatise on Human Nature*, ed. David Norton and Mary Norton (Oxford: Clarendon, 2007), 1:4; "King's College Minutes, 1753–54," 373, 395, quoted in Paul Wood, *The Aberdeen Enlighten-*

ment: The Arts Curriculum in the Eighteenth Century (Aberdeen: Aberdeen University Press, 1993), 67.

10. John Brubacher, *Higher Education in Transition*, 4th ed. (London: Routledge, 2017), 4–5; Thomas Miller, introduction to *Selected Writings of John Witherspoon*, ed. Thomas Miller (Carbondale: Southern Illinois University Press, 2015), 1, and Miller, *Evolution of College English* (Pittsburgh: University of Pittsburgh Press, 2011), 85.

11. Lawrence Cremin, *American Education: The Colonial Experience, 1607–1783* (New York: Harper and Row, 1970), 463–464; Jeffry Morrison, *John Witherspoon and the Founding of the American Republic* (South Bend, IN: University of Notre Dame Press, 2016), 51.

12. Turnbull's commentary in his edition of Johannes Heineccius, *Methodical System of Universal Law*, 2:21, quoted in Miller, *Formation of College English*, 210; THOMAS MIFFLIN, "Notes on Metaphysics and the Laws of Nations," dated March 22–May 31, 1759, Library of Congress manuscript collection MMC-1030, MS 32854.

13. Mailer, *Witherspoon's American Revolution*, 141. See also Norman Fiering, *Moral Philosophy at Seventeenth-Century Harvard: A Discipline in Transition* (Chapel Hill: University of North Carolina Press, 1981); Henry May, "The Problem of the American Enlightenment," *New Literary History* 1 (1970): 201–214; J. David Hoeveler, *Creating the American Mind: Intellect and Politics in the Colonial Colleges* (Lanham, MD: Rowman and Littlefield, 2002); David W. Robson, *Educating Republicans: The College in the Era of the American Revolution* (New York: Praeger, 1985); and Douglas Sloan, *The Scottish Enlightenment and the American College Ideal* (New York: Teachers' College Press, 1971).

Chapter 1. The Framers

1. Jonathan Elliot, ed., *Debates in the Several State Conventions on the Adoption of the Federal Constitution*, 2nd ed. (Philadelphia: Lippincott, 1996), 3:21–22; Akhil Reed Amar, *America's Constitution: A Biography* (New York: Random House, 2005), notes that the earliest draft of the preamble, from July's Committee of Detail (RUTLEDGE, RANDOLPH, ELLSWORTH, WILSON, and GORHAM) is in JAMES WILSON's handwriting, and he points out that WILSON was in many ways the most "populist" of the Framers, citing among other evidence his proposal for direct election of the president. But GOUVERNEUR MORRIS who later acknowledged that the final draft was primarily his work, was also the only other Framer who agreed with WILSON's suggestion for direct presidential election (although MADISON was attracted to it). WILSON's earlier draft claims to speak on behalf of a list of thirteen states (including Rhode Island, which had refused to participate), but MORRIS's draft offers instead the boldly national words, "We the People of the United States . . . ," and introduces the goal of "a more perfect Union" (Amar, *America's Constitution*, 7n3); see Max Farrand, ed., *The Records of the Federal Convention of 1787* (New Haven, NH: Yale University Press, 1937), 2:152.

2. Farrand, ed., *Records*, 1:125, 1:491, 2:649.

3. William T. Hutchinson et al., eds., *The Papers of James Madison* (1st ser.) (Chicago: University of Chicago Press, 1962–77), 8:152

4. John Kaminski, *George Clinton: Yeoman Politician of the New Republic* (Lanham, MD: Rowman and Littlefield, 1993), 119.

5. WASHINGTON to HAMILTON, March 4, 1783, National Archives, Founders Online, https://founders.archives.gov/documents/Hamilton/01-03-02-0171; WASHINGTON to HAMILTON, March 31, 1783, Founders Online, https://founders.archives.gov/documents/Washington/99-01-02-10968.

6. HAMILTON to Jay, July 25, 1783, Founders Online, https://founders.archives.gov/documents/Hamilton/01-03-02-0270; Joseph Ellis, *The Quartet: The Orchestrating of the Second American Revolution* (New York: Random House, 2015), 98.

7. RANDOLPH to MADISON, July 17, 1785, Founders Online, https://founders.archives.gov/documents/Madison/01-08-02-0172; MASON to MADISON, August 9, 1785, Founders Online, https://founders.archives.gov/documents/Madison/01-08-02-0179, December 7, 1785, Founders Online, https://founders.archives.gov/documents/Madison/01-08-02-0226.

8. *The Papers of Alexander Hamilton*, Vol. 3, *1782–1786*, ed. Harold C. Syrett (New York: Columbia University Press, 1962), 690, Founders Online, https://founders.archives.gov/documents/Hamilton/01-03-02-0556; see Jack Rakove, *Revolutionaries* (Boston: Houghton Mifflin Harcourt, 2010), 356–357.

9. Stephen Higginson to John Adams, July 1786, Founders Online, https://founders.archives.gov/?q=%20Recipient%3A%22Adams%2C%20John%22%20Author%3A%22Higginson%2C%20Stephen%22&s=1111311111&r=4; Otto to Vergennes, October 10, 1786, in *Federalists and Antifederalists: The Debate over the Ratification of the Constitution*, ed. John P. Kaminski and Richard Leffler (Madison, WI: Madison House, 1998), 180–183; MADISON to Jefferson, August 12, 1786, Founders Online, https://founders.archives.gov/documents/Madison/01-09-02-0026.

10. Jack Rakove, *The Beginnings of National Politics* (New York: Knopf, 1979), 387; Calvin Johnson, *Righteous Anger at the Wicked States* (New York: Cambridge University Press, 2005). 43.

11. Max Farrand, *The Framing of the Constitution of the United States* (New Haven, CT: Yale University Press, 1913), 89.

12. HAMILTON to MORRIS, February 29, 1802, Founders Online, https://founders.archives.gov/documents/Hamilton/01-25-02-0297.

13. Forrest McDonald, *We the People: The Economic Origins of the Constitution* (Chicago: University of Chicago Press, 1958), 90–91; Ellis, *Quartet*, xiv. But see Robert McGuire, *To Form a More Perfect Union: A New Economic Interpretation of the Constitution* (New York: Oxford, 2003), and Jac C. Heckelman and Keith L. Dougherty, "An Economic Interpretation of the Constitutional Convention of 1787 Revisited," *Journal of Economic History* 73 (2007): 829–848.

14. Mark Noll, *America's God* (New York: Oxford University Press, 2002) 9, 164. See Robert E. Shalhope, "Douglass Adair and the Historiography of Republicanism," in Douglass Adair, *Fame and the Founding Fathers*, ed. Trevor Colbourn (New York: W. W. Norton, 1974), xxix–xliv. On controversy over the Framers' religious beliefs, see, among others, Gregg Frazer, *The Religious Beliefs of America's Founders: Reason, Revelation, and Revolution* (Lawrence: University Press of Kansas, 2012), and

John Fea, *Was America Founded as a Christian Nation? A Historical Introduction* (Louisville: Westminster John Knox Press, 2011).

15. Michael Klarman, *The Framers' Coup* (New York: Oxford University Press, 2016), 247–248, 607, x. Francis D. Cogliano suggests relabeling the Constitution's proponents: "While they were indeed nationalists, I prefer the term 'elitist' to describe them," and he proposes substituting "democrats" for "antifederalists"; Cogliano, *Revolutionary America 1763–1815: A Political History*, 2nd ed. (New York: Routledge, 2009), 208. Given the prominent wealth and status of many Anti-Federalists—and their opposition to a Constitution that replaced state appointment of congressmen with popular election—this seems disingenuous. GERRY warned the Convention against "an excess of democracy," but after he became Massachusetts's leading Anti-Federalist, he did an about-face and decried it as "aristocratic" (Farrand, ed., *Records*, 1:48, 2:286). For an overlooked argument by Virginia's best-known Anti-Federalist that the Constitution was actually *too* democratic, see Robin Einhorn, "Patrick Henry's Case against the Constitution: The Structural Problem of Slavery," *Journal of the Early Republic* 22 (2002): 549–573.

16. Farrand, ed., *Records*, 2:364.

17. THOMAS MIFFLIN, *Notes on Metaphysics and the Elements of the Laws of Nature (1758–1759)*, MS 32854, Mifflin Manuscripts, Library of Congress.

Chapter 2. Educating Demigods

1. Jefferson to Adams, August 30, 1787, National Archives, Founders Online, https://founders.archives.gov/documents/Jefferson/01-12-02-0075. Jefferson and Adams had low opinions of some individual delegates, but it is clear that they and most Americans viewed the Framers, as a body, with respect; see Adams to Benjamin Rush, January 25, 1806, Founders Online, https://founders.archives.gov/documents/Adams/99-02-02-5119.

2. Jefferson to John Trumbull, February 15, 1789, Founders Online, https://founders.archives.gov/documents/Jefferson/01-14-02-0321; Francis Bacon, *The Advancement of Learning*, ed. Steven J. Gould (New York: Penguin Random House, 2001), 72; Douglass Adair, *Fame and the Founding Fathers*, ed. Trevor Colbourn (New York: Norton, 1974), 23; Jack Rakove, *Original Meanings: Politics and Ideas in the Making of the Constitution* (New York: Knopf, 1996), 56.

3. John Adams, "Thoughts on Government," in *Papers of John Adams*, ed. Robert Lint et al. (Cambridge, MA: Harvard University Press, 1980), 4:93. Classical history has fallen far in the last century from its once-central place in American education; it is difficult for modern readers to appreciate how familiar names like Cato or Aristides ("the Just") once were, much as Gandhi or Einstein are today.

4. Gary Wills, *Cincinnatus: George Washington and the Enlightenment* (New York: Doubleday, 1984), 122; David C. Ward, *Charles Willson Peale: Art and Selfhood in the Early Republic* (Berkeley: University of California, 2004), 28; Charles Sellers, *Charles Willson Peale* (New York: Scribner's, 1969), 119.

5. "Invoice of Sundries to be Sent by Robert Cary and Company for the Use of George Washington," in *The Papers of George Washington* (Colonial Series), Vol. 6, *4 September 1758–26 December 1760*, ed. W. W. Abbot (Charlottesville: Uni-

versity Press of Virginia, 1988), 352–358; Adair, *Fame and the Founding Fathers*, 16–17; Adair, *The Intellectual Origins of Jeffersonian Democracy: Republicanism, Class Struggle, and the Virtuous Farmer* (Lanham, MD: Lexington Books, 2000), 24; M. L. Clarke, "Classical Studies," in *The History of the University of Oxford*, Vol. 5, *The Eighteenth Century*, ed. Lucy S. Sutherland and Lesley G. Mitchell (New York: Oxford University Press, 1986), 523; WASHINGTON to George Chapman, December 15, 1784, Founders Online, https://founders.archives.gov/documents/Washington/04-02-02-0149.

6. Rhys Isaac, *The Transformation of Virginia, 1740–1790* (Chapel Hill: University of North Carolina Press, 1982), 130; Caroline Winterer, *American Enlightenments* (New Haven, CT: Yale University Press, 2017), 237; Alison to Stiles, May 7, 1768, in Stiles, *Extracts from the Itineraries*, ed. Franklin Bowditch Dexter (New Haven, CT: Yale University Press, 1916), 433.

7. John Kerr, *Scottish Education: Schools and University from Early Times to 1908* (Cambridge: Cambridge University Press, 1910), 226–257; Martin J. Finkelstein, "From Tutor to Specialized Scholar: Academic Professionalization in Eighteenth and Nineteenth Century America," *History of Higher Education Annual* 3 (1983): 99–121; E. G. W. Bill, *Education at Christ Church College, Oxford, 1660–1800* (London: Oxford University Press, 1988), 247–249.

8. "The Harvard Indian School" (2013), Peabody Museum of Archaeology and Ethnology, http://peabody.harvard.edu; Jack Morpurgo, *Their Majesties Royall Colledge: William and Mary in the Seventeenth and Eighteenth Centuries* (Williamsburg, VA: The College of William and Mary, 1976), 70; Varnum Lansing Collins, *President Witherspoon* (Princeton, NJ: Princeton University Press, 1925), 2:219; James Axtell, *The School upon a Hill: Education and Society in Colonial New England* (New Haven, CT: Yale University Press, 1974), 235n49; Ron Chernow, *Alexander Hamilton* (New York: Penguin, 2004), 48.

9. Thomas Miller, *Formation of College English* (Pittsburgh: University of Pittsburg Press, 1997), 202; John Thelin, *History of Higher Education* (Baltimore: Johns Hopkins University Press, 2004), 25–26; Matthew Hartley and Elizabeth J. Hollander, "The Elusive Ideal: Civic Learning and Higher Education," in *The Institutions of Democracy: The Public Schools*, ed. Susan Fuhrman and Marvin Lazaron (New York: Oxford University Press, 2005), 252–53; Gordon Wood, *The Radicalism of the American Revolution* (New York: Knopf, 1991), 197.

10. The first group includes offspring of great landowning families (LIVINGSTON and MORRIS in the province of New York, CARROLL and SPAIGHT farther south), wealthy merchants (GERRY, KING, MIFFLIN, DAYTON), and southern planters of varying scale (C. C. PINCKNEY, MERCER, MADISON, RANDOLPH). The second group includes WASHINGTON, MASON, DICKINSON, JENIFER, RUTLEDGE, CHARLES PINCKNEY III, and two sons of baronets, HOUSTOUN and BUTLER. The third group includes HAMILTON, PATERSON, WILSON, ELLSWORTH, WILLIAMSON, and BALDWIN (sons of storekeepers, farmers, and a blacksmith), and the last group—men who could well be said to have pulled themselves up by their bootstraps—includes SHERMAN, ROBERT MORRIS, and FRANKLIN.

11. Thelin, *History of Higher Education*, 23; Axtell, *School upon a Hill*, 214–215, 211–212. Franklin Bowditch Dexter published a twenty-three-page pamphlet, *On Some Social Distinctions at Harvard and Yale, Before the Revolution* (Worcester, MA: C. Ham-

ilton, 1894), but the only form he identifies is the ranking of students by parents' status. For the mention of servitors in President Dunster's earliest Harvard law, see Josiah Quincy, *History of Harvard University* (Cambridge, MA: J. Owen, 1840), 1:584.

12. Josiah Quincy 1:440; Samuel Eliot Morison, *Three Centuries of Harvard, 1636–1936* (Cambridge, MA: Harvard University Press,1936), 106–107; WILLIAM PATERSON, untitled essay, Box One, Paterson Family Papers, Seeley G. Mudd Manuscript Library, Princeton University.

13. Axtell, *School upon a Hill*, 213; Miller, *Formation of College English*, 118.

14. "Original Records of the Phi Beta Kappa Society," *William and Mary Quarterly*, 1st series, 4 (1895–96): 238; Thomas Miller, ed., introduction to *Selected Writings of John Witherspoon* (Carbondale: Southern Illinois University Press, 2015) 18; Quincy, *History of Harvard*, 2:133; David Shields, *Civil Tongues and Polite Letters in America* (Chapel Hill: University of North Carolina Press, 1997), 211, 216.

15. Miller, ed., introduction to *Selected Writings*, 17, 5; David W. Robson, *Educating Republicans: The College in the Era of the American Revolution, 1750–1800* (Westport, CT: Greenwood, 1985), 61; Mark Kalthoff, "Liberal Education, the Ordered Soul, and Cicero's *De Officiis:* A Core Text for Every Curriculum" (2014), 2, published online by the Association of Core Texts and Courses, http://www.coretexts.org.

16. Donald S. Lutz, "The Relative Influence of European Writers on Late Eighteenth Century American Political Thought," *American Political Science Review* 78 (1984), 194; David Robson, 16. See also Carl J. Richard, *The Founders and the Classics: Greece, Rome, and the American* Enlightenment (Cambridge, MA: Harvard University Press, 1995). Not all the Framers were committed to imitating classical virtue; HAMILTON scoffed, "It is as ridiculous to seek for models in the simple ages of Greece and Rome as it would be to go in quest of them among the Hottentots and Laplanders"; see "The Continentalist No. VI," July 4, 1782, Founders Online, https://founders.archives.gov/documents/Hamilton/01-03-02-0031#ARHN-01-03-02-0031-fn-0006-ptr.

17. Farrand, ed., *Records*, 2:278; cf. Aristotle, *Aristotle's "Ethics" and "Politics" Comprising His Practical Philosophy*, trans. John Gillies (London: A. Strahan, 1787), 2:282. See Adair, *Intellectual Origins*, 43, 73, and Lawrence Cremin, *American Education: The Colonial Experience, 1607–1783* (New York: Harper and Row, 1970), 460.

18. Trevor Colbourn, *The Lamp of Experience* (Chapel Hill: University of North Carolina Press, 1965), 20; FRANKLIN, *Papers of Benjamin Franklin*, ed. Leonard W. Labaree et al. (New Haven, CT: Yale University Press 1959–), 3:410–412.

19. David Ramsay, *History of the American Revolution* (1789), ed. Lester H. Cohen (Indianapolis: Liberty Fund, 1990), 2:231.

20. WILLIAM LIVINGSTON, *The Independent Reflector*, ed. M. M. Klein (Cambridge, MA: Harvard University Press, 1963), 175.

21. Caroline Robbins, *The Eighteenth-Century Commonwealthman* (Cambridge, MA: Harvard University Press, 1959), 121; Bernard Bailyn, *The Ideological Origins of the American Revolution* (Cambridge, MA: Harvard University Press, 1967), 35; Clinton Rossiter, *Seedtime of the Republic* (New York: Harcourt Brace, 1953), 141; FRANKLIN, *Proposals*, 3:411.

22. Douglas Southall Freeman, *George Washington: A Biography* (New York: Scrib-

ner's, 1948), 1:123. Diary of Nathaniel Ames, July 11, 1758, quoted in Jonathan Walker and Paul D. Streufert, *Early Modern Academic Drama* (London: Ashgate, 2008), 181.

23. Wills, *Cincinnatus*, 100. See Marjorie Hope Nicolson, *Newton Demands the Muse: Newton's Opticks and the 18th Century Poets* (Princeton, MA: Princeton University Press, 1966).

24. Adam Smith, *The Theory of Moral Sentiments*, ed. D. D. Raphael and A. L. Macfie (Oxford: Oxford University Press, 1976 [1790]), 3.1.3; John Witherspoon, *Lectures on Moral Philosophy*, ed. Varnum Lansing Collins (Princeton, NY: Princeton University Press, 1912), 1.

25. Farrand, ed., *Records*, 1:165; HAMILTON to WASHINGTON, March 17, 1783, Founders Online, https://founders.archives.gov/documents/Hamilton/01-03-02-0182; *The Adams Papers, Papers of John Adams*, Vol. 18, *December 1785–January 1787*, ed. Gregg L. Lint et al. (Cambridge, MA: Harvard University Press, 2016), Letter 25.

26. Montesquieu, *The Spirit of the Laws* [*De L'Esprit des Lois*], book 3, chap. 7, quoted in Arthur Lovejoy, *Reflections on Human Nature* (Baltimore: Johns Hopkins University Press, 1961), 39n1; John Witherspoon, *Lectures on Moral Philosophy*, ed. Varnum Lansing Collins (Princeton, NJ: Princeton University Press, 1912), 94; ALEXANDER HAMILTON, JAMES MADISON, and John Jay, *The Federalist Papers*, ed. Clinton Rossiter (New York: Mentor, 1961), 322.

27. Witherspoon, *Lectures on Moral Philosophy*, ed. Collins, 140. See Morton White, *Philosophy, "The Federalist," and the Constitution* (New York: Oxford, 1987), 246, and Susan Manning and Francis Cogliano, *The Atlantic Enlightenment* (London: Ashgate 2008), 74–76.

28. Dumas Malone, *Jefferson and His Time* (Boston: Little, Brown, 1948), 1:52; Clarke quoted in Morison, *Three Centuries*, 135.

29. Barone, *Our First Revolution* (New York: Crown, 2007), 1–2; John Calvin, *Institutes*, 4.20.7, quoted in Jennifer P. McNutt, *Calvin Meets Voltaire* (London: Routledge, 2016), 258n169; Georgio Del Vecchio, "Burlamaqui and Rousseau," *Journal of the History of Ideas* 23 (1962): 421.

30. Hugo Grotius, *De Iure Praedae Commentarius*, trans. Gwladys L. Williams and Walter H. Zeydel (Oxford: Oxford University Press, 1950), 1:8; Grotius *The Rights of War and Peace*, Books I–III, ed. and intro. Richard Tuck (Indianapolis: Liberty Fund, 2005), 93, 150–155.

31. Gordon Wood, *The Creation of the American Republic* (Chapel Hill: University of North Carolina Press, 1969), 236.

32. Anna Haddow, *Political Science in American Colleges and Universities* (New York: Appleton-Century, 1939), 77; Ezra Stiles, *Literary Diary*, ed. Franklin Bowditch Dexter (New York: Scribner's, 1901), March 12, 1789, 3:346; Cabell to David Watson, March 4, 1798, Garret Minor and David Watson Papers, Library of Congress, quoted in Henry May, *The Enlightenment in America* (New York: Oxford University Press, 1976), 247; see Gilbert Chinard, "Polybius and the American Constitution," *Journal of the History of Ideas* 1 (1940): 38–58.

33. Robbins, *Eighteenth-Century Commonwealthman*, 4, 20, 385.

34. *Adams Papers*, ed. Robert J. Taylor et al. (Cambridge, MA: Harvard University Press, 1977), 4:87.

35. Ralph Ketcham, *James Madison* (Charlottesville: University Press of Virginia, 1990), 43, 61; Bradford to MADISON, January 4, 1775, in *The Papers of James Madison*, Congressional Series, ed. T. Hutchinson et al. (Chicago: University of Chicago Press 1962–1977/Charlottesville: University Press of Virginia 1977–1991), 1:125–133, Founders Online, https://founders.archives.gov/documents/Madison/01-01-02-0038; MADISON to Bradford, January 20, 1775, in Hutchinson et al., eds., *Madison Papers*, 1:134–137, Founders Online, https://founders.archives.gov/documents/Madison/01-01-02-0039; "Report on Books for Congress," January 23, 1783, in Hutchinson et al., eds., *Madison Papers*, 6:84–90, Founders Online https://founders.archives.gov/documents/Madison/01-06-02-0031; Roy Branson, "James Madison and the Scottish Enlightenment," *Journal of the History of Ideas* 40 (1979): 236.

36. Robbins, *Eighteenth-Century Commonwealthman*, 266; Robson, *Educating Republicans*, 73–74.

37. MORRIS, "On Wit and Beauty," Gouverneur Morris Papers, MS Coll Morris, Box One, Rare Book and Manuscript Library, Columbia University.

38. Jonathan Elliot, *Debates in the Several State Conventions on the Adoption of the Federal Constitution* (1836), 2nd ed. (Buffalo: Hein, 1996), 5:270–271; Francis Hutcheson, *System of Moral Philosophy* (Glasgow: Foulis, 1755), 2:212–266; *Annals*, Book 13, *Works of Tacitus with Political Discourses upon that Author*, trans. Thomas Gordon (London: Woodward and Peele, 1737), 2:109.

39. Sophia Rosenfeld, *Common Sense: A Political History* (Cambridge, MA: Harvard University Press, 2011), 71. JAMES WILSON, *Works of James Wilson*, ed. Robert McCloskey et al. (Cambridge, MA: Harvard University Press, 1967), 1:214, quoting *A Treatise of Human Nature*, pt. 4, sec. 4.

40. Adair, *Fame and the Founding Fathers*, 132–151; Farrand, ed., *Records*, 2:54; David Hume, *Essays, Moral, Political, and Literary* (1742), ed. Eugene F. Miller (Indianapolis: Liberty Fund, 1987), 34; Rossiter, ed., *Federalist*, no. 51, 322.

41. Rakove, *Original Meanings*, 47.

42. J. J. Walsh, *Education of the Founding Fathers of the Republic: Scholasticism in Colonial Colleges* (New York: Fordham University Press, 1935), 158; reported in *Pennsylvania Chronicle*, October 15, 1770.

43. MADISON, "Vices of the Political System of the United States, April 1787," in *Papers of James Madison*, Vol. 9, *9 April 1786–24 May 1787 and supplement 1781–1784*, ed. Robert A. Rutland and William M. E. Rachal (Chicago: University of Chicago Press, 1975), 351, Founders Online, https://founders.archives.gov/documents/Madison/01-09-02-0187.

44. Daniel Walker Howe, "Why the Scottish Enlightenment Was Useful to the Framers of the American Constitution," *Comparative Studies in Society and History* 31 (1989): 585.

Chapter 3. The Self-Taught and the Tutored

1. BENJAMIN FRANKLIN, *Autobiography*, in *Benjamin Franklin, Writings*, ed. J. A. Leo Lemay (New York: Library of America, 1987), 1313–1317.

2. FRANKLIN, *Autobiography*, 1317.

3. FRANKLIN, 1318–1320; E. Jennifer Monaghan, *Learning to Read and Write in Colonial America* (Amherst: University of Massachusetts Press, 2005), 110; BENJAMIN FRANKLIN, *The Idea of the English School*, in *Papers*, 4:101–104.

4. J. A. Leo Lemay, *The Life of Benjamin Franklin* (Philadelphia: University of Pennsylvania Press, 2006), 1:73–74.

5. FRANKLIN, *Autobiography*, 1353, 1346; Lemay, *Life of Franklin*, 1:261, 272–273.

6. FRANKLIN, *Autobiography*, 1361–1362, 1372.

7. FRANKLIN, 1381.

8. WILLIAM FEW, "Autobiography of Col. William Few of Georgia, From the Original Manuscript in the Possession of William Few Chrystie," *Magazine of American History* 7 (1881): 315; Otto, in Max Farrand, ed., *Records of the Federal Convention of 1787* (New Haven, CT: Yale University Press, 1937), 3:238.

9. PIERCE, in Farrand, ed., *Records*, 3:97, 3:88–89.

10. John Flynn, *Beyond the Blew Hills* (Stoughton, MA: Stoughton Historical Society, 1976), http://www.stoughtonhistory.com; Christopher Collier, *Roger Sherman's Connecticut* (Middleton, CT: Wesleyan University Press, 1971), 7.

11. Collier, *Roger Sherman's Connecticut*, 8, 11; Hugo Paltsits, "Almanacs of Roger Sherman 1750–1761," *Proceedings of the American Antiquarian Society* 18 (1907): 214.

12. Jefferson to John Sanderson, August 31, 1820, National Archives, Founders Online, https://founders.archives.gov/documents/Jefferson/98-01-02-1483; William Wirt, *Sketches of the Life of Patrick Henry* (Philadelphia: James Webster, 1817), 65–66; EDMUND RANDOLPH, *History of Virginia* (Charlottesville: Virginia Historical Society, by the University Press of Virginia, 1970), 190.

13. Theodore Crackel, V. Frederick Rickey, and Joel Silverberg, "George Washington's Use of Trigonometry and Logarithms," *Proceedings of the Canadian Society for History and Philosophy of Mathematics* 26 (2013): 2; Jack D. Warren, "Washington, George, Boyhood Homesite," 16, National Historic Landmark Nomination, July 1, 1999, United States Department of the Interior, http://nps.gov/nhl; Jonathan Boucher, *Reminiscences of an American Loyalist, 1739–1789* (Boston: Houghton, Mifflin, 1925), 49.

14. Edward Kimber, "Itinerant Observations in America," *London Magazine*, July 1746, 329.

15. GEORGE WASHINGTON, *Papers*, Colonial Series, ed. W. W. Abbot (Charlottesville: University Press of Virginia, 1984), 3:202–203; J. Paul Hudson, *George Washington Birthplace National Monument Virginia*, National Park Service Historical Handbook No. 26 (Washington, DC: US Government Printing Office, 1956), 18; WASHINGTON, *Papers*, 3:149; Crackel, Rickey, and Silverberg, "Washington's Use of Trigonometry," 6–7, 12.

16. Appleton Griffin, *Catalogue of the Washington Collection in the Boston Athenaeum* (Cambridge, MA: The Boston Athenaeum, 1897), 555; Paul L. Ford, *The True George Washington* (Philadelphia: J. B. Lippincott, 1896), 63.

17. Jeffry Morrison, *Political Philosophy of George Washington* (Baltimore: Johns Hopkins University Press, 2009), 89; Griffin, *Catalogue of the Washington Collection*, 179, 189, 192.

18. Morrison, *Political Philosophy*, 90; WASHINGTON to Sarah Cary Fairfax, September 25, 1758, Founders Online, https://founders.archives.gov/documents/Washington/02-06-02-0033.

19. Mark Bryan, "'Slideing into Monarchical extravagance': *Cato* at Valley Forge and the Testimony of William Bradford Jr.," *William and Mary Quarterly*, 3rd ser., 67 (2010): 124–125; Morrison, *Political Philosophy*, 91; Richard, *Founders and the Classics*, 58–60; WASHINGTON to HAMILTON, June 26, 1796, Founders Online, https://founders.archives.gov/documents/Hamilton/01-20-02-0151.

20. Morrison, *Political Philosophy*, 88; Griffin, *Catalogue of the Washington Collection*, 23, 35, 53.

21. Prince William County Will Book C, Folios 275–90, Will Book F#1, p. 95; Pamela Copeland, *The Five George Masons* (Charlottesville: University Press of Virginia, 1975), 75; "Miscellaneous Notes from the Records of Prince William and Louisa Counties," *William and Mary Quarterly*, 1st ser., 9 (1900): 241.

22. Copeland, *Five George Masons*, 75, 232, Patricia C. Copeland Mason File, Gunston Hall Library.

23. C. Malcolm Watkins, *Cultural History of Marlborough, Virginia*, Smithsonian Bulletin 253 (Washington, DC: Smithsonian Institution, 1968), 191, 198–208.

24. Helen Hill Miller, *George Mason, Gentleman Revolutionary* (Chapel Hill: University of North Carolina Press, 1975), 31; Copeland, *Five George Masons*, 76; Watkins, *Cultural History of Marlborough*, 198–208.

25. Jefferson, *Autobiography*, Founders Online, https://founders.archives.gov/documents/Jefferson/98-01-02-1756. (The *Autobiography* has not yet been published in the Jefferson *Papers*, Retirement series.)

26. Richard Webster, *History of the Presbyterian Church in America* (Philadelphia: Joseph Wilson, 1857), 440; Wharton Dickinson, "John Dickinson, LL.D.: The Great Colonial Essayist," *Magazine of American History* 10 (1883): 224; Charles J. Stillé, *Life and Times of John Dickinson* (Philadelphia: Pennsylvania Historical Society, 1891), 17–18.

27. *Philip Vickers Fithian Journal and Letters, 1767–1774*, ed. John R. Williams (Princeton, NJ: Princeton University Press, 1900), 50; Milton Flower, *John Dickinson: Conservative Revolutionary* (Charlottesville: University Press of Virginia, 1983), 17–18, 20–21; Trevor Colbourn, "A Pennsylvania Farmer at the Court of King George: John Dickinson's London Letters, 1754–1756," *Pennsylvania Magazine of History and Biography* 86, no. 3 (1962): 247.

28. Alice B. Keith, "Three North Carolina Blount Brothers in Business and Politics" (PhD diss., University of North Carolina, 1940), 37; September 15, 1775, *The Adams Papers*, Diary and Autobiography of John Adams, Vol. 2, *1771–1781*, ed. L. H. Butterfield (Cambridge, MA: Harvard University Press, 1961), 172,

Founders Online, https://founders.archives.gov/documents/Adams/01-02-02-0005-0003.

29. Richard Barry, *Mr. Rutledge of South Carolina* (New York: Duell, Sloan, and Pearce, 1942), 10; David Ramsay, *History of South Carolina* (1809; repr., Whitefish, MT: Kessinger, 2007), 2:510; James Haw, *John and Edward Rutledge of South Caro-*

lina (Athens: University of Georgia Press, 1997) 8; Adams, *Diary*, October 10, 1774, 2:150, Founders Online, https://founders.archives.gov/documents/Adams/01-02-02-0004-0007.

30. Marty Matthews, *Forgotten Founder: The Life and Times of Charles Pinckney* (Columbia: University of South Carolina Press, 2004), 11–12; Robert Brunhouse, ed., "David Ramsay 1749–1815: Selections from his Writings," *American Philosophical Society Transactions*, n.s., 55 (1965): 53.

31. Herbert Schneider and Carol Schneider, eds., *Samuel Johnson, President of King's College: His Career and Writings* (New York: Columbia University Press, 1929), 1:58; Elizabeth McCaughy, *From Loyalist to Founding Father: The Political Odyssey of William Samuel Johnson* (New York: Columbia University Press, 1980), 13; Lawrence Cremin, *American Education: The Colonial Experience, 1607–1783* (New York: Harper and Row, 1970), 296–297.

32. Milton M. Klein, *The American Whig: William Livingston of New York* (New York: Garland, 1993), 36–37.

33. Theodore Sedgwick, *Memoir of the Life of William Livingston* (New York: J. and J. Harper, 1833), 45, 52; John M. Mulder, "William Livingston: Propagandist Against Episcopacy," *Journal of Presbyterian History* 54 (1976): 85; "In Support of Schools," *Journal of the Society for the Propagation of the Gospel* 6 (1731–1735): 233.

34. WILLIAM LIVINGSTON to David Thompson, January 12, 1756, in Sedgwick, *Memoir of William Livingston*, 45.

35. "Autobiography of the Rev. John Barnard," *Collections of the Massachusetts Historical Society* 5 (1836): 220.

36. Mark Valeri, *Law and Providence in Joseph Bellamy's New England: The Origins of the New Divinity in Revolutionary America* (New York: Oxford University Press, 1994), 13.

37. Valeri, *Law and Providence*, 92, 142–143, 148.

38. Joseph Bellamy, *Four Sermons on the Wisdom of God in Permission of Sin* (Morristown, NJ: Henry P. Russell, 1804), 121–130; William Casto, *Oliver Ellsworth and the Creation of the Federal Republic* (New York: Second Circuit Committee on History and Commemorative Events, 1997), 23–26.

39. David Maclay, *Journal of William Maclay* (New York: Appleton, 1890), 388.

40. JAMES MADISON to Reverend Thomas Martin, August 10, 1769, *The Papers of James Madison*, Vol. 1, March 16, 1751–December 16 1779, ed. William T. Hutchinson and William M. E. Rachal (Chicago: The University of Chicago Press, 1962), 1:42–44, Founders Online, https://founders.archives.gov/documents/Madison/01-01-02-0004.

41. George Johnston, *History of Cecil County, Maryland, And the Early Settlements Around the Head of the Chesapeake Bay and on the Delaware River* (Elkton, MD: Dickson and Gilling, 1881) 176–177, 186.

42. Samuel Alexander Harrison and Oswald Tilghman, *History of Talbot County, Maryland, 1661–1861: The Worthies of Talbot* (1915; repr., Baltimore: Regional Publishing, 1967), 68; Ellis Oberholtzer, *Robert Morris, Patriot and Financier* (New York: Macmillan, 1903), 3.

43. Oberholtzer, *Patriot and Financier*, 3; Charles Rappleye, *Robert Morris: Financier of the American Revolution* (New York: Simon and Schuster, 2010), 7–9.

44. Jerry Grundfest, *George Clymer: Philadelphia Revolutionary* (New York: Arno Press, 1987), 15, 19; James McLachlan, *Princetonians, 1748–1768* (Princeton, NJ: Princeton University Press, 1976), 551.

45. Whitfield Bell, *Patriot Improvers, 1743–1768: Biographical Sketches of Members of the American Philosophical Society* (Philadelphia: American Philosophical Society, 1997), 240; Grundfest, *George Clymer*, 18; Benjamin Rush, *Autobiography of Benjamin Rush: His "Travels Through Life" Together with His Commonplace Book for 1789–1813*, ed. George W. Corner (Princeton, NJ: Princeton University Press, 1948), 149; Hopkinson, eulogy delivered April 1813, quoted in John P. Kaminski and Timothy Moore, *Assembly of Demigods* (Madison, WI: Parallel Press, 2012), 100.

Chapter 4. Writing Schools and Grammar Schools

1. Tess Summervell, "Romantic Readings: *The Prelude*, by William Wordsworth," *Wordsworth Grasmere*, https://wordsworth.org.uk/blog/2015/11/19/romantic-readings-the-prelude-by-william-wordsworth/; "James Madison's Autobiography," ed. Douglass Adair, *William and Mary Quarterly*, 3rd ser., 2 (1945): 191.

2. Max Farrand, ed., *The Laws and Liberties of Massachusetts: Reprinted from the Copy of the 1648 Edition in the Henry E. Huntington Library* (Cambridge, MA: Harvard University Press, 1929), 47.

3. Walter H. Small, *Early New England Schools* (Boston: Ginn, 1914), 13; "Autobiography of the Rev. John Barnard," *Collections of the Massachusetts Historical Society*, 3rd ser., 5 (1836): 239–243.

4. Robert Middlekauff, *Ancients and Axioms: Secondary Education in Eighteenth-Century New England* (New Haven, CT: Yale University Press, 1963), 133–134; Charles H. Bell, *History of the Town of Exeter, New Hampshire* (Exeter, NH: Quarter-Millennial Year Committee, 1880), 288, 289.

5. E. Jennifer Monaghan, *Learning to Read and Write in Colonial America* (Amherst: University of Massachusetts Press, 2005), 54–58, 99.

6. Middlekauff, *Ancients and Axioms*, 85–86.

7. Charles W. Brewster, *Rambles about Portsmouth* (Portsmouth, NH: C. W. Brewster & Son, 1859), 1:224–225; see Thomas P. Davis, *Chronicles of Hopkins Grammar School, 1660–1935* (New Haven, CT: Quinnipiac Press, 1938).

8. Emit Grizzell, *Origin and Development of the High School in New England before 1865* (New York: Macmillan, 1923), 28.

9. Henry Cabot Lodge, *A Memoir of Caleb Strong, United States Senator and Governor of Massachusetts* (Cambridge, MA: J. Wilson and Son, 1879), 229; Nehemiah Cleaveland, *A History of the Dummer Academy, Being the Centennial Discourse Delivered by Nehemiah Cleaveland on August 12, 1863* (Newburyport, MA: Herald Press, 1914), 19–20.

10. Cleaveland, *History of the Dummer Academy*, 21.

11. Michael Kammen, *Colonial New York: A History* (New York: Scribner's, 1975), 249.

12. Quoted in Edward A. Fitzpatrick, ed., *The Educational Views of DeWitt Clinton* (New York: Teachers College, 1911), 31.

13. Joel Munsell, *Annals of Albany* (Albany: J. Munsell, 1854), 4:15; Max Farrand, ed., *Records of the Federal Convention of 1787* (New Haven, CT: Yale University Press, 1937), 1:250; "Lansing, John, Jr.," in *Biographical Guide to the United States Congress*, https://bioguideretro.congress.gov/Home/MemberDetails?memIndex =L000087.

14. Jonathan Pearson, *A History of Schenectady Patent in Dutch and English Times* (Albany: J. Munson's Sons, 1883), 437; SPG [Society for the Propagation of the Gospel] Letterbooks, in William Webb Kemp, *The Support of Schools in Colonial New York by the Society for the Propagation of the Gospel in Foreign Parts* (New York: Teachers College Press, 1913), 75. On the changing significance of the terms *triviale* and *illustre schoolen*, see William H. Kirkpatrick, *The Dutch Schools of New Netherlands and Colonial New York* (Washington, DC: United States Bureau of Education, 1912), 211–212.

15. *History of the Province of New York* (1757), ed. Michael Kammen (Cambridge, MA: Harvard University Press, 1972), 1:278.

16. Donald Scarinci, *David Brearley and the Making of the United States Constitution* (Trenton: New Jersey Heritage Press, 2005), 122; William W. Campbell, "Life and Character of Jacob Broom," *Papers of the Delaware Historical Society* 51 (1909): 8–9, 29–33.

17. Thomas Woody, *Early Quaker Education in Pennsylvania* (New York: Teachers College Press, 1920), 182–183; J. William Frost, *The Quaker Family in Colonial America: A Portrait of the Society of Friends* (New York: St. Martin's Press, 1973), 124–125; David Barone, "Before the Revolution: Formal Rhetoric in Philadelphia during the Federal Era," *Pennsylvania History* 54, no. 4 (1987): 248.

18. Pennsylvania Superintendent of Education J. P. Wickenham, quoted in Elmer Brown, *The Making of Our Middle Schools: An Account of the Development of Secondary Education in the United States* (London: Longmans, Green, 1905), 104; Jonathan Boucher, quoted in Bernard Steiner, *History of Education in Maryland* (Washington, DC: US Government Printing Office, 1894), 38; Commissary Thomas Bray, quoted in Steiner, *History of Secondary Education in Maryland*, 22n1; "Daniel of St. Thomas Jenifer," Maryland Archives MSA SC 3520–728.

19. *Virginia Gazette*, May 21, 1751, March 5, 1752, November 5, 1755, quoted in Douglas Southall Freeman, *George Washington* (New York: Scribner's, 1948), 1:129; Cremin, *American Education*, 533, 331–332; Randolph, "Autobiographical Sketch," MS 4263, Albert and Shirley Small Special Collections Library, University of Virginia; see Helen Jones Campbell, "The Syms and Eaton Schools and Their Successors," *William and Mary Quarterly*, 2nd ser., 20 (1940): 1–61.

Chapter 5. The Schools of the Prophets

1. Thomas Shepard, *Works* (Boston: Doctrinal Tract and Book Society, 1853), 104; Kimber, "Itinerant Observations," *London Magazine* (July 1746): 329; J. David Hoeveler, *Creating the American Mind: Intellect and Politics in the Colonial Colleges* (Lanham, MD: Rowman and Littlefield, 2002), 24.

2. E. C. Burnett, ed., *Letters of the Members of the Continental Congress* (Washington, DC: Carnegie Institute, 1921–1936), 8:206–210.

3. Samuel Eliot Morison, *Three Centuries of Harvard* (Cambridge, MA: Harvard University Press, 1936), 102.

4. Morison, *Three Centuries of Harvard*, 60.

5. Morison, 103; Kathryn Sue McDaniel Moore, *Old Saints and Young Sinners: A Study of Student Discipline at Harvard College, 1636–1734* (Madison: University of Wisconsin Press, 1972), 57.

6. Quoted in Arthur O. Norton, "Harvard Text-Books and Reference Books in the Seventeenth Century," *Publications of the Colonial Society of Massachusetts* 28 (1935), 365; Morison, *Three Centuries of Harvard*, 29–31, 67; Thomas Miller, *Evolution of College English* (Pittsburgh: University of Pittsburgh Press, 2011), 34.

7. Louis Tucker, *Puritan Protagonist: President Thomas Clap of Yale College* (Chapel Hill: University of North Carolina Press,1962), 20–21; Ames quoted in Mark Noll, *America's God* (Oxford: Oxford University Press, 2002), 96; Perry Miller, *The New England Mind* (New York: Macmillan, 1939), 1:196, 198, quoting the diary of Cotton Mather, June 28, 1716.

8. Norman Fiering, *Moral Philosophy at Seventeenth-Century Harvard: A Discipline in Transition* (Chapel Hill: University of North Carolina Press, 1981), 199; Morison, *Three Centuries*, 29–31, 89, 135–136; John Adams, November 26, 1760, *The Adams Papers, Diary and Autobiography of John Adams*, Vol. 1, *1755–1770*, ed. L. H. Butterfield (Cambridge, MA: Harvard University Press, 1961), 174, Founders Online, https://founders.archives.gov/documents/Adams/01-01-02-0005-0007. There is a telling index entry in Fiering's book: "Politics, teaching of, rare."

9. Ellis Sandoz, ed., *Political Sermons of the Founding Era, 1730–1785* (Indianapolis: Liberty Fund, 1991), 240–241; François-Jean de Chastellux, *Travels in North America* (New York, 1828), 130.

10. Morison, *Three Centuries*, 89, 82, 92–93.

11. Morison, 32, 85, 90, 108.

12. Benjamin Wadsworth, *Abridgement of What I extracted while an Undergraduate at Harvard College*, manuscript, Harvard University Library, HUC8766.314 mf/N, https://iiif.lib.harvard.edu/manifests/view/drs:46471858$1i.

13. Wadsworth, *Abridgement*.

14. Anna Haddow, *Political Science in American Colleges and Universities* (New York: Appleton-Century, 1939) 5; John Adams, April 24, 1756, *Adams Diary and Autobiography*, 1:173–74, Founders Online, https://founders.archives.gov/documents/Adams/01-01-02-0002-0004-0024.

15. Haddow, *Political Science in American Colleges*, 5; Hollis to Mayhew, January 7, 1766, in *Memoirs of Thomas Hollis, Esq.*, ed. Francis Blackburne (London: J. Nichols, 1780; repr., Detroit: Gale ECCO Print Editions, 2010), 1:319, 1:396.

16. Robert Ernst, *Rufus King: American Federalist* (Chapel Hill: University of North Carolina Press, 1968), 18.

17. Morison, *Three Centuries*, 112–113; Moore, *Old Saints*, 657.

18. Samuel Eliot Morison, *The Founding of Harvard College* (Cambridge, MA: Harvard University Press, 1935), 136; Harvard University Archives HUC 6642.

19. Minor Meyer Jr., "A Source for Eighteenth Century Harvard Master's Questiones," *William and Mary Quarterly* 38 (1981): 261–267; David Robson, *Educating Re-*

publicans: *The College in the Era of the American Revolution, 1750–1800* (Westport, CT: Greenwood, 1985), 17–18.

20. Morison, *Three Centuries*, 138–140; Ernst, *Rufus King*, 18.

21. Ernst, *Rufus King*, 20; Morison, *Three Centuries*, 145, 147–148; Robson, *Educating Republicans*, 72; Robert Wright and Morris MacGregor, *Soldier Statesmen of the Constitution* (Washington, DC: Center of Military History, US Army, 1987), 98; Hoeveler, *Creating the American Mind*, 258–260.

22. *Abstract of Wills on File in the Surrogate's Office, City of New York, 1760–1766* (New York: New York Historical Society, 1898), 6:174. See Clinton Rossiter, *1787: The Grand Convention* (New York: Macmillan, 1966), 215–216.

23. Judith Schiff, Chief Research Archivist, "A Brief History of Yale," http://guides.library.yale.edu/yalehistory; Franklin Bowditch Dexter, *Documentary History of Yale University* (New Haven, CT: Yale University Press, 1916), 16–19; Brooks Mather Kelley, *Yale: A History* (New Haven, CT: Yale University Press, 1999), 6.

24. Kelley, *Yale: A History*, 10.

25. Kelley, 17; Samuel Johnson, "Autobiography," in *Samuel Johnson, President of King's College: His Career and Writings*, ed. Herbert Schneider and Carol Schneider (New York: Columbia University Press, 1929), 1:6–7.

26. Kelley, *Yale: A History*, 34.

27. John M. Mulder, "William Livingston: Propagandist Against Episcopacy," *Journal of Presbyterian History* 54 (1976): 85; Yale Laws quoted in Kelley, *Yale: A History*, 42.

28. Kelley, *Yale: A History*, 43.

29. Jonathan Edwards to Timothy Edwards, March 1, 1721, in *A Jonathan Edwards Reader*, ed. John E. Smith, Harry S. Stout, and Kenneth P. Minkema (New Haven, CT: Yale University Press, 1995), xxvii.

30. Ezra Stiles, *Literary Diary of Ezra Stiles*, ed. Franklin Bowditch Dexter (New York: Scribner's, 1901), 2:349.

31. William Livingston, to the Rev. James Dana, November 26, 1787, Livingston Papers Box 15, Massachusetts Historical Society; WILLIAM LIVINGSTON, *The Independent Reflector*, ed. M. M. Klein (Cambridge, MA: Harvard University Press, 1963), 175; Yale University, "Giving to Yale," http://yale.edu/development/gifts/capital_trad.html.

32. Elizabeth McCaughey, *From Loyalist to Founding Father: The Political Odyssey of William Samuel Johnson* (New York: Columbia University Press, 1980), 17, 19; Samuel Johnson, quoted in Eben Edwards Beardsley, *Life and Times of William Samuel Johnson, LL.D.* (New York: Hurd and Houghton, 1876), 4.

33. McCaughey, *Loyalist to Founding Father*, 18–19, 14; Tucker, *Puritan Protagonist*, 98.

34. Tucker, *Puritan Protagonist*, 29; Thomas Clap, *The Annals or History of Yale-College* (New Haven, CT: John Hotchkiss and B. Mecom, 1766), 62.

35. Kelley, *Yale: A History*, 53; LIVINGSTON, *The Independent Reflector*, 430; LIVINGSTON to Noah Welles, March 27, 1742, quoted in Mulder, "Propagandist Against Episcopacy," 86.

36. McCaughey, *Loyalist to Founding Father*, 25.

37. Guy Howard Miller, *The Revolutionary College: American Presbyterian Higher Education 1707–1837* (New York: New York University Press, 1976), 179–181; Christopher Grasso, *A Speaking Aristocracy: Transforming Public Discourse in Eighteenth-Century Connecticut* (Chapel Hill: University of North Carolina Press, 1999), 152; Richard L. Bushman, *From Puritan to Yankee: Character and the Social Order in Connecticut, 1690–1765* (Cambridge, MA: Harvard University Press, 2009), 243.

38. Stiles, *Literary Diary*, 2:349; 2:388; Franklin Bowditch Dexter, *Biographical Sketches of the Graduates of Yale College* (New York: Holt, 1896) 2:5–6.

39. Clap, *Annals*, 80; *Catalog of the Officers and Graduates of Yale University in New Haven, Connecticut 1701–1910* (New Haven, CT: Tuttle, Morehouse, and Taylor, 1910), 21.

40. Mulder, "Propagandist Against Episcopacy," 85; Dexter, *Documentary History*, 345; Thomas Darling, *Some Remarks on Mr. President Clap's History and Vindication of the Doctrines etc. of the New-England Churche* (New Haven, CT: J. Parker, 1757), 127; Stiles to Jared Eliot, September 24, 1759, MS in Yale University Library, quoted in Tucker, *Puritan Protagonist*, 157; Clap, *Annals*, 86.

41. Clap, *Annals*, 88; Tucker, *Puritan Protagonist*, 77–80.

42. Thomas Clap, *Essay on the Foundation of Moral Virtue and Obligation: Being a Short Introduction to the Study of Ethics for the Use of Students at Yale-College* (New Haven, CT: B. Mecum, 1765), quoted in Haddow, *Political Science*, 23.

43. Clap, *Annals*, 84.

44. John Brubacher, *Higher Education in Transition*, 4th ed. (London: Routledge, 2017), 4; Abiel Holmes, *The Life of Ezra Stiles* (Boston: Thomas and Anderson, 1798), 14; George Groce Jr., *William Samuel Johnson: A Maker of the Constitution* (New York: Columbia University Press, 1937), 11; McCaughey, *From Loyalist to Founding Father*, 28.

45. Dexter, *Documentary History*, 346–347, 351; Hoeveler, *American Mind*, 71; Tucker, *Puritan Protagonist*, 75–77; Clap, *Annals*, 57.

46. WILLIAM S. JOHNSON to William Smith Jr. 1748, in Johnson Papers, Connecticut Historical Society, quoted in Groce, 8–9.

47. Tucker, *Puritan Protagonist*, 69–70.

48. Tucker, 67–68; Clap, *Annals*, 92–93.

49. Henry Cabot Lodge, "Oliver Ellsworth," in *A Fighting Frigate and Other Essays* (New York: Scribner's, 1902), 70; Dexter, *Biographical Sketches*, 2:682.

50. Will G. Brown, *Life of Oliver Ellsworth* (New York: Macmillan, 1905), 15–16; W. S. Pearson, "Waightstill Avery," *Biographical History of North Carolina*, ed. Samuel Ashe (Greensboro, NC: Charles L. Van Noppen, 1908), 2–6.

51. Benjamin Gale to JARED INGERSOLL, August 9, 1762, in Franklin Bowditch Dexter, ed., "A Selection from the Correspondence and Miscellaneous Papers of Jared Ingersoll," *Papers of the New Haven Colony Historical Society* (New Haven, CT: Printed for the Society, 1918), 9:276; Strother E. Roberts, "Pines, Profits, and Popular Politics: Responses to the White Pine Acts in the Colonial Connecticut River Valley," *New England Quarterly* 83, no. 1 (2010): 85–89; David Alan Richards, "New Haven and the Stamp Act Crisis of 1765–1766," *Yale University Library Gazette* 46, no. 2 (1971): 69.

52. Lawrence Gipson, *Jared Ingersoll: A Study of American Loyalism* (New Haven, CT: Yale University Press, 1920), 158–159; Richards, "New Haven and the Stamp Act Crisis," 75; INGERSOLL to LIVINGSTON, October 1, 1765, "Letters on the Stamp Act," *The Historical Magazine* 6 (1862): 138; Dexter, "Correspondence and Miscellaneous Papers," 9:349; Michael Sletcher, *New Haven: From Puritanism to the Age of Terrorism* (Charleston, SC: Arcadia, 2004), 31.

53. Stiles, *Literary Diary*, 2:336–337; Clap, *Annals*, 85; Tucker, *Puritan Protagonist*, 254–260; James E. Scanlon, "American College Presidents in the Eighteenth Century," *History of Education Quarterly* 2 (1971): 74; James Axtell, *The School upon a Hill: Education and Society in Colonial New England* (New Haven, CT: Yale University Press, 1974), 238–244.

54. Beverly McAnear, "The Selection of an Alma Mater by Pre-Revolutionary Students," *Pennsylvania Magazine of History and Biography* 73 (1949): 436.

55. Hoeveler, *American Mind*, 269; Robson, *Educating Republicans*, 48–49.

56. Stiles, *Literary Diary*, 2:387–388; Trumbull, *Progress of Dulness*, quoted in Geiger, *History of American Higher Education: Learning and Culture from the Founding to World War II* (Princeton, NJ: Princeton University Press, 2014), 54.

57. Stiles, *Literary Diary*, 2:349, 2:387–88, 3:346, 3:487.

58. Samuel Johnson to WILLIAM S. JOHNSON, March 4, 1773, in James Boswell, *The Life of Samuel Johnson*, ed. David P. Womersley (New York: Penguin Random House, 2008), 121.

59. For KING and the Missouri Compromise, see Andrew H. Browning, *The Panic of 1819* (Columbia: University of Missouri Press, 2019), 340, 346.

60. Stiles, *Literary Diary*, 2:209.

Chapter 6. Their Majesties' College in Williamsburg

1. Edward Kimber, "Itinerant Observations in America," *London Magazine*, July 1746, 329.

2. Dumas Malone, *Jefferson and His Time* (Boston: Little, Brown, 1948), 1:60.

3. Jack Morpurgo, *Their Majesties' Royall Colledge: William and Mary in the Seventeenth and Eighteenth Centuries* (Williamsburg, VA: College of William and Mary, 1976), 98–99.

4. Lyon Tyler, "Education in Colonial Virginia: Part IV," *William and Mary Quarterly*, 1st ser., 6 (1898): 176–177.

5. Stith to the Rt. Rev. Thomas Sherlock, August 18, 1753, quoted in Morpurgo, *Royall Colledge*, 118.

6. "Academicus," *Virginia Gazette*, May 19, 1774; Morpurgo, *Royall Colledge*, 77.

7. Tyler, "Education in Colonial Virginia," 177; David Robson, *Educating Republicans: The College in the Era of the American Revolution, 1750–1800* (Westport, CT: Greenwood, 1985), 22.

8. Morpurgo, *Royall Colledge*, 107; Courtland Canby, "A Note on the Influence of Oxford at William and Mary," *William and Mary Quarterly*, 2nd ser., 21 (1941): 243–44; Malone, *Jefferson*, 1:51–52.

9. October 6, 1763, "Journal of the Meetings of the President and Masters of the College, 1729–1784," *William and Mary Quarterly*, 1st ser., 1 (1893): 130–137.

10. James McCaw, *A Memoir of James McClurg, M.D.* (Richmond, VA: Colin and Nowlan, 1854), 163.

11. Morpurgo, *Royal College*, 83; Tyler, "Education in Colonial Virginia," 176–177; Lawrence Cremin, *American Education: The Colonial Experience, 1607–1783* (New York: Harper and Row, 1970), 54.

12. Robson, *Educating Republicans*, 76–77, 153.

13. Jefferson, *Autobiography*, National Archives, Founders Online, https://founders.archives.gov/documents/Jefferson/98-01-02-1756; Tyler, "Education in Colonial Virginia," 177; Morpurgo, *Royall Colledge*, 193–194.

14. Morpurgo, *Royall Colledge*, 81, 167.

15. Kimber, "Itinerant Observations," 55; Jefferson to John Page, October 7, 1763, *Papers of Thomas Jefferson*, ed. Julian P. Boyd (Princeton, NJ: Princeton University Press, 1950), 1:11, National Archives, Founders Online, https://founders.archives.gov/documents/Jefferson/01-01-02-0005; *Diary of Landon Carter of Sabine Hall, 1752–1778*, ed. Jack P. Green (Richmond: William Byrd Press for the Virginia Historical Society, 1987), 2:765.

16. Morpurgo, *Royall Colledge*, 101; Jefferson to Thomas McCauley, June 14, 1819, Founders Online, https://founders.archives.gov/documents/Jefferson/03-14-02-0392; Malone, *Jefferson*, 1:57; Jane Carson, *James Innes and His Brothers of the F.H.C.* (Williamsburg, VA: Colonial Williamsburg, 1965), 5.

17. Tucker-Coleman Collection, Swem Library Special Collections; Carson, *James Innes and His Brothers*, 72.

18. Proceedings of the Visitors and Governors of William and Mary College, April 26, 1760, *General Correspondence, Virginia*, 13:284, Fulham Papers, Lambeth Palace Library, London; William T. Walker, "Professor William Small 1735–1775," William and Mary, https://www.wm.edu/as/physics/about_physics/williamsmall/index.php; R. A. Brock, *Virginia and Virginians* (Richmond, VA: H. H. Hardesty, 1888), 1:56; "Journal of the Meetings of the President and Masters of William and Mary College," *William and Mary Quarterly*, 1st ser., 13 (1904–1905): 149.

19. John J. Reardon, *Edmund Randolph: A Biography* (New York: Macmillan, 1975), 6–7; Moncure Conway, *Omitted Chapters of History Disclosed in the Life and Papers of Edmund Randolph* (New York: Putnam, 1888), 3.

20. Samuel K. Fore, Harlan Crow Library, personal communication, January 31, 2013; Charles Willson Peale, *Selected Papers of Charles Willson Peale and His Family*, ed. Lillian Miller et al. (New Haven, CT: Yale University Press, 1996), 135; Charles C. Sellers, *Charles Willson Peale* (Philadelphia: American Philosophical Society, 1947), 1:119. See Samuel Fore, "William Pierce (1753–1789)," *New Georgia Encyclopedia*, http://www.georgiaencyclopedia.org/articles/history-archaeology/william-pierce-1753-1789.

21. Charles T Cullen, *St. George Tucker and Law in Virginia, 1772–1804* (New York: Garland Publishing, 1987), 18.

22. "The Southern Campaign of Major-General Greene, 1781–2: Letters of Major William Pierce to St. George Tucker," *Magazine of American History* 7 (1891): 431–445; Fore, "William Pierce"; James Hutson, ed., *Supplement to Max Farrand's Records of the Federal Convention of 1787* (New Haven, CT: Yale University Press,

1987), 123; Max Farrand, ed., *Records of the Federal Convention of 1787* (New Haven, CT: Yale University Press, 1937), 3:100.

23. Monroe to Lee, June 15, 1780, in *Writings of James Monroe*, ed. Stanislaus Murray Hamilton (New York: Putnam's, 1898), 1:2; George Morgan, *The Life of James Monroe* (Boston: Small, Maynard, 1921), 68, 70.

24. *Papers of James Madison*, Congressional Series, ed. William Hutcheson and William Rachal (Chicago: University of Chicago Press, 1973, 1975), November 12, 1784, 8:152; December 23, 1786, 9:221–224; January 16, 1787, 9:246–247.

25. Monroe to Jefferson, July 27, 1787, in *Selected Correspondence and Papers of James Monroe*, ed. Daniel Preston et al. (Westport, CT: Greenwood Press, 2006), 2:378, Founders Online, https://founders.archives.gov/documents/Jefferson/01-11-02-0556.

26. Monroe, *Selected Correspondence and Papers*, 2:56.

27. Washington to Hamilton, July 29, 1792, *Papers of George Washington*, Presidential Series, ed. Robert F. Haggard and Mark A. Mastromarino (Charlottesville: University of Virginia Press, 2002), 10:588–592, Founders Online, https://founders.archives.gov/documents/Washington/05-10-02-0401.

28. Malone, *Jefferson*, 1:50.

29. Morpurgo, *Royall Colledge*, 174.

30. February 12, 1783, in Marshall, *Writings*, ed. Charles F. Hobson (New York: Library of America, 2010), 4; "Original Records of the Phi Beta Kappa Society," *William and Mary Quarterly*, 1st ser., 4 (1896): 236–239. PIERCE's duel was called off after the intervention of his adversary's second—ALEXANDER HAMILTON.

31. Morpurgo, *Royall Colledge*, 204.

32. GEORGE WASHINGTON to Jonathan Boucher, January 7, 1773, Founders Online, https://founders.archives.gov/documents/Washington/02-09-02-0116; WASHINGTON to the Rev. James Madison, October 27, 1781, Founders Online, https://founders.archives.gov/documents/Washington/99-01-02-07304; WASHINGTON to David Stuart, January 22, 1798, Founders Online, https://founders.archives.gov/documents/Washington/06-02-02-0036.

33. Morpurgo, *Royall Colledge*, 99.

Chapter 7. The Old World's Old Schools

1. ACAD: A Cambridge Alumni Database (https://venn.lib.cam.ac.uk), containing the ten volumes of *Alumni Cantabrigienses*, ed. John Venn (Cambridge: Cambridge University Press, 1922–27), lists only Jonathan Belcher, son of the royal governor, who took a second MA at Cambridge in 1733, after receiving his BA and MA from Harvard.

2. Douglas Southall Freeman, *George Washington: A Biography* (New York: Scribner's, 1948), 1:133; "Some Virginians Educated in Great Britain," *Virginia Magazine of History and Biography* 21 (1913): 196–199; W. G. Stanard, "Virginians at Oxford," *William and Mary Quarterly* 2 (1893): 22–24, 49–153; Harriott Horry Ravenel, *Charleston: The Place and the People* (New York: Macmillan, 1906), 148–149.

3. V. H. H. Green, "The University and Social Life," in *The History of the University of Oxford*, Vol. 5, *The Eighteenth Century*, ed. Lucy Sutherland and Lesley G. Mitch-

ell (New York: Oxford University Press, 1986), 309–311; Graham Midgely, *University Life in Eighteenth-Century Oxford* (New Haven, CT: Yale University Press, 1996), x; Lesley G. Mitchell, "Introduction," in Sutherland and Mitchell, eds., *History of the University of Oxford*, 5:4, 18; Edward Gibbon, *Autobiography of Edward Gibbon* (New York: Oxford University Press, 1978), 36; Ezra Stiles, *Literary Diary of Ezra Stiles*, ed. Franklin Bowditch Dexter (New York: Scribner's, 1901), 3:304.

4. Gibbon, *Autobiography*, 55; E. G. W. Bill, *Education at Christ Church College, Oxford, 1660–1800* (London: Oxford University Press, 1988), 56.

5. Max Farrand, ed., *Records of the Federal Convention of 1787* (New Haven, CT: Yale University Press, 1937), 3:97; Eric Stockdale and Randy Holland, *Middle Temple Lawyers and the American Revolution* (Eagan, MN: Thomson-West, 2007), 187; Harriot Ravenel, *Eliza Lucas Pinckney* (New York: Scribner's, 1896), 160.

6. Philip Stanhope, Lord Chesterfield, *Letters to His Son* (London: Walter Dunne, 1901), 381; Alexander Garden, *Eulogy on Gen. Charles Cotesworth Pinckney, President-General of the Society of the Cincinnati* (Charleston, SC: A. E. Miller, 1825), 32.

7. Quoted in Ravenel, *Eliza Lucas Pinckney*, 149–151.

8. Lawrence Stone, "Size and Composition," in *The University in Society*, ed. Lawrence Stone (Princeton, NJ: Princeton University Press, 1974), 1:53; I. G. Doolittle, "College Administration," in Sutherland and Mitchell, eds., *History of the University of Oxford*, Vol. 5, 260–261; Keith Krawczynski, *William Henry Drayton: South Carolina Revolutionary Patriot* (Baton Rouge: Louisiana State University Press, 2001), 16.

9. Quoted in Bill, *Education at Christ Church*, 220; Doolittle, "College Administration," 262–263; Eliza Pinckney, *The Letter Book of Eliza Pinckney, 1739–1762* (Chapel Hill: University of North Carolina Press, 1972), 168; Green, "The University and Social Life," 330.

10. Judith Curthoys, Christ Church College Archivist, personal communication, November 7, 2013.

11. Doolittle, "College Administration," 258–259; Farrand, ed., *Records*, 1:426–427.

12. Green, "University and Social Life," 342.

13. Bill, *Education at Christ Church*, 233, 237–239; MS 2564, folio 319, Secker Papers, Lambeth Palace Library.

14. P. Quarrie, "The Christ Church Collections Books," in Sutherland and Mitchell, eds., *History of the University of Oxford*, 5:478. A stubbornly persistent error, traceable at least to James Longacre and James Herring, *National Portrait Gallery of Distinguished Americans* (Philadelphia: Henry Perkins, 1834), 4:3, has the future dean Cyril Jackson tutoring PINCKNEY. The assertion has since been repeated frequently, including by Marvin Zahnhiser, *Charles Cotesworth Pinckney, Founding Father* (Chapel Hill: University of North Carolina Press, 1967), still the best biography. The records of Christ Church make clear that Jackson was never a tutor; moreover Jackson, who was actually younger than PINCKNEY, did not even matriculate as an undergraduate at Christ Church until six months after PINCKNEY did. One of the responsibilities of a tutor was to pay a pupil's caution money, and PINCKNEY's caution money was paid by Henry Reginald Courtenay, another Westminster alumnus (Bill, *Education at Christ Church*, 227–228; Curthoys, personal communication, August 28, 2013.)

15. Quarrie, "Christ Church Collection Books," 499–501; Bill, *Education at Christ Church*, 211; Boswell, *Life of Johnson*, 2:68.

16. Bill, *Education at Christ Church*, 298–99; J. Yolton, "Schoolmen, Logic, and Philosophy," in Sutherland and Mitchell, eds., *History of the University of Oxford*, 5:581, 585.

17. Longacre and Herring, *Portrait Gallery*, 4:3.

18. Quarrie, "Christ Church Collection Books," 473.

19. Ronald Hoffman and Sally D. Mason, *Princes of Ireland, Planters of Maryland: A Carroll Saga* (Chapel Hill: University of North Carolina Press, 2000), 143.

20. Hoffman and Mason, *Princes of Ireland, Planters of Maryland*, 153; John Gerard, *Stonyhurst College, Its Life Beyond the Seas, 1592–1794, and on English Soil, 1794–1894* (Belfast: Marcus Ward, 1894), 31–32, 24; Thomas Muir, *Stonyhurst College 1593–1993* (London: James and James, 1992), 12.

21. Edward Copleton, quoted in Bill, *Education at Christ Church*, 275.

22. Burke to Sir Hercules Langrishe, Bart., M.P., January 3, 1792, in Burke, *Selected Writings and Speeches*, ed. Peter J. Stanlis (Washington, DC: Regnery, 1997), 319.

23. J. C. Beckett, *Protestant Dissent in Ireland* (London: Faber, 1948), 40–41; David Steers, "'The very life-blood of Nonconformity is education': The Killyleagh Philosophy School, County Down," *Familia* 28 (2012): 67; J. R. R. Adams, "Swine-Tax and Eat-Him-All-Magee: The Hedge Schools and Popular Education in Ireland," in *Irish Popular Culture 1650–1850*, ed. James S. Donnelly Jr. and Kerby A. Miller (Dublin: Irish Academic Press, 1998), 99–100.

24. Peter Clarke, "Teaching of Bookkeeping," Estudios Irlandeses 5 (2010): 4–5; Timothy Corcoran, Select Texts on Education Systems in Ireland from the Close of the Middle Ages (Dublin: University College Press, 1928), 30; Benjamin Rush, commonplace book, quoted in John P. Kaminski and Timothy Moore, Assembly of Demigods (Madison, WI: Parallel Press, 2012), 101.

25. Francis McKee, "Francis Hutcheson and Bernard Mandeville," *Eighteenth-Century Ireland* 3 (1988): 124; Bernard Steiner, *Life and Correspondence of James McHenry, Secretary of War under Washington and Adams* (Cleveland: Burrows Brothers, 1907), 1–2.

26. Nicholas Hans, *New Trends in Education in the Eighteenth Century* (London: Rutledge, Kegan Paul, 1951), 24–32.

27. BUTLER to Andrew Pickens, August 24, 1794, quoted in Terry W. Lipscomb, ed., *Letters of Pierce Butler, 1790–1794* (Columbia: University of South Carolina Press, 2007), xi; Malcolm Bell, Major Butler's Legacy: Five Generations of a Slaveholding Family (Athens: University of Georgia Press, 1987), 1–2; Lipscomb, *Letters of Pierce Butler, 1790–1794*, xvi.

28. Justina Dobbs to Conway Richard Dobbs, May 14, 1765, Desmond Clarke Papers #3340, Southern Historical Collection, Wilson Library, University of North Carolina.

29. See Mary Ellen Gadski, The History of New Bern Academy (Raleigh: Department of Archives and History, North Carolina Department of Cultural Resources, 1977).

30. Hutcheson, System of Moral Philosophy (Glasgow: R. & A. Foulis, 1755), 1:xlx; Jane Ohlmeyer, Political Thought in Seventeenth Century Ireland (Cambridge: Cambridge University Press, 2000), 15.

31. J. C. Ballantyne (University of Glasgow) to Alexander B. Andrews, September 21, 1912, North Carolina Archives, Richard Dobbs Spaight Papers, reprinted in Alexander B. Andrews, RICHARD DOBBS SPAIGHT: Governor of North Carolina, 1792–1795 (Raleigh, NC: Edwards and Broughton, 1924), 97; Thomas Irving, Controversy between Gen. RICHARD D. SPAIGHT and John Stanly, Esq., To Which is Attached a Funeral Discourse . . . (New Bern, NC: John S. Pasteur, 1802), 29. See Andrew Browning, "Richard Dobbs Spaight in Ireland and Scotland," North Carolina Historical Review 94 (2017): 137.

32. Viscount Harcourt to Lord North, October 11, 1775, quoted in Charles Augustus Hanna, The Scotch-Irish: Or, the Scot in North Britain, North Ireland, and North America (New York: G. P. Putnam's Sons, 1902), 184.

Chapter 8. The Inns of Court and Legal Apprenticeship

1. Edmund Burke, On Moving His Resolutions for Conciliation with the Colonies (London: J. Dodsley, 1784), 30.

2. Burke, On Moving His Resolutions, 30.

3. John Colyer, "The American Connection," in A History of the Middle Temple, ed. Richard Havery (London: Hart, 2011), 248.

4. Milton M. Klein, American Whig: William Livingston of New York (New York: Garland, 1993), 59.

5. JOHN DICKINSON to Samuel Dickinson, May 25, 1754, quoted in Trevor Colbourn, ed., "A Pennsylvania Farmer at the Court of King George: John Dickinson's London Letters, 1754–1756," Pennsylvania Magazine of History and Biography 86 (1962): 269–270.

6. William M. Meigs, Life of Charles Jared Ingersoll (Philadelphia: Lippincott, 1897), 18; Joseph Reed to JARED INGERSOLL, December 15, 1777, in William Bradford Reed, Life and Correspondence of Joseph Reed (Philadelphia: Lindsay and Blackstone, 1847), 2:39.

7. C. E. A. Bedwell, "American Middle Templars," American Historical Review 25 (1920): 680–689.

8. James Haw, John and Edward Rutledge of South Carolina (Athens: University of Georgia Press, 1997), 8–9; Colyer, "American Connection," 243–246; Eliza Pinckney to CHARLES COTESWORTH PINCKNEY, December 1768, in William Gilmore Simms, "A Memoir of the Pinckney Family of South Carolina," Historical Magazine and Notes and Queries, 2nd ser., 2 (1867): 136–137.

9. Julie Flavell, When London Was Capital of America (New Haven, CT: Yale University Press: 2010), 11; James Raven, London Booksellers and American Customers: Transatlantic Literary Community and the Charleston Library Society, 1748–1811 (Columbia: University of South Carolina Press, 2002) 127, 145; Bedwell, "American Middle Templars," 688.

10. Marty D. Matthews, Forgotten Founder: The Life and Times of Charles Pinckney (Columbia: University of South Carolina Press, 2004), 11.

11. William S. Henwood, "William Houstoun: A Powerful Statesman with a Colorful Personality," *Georgia Journal of Southern Legal History* 1, no. 1 (1991): 215; *Papers of Henry Laurens*, ed. David R. Chesnutt (Columbia: University of South Carolina Press 1968), 11:209; Monroe to Jefferson, November 1, 1784, Founders Online, https://founders.archives.gov/?q=%20Author%3A%22Monroe%2C%20James%22%20Recipient%3A%22Jefferson%2C%20Thomas%22&s=1111311111&sa=&r=15&sr=.

12. Ralph M. Stein, "The Path of Legal Education from Edward I to Langdell: A History of Insular Reaction," *Chicago-Kent Law Review* 57 (1981): 430–431; H. S. Richards, *Legal Education in Great Britain*, U.S. Bureau of Education Bulletin 18 (Washington, DC: Government Printing Office, 1915), 8; Brian Abel-Smith and Robert Stevens, *Lawyers and the Courts: A Sociological Study of the English Legal System, 1750–1965* (London: Heineman, 1967), 16–17.

13. Wilfrid Prest, "The Unreformed Middle Temple," in Havery, *History of the Middle Temple*, 227.

14. Stein, "Path of Legal Education," 434–35; Prest, "Unreformed Middle Temple," 221.

15. Abel-Smith and Stevens, *Lawyers and the Courts*, 25.

16. Haw, *John and Edward Rutledge*, 9; Prest, "Unreformed Middle Temple," 228, 231.

17. Blackstone, *Commentaries on the Laws of England* (Oxford: Clarendon, 1765), 1:31.

18. JOHN RUTLEDGE to Edward Rutledge, July 30, 1769, in John Belton O'Neall, *Bench and Bar of South Carolina* (Charleston: Courtenay, 1859), 123–124.

19. Adams, *Diary*, September 3, 1774, in *The Adams Papers: Diary and Autobiography of John Adams*, Vol. 2, *1771–1781*, ed. L. H. Butterfield (Cambridge, MA: Harvard University Press, 1961) 120–122, National Archives, Founders Online, https://founders.archives.gov/documents/Adams/01-02-02-0004-0006-0003.

20. JOHN DICKINSON to Samuel Dickinson, March 8, 1754, in Colbourn, "Pennsylvania Farmer," 257.

21. JOHN DICKINSON to Judith Dickinson, March 8, 1754, August 15, 1754, and January 22, 1755, in Colbourn, 246, 280, 423.

22. Stein, "Path of Legal Education," 434; Colbourn, "Pennsylvania Farmer," 246; JOHN RUTLEDGE to Edward Rutledge, July 30, 1769, in O'Neall, *Bench and Bar*, 125–127.

23. JOHN DICKINSON to Samuel Dickinson, April 22, 1754, in Colbourn, "Pennsylvania Farmer," 267; Haw, *John and Edward Rutledge*, 9.

24. JOHN DICKINSON to Samuel Dickinson, March 8, 1754, in Colbourn, "Pennsylvania Farmer," 258; JOHN RUTLEDGE to Edward Rutledge, July 30, 1769, in O'Neall, *Bench and Bar*, 125–127; Haw, *John and Edward Rutledge*, 10.

25. JOHN DICKINSON to Samuel Dickinson, March 8, 1754, August 2, 1756, in Colbourn, "Pennsylvania Farmer," 258, 453.

26. "Six Letters of Peter Manigault," *South Carolina Historical and Genealogical Magazine* 15 (1914): 123.

27. JOHN DICKINSON to Judith Dickinson, January 18, 1754, in Colbourn, "Pennsylvania Farmer," 254.

28. Prest, "Unreformed Middle Temple," 211–213; JOHN DICKINSON to Samuel Dickinson, May 25, 1754, in Colbourn, "Pennsylvania Farmer," 269.

29. Prest, "Unreformed Middle Temple," 235; JOHN RUTLEDGE to Edward Rutledge, July 30, 1769, in O'Neall, *Bench and Bar*, 123.

30. JOHN DICKINSON to Judith Dickinson, January 19, 1754, to Samuel Dickinson, April 22, 1754, January 21, 1755, in Colbourn, "Pennsylvania Farmer," 254, 268, 421; JOHN RUTLEDGE to Edward Rutledge, July 30, 1769, in O'Neall, *Bench and Bar*, 122–123.

31. Max Farrand, ed., *Records of the Federal Convention of 1787* (New Haven, CT: Yale University Press, 1937), 2:202, 204, 216, 1:150; JOHN DICKINSON to Samuel Dickinson, March 8, 1754, in Colbourn, "Pennsylvania Farmer," 259.

32. See "James Madison's Autobiography," ed. Douglass Adair, *William and Mary Quarterly*, 3rd ser., 2 (1945): 198.

33. Charles A. Warren, *A History of the American Bar* (Boston: Little, Brown: 1911), 195; Stein, "Path of Legal Education," 438–439; Bruce A. Kimball, *The "True Professional Ideal" in America: A History* (Cambridge, MA, and Oxford: Blackwell, 1992), 85; *Public Records of Connecticut*, 7:279–280 (1730).

34. Stein, "Path of Legal Education," 440; Brian Moline, "Early American Legal Education," *Washburn Law Journal* 42 (2004): 780–781.

35. Charles R. McKirdy, "The Lawyer as Apprentice: Legal Education in Eighteenth Century Massachusetts," *Journal of Legal Education* 28 (1976): 129; New York *Gazette and Post-Boy*, August 19, 1745, February 18, 1751.

36. John E. O'Conner, *William Paterson: Lawyer and Statesman, 1745–1806* (New Brunswick, NJ: Rutgers University Press, 1979) 20, 32; Donald Scarinci, *David Brearley and the Making of the United States Constitution* (Trenton: New Jersey Heritage Press, 2005) 45; PATERSON to MacPherson, January 17, 1767, original letter book, box 1, Paterson Family Collection, Princeton University Library; John McLachlan, *Princetonians, 1748–1768: A Biographical Dictionary* (Princeton, NJ: Princeton University Press, 1976), 576.

37. Broadus Mitchell, *Alexander Hamilton: Youth to Maturity* (New York: Macmillan, 1957), 269; Moline, "Early American Legal Education," 785; Thomas A. Glenn, *William Churchill Houston 1746–1788* (Norristown, PA: privately printed, 1903), 66–67.

38. Morris L. Cohen, "Legal Literature in Colonial Massachusetts," in *Law in Colonial Massachusetts 1630–1800*, ed. Daniel R. Coquillette (Boston: Colonial Society of Massachusetts, 1984), 243; W. Hamilton Bryson, "Private Law Libraries Before 1776," in *Virginia Law Books: Essays and Bibliographies*, ed. W. H. Bryson (Philadelphia: American Philosophical Society, 2000), 487; McKirdy, "Lawyer as Apprentice," 130; Ralph Ketcham, *James Madison* (Charlottesville: University of Virginia Press, 1990), 149–150; *Miscellaneous Writings of Joseph Story*, ed. William W. Story (Boston: Little, Brown, 1852), 20.

39. Jefferson to John Page, December 25, 1762, in *Papers of Thomas Jefferson*, ed. Julian Boyd (Princeton, NJ: Princeton University Press, 1950) 1:5, Founders Online, https://founders.archives.gov/documents/Jefferson/01-01-02-0002; Jefferson to MADISON, February 17, 1826, Founders Online, https://founders.archives.gov/documents/Jefferson/98-01-02-5912.

40. Ian Williams, "Dr. Bonham's Case and 'Void' Statutes," *Journal of Legal History* 27 (2006): 111–128.

41. George Groce, *William Samuel Johnson: A Maker of the Constitution* (New York: Columbia University Press, 1937), 17–19; "William Smith Jr. Letters and Documents 1771–1775, MSS Col 15660, 'Miscellaneous,'" New York Public Library; Paul Hamlin, *Legal Education in Colonial New York* (New York: New York University Law Quarterly Review, 1939), 197–200.

42. Martin Clagett, "James Wilson—His Scottish Background: Corrections and Additions," *Pennsylvania History: A Journal of Mid-Atlantic Studies* 79, no. 2 (2012): 163–164.

43. William Ewald, "James Wilson and the Drafting of the Constitution," *University of Pennsylvania Journal of Constitutional Law* 10 (2008): 904. See James E. Pfander and Donald D. Birk, "Article III and the Scottish Judiciary," *Harvard Law Review* 124 (2011): 1613–1687.

44. W. Hamilton Bryson, "The History of Legal Education in Virginia," *University of Richmond Law Review* 14 (1979):162; Warren, *American Bar*, 165; Moline, "Early American Legal Education," 780.

45. Jefferson to MADISON, April 25, May 7, 1784, in
The Papers of Thomas Jefferson, Vol. 7, *2 March 1784–25 February 1785*, ed. Julian P. Boyd (Princeton, NJ: Princeton University Press, 1953), 120, 228, Founders Online, https://founders.archives.gov/documents/Jefferson/01-07-02-0129, https://founders.archives.gov/documents/Jefferson/01-07-02-0169.

46. *Documentary History of the Supreme Court of the United States*, ed. Maeva Marcus (New York: Columbia University Press, 1985–2003), 2:886n2; Paul Clarkson and Samuel Jett, *Luther Martin of Maryland* (Baltimore: Johns Hopkins University Press, 1970), 22–23, 28, 58; LUTHER MARTIN, *Modern Gratitude* (1801) (Whitefish, MT: Kessinger, 2010), 144, 147.

47. WILLIAM FEW, "Autobiography of Col. William Few of Georgia, From the Original Manuscript in the Possession of William Few Chrystie," *Magazine of American History* 7 (1881): 352.

48. FEW, "Autobiography of Col. William Few," 352.

49. After months in which the Convention stayed with the idea of Congress choosing (and overshadowing) the executive, the method of electing a president would ultimately resemble what JAMES WILSON had first proposed back at the beginning of June; in committee, it would be GOUVERNEUR MORRIS's efforts that revived the idea of an electoral college, potentially chosen by the people themselves. See Jack Heyburn, "Gouverneur Morris and James Wilson at the Constitutional Convention," *Journal of Constitutional Law* 20 (2017): 179–180.

Chapter 9. The New Old World

1. Benjamin Rush, *Autobiography of Benjamin Rush: His "Travels Through Life" Together with His Commonplace Book for 1789–1813*, ed. George W. Corner (Princeton, NJ: Princeton University Press, 1948), 64, 43.

2. Garry Wills, *Explaining America* (Garden City, NY: Doubleday, 1981), 63; M. E. Bradford, *A Worthy Company: Brief Lives of the Framers of the U.S. Constitution* (Marl-

borough, NH: Plymouth Rock Foundation, 1982), 194; Iain McLean, "Adam Smith, James Wilson, and the U.S. Constitution," *Adam Smith Review* 8 (2015): 141.

3. JAMES MADISON, *Papers of James Madison*, ed. Robert A. Rutland and William M. E. Rachal (Chicago: University of Chicago Press, 1967), 6:62–115; McLean, "Adam Smith, James Wilson, and the U.S. Constitution," 152–154; Douglass Adair, "James Madison," in *Fame and the Founding Fathers*, ed. Trevor Colbourn (New York: Norton, 1974), 161. See Samuel Fleischaker, "Adam Smith's Reception among the American Founders," *William and Mary Quarterly* 59 (2002): 897–924, esp. 909–910; Iain McDaniel, *Adam Ferguson in the Scottish Enlightenment: The Roman Past and Europe's Future* (Cambridge, MA: Harvard University Press, 2013); and Max Skjonsberg, "Adam Ferguson on the Perils of Popular Factions and Demagogues in a Roman Mirror," *History of European Ideas* 45 (2019): 842–865.

4. Gouverneur Morris Papers, MS Coll Morris, Box 1, Rare Book and Manuscript Library, Columbia University.

5. Max Farrand, *The Framing of the Constitution of the United States* (New Haven, CT: Yale University Press, 1913), 198; William Lee Miller, *The Business of May Next: James Madison and the Founding* (Charlottesville: University of Virginia Press, 1992), 62.

6. Martin Clagett, "James Wilson, His Scottish Background: Corrections and Additions," *Pennsylvania History: A Journal of Mid-Atlantic Studies* 79, no. 2 (2012):159–160; James Beale, *A History of the Burgh and Parochial Schools of Fife*, ed. Donald Witherington (Edinburgh: Lindsay, 1983), 150.

7. Robert Annan to Bird Wilson, May 16, 1805, Benjamin Rush Papers, 43:133, Historical Society of Pennsylvania, Philadelphia.

8. Clagett, "Scottish Background," 161.

9. Bradford, *Worthy Company*, 82; Michael Klarman, *The Framers' Coup* (New York: Oxford, 2016), 146n; Clagett, "Scottish Background," 156, 161.

10. Clagett, "Scottish Background,"163; RH9/1/121 and Cupar Burgh Records (1762) 119, 127, (1764) 213, National Archives of Scotland, in Clagett, 163.

11. Robert Heron, *Observations Made in a Journey through the Western Counties of Scotland in 1792* (Perth: R. Morison, Jr., 1793), 2:418; Trustees of the University of Pennsylvania, Minute Books 1749–1768, 309, University of Pennsylvania Archives, https://archives.upenn.edu/digitized-resources/docs-pubs/trustees-minutes.

12. William Stewart, ed., *University of Glasgow Old and New* (Glasgow: T. & R. Annan & Sons, James MacLehose & Sons, 1891), xxiii; Caroline Robbins, *Eighteenth Century Commonwealthman* (Cambridge, MA: Harvard University Press, 1959), 7.

13. Norman Fiering, *Moral Philosophy at Seventeenth Century Harvard: A Discipline in Transition* (Chapel Hill: University of North Carolina Press, 1981), 199; Douglas Sloan, *The Scottish Enlightenment and the American College Ideal* (New York: Teachers College Press, 1971), 92.

14. W. R. Scott, *Francis Hutcheson, His Life, Teaching, and Position in the History of Philosophy* (Cambridge: Cambridge University Press, 1900), 234–235; Sophia Rosenfeld, *Common Sense: A Political History* (Cambridge, MA: Harvard University Press, 2011), 71–72.

15. Reid to Andrew Skene, November 14, 1764, in *Correspondence of Thomas Reid*, ed. Paul Wood (Edinburgh: University of Edinburgh Press, 2002), 36.

16. John Millar, *An Historical View of the English Government: From the Settlement of the Saxons in Britain to the Revolution of 1688*, ed. Mark Salber Phillips and Dale R. Smith (Indianapolis: Liberty Fund, 2006), 481.

17. Alexander Peters to James Beattie, December 8, 1778, MS 30/2/322, National Library of Scotland, in Kathleen Holcomb, "Thomas Reid in the Glasgow Literary Society," in *The Glasgow Enlightenment*, ed. Andrew Hook and Richard Sher (East Linton, Scotland: Tuckwell Press, 1995), 95, 99; Robbins, *Commonwealthman*, 219; Reid, *Correspondence*, 46.

18. *Student Receipt Books 1758–1763* [mislabeled; they extend to 1765], Glasgow University Library, cited in Clagett, "Scottish Background," 167; Sarah Hepworth, librarian, University of Glasgow Library, private communication, September 27, 2016. See Andrew Browning, "Richard Dobbs Spaight in Ireland and Scotland: The Education of a North Carolina Founding Father," *North Carolina Historical Review* 94 (2017): 144, 147–149.

19. Clagett, "Scottish Background," 171. See William Ewald, "James Wilson and the Scottish Enlightenment," *University of Pennsylvania Journal of Constitutional Law* 12 (2010): 1053–1114; Ewald, "James Wilson and the Drafting of the Constitution," *University of Pennsylvania Journal of Constitutional Law* 10 (2008): 901–1004; and Iain McLean, "Adam Smith, James Wilson, and the U.S. Constitution," *Adam Smith Review* 8 (2015): 141–160.

20. JAMES WILSON, *The Works of James Wilson*, ed. Robert McCloskey et al. (Cambridge, MA: Harvard University Press, 1967), 1:60–79; McLean, "Adam Smith, James Wilson, and the U.S. Constitution," 151n13, 157,158.

21. WILSON, *Works*, 1:513; Thomas Reid, *Essays on the Intellectual Powers of Man, a Critical Edition*, ed. Derek R. Brookes (Edinburgh: University of Edinburgh Press, 2000), 551.

22. James Pfander and Daniel Birk, "Article III and the Scottish Judiciary," *Harvard Law Review* 124 (2011): 1624, 1677; Leonard Ratner, "Congressional Power over the Appellate Jurisdiction . . ." *University of Pennsylvania Law Review* 109 (1960): 172; Alex Glashauser, "A Return to Form for the Exceptions Clause," *Boston College Law Review* 51 (2010): 1383, 1409.

23. Pfander and Birk, "Article III and the Scottish Judiciary," 1617, 1618.

24. WILSON, *Works*, 1:149, 1:719; Reid, *Intellectual Powers*, 461.

25. WILSON, *Works*, 1:213; Rosenfeld, *Common Sense* (quoting Reid), 80; Max Farrand, ed., *Records of the Federal Convention of 1787* (New Haven, CT: Yale University Press, 1937), 2:56–57. On the evolution from parliamentary sovereignty to sovereignty of the people, see Gordon Wood, *Creation of the American Republic* (Chapel Hill: University of North Carolina Press, 1969), 372–389.

26. Sloan, *Scottish Enlightenment*, 186. See Gillian Hull, "William Small 1734–1775: No Publications, Much Influence," *Journal of the Royal Society of Medicine* 90 (1997): 102–105.

27. Rush, *Autobiography*,19–20; Bernard Steiner, *The Life and Correspondence of*

James McHenry, Secretary of War under Washington and Adams (Cleveland: Burrows Brothers, 1907) 5.

28. Rush, *Autobiography*, 80–84.

29. Rush, 80–84, 89–90.

30. Samuel Lewis, "List of the American Graduates in Medicine of the University of Edinburgh, from 1705 to 1866, With the Titles of their Theses," *New England Historical and Genealogical Register* 42 (1888): 159–160; Marynita Anderson Nolosco, *Physician Heal Thyself: Medical Practitioners of Eighteenth-Century* (New York: Peter Long, 2004), 213n30.

31. Julie Flavell, "'School of Modesty and Humility': Colonial American Youth in London and Their Parents, 1755–1775," *The Historical Journal* 42, no. 2 (1999): 379.

32. David Hosack, *Biographical Memoir of Hugh Williamson, M.D., LL.D.* (New York: C. S. Van Winkle, 1820), 16–17; James Buchan, *Capital of the Mind: How Edinburgh Changed the World* (London: John Murray, 2003), 273; Nolosco, *Physician Heal Thyself*, 58; Lisa Rosner, *Medical Education in the Age of Improvement: Edinburgh Students and Apprentices, 1760–1824* (Edinburgh: Edinburgh University Press, 1991), 58.

33. *Album Promotorum . . . Rheno-Trajectina* (Utrecht: Broekhoff, 1936), 176; Hosack, *Biographical Memoir*, 23–24.

34. Voltaire, in *Gazette littéraire de l'Europe*, quoted in Buchan, *Capital of the Mind*, 2; J. W. Archenholz, *England und Italien* (1787; repr., Heidelberg: C. Winter, 1993), 3:224.

35. Public Record Office (UK) London, ADM 97/85 (pages unnumbered), quoted in James D. Alsop, "Royal Naval Morbidity in Early Eighteenth Century Virginia," in *Colonial Chesapeake: New Perspectives*, ed. Debra Meyers and Melanie Perrault (Lanham, MD: Lexington Books, 2006), 141–142; MADISON to Samuel Miller (n.d.), quoted in Samuel Miller, *Brief Retrospect of the Eighteenth Century* (New York: T. and J. Swords, 1803), 1:491. See Bernice Hamilton, "Medical Professions in the Eighteenth Century," *Economic History Review*, 2nd ser., 4 (1951): 141–169.

36. Rush, *Autobiography*, 25.

37. Thomas Tucker to St. George Tucker, January 10, 1768, in Tucker MSS, Tucker-Coleman Collection, College of William and Mary Swem Library; Rosner, *Medical Education*, 58, 115.

38. Whitfield Bell, "Thomas Parke's Student Life in England and Scotland," *Pennsylvania Magazine of History and Biography* 75 (1951): 250; Elizabeth Singh, Permanent Secretary, Royal Medical Society, personal communication, December 11, 2014.

39. Alexander Monro, preface to *Essays and Observations*, Vol. 5 (1742), reprinted in *The Scots Magazine*, April 1754, 184–185; Davis D. McElroy, "The Literary Clubs and Societies of Eighteenth-Century Scotland" (PhD diss., Edinburgh University, 1952), 83–84, 98–102.

40. McElroy, "Literary Clubs," 138–144; Buchan, *Capital of the Mind*, 121–122.

41. Lord MacKenzie-Stuart, "Ben Franklin in Scotland," *Denning Law Journal* 6 (1991): 123.

42. Bell, "Thomas Parke's Student Life," 128, 251.

43. Rush, *Autobiography*, 25.

Chapter 10. Presbyterian Schools and Scottish Schoolmasters

1. Bernard Steiner, *Life and Correspondence of James McHenry* (Cleveland: Burrows Brothers, 1907), 1–2.

2. *Pennsylvania Packet*, October 12, 1772.

3. Patrick Griffin, *The People with No Name* (Princeton, NJ: Princeton University Press, 2001), 1; Richard Webster, *History of the Presbyterian Church in America* (Philadelphia: Joseph Wilson, 1857), 679, cited in Douglas Sloan, *The Scottish Enlightenment and the American College Ideal* (New York: Teachers College Press, 1971), 37. See Aaron Fogleman, "Migrations to the Thirteen British North American Colonies, 1700–1775: New Estimates," *Journal of Interdisciplinary History* 22 (1992): 691–709; twenty-eight years later, Fogleman sees no reason to revise those numbers (personal communication, February 19, 2020).

4. Garry Wills, *Inventing America: Jefferson's Declaration of Independence* (Garden City, NY: Doubleday, 1978), 177.

5. Sloan, *Scottish Enlightenment*, 42–44.

6. Sloan, 47. See Richard Warch, "The Shepherd's Tent: Education and Enthusiasm in the Great Awakening," *American Quarterly* 30 (1978): 177–198.

7. Sloan, *Scottish Enlightenment*, 44–45.

8. "Francis Alison," University Archives and Records Center, University of Pennsylvania http://www.archives.upenn.edu/exhibits/penn-people/biography/francis-alison.

9. *Pennsylvania Gazette*, November 24, 1743.

10. Matthew Wilson, "The Character of the Rev. Francis Alison, D.D., Vice-Provost of the College of Philadelphia," *Pennsylvania Journal*, April 19, 1780; McKean quoted in Thomas C. Pears, "Francis Alison," *Journal of the Presbyterian Historical Society* 29 (1951): 220–221.

11. Ezra Stiles, *Literary Diary of Ezra Stiles*, ed. Franklin Bowditch Dexter (New York: Scribner's, 1901), 2:338; *Records of the Presbyterian Church in the United States, Embracing the Minutes of the General Presbytery and General Synod, 1786–1788* (Philadelphia: Presbyterian Board of Publications, 1904), 213; George H. Ryden, "The Newark Academy in Colonial Days," *Pennsylvania History* 2 (1935): 208.

12. Ryden, "Newark Academy in Colonial Days," 208; W. R. Scott, *Francis Hutcheson, His Life, Teaching, and Position in the History of Philosophy* (Cambridge: Cambridge University Press, 1900), 136–137; Ezra Stiles, *Extracts from the Itineraries and Other Miscellanies of Ezra Stiles, D.D., LL.D. 1755–1794*, ed. Franklin Bowditch Dexter (New Haven, CT: Yale University Press, 1916), 433.

13. *Pennsylvania Journal*, July 7, 1768; James J. Kirschke, *Gouverneur Morris: Author, Statesman, Man of the World* (New York: Macmillan, 2005), 6.

14. Alison quoted in Thomas Pears, "Presbyterians and American Freedom," *Journal of the Presbyterian Historical Society* 29 (1951): 87; David Hume, *History of England* (London: A. Miller, 1757), 6:165; John Witherspoon, *An Annotated Edition of Lectures on Moral Philosophy*, ed. Jack Scott (Newark: University of Delaware Press, 1982), 144. See Elizabeth I. Nybakken, ed., *The "Centinel": Warnings of a Revolution* (Newark: University of Delaware Press, 1980), and Richard H. Dees, "The Paradox-

ical Principle and Salutary Practice: Hume on Toleration," *Hume Studies* 31 (2005): 145–164.

15. Charles Rodenbough, *Governor Alexander Martin: Biography of a Revolutionary War Statesman* (Jefferson, NC: McFarland, 2004), 14–15, 19–23; WILLIAMSON to Iredell, July 8,1787, in *Records of the Federal Convention of 1787*, ed. Max Farrand (New Haven, CT: Yale University Press, 1937), 3:55.

16. Farrand, ed., *Records*, 1:37, 3:574–576.

17. David Hosack, *Biographical Memoir of Hugh Williamson, M.D., LL.D.* (New York: C. S. Van Winkle, 1820), 14–17.

18. Hosack, *Biographical Memoir of Hugh Williamson*, 21.

19. Hosack, 32–36; Beverly McAnear, "Raising of Funds by the Colonial Colleges," *Mississippi Valley Historical Review* 38 (1952): 602–604; Sloan, *Scottish Enlightenment*, 81.

20. Stiles, *Itineraries*, 422–423; Alison to Stiles, March 24, 1762, Stiles MSS in Yale University Library, quoted in *Annals of the American Pulpit*, ed. William Buell Sprague (New York: Robert Carter, 1858), 3:78; Whitfield Bell, *Patriot Improvers,1743–1768: Biographical Sketches of Members of the American Philosophical Society* (Philadelphia: American Philosophical Society, 1997), 153.

21. Sloan, *Scottish Enlightenment*, 61, 181; Rodenbough, *Governor Martin*, 15; Guy Klett, *Presbyterians in Colonial Pennsylvania* (Philadelphia: University of Pennsylvania Press, 1937), 207; Benjamin Rush, *Autobiography of Benjamin Rush: His "Travels Through Life" Together with His Commonplace Book for 1789–1813*, ed. George W. Corner (Princeton, NJ: Princeton University Press, 1948), 32–37.

22. James McLachlan, *Princetonians, 1748–1768: A Biographical Dictionary* (Princeton, NJ: Princeton University Press, 2015), 156; Varnum Lansing Collins, *Princeton* (Oxford: Oxford University Press, 1914), 61n1.

23. Sloan, *Scottish Enlightenment*, 281.

24. John C. Hamilton, *Life of Alexander Hamilton* (New York: Appleton, 1840), 1:6, 42.

25. ALEXANDER HAMILTON, *Papers*, ed. David Syrett (New York: Columbia University Press, 1962), 1:41–42; New-York *Gazette and Weekly Mercury*, January 6, 1772, in *Extracts from American Newspapers Relating to New Jersey*, ed. William Nelson (Trenton: New Jersey Historical Commission, 1914), 28:7. See Broadus Mitchell, "The Man Who Discovered Alexander Hamilton (Hugh Knox)," *Proceedings of the New Jersey Historical Society* 69 (1951): 88–114.

26. Dumas Malone, *Jefferson and His Time* (Boston: Little, Brown, 1948), 1:42; Willard Randall, *Thomas Jefferson: A Life* (New York: Henry Holt, 1993), 1:17–18. See Donald Come, "Influence of Princeton on Higher Education in the South Before 1825," *William and Mary Quarterly*, 3rd ser., 3 (1945): 35–96; the Framers were LUTHER MARTIN, WILLIAM C. HOUSTON, WILLIAM RICHARDSON DAVIE, and JAMES MADISON.

27. Jefferson, *Autobiography*, January 6, 1821, National Archives, Founders Online, https://founders.archives.gov/documents/Jefferson/98-01-02-1756; MADISON quoted by John C. Payne to John Quincy Adams, August 1836, Adams MSS, Massachusetts Historical Society, in Ralph Ketcham, *James Madison: A Life* (Charlottesville: University of Virginia Press, 1990 [1971]), 21; Irving Brant, *James Madison*

(Indianapolis: Bobbs-Merrill, 1941), 1:60; Douglass Adair, ed., "James Madison's Autobiography," *William and Mary Quarterly*, 3rd ser., 11 (1945): 197. See *Bulletin of the King and Queen County Historical Society of Virginia* 14 (1963): 1–12, and 44 (1993): 1–10. DANIEL OF ST. THOMAS JENIFER evidently read French also; he bequeathed all of his books in French to MADISON (Archives of Maryland, MSA SC 3520-728).

28. "Donald Robertson's . . . Account Book," *Virginia Magazine of History and Biography* 33 (1925): 288–292; "Donald Robertson's School," King and Queen Courthouse Tavern Museum, http://www.kingandqueenmuseum.org/donald-robert sons-school/; Adair, ed., "James Madison's Autobiography," 197.

29. Alexander Leitch, *A Princeton Companion* (Princeton, NJ: Princeton University Press, 1978), 524.

30. Henry White, *Southern Presbyterian Leaders* (New York: Neale, 1911), 104; Come, "Influence of Princeton," 366–368; W. Gordon McCabe, *Virginia's Schools before and after the Revolution* (Charlottesville: Society of the Alumni of the University of Virginia, 1890), 20.

31. Neill R. McGeachy, *History of the Sugaw Creek Presbyterian Church* (Rock Hill, SC: Record Print Co., 1954), 36–37; C. G. Davidson, *Piedmont Partisan: The Life and Times of Brigadier-General William Lee Davidson* (Davidson, NC: Davidson College, 1951), 17; W. H. Foote, *Sketches of North Carolina* (New York: R. Carter, 1846), 513; White, *Southern Presbyterian Leaders*, 78; William S. Harris, *Historical Sketch of Poplar Tent Church* (Concord, NC: Times Press, 1924), 24; Thomas Allen Glenn, *William Churchill Houston, 1746–1788* (Norristown, PA: privately printed, 1903), 5–8.

32. Marshall D. Haywood, "The Story of Queen's College or Liberty Hall in the province of North Carolina," *North Carolina Booklet* 11 (1911), 169–170; Francis Lister Hawks Papers, "Collection 1726–1854," 147 (microfilm image 125), New-York Historical Society; James H. Williams, personal communication, June 3, 2019. See Elizabeth Leland, "Princeton of the South," *Our State* (July 1, 2010); James H. Williams, "Queen's College," *Olde Mecklenburg Genealogical Society Quarterly* 34 (2016): 3–8, and Andrew Browning, "The Princeton Connections of William Richardson Davie: The Education of a North Carolina Founding Father," *North Carolina Historical Review* 95 (2018): 284–318.

33. Quoted in Haywood, "Story of Queen's College," 170.

34. Francis Lister Hawks Papers, "Collection 1726–1854," 379 (microfilm frames 310–11) New-York Historical Society; Stewart Lillard, "Queen's College," *Encyclopedia of North Carolina* (Chapel Hill: University of North Carolina Press, 2006), https://www.ncpedia.org/queens-college.

35. Haywood, "Story of Queen's College," 174; *Luigi Castiglioni's Viaggio, Travels in the United States of North America 1785–87*, trans. and ed. Antonia Pace (Syracuse, NY: Syracuse University Press, 1983), 173; *The Diaries of George Washington, Vol. 6, 1 January 1790–13 December 1799*, ed. Donald Jackson and Dorothy Twohig (Charlottesville: University Press of Virginia 1979), 150–151, Founders Online, https://founders.archives.gov/documents/Washington/01-06-02-0002-0004-0028. It is puzzling that Harry Watson considers DAVIE's matriculation at Princeton "highly unusual for that place and time," given the number of influential alumni who surrounded him in Mecklenburg County's Presbyterian community and the several neighbors

who had recently preceded him; see Watson, "William Richardson Davie and the University of the People," Gladys Hall Coates University History Lecture, UNC University Libraries, University of North Carolina at Chapel Hill, 2006), 3, https://dcr.lib.unc.edu/indexablecontent/uuid:23e4c064-d0e6-4347-a004-53700af7a3cc.

36. Lawrence Cremin, *American Education: The Colonial Experience, 1607–1783* (New York: Harper and Row, 1970), 327.

Chapter 11. Mirania in America

1. BENJAMIN FRANKLIN, *Autobiography, Poor Richard, and Later Writings*, ed. J. A. Leo Lemay (New York: Library of America, 1987), 1410–1411.

2. J. A. Leo Lemay, *Life of Benjamin Franklin* (Philadelphia: University of Pennsylvania Press, 2006), 3:178.

3. BENJAMIN FRANKLIN, *Proposals Relating to the Education of Youth in Pennsylvania*, in *The Papers of Benjamin Franklin*, ed. Leonard Labaree et al. (New Haven, CT: Yale University Press, 1959-2018), 3:404–419; FRANKLIN, *Idea of the English School*, in FRANKLIN, *Papers*, 4:101–104; FRANKLIN, *Autobiography*, 1319.

4. FRANKLIN to Johnson, July 2, 1752, quoted in Thomas Montgomery, *History of the University of Pennsylvania* (Philadelphia: Jacobs, 1900), 163; Joseph Ellis, *The New England Mind in Transition: Samuel Johnson of Connecticut* (New Haven, CT: Yale University Press, 1973), 180; Lemay, *Life of Benjamin Franklin*, 3:178.

5. Francis Jennings, *Benjamin Franklin, Politician* (New York: Norton: 1996), 69.

6. Jennings, *Benjamin Franklin, Politician*, 68.

7. Lemay, *Life of Benjamin Franklin*, 3:202, 212; Collinson to FRANKLIN, August 12, 1753, in FRANKLIN, *Papers*, 5:68–79, National Archives, Founders Online, https://founders.archives.gov/documents/Franklin/01-05-02-0009; FRANKLIN to Collinson, May 28, 1754, in FRANKLIN *Papers*, 5:331, Founders Online, https://founders.archives.gov/documents/Franklin/01-05-02-0090.

8. Jennings, *Benjamin Franklin*, 70, 98; Lemay, *Life of Benjamin Franklin*, 3:200–203; Collinson to FRANKLIN, January 26, 1754, in FRANKLIN, *Papers*, 5:190–193, Founders Online, https://founders.archives.gov/documents/Franklin/01-05-02-0056.

9. Jennings, *Benjamin Franklin*, 70–71.

10. Lemay, *Life of Benjamin Franklin*, 3:208–209; Horace Wemyss Smith, *Life and Correspondence of the Rev. William Smith* (Philadelphia: S. A. George,1879), 1:143.

11. Douglas Sloan, *The Scottish Enlightenment and the American College Ideal* (New York: Teachers College Press, 1971), 83–84; Lawrence Cremin, *American Education: The Colonial Experience, 1607–1783* (New York: Harper and Row, 1970), 381.

12. David Norton, "Francis Hutcheson in America," *Studies on Voltaire and the Eighteenth Century* 154 (1976): 1554; Anna Haddow, *Political Science in American Colleges and Universities* (New York: Appleton-Century, 1939), 14, 24; Cremin, *American Education*, 463–464.

13. Charlotte Fletcher, *Cato's Mirania: A Life of Provost Smith* (Lanham, MD: University Press of America, 2002), 29; Charles Stillé, *Memoir of the Rev. William Smith, D.D.* (Philadelphia: Moore and Sons,1869), 12–13.

14. Smith, *Life and Correspondence*, 1:49; Montgomery, *History of the University of Pennsylvania*, 204–206.

15. Stillé, *Memoir of William Smith*, 11; Henry May, *Enlightenment in America* (New York: Oxford University Press, 1976), 83; William Smith, "Account of the College and Academy," *Discourses on Several Public Occasions*, 2nd ed. (London: Millar, 1762), appendix, 2:116–117.

16. Smith, "Account of the College and Academy," 2:116–117.

17. FRANKLIN to Peters, July 1754, in Smith, *Life and Correspondence*, 1:49.

18. Sloan, *Scottish Enlightenment*, 89; THOMAS MIFFLIN, *Notes on Metaphysics and the Laws of Nations*, Library of Congress Manuscript Collection MMC-1030 MS 32854; Hutcheson, *Short Introduction to Moral Philosophy in Three Books* (Glasgow: Foulis, 1753), 1:v.

19. MIFFLIN, *Notes*.

20. July 2, 1787, MADISON notes, in *Records of the Federal Convention of 1787*, ed. Max Farrand (New Haven, CT: Yale University Press, 1937), 1:512; Yates notes, in Farrand, ed., *Records*, 1:517; July 5, 1787, MADISON notes, in Farrand, ed., 1:533.

21. Kenneth R. Rossman, *Thomas Mifflin and the Politics of the American Revolution* (Chapel Hill: University of North Carolina Press, 1952), 6; Cremin, *American Education*, 465; John Adams to Abigail Adams, May 24, 1775, in *The Adams Papers: Adams Family Correspondence*, Vol. 1, *December 1761–May 1776*, ed. Lyman H. Butterfield (Cambridge, MA: Harvard University Press, 1963), 204–206, Founders Online, https://founders.archives.gov/documents/Adams/04-01-02-0136.

22. W. H. Adams, *Gouverneur Morris: An Independent Life* (New Haven, CT: Yale University Press, 2003), 14.

23. Smith, *Life and Correspondence*, 1:49; Beverly McAnear, "The Selection of an Alma Mater by Pre-Revolutionary Students," *Pennsylvania Magazine of History and Biography* 73 (1949): 436; Richard Peters to Smith, May 25, 1763, and Smith to Peters, February 25, 1764, Smith Papers, Jasper Yeates Brinton Collection 1619, Series 2, 2:130–132, 162, Historical Society of Pennsylvania; Minutes of the Trustees, January 13, 1761 and January 19, 1768, University of Pennsylvania Archives, https://archives.upenn.edu/digitized-resources/docs-pubs/trustees-minutes; George Pilcher, *The Reverend Samuel Davies Abroad: A Diary of a Journey to England and Scotland* (Champaign: University of Illinois Press, 1967), 19–20; MacPherson to PATERSON, November 17, 1767, in William MacPherson Horner, "Extracts from Letters of John MacPherson, Jr., to WILLIAM PATERSON, 1765–1773," *Pennsylvania Magazine of History and Biography* 23 (1899): 53.

24. Josiah Quincy, *History of Harvard University* (Cambridge MA: John Owen, 1840), 2:180; *Pennsylvania Gazette*, February 6, 1757, quoted in David Barone, "Before the Revolution: Formal Rhetoric in Philadelphia During the Federal Era," *Pennsylvania History* 54, no. 4 (1987): 253; William Smith, *Discourses*, 216.

25. William Hedges, "The Old World Yet: Writers and Writing in Post-Revolutionary America," *Early American Literature* 16 (1981): 7; Farrand, ed., *Records*, 1:531; M. E. Bradford, *A Worthy Company: Brief Lives of the Framers of the U.S. Constitution* (Marlborough, NH: Plymouth Rock Foundation, 1982), 185; MADISON to Jared Sparks, April 8, 1831, in Farrand, ed., *Records*, 3:449.

26. FRANKLIN to Collinson, November 5, 1756, in *Papers*, 7:9–15, Founders Online, https://founders.archives.gov/documents/Franklin/01-07-02-0004; May 24, 1779,

in *Literary Diary of Ezra Stiles*, ed. Franklin Bowditch Dexter (New York: Scribner's, 1901), 338; Smith to Peters, July 18, 1754, in Smith, *Life and Correspondence*, 1:49; Carl Bridenbaugh and Jessica Bridenbaugh, *Rebels and Gentlemen: Philadelphia in the Age of Benjamin Franklin* (New York: Reynal and Hitchcock, 1942), 62.

27. Lewis Morris to John Chamberlyn, June 1704, SPG Archives, 1:171, College Papers 1, Columbia University Library; Ellis, *New England Mind in Transition*, 175. See Robert McCaughey, *Stand, Columbia: A History of Columbia University in the City of New York* (New York: Columbia University Press, 2003), 1–4.

28. Milton Klein, introduction to *The Independent Reflector or, Weekly Essays on Sundry Important Subjects More Particularly Adapted to the Province of New York*, ed. Milton M. Klein (Cambridge, MA: Harvard University Press, 1963), 10, 35; Cremin, *American Education*, 429.

29. Edwin Gaustad, *Historical Atlas of Religion in America*, rev. ed. (New York: Harper and Row, 1976), 167; David Humphrey, *From King's College to Columbia, 1746–1800* (New York: Columbia University Press, 1976), 37, 28; Samuel Johnson to WILLIAM SAMUEL JOHNSON, January 20, 1755, in *Samuel Johnson, President of King's College: His Career and Writings*, ed. Herbert Schneider and Carol Schneider (New York: Columbia University Press, 1929), 1:209; Samuel Johnson to Cadwallader Colden, April 15, 1747, in *Collections of the New-York Historical Society* (New York: New-York Historical Society, 1871), 52:375.

30. Ellis, *New England Mind*, 161.

31. Fletcher, *Cato's Mirania*, 9, 11.

32. LIVINGSTON, *Independent Reflector*, 174.

33. LIVINGSTON, 172.

34. LIVINGSTON, 232.

35. New York *Mercury*, October 22, 1753, 8, 15; see Ellis, *New England Mind*, 184–187.

36. Humphrey, *From King's College to Columbia*, 75.

37. Minutes of the Vestry of Trinity Church, New York, December 20, 1753, in Ellis, *New England Mind*, 181; Humphrey, *From King's College to Columbia*, 31; "Extract from the Journal of the General Assembly of New York, 16 May 1754," in H. Schneider and C. Schneider, eds., *Samuel Johnson*, 4:177–190.

38. Humphrey, *From King's College to Columbia*, 167.

39. Humphrey, 95–97, 115, 196; Nathan Schachner, "Alexander Hamilton Viewed by His Friends: The Narratives of Robert Troup and Hercules Mulligan," *William and Mary Quarterly* 4, no. 2 (1947): 204; Robert McCaughey, *Stand, Columbia*, 35; Vardill, *Candid Remarks on Dr. Witherspoon's Address to the Inhabitants of Jamaica*, 41–42, quoted in Humphrey, *From King's College to Columbia*, 209.

40. Schneider and Schneider, eds., *Samuel Johnson*, 1:37–40, 4:98; Johnson, "Autobiography," in Schneider and Schneider, eds., 1:40–42; George H. Moore, *Collegium Regale Novi Eboraci: The Origin and Early History of Columbia College* (New York: privately printed, 1890), 23–25; Jones, "How President Myles Cooper Ran Away," in Thomas Jones, *History of New York During the Revolutionary War*, ed. Edward De Lancey (New York: New York Historical Society, 1879), 1:61.

41. Brander Matthews, *A History of Columbia University, 1754–1904* (New York:

Columbia University Press, 1904), 450–451; Louis Snow, *The College Curriculum in the United States* (New York: Teachers College Press, 1907), 58–59; Humphrey, *From King's College to Columbia*, 134–135.

42. Cooper to Boucher, March 22, 1773, in *The Papers of George Washington*, Colonial Series, Vol. 9, *8 January 1772–18 March 1774*, ed. W. W. Abbot and Dorothy Twohig (Charlottesville: University Press of Virginia, 1994), 9:215n2, Founders Online, https://founders.archives.gov/documents/Washington/02-09-02-0159; J. Yolton, "Schoolmen, Logic, and Philosophy," in *History of the University of Oxford*, Vol. 5, *The Eighteenth Century*, ed. Lucy S. Sutherland and Leslie G. Mitchell (New York: Oxford University Press, 1986), 581–582.

43. Humphrey, *From King's College to Columbia*, 131–132.

44. Jared Sparks, *The Life of Gouverneur Morris* (Boston: Gray and Bowen, 1832), 5; William Adams, *Gouverneur Morris: An Independent Life* (New Haven, CT: Yale University Press, 2003), 14.

45. Humphrey, *From King's College to Columbia*, 202; Thomas Mittelsey, "The Black Book of King's College," *Columbia University Quarterly* 23 (1931): 7; *Minutes of the Governors of the College in the Province of New York . . . and of the Corporation of King's College in the City of New York* (New York: Columbia University, 1932), May 13, 1766, February 6, 1767 (n.p.).

46. MORRIS, "On Wit and Beauty," Gouverneur Morris Papers, MS Coll Morris, Box 1, Rare Book and Manuscript Library, Columbia University; Max Mintz, *Gouverneur Morris and the American Revolution* (Norman: University of Oklahoma Press, 1970), 31.

47. Broadus Mitchell, *Alexander Hamilton: Youth to Maturity* (New York: Macmillan, 1957), 54–55; Willard Randall, *Alexander Hamilton: A Life* (New York: HarperCollins, 2003),

52; Robert McCaughey, "The Education of Alexander Hamilton," *New-York Journal of American History* (Fall 2004), 28; Troup to John Mason, March 22, 1810, in Schachner, "Alexander Hamilton Viewed by his Friends," 212; Ron Chernow, *Alexander Hamilton* (New York: Penguin, 2004), 56; Cooper to Boucher, March 22, 1773, in WASHINGTON, *Papers*, 9:215n2.

48. Chernow, *Alexander Hamilton*, 27–30; Schachner, "Alexander Hamilton Viewed by His Friends," 209, 212–213; Farrand, ed., *Records*, 1:282–293.

49. November 24, 1772, in *Documents Relating to the Colonial History of New Jersey*, ed. William Nelson (Paterson, NJ: Call Printing and Publishing, 1916), 28:353; Cooper, "Draft Address of the Governors of the College," October 12, 1771, quoted in Humphrey, *From King's College to Columbia*, 141.

50. McCaughey, *Stand Columbia*, 29, 45; Humphrey, *From King's College to Columbia*, 228; *Minutes of the Governors of the College . . . in New York*, September 2, 1773 (n.p.); Cooper, *A Friendly Address*, in Matthews, *History of Columbia*, 46.

51. Humphrey, *From King's College to Columbia*, 153.

52. Humphrey, 153–154.

53. Cooper, Oxford sermon (1776), published in 1777 as *National Humiliation and Repentance Recommended* (Oxford: Clarendon, 1777), 22–23; Chernow, *Alexander Hamilton*, 71–72, 52; HAMILTON TO WASHINGTON, September 15, 1790, in HAMILTON, *Pa-*

pers, 7:40, Founders Online, https://founders.archives.gov/documents/Washington/05-06-02-0212-0002.

54. Douglass Adair, *Intellectual Origins of Jeffersonian Democracy: Republicanism, Class Struggle, and the Virtuous Farmer*, ed. Mark E. Yellin (Lanham, MD: Lexington Books, 2000 [1944]), 70, 112; Adair, "Disputed Federalist Papers," in Douglass Adair, *Fame and the Founding Fathers*, ed. Trevor Colbourn (New York: W. W. Norton, 1974), 87n91.

55. Chernow, *Alexander Hamilton*, 52; Mark E. Yellin, introduction to Adair, *Intellectual Origins*, xvii; MORRIS to Robert Walsh, February 15, 1811, in Sparks, *Life of Morris*, 2:260–261.

56. Humphrey, *From King's College to Columbia*, 223; Gordon Wood, *Creation of the American Republic* (Chapel Hill: University of North Carolina Press, 1998), 479.

57. Wood, *Creation of the American Republic*, 16; Vardill to Peter Van Schaack, September 15, 1774, Peter Van Schaack Papers, Columbia University, quoted in Humphrey, *From King's College to Columbia*, 220.

58. KING to MORRIS, March 21, 1810, in Charles King, *Life and Correspondence of Rufus King* (New York: Putnam, 1894), 215–216.

Chapter 12. Princeton in the Nation's Service

1. Jeffry Morrison, *John Witherspoon and the Founding of the American Republic* (South Bend, IN: University of Notre Dame Press, 2005), 4; Ezra Stiles, *Literary Diary of Ezra Stiles*, ed. Franklin Bowditch Dexter (New York: Scribner's, 1901), 72; Varnum Lansing Collins, *President Witherspoon* (Princeton, NJ: Princeton University Press, 1925), 1:138. See *Journals of the Continental Congress*, ed. Steven D. Tilley et al. (Washington, DC: US Government Printing Office, 1904–1937), 19:110.

2. MADISON to James Monroe, August 11, 1786, in *The Papers of James Madison*, Vol. 9, *9 April 1786–24 May 1787 and supplement 1781–1784*, ed. Robert A. Rutland and William M. E. Rachal (Chicago: University of Chicago Press, 1975), 90, Founders Online, https://founders.archives.gov/documents/Madison/01-09-02-0024; WASHINGTON to Witherspoon, March 10, 1784, in *The Papers of George Washington*, Confederation Series, Vol. 1, *1 January 1784–17 July 1784*, ed. W. W. Abbot (Charlottesville: University Press of Virginia, 1992), 197–201, Founders Online, https://founders.archives.gov/documents/Washington/04-01-02-0149-0001; Fred J. Hood, *Reformed America: The Middle and Southern States 1783–1837* (Tuscaloosa: University of Alabama Press, 1980), 10, 17; Witherspoon to HAMILTON, October 20, 1789, *The Papers of Alexander Hamilton*, ed. Harold C. Syrett. (New York: Columbia University Press, 1961–1987), 5:464–465, Founders Online, https://founders.archives.gov/documents/Hamilton/01-05-02-0258; *Papers of Alexander Hamilton*, 6:56. MADISON had submitted a draft address at WASHINGTON's request when the president considered retiring at the end of his first term; in a letter to Jefferson in 1823, MADISON assumed that WASHINGTON had given HAMILTON that earlier draft to work from; see *Papers of Alexander Hamilton*, 20:169–173, and MADISON to Jefferson, March 27, 1823, Founders Online, https://founders.archives.gov/documents/Jefferson/98-01-02-3597.

3. Woodrow Wilson, *Papers of Woodrow Wilson*, Vol. 10, *1896–1898*, ed. Arthur S. Link (Princeton, NJ: Princeton University Press, 1971), 29–30.

4. Donald Scarinci, *David Brearley and the Making of the United States Constitution* ('Trenton: New Jersey Heritage Press, 2005), 44–45; James McLachlan, *Princetonians, 1748–1768: A Biographical Dictionary* (Princeton, NJ: Princeton University Press, 1976), xi, xx; Richard A. Harrison, *Princetonians, 1769–1795: A Biographical Dictionary* (Princeton, NJ: Princeton University Press, 1980), xxii–xxv; John M. Murrin, preface to Thomas Jefferson Wertenbaker, *Princeton 1746–1896*, rev. ed. (Princeton, NJ: Princeton University Press, 1996 [1946]), xxiv.

5. McLachlan, *Princetonians, 1748–1768*, xix; Harrison, *Princetonians, 1769–1795*, xx; Varnum Lansing Collins, ed., *A General Catalogue of Princeton University, 1746–1906* (Princeton, NJ: Princeton University Press, 1908), 89–92, 94–96, 396–404.

6. Guy Howard Miller, *The Revolutionary College: American Presbyterian Higher Education 1707–1837* (New York: New York University Press, 1976), 124; unidentified college trustee, 1748, Princeton University Library MS AM 1424, quoted in Francis L. Broderick, "Pulpit, Physics, and Politics: The Curriculum of the College of New Jersey, 1746–1794," *William and Mary Quarterly*, 3rd ser., 6 (1949): 56–57; John Rodgers to John Witherspoon, December 24, 1766, in Lyman H. Butterfield, *John Witherspoon Comes to America* (Princeton, NJ: Princeton University Press, 1953), 21–22.

7. McLachlan, *Princetonians, 1748–1768*, xxiii; Harrison, *Princetonians, 1769–1796*, xxxi; Varnum Lansing Collins, *President Witherspoon: A Biography* (Princeton, NJ: Princeton University Press, 1925), 2:229; David Robson, *Educating Republicans: The College in the Era of the American Revolution, 1750–1800* (Westport, CT: Greenwood, 1985), 70.

8. Wertenbaker, *Princeton, 1746–1796*, 31–34; Stiles, *Literary Diary*, 337.

9. Stiles, *Literary Diary*, 87; Ralph Ketcham, *James Madison* (Charlottesville: University of Virginia Press, 1990), 29; Tessa Whitehouse, *The Textual Culture of English Protestant Dissent, 1720–1800* (New York: Oxford University Press, 2016), 85–86; Samuel Davies, *A General Account of the Rise and State of the College, Lately Established in the Province of New Jersey, in America*, quoted in Whitehouse, *Textual Culture of English Protestant Dissent*, 6; Broderick, "Pulpit, Physics, and Politics," 49–52.

10. Caroline Winterer, *American Enlightenments* (New Haven, CT: Yale University Press, 2017), 237; Trustee Minutes, 1:44, Seeley G. Mudd Manuscript Library, Princeton University, https://library.princeton.edu/special-collections/databases/trustees-minutes-1746-1894.

11. Trustee Minutes, 1:15; McLachlan, *Princetonians, 1748–1768*, 101–104; Samuel Miller, *Memoirs of the Rev. John Rodgers, D.D.* (New York: Whiting and Whiting, 1813), 97.

12. John E. O'Connor, *William Paterson, Lawyer and Statesman, 1745–1806* (New Brunswick, NJ: Rutgers University Press, 1979), 18; Julie Flavell, *When London Was Capital of America* (New Haven, CT: Yale University Press, 2010), 117, 159–63. Flavell employs the same formula as O'Connor to characterize Sayre's fellow students, but most were, like Sayre and MARTIN, the sons of modest farmers. See John R. Alden, *Stephen Sayre: American Revolutionary Adventurer* (Baton Rouge: Louisiana State University Press, 1983).

13. John Maclean, *History of the College of New Jersey From Its Origins in 1746 to the Commencement of 1854* (Philadelphia: Lippincott, 1877), 219–220; Sanford H. Cobb,

Rise of Religious Liberty in America: A History (New York: Macmillan, 1902), 104n; William Foote, *Sketches of Virginia, Historical and Biographical* (Philadelphia: J. B. Lippincott, 1856), 1:299.

14. Samuel Davies, October 8, 1753, in George W. Pilcher, ed., *The Reverend Samuel Davies Abroad: A Diary of a Journey to England and Scotland* (Champaign: University of Illinois Press, 1967), 19–20; Thomas Miller, *The Formation of College English* (Pittsburgh: University of Pittsburgh Press,1997), 175.

15. Samuel Davies, *Religion and the Public Spirit. A Valedictory Address to the Senior Class, delivered in Nassau-Hall, September 21, 1760* (Portsmouth, NH: Daniel Fowles, 1762), 5–7.

16. Woodrow Wilson, "Commemorative Address Delivered October 21, 1896," in Link, ed. *Papers of Woodrow Wilson*, 10:29–30; Collins, *Princeton*, 64; Maclean, *College of New Jersey*, 1:264; New York *Gazette*, October 2, 1766, in New Jersey Archives, 1st ser., 25:219.

17. Max Farrand, ed., *Records of the Federal Convention of 1787* (New Haven, CT: Yale University Press, 1937), 3:90.

18. Box one, Paterson Family Papers, Seeley G. Mudd Manuscript Library, Princeton University.

19. McLachlan, *Princetonians, 1748–1768*, 578–579.

20. LUTHER MARTIN, *Modern Gratitude in Five Numbers* (Whitefish, MT: Kessinger, 2010 [1801]), 134.

21. Samuel Davies, "A General Account of the Rise and State of the College in the Province of New Jersey, in America," *New American Magazine* 27 (March 1760): 103; Broderick, "Pulpit, Physics, and Politics," 54; Douglas Sloan, *The Scottish Enlightenment and the American College Ideal* (New York: Teachers College Press, 1971), 64; Samuel Blair, *Account of the College of New Jersey* (Woodbridge, NJ: James Parker, 1764), 23–30.

22. Beverly McAnear, "The Selection of an Alma Mater by Pre-Revolutionary Students," *Pennsylvania Magazine of History and Biography* 73 (1949): 431; Blair, *Account of the College of New Jersey*, 25–30.

23. Blair, *Account of the College of New Jersey*, 23–24, 25–30.

24. Blair, 23–30.

25. Collins, *Princeton*, 61; Blair, *Account of the College of New Jersey*, 30. These roles are somewhat similarly assigned at Princeton to this day, but a concession has been made to the reality that Latin is no longer the universal language of scholarship: each graduating senior—but no one else—is provided a copy of the Latin salutation address with parenthetical hints, such as *"hic plaudite"* and *"hic ridete."* See Anthony Grafton, "Veni, Vidi, Vici: How Latin Lives On," *London Review of Books*, October 25, 2001, https://www.theguardian.com/books/2001/oct/25/londonreviewofbooks.

26. McLachlan, *Princetonians, 1748–1768*, 648.

27. Maclean, *History of the College of New Jersey*, 1:314; Ashbel Green, *Discourses Delivered in the College of New Jersey . . . Including A Historical Sketch of the College from its Origin the Accession of President Witherspoon* (Philadelphia: Littel, 1822), 392. For an account of Rush's campaign, see Butterfield, *John Witherspoon Comes to America*.

28. Sloan, *Scottish Enlightenment*, 11, 118; Roy Branson, "James Madison and the Scottish Enlightenment," *Journal of the History of Ideas* 40 (1979): 236; Mark Noll, *Princeton and the Republic, 1768–1822: The Search for a Christian Enlightenment in the Era of Samuel Stanhope Smith* (Princeton, NJ: Princeton University Press, 1989), 36; Collins, *President Witherspoon*, 1:90.

29. John Witherspoon, *Address to the Inhabitants of Jamaica*, in *Selected Writings of John Witherspoon*, ed. Thomas Miller (Carbondale: Southern Illinois University Press, 1990), 109.

30. Roger L. Geiger, *A History of American Higher Education: Learning and Culture from the Founding to World War II* (Princeton, NJ: Princeton University Press, 2014), 74; Morrison, *John Witherspoon*, 4.

31. Trustee Minutes, September 24, 1760, in Broderick, "Pulpit, Physics, and Politics," 53; Trustee Minutes, September 29, 1762, December 9, 1767, in Maclean, *History of the College of New Jersey*, 1:255, 298; Ron Chernow, *Alexander Hamilton* (New York: Penguin, 2004), 47–48.

32. Douglass Adair, ed., "James Madison's Autobiography," *William and Mary Quarterly*, 3rd ser., 11 (1945): 197–198.

33. Farrand, ed., *Records*, 3:94–95; Ames to George Minor, March 29, 1789, in *The Papers of James Madison*, ed. William Hutchinson et al. (Charlottesville: University of Virginia Press, 1979) 12:53; French Archives: Ministère des Affaires Étrangères, Archives États Unis, Correspondence, Supplement, 2e Série, 25:314ff., in Farrand, ed., *Records*, 3:237 (my translation).

34. Douglass Adair, *Fame and the Founding Fathers*, ed. Trevor Colbourn (New York: W. W. Norton, 1974), 176–77, 180.

35. JAMES MADISON to James Madison Sr., July 23, 1770, in Hutchinson et al., eds., *Papers of James Madison*, 1:49–50, Founders Online, https://founders.archives.gov /documents/Madison/01-01-02-0008; Maclean, *History of the College of New Jersey*, 1:298.

36. Philip Vickers Fithian, November 30, 1770, in John R. Williams, ed., *Philip Vickers Fithian, Journal and Letters, 1767–1774* (Princeton, NJ: Princeton University Press, 1900), 7–9.

37. Maclean, *History of the College of New Jersey*, 1:363.

38. Williams, ed., *Fithian*, 256–257.

39. Williams, ed., 256–257.

40. Charles Richard Williams, *The Cliosophic Society, Princeton University* (Princeton, NJ: Princeton University Press, 1916), 3.

41. Williams, *Cliosophic Society*, 6, 29, 41; Henry Clay Cameron, *History of the American Whig Society from 1769 to 1869* (Princeton, NJ: Stelle and Smith, 1871), 6–7. See J. Jefferson Looney, *Nursery of Letters and Republicanism: A Brief History of the American Whig-Cliosophic Society and Its Predecessors, 1765–1941* (Princeton, NJ: American Whig-Cliosophic Society, 1996).

42. Harry Watson, "William Richardson Davie and the University of the People," 3, 2006 Gladys Hall Coates University History Lecture, UNC University Libraries, University of North Carolina at Chapel Hill, https://dcr.lib.unc.edu/in dexablecontent/uuid:23e4c064-d0e6-4347-a004-53700af7a3cc.

43. Williams, ed., *Cliosophic Society*, 12, 15.

44. Ashbel Green, *Life of Ashbel Green* (New York: Robert Carter Brothers, 1849) 141. A sample of MADISON's contributions, predicting the future of Clio leader Moses Allen:

> Great Allen founder of the crew
> If right I guess must keep a stew [i.e., brothel]
> The lecherous rascal there will find
> A place just suited to his mind
> May whore and pimp and drink and swear
> Nor more the garb of Christians wear
> And free Nassau from such a pest
> A dunce a fool an ass at best.
> (Notebook of William Bradford, Princeton University Library,
>   quoted in Ketcham, *James Madison*, 36)

In sad fact, it was the fate of Allen (by then a clergyman and patriot in Savannah, Georgia) to drown in 1779 while trying to escape from a British prison ship during the Revolution.

45. *Pennsylvania Chronicle*, October 15, 1771.

46. Diary entry December 23, 1777, in *Historical Memoirs of William Smith*, ed. William H. W. Sabine (New York: *New York Times*, 1971), 277; Witherspoon, "Address to the Inhabitants of Jamaica," in Witherspoon, *Selected Writings*, 103.

47. Adair, *Fame and the Founding Fathers*, 181; John Witherspoon, *Lectures on Moral Philosophy*, ed. Varnum Lansing Collins (Princeton, NJ: Princeton University Press, 1912), xxii; Broderick, "Pulpit, Physics, and Politics," 59; Ashbel Green, *Life of the Reverend John Witherspoon D.D., LL.D.*, ed. Henry Lyttelton Savage (Princeton, NJ: Princeton University Press, 1973), 126.

48. Ferguson to Alexander Carlyle, quoted in Holly Nelson et al., *Robert Burns and Transatlantic Culture* (Farnham: Ashgate, 2013), 37; Sir Guy Carleton Papers, Colonial Williamsburg, Vol. 83, Paper 9294, quoted in Green, *Life of John Witherspoon*, 2.

49. Henry May, *American Enlightenment* (New York: Oxford University Press, 1976), 63; Ketcham, *James Madison*, 48, 42–43. See Ralph Ketcham, "James Madison at Princeton," *The Princeton University Library Chronicle* 28 (1966): 24–54.

50. Lawrence Cremin, *American Education: The Colonial Experience, 1607–1783* (New York: Harper and Row, 1970), 464–465; Mark Noll, *America's God* (New York: Oxford University Press, 2002), 106.

51. Witherspoon, *Lectures on Moral Philosophy*, ed. Collins, 142–144.

52. Ralph Ketcham, "James Madison and the Nature of Man," *Journal of the History of Ideas* 19 (1958): 72–73; Branson, "James Madison and the Scottish Enlightenment," 248–249. See Morton White, *Philosophy, the "Federalist," and the Constitution* (New York: Oxford, 1989), 92–95, and Lisa Hill, "Ideas of Corruption in the Eighteenth Century: The Competing Conceptions of Adam Ferguson and Adam

Smith," in *Corruption: Expanding the Focus*, ed. Manuhuia Barcham et al. (Canberra: ANU Press, 2012), 97–112.

53. Gideon Mailer, *John Witherspoon's American Revolution* (Chapel Hill: University of North Carolina, 2019), 359.

54. Witherspoon, *Lectures on Morality*, ed. Collins, 94 (emphasis added).

55. Witherspoon, 94.

56. Thomas P. Miller, "Witherspoon, Blair and the Rhetoric of Civic Humanism," in *Scotland and America in the Age of the Enlightenment*, ed. Richard B. Sher and Jeffrey R. Smitten (Princeton, NJ: Princeton University Press, 1990), 101.

57. David C. Hendrickson, *Peace Pact: The Lost World of American Founding* (Lawrence: University Press of Kansas, 2003), 141; Witherspoon, speech in Congress, July 30, 1776, in *Letters of the Delegates to Congress 1774–1789*, ed. Paul H. Smith (Washington, DC: Library of Congress, 1976–2000), 4:587; Wertenbaker, *Princeton University*, 57.

58. *Papers of George Washington: Colonial Series*, ed. W. W. Abbot and Dorothy Twohig (Charlottesville: University Press of Virginia, 1994), 9:227n, 9:161–165.

59. Samuel Stanhope Smith, *Lectures . . . on the Subjects of Moral and Political Philosophy* (New York: Whiting and Watson, 1812), 2:329.

Chapter 13. At the Convention

1. Forrest McDonald, *We the People: The Economic Origins of the Constitution* (Chicago: University of Chicago Press, 1958), 106, 109. Robert McGuire, *To Form a More Perfect Union: A New Economic Interpretation of the Constitution* (New York: Oxford, 2003), demonstrates that at the Convention and in the states' ratification conventions, those involved in commerce were a little more likely to support the Constitution and slaveholders a little less so; he warns that the data "do *not* a support a narrow 'Beardian' view of the Framers'" (211; emphasis original). Jac C. Heckelman and Keith L. Dougherty, "An Economic Interpretation of the Constitutional Convention of 1787 Revisited," *Journal of Economic History* 73 (2007): 829–848, acknowledge that it is unclear whether McGuire's "analysis actually tests for factors that affected voting behavior, strictly speaking" (831). They in turn present an elaborate statistical demonstration of what turns out to be a very general state-by-state voting trend. None of these studies, however, is very helpful in explaining the significant differences on many questions—often revealed in debate but obscured by states' unitary votes—between *particular individuals* who shared similar economic interests.

2. WASHINGTON TO HAMILTON, March 31, 1781, in *The Papers of Alexander Hamilton*, ed. Harold C. Syrett (New York: Columbia University Press, 1961–1987), 3:310, Founders Online, https://founders.archives.gov/documents/Hamilton/01-03-02-0197; KING, September 3, 1785, in *Letters of Members of the Continental Congress*, ed. Edmund Cody Burnett (Washington, DC: Carnegie Institution, 1921), 8:206–210; e.g., Max Farrand, ed., *Records of the Federal Convention of 1787* (New Haven, CT: Yale University Press, 1937), 1:48; Forrest McDonald, "The Constitution and Hamiltonian Capitalism," in *How Capitalistic Is the Constitution?*, ed. Robert Godwin and William Schambra (Washington, DC: American Enterprise Institute, 1982), 61.

3. Clinton Rossiter, *1787: The Grand Convention* (New York: Macmillan, 1966), 79–80, 99.

4. Marjorie Hope Nicholson, *Newton Demands the Muse: Newton's Opticks and the 18th Century Poets* (Princeton, NJ: Princeton University Press, 1946), 4; Douglass Adair to Robert E. Brown 1965, quoted in introduction to Douglass Adair, *Fame and the Founding Fathers*, ed. Trevor Colbourn (New York: W. W. Norton, 1974), xiv.

5. Daniel Walker Howe, "Why the Scottish Enlightenment Was Useful to the Framers of the American Constitution," *Comparative Studies of Society and History* 31 (1989), 582; Farrand, ed., *Records*, 3:93.

6. Noah Webster, "On the Education of Youth in America," quoted in Carl Richard, "Cicero and the American Founders," in *Brill's Companion to the Reception of Cicero*, ed. William H. Altman (Leiden: Brill, 2015), 125; JAMES WILSON, *The Works of James Wilson*, ed. Robert Green McCloskey (Cambridge, MA: Harvard University Press, 1967), 1:643; Hume to Hutcheson, September 17, 1739, in *The Letters of David Hume*, ed. J. Y. T. Greig (Oxford: Clarendon, 1932), 1:32; Mayhew quoted in William Tudor, *Life of James Otis, of Massachusetts* (Boston: Wells and Lilly, 1823), 144.

7. Farrand, ed., *Records*, 3:92, 91, 88.

8. Gilbert Chinard, "Polybius and the American Constitution," in *American Enlightenment*, ed. Frank Shuffelton (Rochester, NY: University of Rochester Press, 1993), 219.

9. Farrand, ed., *Records*, 1:48–50, 2:248–251, 2:267–272.

10. Samuel Fleischaker, "Adam Smith's Reception among the American Founders," *William and Mary Quarterly* 59 (2002): 915, 918–19; Farrand, ed., *Records*, 1:71, 1:308, 1:391, 1:485, 1:497, 1:580, 2:34, 2:530; Colleen Sheehan, "Madison and the French Enlightenment: The Authority of Public Opinion," *William and Mary Quarterly* 59 (2002): 926.

11. Donald S. Lutz, "The Relative Influence of European Writers on Later Eighteenth-Century Political Thought," *American Political Science Review* 78 (1984): 189–190; Fleischaker, "Adam Smith's Reception," 913.

12. *Selected Correspondence and Papers of James Monroe*, ed. Daniel Preston et al. (Westport, CT: Greenwood Press, 2006), 2:56

13. Farrand, ed., *Records*, 1:135, 317, 319, 448, 485, 254, 343, 399–402, 283–308, 437–441.

14. Farrand, ed., 1:553, 153, 165, 100, 125, 391.

15. George Billias, *Elbridge Gerry: Founding Father and Republican Statesman* (New York: McGraw-Hill, 1976), 41; Farrand, ed., *Records*, 1:48.

16. Forrest McDonald, *Novus Ordo Seclorum: The Intellectual Origins of the Constitution* (Lawrence: University Press of Kansas, 1985), 199.

17. Howe, "Why the Scottish Enlightenment Was Useful to the Framers," 584–585; Farrand, ed., *Records*, 2:53.

18. J. G. A. Pocock, *The Machiavellian Moment: Florentine Political Thought and the Atlantic Republican Tradition*, 2nd ed. (Princeton, NJ: Princeton University Press, 2016), 509; Thomas Miller, *Formation of College English* (Pittsburgh: University of Pittsburgh Press, 1997), 179–182, and Thomas Miller, introduction to *Selected Writings of John Witherspoon* (Carbondale: Southern Illinois University Press, 2015), 36, 38; Richard Matthews, *If Men Were Angels* (Lawrence: University Press of Kansas,

1995), 17, 19n49, 5, 23; David Epstein, *The Political Theory of the Federalist* (Chicago: University of Chicago Press, 1984) 3, 5–6. See Pocock, *Machiavellian Moment*, 461–552, Hans Baron, *The Crisis of the Early Italian Renaissance: Civic Humanism and Republican Liberty in an Age of Classicism and Tyranny*, rev. ed. (Princeton, NJ: Princeton University Press, 1966), Christopher J. Finlay, "Hume's Theory of Civil Society," *European Journal of Political Theory* 3 (2004): 369–391, Craig Smith, "The Scottish Enlightenment, Unintended Consequences, and the Science of Man," *Journal of Scottish Philosophy* 7 (2009): 9–29; Lance Banning, *The Jeffersonian Persuasion* (Ithaca, NY: Cornell University Press, 1978); Drew McCoy, *The Elusive Republic: Political Economy in Jeffersonian America* (Chapel Hill: University of North Carolina Press, 1980); and Drew McCoy, *The Last of the Fathers: James Madison and the Republican* Legacy (New York: Cambridge University Press, 1989).

19. Pocock, *Machiavellian Moment*, 523.

20. McDonald, *Novus Ordo Seclorum*, 200; Adams to John Sanderson, November 19, 1822, in *Sanderson's Biography of the Signers to the Declaration of Independence*, rev. ed., ed. Robert T. Conrad (Philadelphia: Thomas Cowperthwait, 1846) 176. It is a little confusing that McDonald, who chooses to call MADISON's opponents "the ideologues," then describes MADISON himself as "an ideologue in search of an ideology" (203).

21. David Hume, "That Politics May Be Reduced to a Science," in *Essays Moral and Political*, ed. Eugene F. Miller (Indianapolis: Liberty Fund, 1987 [1764]), 34; *Federalist*, no., 51, 322; Farrand, ed., *Records*, 2:41–43, 52.

22. EBRIDGE GERRY to President of Senate and Speaker of House of Representatives of Massachusetts, October 18, 1787, quoted in Farrand, ed., *Records*, 3:128–129; GEORGE MASON, "Objections to this Constitution of Government," quoted in Farrand, ed., 2:637–640; EDMUND RANDOLPH to the Speaker of the Virginia House of Delegates, October 10, 1787, quoted in Farrand, ed., 3:127; LUTHER MARTIN, before the Maryland House of Representatives, November 29, 1787, quoted in Farrand, ed., 3: 151–159.

23. *Federalist*, no. 38, 236.

24. Farrand, ed., *Records*, 2:64–69; 2:551.

25. Rossiter, *1787: The Grand Convention*, 182.

26. See David Gelman, "Ideology and Participation: Examining the Constitutional Convention of 1787," *Political Research Quarterly* 71, no. 3 (2018): 546–559.

27. Marshall quoted in William C. Rives, *History of the Life and Times of James Madison* (Boston: Little, Brown, 1859–1868), 2:612n; Farrand, ed., *Records*, 3:87–97.

28. May, *Enlightenment in America*, 99; Farrand, ed., *Records*, 2:370–372. Enlightenment philosophers stressed the equality of all men; Witherspoon privately tutored two Black students at Princeton and publicly declared it "unlawful to make inroads upon others, unprovoked, and take away their liberty by no better right than superior power," but he nonetheless purchased two slaves shortly after he arrived in New Jersey. See Lesa Redmond, "John Witherspoon," Princeton & Slavery Project, https://slavery.princeton.edu/stories/john-witherspoon.

29. John Kaminski and Gaspare Saladino, eds., *Documentary History of the Ratification of the Constitution* (Madison: University of Wisconsin Press 1990, 1993),

10:1476–1477; Farrand, ed., *Records*, 2:375, 2:417; Jonathan Elliot, *Debates in the Several State Conventions on the Adoption of the Federal Constitution*, 2nd ed. (Buffalo: Hein, 1996 [1836]), 4:30; William Casto, "Oliver Ellsworth's Calvinism," *Journal of Church and State* 36 (1994): 519. See Robin Einhorn, "Patrick Henry's Case against the Constitution: The Structural Problem of Slavery," *Journal of the Early Republic* 22 (2002): 549–573; Sean Wilentz, *No Property in Man: Slavery and Antislavery at the Nation's Founding* (Cambridge, MA: Harvard University Press, 2018); and David Waldstreicher, *Slavery's Constitution: From Revolution to Ratification* (New York: Hill and Wang, 2009).

30. Casto, "Ellsworth's Calvinism," 519; Farrand, ed., *Records*, 1:468, 488. For confusion of DAYTON with DAVIE as the speaker, see, e.g., "The Connecticut Compromise," http://teachingamericanhistory.org; see also Calvin Jillson and Thornton Anderson, "Voting Bloc Analysis in the Constitutional Convention," *Western Political Quarterly* 31 (1978): 535–547, and Gerald Pomper, "Conflict and Coalition at the Constitutional Convention," in *The Study of Coalition Behavior: Theoretical Perspectives and Cases from Four Continents*, ed. S. O. Groennings et al. (New York: Holt, Rinehart, and Winston, 1970), 209–225.

31. Michael Klarman, *The Framers' Coup* (New York: Oxford, 2016), 196, 146; McDonald, *Novus Ordo Seclorum*, 200; Farrand, ed., *Records*, 3:396, 1:526. For an argument that SHERMAN's personal influence at the Convention is overrated, see Keith L. Dougherty and Jac C. Heckelman, "A Pivotal Voter from a Pivotal State: Roger Sherman at the Constitutional Convention," *American Political Science Review* 100 (2006): 297–302.

32. James Hutson, *Supplement to Max Farrand's Records of the Federal Convention of 1787* (New Haven, CT: Yale University Press, 1987), 143; Farrand, ed., *Records*, 2:15; Manasseh Cutler, *Life, Journals and Correspondence*, ed. William Parker Cutler et al. (Cincinnati: Clarke, 1888), 1:254; Richard Beeman, *Plain Honest Men: The Making of the American Constitution* (New York: Random House, 2009), 78.

33. McDonald, *Novus Ordo Seclorum*, 235, 237n43; Forrest McDonald, *E Pluribus Unum: The Formation of the American Republic, 1776–1790*, 2nd ed. (Indianapolis: Liberty Fund, 1979), 292, 292–293n54, 29n58, 300n66; Richard Barry, *Mr. Rutledge of South Carolina* (New York: Duell, Sloan, and Pearce, 1942), 329–332; BLOUNT to Caswell, July 10, 1787, in Farrand, ed., *Records*, 3:57.

34. Beeman, *Plain, Honest Men*, 219–220; KING quoted in Delbert Gilpatrick, "Contemporary Opinion of Hugh Williamson," *North Carolina Historical Review* 17 (1940): 28; David O. Stewart, *The Summer of 1787: The Men Who Invented the Constitution* (New York: Simon and Schuster, 2007), 125; Farrand, ed., *Records*,1:593, 579, 581, 588; Barry, *Mr. Rutledge*, 334–335; Jeremy C. Pope and Shawn Trier, "Reconsidering the Great Compromise at the Federal Convention of 1787: Deliberation and Agenda Effects on the Senate and Slavery," *American Journal of Political Science* 55, no. 2 (2011): 300n16, 301, 304; Klarman, *Framers' Coup*, 201.

35. Farrand, ed., *Records*, 1:510, 2:15; see Browning, "William Richardson Davie's Princeton Connections," 303–307. Between the meeting of the committee and the July 16 vote, New York's delegation, which had supported the Compromise, abandoned the Convention; only 10 states were represented until delegates from the

small state of New Hampshire arrived five days later, on July 21. Had these two states been present, the Compromise would likely have passed by a wider margin.

36. Rossiter, *1787: The Grand Convention*, 169.

37. Herbert Storing and Murray Dry, eds., *The Complete Anti-Federalist* (Chicago: University of Chicago Press, 1981), 2:5n.

38. Farrand, ed., *Records*, 2:616; JAMES MADISON, "Notes for the *National Gazette* Essays," in *Papers of James Madison*, Congressional Series, ed. William T. Hutchinson, Robert A. Rutland, et al., (Charlottesville: University Press of Virginia, 1962–1991), 14:168, Founders Online, https://founders.archives.gov/documents/Madison/01-14-02-0144.

Conclusion

1. Carl J. Richard, *The Founders and the Classics: Greece, Rome, and the American Enlightenment* (Cambridge, MA: Harvard University Press, 1995), 118; Douglass Adair, *Fame and the Founding Fathers*, ed. Trevor Colbourn (New York: W. W. Norton, 1974), 87n9.

It is the argument of this book that the different educations of the Framers of the Constitution had important effects at the Constitutional Convention. It follows that the sources I have drawn on divide themselves into three categories (with some inevitable overlap): (1) education in the eighteenth century, (2) the lives of the Framers themselves, and (3) the events surrounding the Convention. The work of anyone who looks into the last of these is made infinitely easier by Max Farrand's indispensable three volumes of *The Records of the Federal Convention of 1787* (New Have, CT: Yale University Press, 1937). Farrand's compilation of MADISON's daily notes, occasional notes taken by other participants, and more than 400 other documents was first published in 1911, revised in 1937, and supplemented in 1987 by James Hutson, ed., *Supplement to Max Farrand's Records of the Federal Convention of 1787* (New Haven, CT: Yale University Press, 1987). (For the controversy over MADISON's late revisions to those notes, see Mary Sarah Bilder, *Madison's Hand* (Cambridge, MA: Harvard University Press, 2015), and Lyn Uzzell, "Madison's Notes: At Last, a New and Improved Look," *Law and Liberty*, March 8, 2018, https://lawliberty.org/madisons-notes-at-last-a-new-and-improved-look/.) Scholars have depended on Farrand for generations; gradually over the past ten years another invaluable compilation has made instantly available the correspondence (and other documents) of the four most prominent of the Framers: the National Archives' website Founders Online (https://founders.archives.gov). Still a work in progress, it is already the most efficient and comprehensive source for the writings of GEORGE WASHINGTON, BENJAMIN FRANKLIN, JAMES MADISON, and ALEXANDER HAMILTON, and also John Adams and John Jay. Founders Online will eventually reproduce the entire printed papers of those Founders (for the most part still incomplete) along with other sources, published and unpublished; it may eventually expand to include the works of more of the Framers. Wherever possible in my footnotes I have cited it along with print locations.

Sadly, there is no similar gold mine for primary sources relating to eighteenth-century education. For that category, as for the lives of the less familiar Framers, one must be prepared to hunt—sometimes in older, out-of-the-way publications, but often in the as-yet unpublished archives of universities, libraries, and historical societies. I would be remiss if I did not acknowledge the thoughtful help of the staffs of the following repositories of unpublished manuscripts and documents: the Library of Congress Manuscript Division (THOMAS MIFFLIN, *Notes on Metaphysics and the Elements of the Laws of Nature [1758–1759]* MS 32854, Mifflin Manuscripts); the Seeley G. Mudd Manuscript Library, Princeton University (WILLIAM PATERSON commonplace book and original letter book, box one, Paterson Family Papers); the Rare Book and Manuscript Library, Columbia University (GOUVERNEUR MORRIS manuscript "On Wit and Beauty," MS Coll. Morris, box one); the Albert and Shirley Small Special Collections Library, University of Virginia (EDMUND RANDOLPH, "Autobiographical Sketch," MS 4263); the Earl Gregg Swem Library of the College of William and Mary (Tucker MSS, Tucker-Coleman Collection); the Southern Historical Collection, Wilson Library, University of North Carolina (letter from Justina Dobbs to Conway Richard Dobbs, May 14, 1765, Desmond Clarke Papers #3340); the Massachusetts Historical Society (letter from WILLIAM LIVINGSTON to the Rev. James Dana, November 26, 1787, Livingston Family Papers box fifteen); the New-York Historical Society (Francis Lister Hawks Papers, Collection 1726–1854 [microfilm], construction contract, Queen's College hall); and generous personal communications from Samuel K. Fore of the Harlan Crow Library; Aaron Fogleman of Northern Illinois University; James H. Williams of the Mecklenburg Historical Association; Alison Heinbaugh of the John D. Rockefeller Library of Colonial Williamsburg; Elizabeth Singh of the Royal Medical Society, Edinburgh; Sarah Hepworth of the University of Glasgow Library; Michel Frost of the library of the Inner Temple; Frans Sellies of the University of Utrecht Library; and Judith Curthoys of the Christ Church College Archives, University of Oxford. I must also record my gratitude to the staff of the Jefferson County Library in Port Hadlock, Washington, who processed countless interlibrary loans for me during a two-year residence on the Olympic Peninsula.

In addition to primary sources, there are a vast number of secondary sources available; the Constitution has always generated tremendous interest among both academic historians and the public at large. Some of these are classics, some are the product of very recent research, and many are, unfortunately, of very little value to the serious student. Antiquarianism was being replaced by modern historical scholarship toward the end of the nineteenth century, and many resources from that period have not been superseded and remain invaluable, as do some seminal works of the 1940s and 1950s. More recent information in print and online regarding the Framers, their education, and their activities is daunting in its extent, and the quantity of misinformation is discouraging, to say the least. In the preceding chapters I have often cited works that may be otherwise valuable in order to correct persistent errors; in the brief essay that follows, I have winnowed down countless books and articles to list only those that I have found to be both trustworthy and particularly helpful, keeping the focus strictly on my narrow topic: the education of the Framers and its effect on their actions at the Convention of 1787. Much excellent scholarship on the era has perforce been left out.

Education

Four valuable accounts of American colleges, written by their early presidents, are Thomas Clap, *Annals of Yale College* (New Haven, CT: Hotchkiss and Mecom, 1766); William Smith, "Account of the College and Academy [of Philadelphia]," in *Discourses on Several Public Occasions*, 2nd ed. (London: Millar, 1762); Ashbel Green, *Discourses Delivered in the College of New Jersey . . . Including A Historical Sketch of the College from its Origin the Accession of President Witherspoon* (Philadelphia: Littel,

1822); and Josiah Quincy, *History of Harvard University* (Cambridge, MA: J. Owen, 1840); the authorized description of Princeton's early practices is Samuel Blair, *Account of the College of New Jersey* (Woodbridge, NJ: James Parker, 1764). See also Samuel Davies, "A General Account of the Rise and State of the College Lately Established in the Province of New Jersey, in America," *New American Magazine* 27 (March 1760), and *Laws of Harvard College* (Boston: Samuel Hall, 1790). A brief description of William and Mary appears in Edward Kimber, "Itinerant Observations in America," *London Magazine* (July 1746), Kevin J. Hayes, ed., *Itinerant Observations in America* (Newark: University of Delaware Press, 1998). Ezra Stiles, Yale's late eighteenth-century president, kept current on the events and personalities of not only that institution but most of America's early colleges. Two very useful sources for all things education-related are *Extracts from the Itineraries and Other Miscellanies of Ezra Stiles, D.D., LL.D. 1755–1794*, ed. Franklin Bowditch Dexter (New Haven, CT: Yale University Press, 1916), and *The Literary Diary of Ezra Stiles*, 3 vols., ed. Franklin Bowditch Dexter (New York: Scribner's, 1901). For records of administrative decision-making, see *Minutes of the Governors of the College in the Province of New York . . . and of the Corporation of King's College in the City of New York* (New York: Columbia University, 1932); "Journal of the Meetings of the President and Masters of William and Mary College," *William and Mary Quarterly*, 1st ser., 13 (1904–1905): 15–22, 133–138, 148–157, 230–238; Trustees of the University of Pennsylvania, Minute Books 1749–1768, University of Pennsylvania Archives https://archives.upenn.edu /digitized-resources/docs-pubs/trustees-minutes; and Trustee Minute Books, College of New Jersey, https://library.princeton.edu/special-collections/databases /trustees-minutes-1746–1894. See also the William Smith Papers (Jasper Yeates Brinton Collection 1619, Pennsylvania Historical Society), and Franklin Bowditch Dexter, *Documentary History of Yale University* (New Haven, CT: Yale University Press, 1916). *Catalog of the Officers and Graduates of Yale University in New Haven, Connecticut, 1701–1910* (New Haven, CT: Tuttle, Morehouse, and Taylor, 1910), and Varnum Lansing Collins, ed., *A General Catalogue of Princeton University, 1746–1906* (Princeton, NJ: Princeton University Press, 1908), list both graduates and faculty members for each year.

The best modern survey of education in general in the Framers' time is Lawrence Cremin, *American Education: The Colonial Experience, 1607–1783* (New York: Harper And Row, 1970), but see also Lawrence Stone, ed., *The University in Society* (Princeton, NJ: Princeton University Press, 1974). For colonial colleges, essential sources are Douglas Sloan, *The Scottish Enlightenment and the American College Ideal* (New York: Teachers College Press, 1971), J. David Hoeveler, *Creating the American Mind: Intellect and Politics in the Colonial Colleges* (Lanham, MD: Rowman and Littlefield, 2002), and David W. Robson, *Educating Republicans: The College in the Era of the American Revolution, 1750–1800* (Westport, CT: Greenwood, 1985). Histories of specific schools and colleges include Samuel Eliot Morison, *Three Centuries of Harvard, 1636–1936* (Cambridge, MA: Harvard University Press,1936), Brooks Mather Kelley, *Yale: A History* (New Haven, CT: Yale University Press, 1999), Varnum Lansing Collins, *Princeton* (Oxford: Oxford University Press, 1914), Thomas Jefferson Wertenbaker, *Princeton 1746–1896*, rev. ed. (Princeton, NJ: Princeton University Press: 1996

[1946]), and Robert McCaughey, *Stand, Columbia: A History of Columbia University in the City of New York* (New York: Columbia University Press, 2003).

Valuable studies focused on education in the eighteenth century include Beverly McAnear, "The Selection of an Alma Mater by Pre-Revolutionary Students," *Pennsylvania Magazine of History and Biography* 73 (1949): 429–440, and Beverly McAnear, "Raising of Funds by the Colonial Colleges," *Mississippi Valley Historical Review* 38 (1952): 591–612; Jack Morpurgo, *Their Majesties Royall Colledge: William and Mary in the Seventeenth and Eighteenth Centuries* (Williamsburg, VA: The College of William and Mary, 1976); Courtland Canby, "A Note on the Influence of Oxford at William and Mary," *William and Mary Quarterly*, 2nd ser., 21 (1941): 243–247; Lucy Sutherland and Lesley G. Mitchell, eds., *The History of the University of Oxford*, Vol. 5, *The Eighteenth Century* (New York: Oxford University Press, 1986); E. G. W. Bill, *Education at Christ Church College, Oxford, 1660–1800* (London: Oxford University Press, 1988); John Kerr, *Scottish Education: Schools and University from Early Times to 1908* (Cambridge: Cambridge University Press, 1910); *Correspondence of Thomas Reid*, ed. Paul Wood (Edinburgh: University of Edinburgh Press, 2002); John Maclean, *History of the College of New Jersey from Its Origins in 1746 to the Commencement of 1854* (Philadelphia: Lippincott, 1877); Mark Noll, *Princeton and the Republic, 1768–1822: The Search for a Christian Enlightenment in the Era of Samuel Stanhope Smith* (Princeton, NJ: Princeton University Press, 1989); David Humphrey, *From King's College to Columbia, 1746–1800* (New York: Columbia University Press, 1976); Guy Howard Miller, *The Revolutionary College: American Presbyterian Higher Education, 1707–1837* (New York: New York University Press, 1976); Donald Come, "Influence of Princeton on Higher Education in the South Before 1825," *William and Mary Quarterly*, 3rd ser., 3 (1945): 35–96; and Jonathan Boucher, *Reminiscences of an American Loyalist, 1739–1789* (Boston: Houghton, Mifflin, 1925). Two books that provide insight into St. Omer's College, in Flanders, are Hubert Chadwick, *St. Omers to Stonyhurst* (London: Burns and Oates, 1962), and Thomas Muir, *Stonyhurst College, 1593–1993* (London: James and James, 1992).

College administrators in the eighteenth century left indelible impressions on their students, for better or for worse; see Louis Tucker, *Puritan Protagonist: President Thomas Clap of Yale College* (Chapel Hill: University of North Carolina Press, 1962); Herbert Schneider and Carol Schneider, eds., *Samuel Johnson, President of King's College: His Career and Writings* (New York: Columbia University Press, 1929); Lyman H. Butterfield, *John Witherspoon Comes to America* (Princeton, NJ: Princeton University Press, 1953); Varnum Lansing Collins, *President Witherspoon* (Princeton, NJ: Princeton University Press, 1925); Ashbel Green, *Life of the Reverend John Witherspoon D.D., LL.D.*, ed. Henry Lyttelton Savage (Princeton, NJ: Princeton University Press, 1973); Jeffry Morrison, *John Witherspoon and the Founding of the American Republic* (South Bend, IN: University of Notre Dame Press, 2005); Gideon Mailer, *John Witherspoon's American Revolution* (Chapel Hill: University of North Carolina, 2019); Thomas Miller, ed., *Selected Writings of John Witherspoon* (Carbondale: Southern Illinois University Press, 2015); George W. Pilcher, ed., *The Reverend Samuel Davies Abroad: A Diary of a Journey to England and Scotland* (Champaign: University of Illinois Press, 1967); Charles Stillé, *Memoir of the Rev. William Smith, D.D.* (Philadelphia:

Moore and Sons, 1869); William H. W. Sabine, ed., *Historical Memoirs of William Smith* (New York: New York Times, 1971); Horace Wemyss Smith, *Life and Correspondence of the Rev. William Smith* (Philadelphia: S. A. George,1879); Charlotte Fletcher, *Cato's Mirania: A Life of Provost Smith* (Lanham, MD: University Press of America, 2002); Thomas C. Pears, "Francis Alison," *Journal of the Presbyterian Historical Society* 29 (1951): 115–126; and Joseph Ellis, *The New England Mind in Transition: Samuel Johnson of Connecticut* (New Haven, CT: Yale University Press, 1973).

Legal and medical educations have received their share of attention; they often drew colonial students to travel to England or Scotland, an experience that was an education in itself. See Ralph M. Stein, "The Path of Legal Education from Edward I to Langdell: A History of Insular Reaction," *Chicago-Kent Law Review* 57 (1981): 429–454; Brian Abel-Smith and Robert Stevens, *Lawyers and the Courts: A Sociological Study of the English Legal System, 1750–1965* (London: Heineman, 1967); John Colyer, "The American Connection," in *A History of the Middle Temple*, ed. Richard Havery (London: Hart, 2011) 267–286; Wilfrid Prest, "The Unreformed Middle Temple," in Havery, ed., *A History of the Middle Temple*, 205–238; C. E. A. Bedwell, "American Middle Templars," *American Historical Review* 25 (1920): 680–689; Eric Stockdale and Randy Holland, *Middle Temple Lawyers and the American Revolution* (Eagan, MN: Thomson-West, 2007); Brian Moline, "Early American Legal Education," *Washburn Law Journal* 42 (2004): 775–802; Charles R. McKirdy, "The Lawyer as Apprentice: Legal Education in Eighteenth-Century Massachusetts," *Journal of Legal Education* 28 (1976): 124–136; W. Hamilton Bryson, "The History of Legal Education in Virginia," *University of Richmond Law Review* 14 (1979): 155–210; and Lisa Rosner, *Medical Education in the Age of Improvement: Edinburgh Students and Apprentices, 1760–1824* (Edinburgh: Edinburgh University Press, 1991). Several of the Framers experienced religious discrimination in education in Ireland, or left Maryland in order to avoid it there. See M. J. Farrelly, *Papist Patriots: The Making of an American Catholic Identity* (New York: Oxford University Press, 2012); J. R. R. Adams, "Swine-Tax and Eat-Him-All-Magee: The Hedge Schools and Popular Education in Ireland," in *Irish Popular Culture 1650–1850*, ed. James S. Donnelly Jr. and Kerby A. Miller (Dublin: Irish Academic Press, 1998) 99–100; and J. C. Beckett, *Protestant Dissent in Ireland* (London: Faber, 1948).

Higher education has always received the lion's share of attention from historians, but more than half of the Framers never went to college. For accounts of elementary and secondary education in the eighteenth century, see E. Jennifer Monaghan, *Learning to Read and Write in Colonial America* (Amherst: University of Massachusetts Press, 2005); James Axtell, *The School upon a Hill: Education and Society in Colonial New England* (New Haven, CT: Yale University Press, 1974); William Webb Kemp, *The Support of Schools in Colonial New York by the Society for the Propagation of the Gospel in Foreign Parts* (New York: Teachers College Press, 1913); Robert Middlekauff, *Ancients and Axioms: Secondary Education in Eighteenth-Century New England* (New Haven, CT: Yale University Press, 1963); Nehemiah Cleaveland, *A History of the Dummer Academy, Being the Centennial Discourse Delivered by Nehemiah Cleaveland on August 12, 1863* (Newburyport, MA: Herald Press, 1914); W. Gordon McCabe, *Virginia's Schools before and after the Revolution* (Charlottesville: Society of the Alumni of the University of Virginia, 1890); Fred J. Hood, *Reformed America: The Middle and Southern States, 1783–1837* (Tuscaloosa, AL: University of Alabama Press, 1980); Marshall D. Haywood, "The Story of Queen's College or Liberty Hall in the Province of North Carolina," *North Carolina Booklet* 11 (1912): 169–175; James Williams, "Queen's College," *Olde Mecklenburg Genealogical Society Quarterly* 34 (2016): 3–8; and Thomas Woody, *Early Quaker Education in Pennsylvania* (New York: Teachers College Press, 1920).

Several of the most influential Framers, including WASHINGTON, FRANKLIN, SHERMAN, and MASON, were essentially self-taught; others were educated entirely by private tutors. Autobiographical accounts of two very different self-educations are FRANKLIN's classic *Autobiography*, in BENJAMIN FRANKLIN, *Autobiography, Poor Richard, and Later Writings*, ed. J. A. Leo Lemay (New York: Library of America, 1987) and the "Autobiography of Col. William Few of Georgia, From the Original Manuscript in the Possession of William Few Chrystie," *Magazine of American History* 7 (November, 1881): 343–58. An idea of the resources available to WASHINGTON and MASON can be gotten from Appleton Griffin, *Catalogue of the Washington Collection in the Boston Athenaeum* (Cambridge, MA: The Boston Athenaeum, 1897), and C. Malcolm Watkins, *Cultural History of Marlborough, Virginia*, Smithsonian Bulletin 253 (Washington, DC: Smithsonian Institution, 1968), 191, 198–208. For the consequences of WASHINGTON's reading, see Jeffry Morrison, *Political Philosophy of George Washington* (Baltimore: Johns Hopkins University Press, 2009), and Mark Bryan, "'Slideing into Monarchical extravagance': *Cato* at Valley Forge and the Testimony of William Bradford Jr." *William and Mary Quarterly*, 3rd ser., 67 (2010): 123–144. Philip Vickers Fithian, a Princeton classmate of MADISON, left a diary of a year as a private tutor in Virginia that gives a good idea of what the children of well-to-do parents (such as MADISON or DICKINSON) might have expected from a tutor: *Philip Vickers Fithian Journal and Letters, 1767–1774*, ed. John R. Williams (Princeton, NJ: Princeton University Press, 1900). The Rev. Joseph Bellamy, tutor of OLIVER ELLSWORTH, had a lasting influence on his pupil. Two good studies of Bellamy and his teaching are Mark Valeri, *Law and Providence in Joseph Bellamy's New England: The Origins of the New Divinity in Revolutionary America* (New York: Oxford University Press, 1994), and William Casto, "Oliver Ellsworth's Calvinism: A Biographical Essay on Religion and Political Psychology in the Early Republic," *Journal of Church and State* 36 (1994): 507–26. For the text of the series of sermons that made him famous, see Joseph Bellamy, *Four Sermons on the Wisdom of God in Permission of Sin* (Morristown, NJ: Henry P. Russell, 1804).

Two aspects of education require particular attention. The first of these is the curriculum itself. An early but still useful introduction is Louis Snow, *The College Curriculum in the United States* (New York: Teachers College Press, 1907). Useful reviews of college curriculum include Norman Fiering, *Moral Philosophy at Seventeenth-Century Harvard: A Discipline in Transition* (Chapel Hill: University of North Carolina Press, 1981), Francis L. Broderick, "Pulpit, Physics, and Politics: The Curriculum of the College of New Jersey, 1746–1794," *William and Mary Quarterly*, 3rd ser., 6 (1949): 42–60, and Thomas Miller, *Evolution of College English* (Pittsburgh: University of Pittsburgh Press, 2011). Another older but helpful survey of one especially important element of instruction is Anna Haddow, *Political Science in American Colleges and Universities* (New York: Appleton-Century, 1939).

Traditional grammar schools and colleges focused their attention primarily on the grammar of Latin and Greek, secondarily on the literature of those languages in the ancient world. The best study of classical instruction is Carl J. Richard, *The Founders and the Classics: Greece, Rome, and the American Enlightenment* (Cambridge, MA: Harvard University Press, 1995), and a more recent, popular account is Thomas E. Ricks, *First Principles: What America's Founders Learned from the Greeks and Romans and How That Shaped Our Country* (New York: Harper, 2020). Particularly useful is Mark Kalthoff, "Liberal Education, the Ordered Soul, and Cicero's *De Officiis:* A Core Text for Every Curriculum" (2014), Association of Core Texts and Courses, http://www.coretexts.org. See also Carl J. Richard, "Cicero and the American Founders," in *Brill's Companion to the Reception of Cicero*, ed. William H. Altman (Leiden: Brill, 2015), and Gilbert Chinard, "Polybius and the American Constitution, "*Journal of the History of Ideas* 1 (1940): 38–58.

Gradually, the Scottish universities and new American colleges were beginning to incorporate the newer philosophy into their curriculum; see Paul Wood, *The Aberdeen Enlightenment: The Arts Curriculum in the Eighteenth Century* (Aberdeen: Aberdeen University Press, 1993), and Martin J. Finkelstein, "From Tutor to Specialized Scholar: Academic Professionalization in Eighteenth and Nineteenth Century America," *History of Higher Education Annual* 3 (1983): 99–121. Useful overviews are Susan Manning and Francis Cogliano, *The Atlantic Enlightenment* (London: Ashgate 2008), Caroline Winterer, *American Enlightenments* (New Haven, CT: Yale University Press, 2017), and Henry May, *The Enlightenment in America* (New York: Oxford University Press, 1976).

The important influences from Scotland are analyzed in Sloan, *The Scottish Enlightenment and the American College Ideal;* Roy Branson, "James Madison and the Scottish Enlightenment," *Journal of the History of Ideas* 40 (1979): 235–250; Daniel Walker Howe, "Why the Scottish Enlightenment Was Useful to the Framers of the American Constitution," *Comparative Studies in Society and History* 31 (1989): 572–587; and Thomas Miller, *Formation of College English* (Pittsburgh: University of Pittsburg Press, 1997), a book that goes well beyond what its title suggests. For specific Scottish philosophers, see Thomas Reid, *Essays on the Intellectual Powers of Man, a Critical Edition*, ed. Derek R. Brookes (Edinburgh: University of Edinburgh Press, 2000); Kathleen Holcomb, "Thomas Reid in the Glasgow Literary Society," in *The Glasgow Enlightenment*, ed. Andrew Hook and Richard Sher (East Linton, Scotland: Tuckwell Press, 1995), 95–110; Sophia Rosenfeld, *Common Sense: A Political History* (Cambridge, MA: Harvard University Press, 2011); Samuel Fleischaker, "Adam Smith's Reception among the American Founders," *William and Mary Quarterly* 59 (2002): 897–924; Max Skjonsberg, "Adam Ferguson on the Perils of Popular Factions and Demagogues in a Roman Mirror," *History of European Ideas* 45 (2019): 842–65; W. R. Scott, *Francis Hutcheson, His Life, Teaching, and Position in the History of Philosophy* (Cambridge: Cambridge University Press, 1900); David Norton, "Francis Hutcheson in America," *Studies on Voltaire and the Eighteenth Century* 154 (1976): 1547–1568; Garry Wills, *Inventing America: Jefferson's Declaration of Inde-*

pendence (Garden City, NY: Doubleday, 1978); Richard H. Dees, "The Paradoxical Principle and Salutary Practice: Hume on Toleration," *Hume Studies* 31 (2005): 145–64; David Hume, "That Politics May Be Reduced to a Science," *Essays Moral and Political* (1764), ed. Eugene F. Miller (Indianapolis: Liberty Fund, 1987); Douglass Adair, "'That Politics May Be Reduced to a Science': David Hume, James Madison, and the Tenth Federalist," *Huntington Library Quarterly* 20, no. 4 (1957): 343–360; and Craig Smith, "The Scottish Enlightenment, Unintended Consequences, and the Science of Man," *Journal of Scottish Philosophy* 7 (2009): 9–29.

The most important American teacher of Scottish philosophy was the Scottish-born president of Princeton, John Witherspoon. His lectures, heard by five of the Framers, may be found in Witherspoon, *Lectures on Moral Philosophy*, ed. Varnum Lansing Collins (Princeton, NJ: Princeton University Press, 1912), and Witherspoon, *An Annotated Edition of Lectures on Moral Philosophy*, ed. Jack Scott (Newark: University of Delaware Press, 1982). Witherspoon was also instrumental in the new approach to teaching rhetoric and public speaking; see Thomas Miller, "Witherspoon, Blair, and the Rhetoric of Civic Humanism," in *Scotland and America in the Age of the Enlightenment*, ed. Richard B. Sher and Jeffrey R. Smitten (Princeton, NJ: Princeton University Press, 1990), 100–114, and David Barone, "Before the Revolution, Formal Rhetoric in Philadelphia during the Federal Era," *Pennsylvania History* 54, no. 4 (1987): 244–262. A useful study of rhetoric and belles lettres in eighteenth-century America is David Shields, *Civil Tongues and Polite Letters in America* (Chapel Hill: University of North Carolina Press, 1997), and see Christopher Grasso, *A Speaking Aristocracy: Transforming Public Discourse in Eighteenth-century Connecticut* (Chapel Hill: University of North Carolina Press, 1999).

For an idea of the usual materials studied by prospective lawyers, see W. H. Bryson, ed., *Virginia Law Books: Essays and Bibliographies* (Philadelphia: American Philosophical Society, 2000), and Morris L. Cohen, "Legal Literature in Colonial Massachusetts," in *Law in Colonial Massachusetts, 1630–1800*, ed. Daniel R. Coquillette (Boston: Colonial Society of Massachusetts, 1984). Marjorie Hope Nicolson, *Newton Demands the Muse: Newton's Opticks and the 18th Century Poets* (Princeton, NJ: Princeton University Press, 1966), and Arthur Lovejoy, *Reflections on Human Nature* (Baltimore: Johns Hopkins University Press, 1961), provide reminders that Newton's new science was important to more people than physicists.

The student experience, social as well as academic, is a second important aspect of education. Commonplace books give a student perspective on curriculum: at Harvard by Benjamin Wadsworth, *Abridgement of What I Extracted while an Undergraduate at Harvard College*, manuscript, Harvard University Library, HUC8766.314 mf/N (https://iiif.lib.harvard.edu/manifests/view/drs:46471858$1i); at Princeton by the Framer WILLIAM PATERSON, Paterson Family Papers, box one, Seeley G. Mudd Document Library, Princeton University; and at the College of Philadelphia by the Framer THOMAS MIFFLIN, *Notes on Metaphysics and the Elements of the Laws of Nature (1758–1759)*, MS 32854, Mifflin Manuscripts, Library of Congress.

Letters between friends and family members reveal what life was really like: see *Philip Vickers Fithian Journal and Letters, 1767–1774*, ed. John R. Williams (Princeton, NJ: Princeton University Press, 1900), and Eliza Pinckney, *The Letter Book of Eliza*

Pinckney, 1739–1762 (Chapel Hill: University of North Carolina Press, 1972), and correspondence collected in individual Framers' published papers and in Founders Online. The popularity of clubs and secret societies is evident in the "Original Records of the Phi Beta Kappa Society," *William and Mary Quarterly*, 1st ser., 4 (1896): 213–259, and is the subject of Jane Carson, *James Innes and His Brothers of the F.H.C.* (Williamsburg, VA: Colonial Williamsburg, 1965); Henry Clay Cameron, *History of the American Whig Society from 1769 to 1869* (Princeton, NJ: Stelle and Smith, 1871); Charles Richard Williams, *The Cliosophic Society, Princeton University: A Study of Its History in Commemoration of Its Sesquicentennial Anniversary* (Princeton, NJ: Princeton University Press, 1916); and J. Jefferson Looney, *Nursery of Letters and Republicanism: A Brief History of the American Whig-Cliosophic Society and Its Predecessors, 1765–1941* (Princeton, NJ: American Whig-Cliosophic Society, 1996). Readers may learn about inevitable student misbehavior (and varying administrative response) in Kathryn Sue McDaniel Moore, *Old Saints and Young Sinners: A Study of Student Discipline at Harvard College, 1636–1734* (Madison: University of Wisconsin Press, 1972), and the rigidity of social rank in New England's colleges is examined in Franklin Bowditch Dexter, *On Some Social Distinctions at Harvard and Yale, before the Revolution* (Worcester, MA: C. Hamilton, 1894).

Law students at the Inns of Court and in attorneys' offices had mixed feelings about their experiences—complacent in the case of JOHN DICKINSON: Trevor Colbourn, "A Pennsylvania Farmer at the Court of King George: John Dickinson's London Letters, 1754–1756," *Pennsylvania Magazine of History and Biography* 86 (1962): 241–286, 417–453 and his South Carolinian contemporary, Peter Manigault: "Six Letters of Peter Manigault," *South Carolina Historical and Genealogical Magazine* 15 (1914): 113–123; less satisfied in the case of two Princeton classmates clerking for DICKINSON and for Richard Stockton: see William MacPherson Horner, "Extracts from Letters of John MacPherson, Jr., to William Paterson, 1765–1773," *Pennsylvania Magazine of History and Biography* 33 (1910): 53. A Pennsylvania medical student at Edinburgh had a mixed experience: see Whitfield Bell, "Thomas Parke's Student Life in England and Scotland," *Pennsylvania Magazine of History and Biography* 75 (1951): 237–259. For an appreciation of the expatriate students' world, see Julie Flavell, *When London Was Capital of America* (New Haven, CT: Yale University Press: 2010), and Julie Flavell, "'The School of Modesty and Humility': Colonial American Youth in London and Their Parents, 1755–1775," *The Historical Journal* 42, no. 2 (1999): 377–403. The social milieu at Edinburgh is described in Davis D. McElroy, "The Literary Clubs and Societies of Eighteenth-Century Scotland" (PhD diss., Edinburgh University, 1952), and the more extravagant possibilities of London in John R. Alden, *Stephen Sayre: American Revolutionary Adventurer* (Baton Rouge: Louisiana State University Press, 1983).

The Framers

There were fifty-five Framers who participated in the Constitutional Convention. Most but not all have been the subjects of published biographies; the following are particularly helpful on the subject of their educations: Douglas Southall Freeman, *George Washington*, Vol. 1 (New York: Scribner's 1948); Irving Brant, *James*

Madison, Vol. 1 (Indianapolis: Bobbs-Merrill, 1941); J. A. Leo Lemay, *The Life of Benjamin Franklin* (Philadelphia: University of Pennsylvania Press, 2006); James Haw, *John and Edward Rutledge of South Carolina* (Athens: University of Georgia Press, 1997); Christopher Collier, *Roger Sherman's Connecticut* (Middleton, CT: Wesleyan University Press, 1971); Pamela Copeland, *The Five George Masons* (Charlottesville: University Press of Virginia, 1975); William Casto, *Oliver Ellsworth and the Creation of the Federal Republic* (New York: Second Circuit Committee on History and Commemorative Events, 1997); Milton M. Klein, *American Whig: William Livingston of New York* (New York: Garland, 1993); Ralph Ketcham, *James Madison: A Biography* (Charlottesville: University of Virginia Press, 1990 [1971]); and Broadus Mitchell, *Alexander Hamilton: Youth to Maturity* (New York: Macmillan, 1971 [1957]). Samuel K. Fore, "William Pierce (1753–1789)," *New Georgia Encyclopedia*, http://www.georgia encyclopedia.org/articles/history-archaeology/william-pierce-1753–1789, clears up a number of long-standing confusions about the little-known Georgia Framer. Sometimes prone to exaggeration or surmise are Richard Barry, *Mr. Rutledge of South Carolina* (New York: Duell, Sloan, and Pearce, 1942), and Ron Chernow, *Alexander Hamilton* (New York: Penguin, 2004). Page Smith, *James Wilson, Founding Father* (Chapel Hill: University of North Carolina Press, 1956), is best avoided.

A few much older works have value for data that is not available elsewhere: John C. Hamilton, *Life of Alexander Hamilton* (New York: Appleton, 1840), Charles J. Stillé, *Life and Times of John Dickinson* (Philadelphia: Pennsylvania Historical Society, 1891), Paul L. Ford, *The True George Washington* (Philadelphia: J. B. Lippincott, 1896), David Hosack, *A Biographical Memoir of Hugh Williamson, M.D., LL.D.* (New York: C. S. Van Winkle, 1820), Joel Munsell, *Annals of Albany* (Albany: J. Munsell, 1854), Bernard Steiner, *Life and Correspondence of James McHenry, Secretary of War under Washington and Adams* (Cleveland: Burrows Brothers, 1907), Thomas Irving, *Controversy between Gen. Richard D. Spaight and John Stanly, Esq., To Which is Attached a Funeral Discourse . . .* (New Bern, NC: John S. Pasteur, 1802), George Johnston, *History of Cecil County, Maryland, And the Early Settlements Around the Head of the Chesapeake Bay and on the Delaware River* (Elkton, MD: Dickson and Gilling, 1881), Samuel Alexander Harrison and Oswald Tilghman, *History of Talbot County, Maryland 1661–1861: The Worthies of Talbot* (Baltimore: Regional Publishing, 1967 [1915]), John Flynn, *Beyond the Blew Hills* (Stoughton, MA: Stoughton Historical Society, 1976), http://www.stoughtonhistory.com.

In addition to the autobiographies of FRANKLIN and FEW, there are these relatively brief autobiographical sketches: "James Madison's Autobiography," ed. Douglass Adair, *William and Mary Quarterly*, 3rd ser., 2 (1945); EDMUND RANDOLPH, "Autobiographical Sketch," MS 4263, Albert and Shirley Small Special Collections Library, University of Virginia; and LUTHER MARTIN, *Modern Gratitude* (Whitefish, MT: Kessinger, 2010 [1801]). There is useful information about several Framers in Benjamin Rush, *Autobiography of Benjamin Rush: His "Travels Through Life" Together with His Commonplace Book for 1789–1813*, ed. George W. Corner (Princeton, NJ: Princeton University Press, 1948); *The Adams Papers*, Diary and Autobiography of John Adams, ed. L. H. Butterfield (Cambridge, MA: Harvard University Press, 1961); and *The Autobiography of Thomas Jefferson*, ed. Paul Leicester Ford (Philadelphia: University of Pennsylvania Press, 2005 [1914]), which has not yet been published in the ongoing *Papers of Thomas Jefferson* but can be accessed at Founders Online, https://founders.archives.gov/documents/Jefferson/98-01-02-1756.

Studies of the educations of individual Framers include Robert McCaughey, "The Education of Alexander Hamilton," *New-York Journal of American History* (Fall 2004): 25–31; Ralph Ketcham, "James Madison at Princeton," *The Princeton University Library Chronicle* 28 (1966): 24–54; Martin Clagett, "James Wilson—His Scottish Background: Corrections and Additions," *Pennsylvania History: A Journal of Mid-Atlantic Studies* 79, no. 2 (2012): 154–176; Andrew H. Browning, "Richard Dobbs Spaight in Ireland and Scotland: The Education of a North Carolina Founding Father," *North Carolina Historical Review* 94 (2017): 127–149, and Browning, "The Princeton Connections of William Richardson Davie: The Education of a North Carolina Founding Father," *North Carolina Historical Review* 95 (2018): 284–318.

Correspondence, diaries, and other writings can be found in the Founders' collected papers: William T. Hutchinson et al., eds., *The Papers of James Madison* (Chicago: University of Chicago Press, 1962–1977/Charlottesville: University of Virginia Press, 1977–); Leonard W. Labaree et al., eds., *The Papers of Benjamin Franklin* (New Haven, CT: Yale University Press 1959-); Donald Jackson et al., eds., *The Papers of George Washington* (Charlottesville: University of Virginia Press, 1968–); David Syrett, ed., *The Papers of Alexander Hamilton* (New York: Columbia University Press, 1961–1987). Also useful are Terry W. Lipscomb, ed., *Letters of Pierce Butler, 1790–1794* (Columbia: University of South Carolina Press, 2007); "The Southern Campaign of General Greene, 1781–2: Letters of Major William Pierce to St. George Tucker," *Magazine of American History* 7 (1891): 431–445; *Selected Correspondence and Papers of James Monroe*, ed. Daniel Preston et al. (Westport, CT: Greenwood Press, 2006); E. C. Burnett, ed., *Letters of the Members of the Continental Congress*, 8 vols. (Washington, DC: Carnegie Institute, 1921–1936); WILLIAM LIVINGSTON, *Independent Reflector*, ed. M. M. Klein (Cambridge, MA: Harvard University Press, 1963); JAMES WILSON, *Works*, ed. Robert McCloskey et al. (Cambridge, MA: Harvard University Press, 1967). Contemporary commentary on the Framers (marred by a few errors) has been collected in John P. Kaminski and Timothy Moore, *Assembly of Demigods* (Madison, WI: Parallel Press, 2012); see also Nathan Schachner, "Alexander Hamilton Viewed by His Friends: The Narratives of Robert Troup and Hercules Mulligan," *William and Mary Quarterly* 4, no. 2 (1947): 203–25, and Robert T. Conrad, ed., *Sanderson's Biography of the Signers to the Declaration of Independence*, rev. ed. (Philadelphia: Thomas Cowperthwait, 1846).

Of the many secondary sources on the lives of the Framers, several are particularly valuable on their education: Broadus Mitchell, "The Man Who Discovered Alexander Hamilton (Hugh Knox)," *Proceedings of the New Jersey Historical Society* 69 (1951): 88–114; John M. Mulder, "William Livingston: Propagandist Against Episcopacy," *Journal of Presbyterian History* 54 (1976); Garry Wills, *Cincinnatus: George Washington and the Enlightenment* (New York: Doubleday, 1984); and William Ewald, "James Wilson and the Scottish Enlightenment," *University of Pennsylvania Journal of Constitutional Law* 12 (2010): 1053–1114. A thoughtful analysis that I cannot ultimately agree with is Richard Matthews, *If Men Were Angels: James Madison and the*

Heartless Empire of Reason (Lawrence: University Press of Kansas, 1995). Some classic studies that remain useful include Gordon Wood, *The Creation of the American Republic* (Chapel Hill: University of North Carolina Press, 1969), Carl Bridenbaugh and Jessica Bridenbaugh, *Rebels and Gentlemen: Philadelphia in the Age of Benjamin Franklin* (New York: Reynal and Hitchcock, 1942), and Douglass Adair, *Fame and the Founding Fathers*, ed. Trevor Colbourn (New York: W. W. Norton, 1974).

The Constitutional Convention

The most important sources for the Constitutional Convention and the state ratifying conventions that followed are Max Farrand, ed., *The Records of the Federal Convention of 1787* (New Haven, CT: Yale University Press, 1937); James Hutson, ed., *Supplement to Max Farrand's Records of the Federal Convention of 1787* (New Haven, CT: Yale University Press, 1987); C. C. Tansill, ed., *Documents Illustrative of the Formation of the Union of the American States* (House Doc. 398, 69th Congress, 1st Session, 1927); Jonathan Elliot, ed., *Debates in the Several State Conventions on the Adoption of the Federal Constitution*, 2nd ed. (Philadelphia: Lippincott, 1996); John Kaminski and Gaspare Saladino, eds., *Documentary History of the Ratification of the Constitution* (Madison: University of Wisconsin Press 1990,1993); Herbert Storing and Murray Dry, *The Complete Anti-Federalist* (Chicago: University of Chicago Press, 1981). Of obvious importance is ALEXANDER HAMILTON, JAMES MADISON, and John Jay, *The Federalist Papers*, ed. Clinton Rossiter (New York: Mentor, 1961). Thought-provoking observations by a visitor to the Convention are found in Manasseh Cutler, *Life, Journals and Correspondence*, ed. William Parker Cutler et al. (Cincinnati: Clarke, 1888).

Many studies of greatly varying quality have been written about ideas and events that led to the Convention and may have been among the Framers' motives—especially their economic interests. These are some that are well worth reading: Akhil Reed Amar, *America's Constitution: A Biography* (New York: Random House, 2005); Joseph Ellis, *The Quartet: The Orchestrating of the Second American Revolution* (New York: Random House, 2015); David C. Hendrickson, *Peace Pact: The Lost World of American Founding* (Lawrence: University Press of Kansas, 2003); Charles A. Beard, *An Economic Interpretation of the Constitution of the United States* (New York: Macmillan, 1913); Forrest McDonald, *We the People: The Economic Origins of the Constitution* (Chicago: University of Chicago Press, 1958); Trevor Colbourn, *The Lamp of Experience* (Chapel Hill: University of North Carolina Press, 1965); Caroline Robbins, *The Eighteenth-Century Commonwealthman* (Cambridge, MA: Harvard University Press, 1959); J. G. A. Pocock, *The Machiavellian Moment: Florentine Political Thought and the Atlantic Republican Tradition* (Princeton, NJ: Princeton University Press, 1975); Stanley Elkins and Eric McKitrick, "Young Men of the Revolution," *Political Science Quarterly* 76, no. 2 (1961): 181–216; Jack Rakove, *Original Meanings: Politics and Ideas in the Making of the Constitution* (New York: Knopf, 1996); Robert McGuire, *To Form a More Perfect Union: A New Economic Interpretation of the Constitution* (New York: Oxford, 2003); and Mark Noll, *America's God: From Jonathan Edwards to Abraham Lincoln* (New York: Oxford University Press, 2002).

Of the numerous accounts of the events of the Convention itself, the best remains Clinton Rossiter, *1787: The Grand Convention* (New York: Macmillan, 1966). The most thorough account of the ideas behind the arguments is Forrest McDonald, *Novus Ordo Seclorum: The Intellectual Origins of the Constitution* (Lawrence: University Press of Kansas, 1985), and the most recent analysis is Michael Klarman, *The Framers' Coup: The Making of the Unites States Constitution* (New York: Oxford University Press, 2016). Catherine Drinker Bowen, *Miracle at Philadelphia: The Story of the Constitutional Convention May to September 1787* (Boston: Little, Brown, 1966), Richard Beeman, *Plain, Honest Men: The Making of the American Constitution* (New York: Random House, 2009), and David O. Stewart, *The Summer of 1787: The Men Who Invented the Constitution* (New York: Simon and Schuster, 2007), are readable if not particularly original. For a few closer, scholarly analyses of the debates that took place during the Convention and their connection to the Framers' education, readers should consult Jack Heyburn, "Gouverneur Morris and James Wilson at the Constitutional Convention," *Journal of Constitutional Law* 20 (2017): 169–199; William Ewald, "James Wilson and the Drafting of the Constitution," *University of Pennsylvania Journal of Constitutional Law* 10 (2008): 901–1004; James E. Pfander and Donald D. Birk, "Article III and the Scottish Judiciary," *Harvard Law Review* 124 (2011): 1613–1687; Jeremy C. Pope and Shawn Trier, "Reconsidering the Great Compromise at the Federal Convention of 1787: Deliberation and Agenda Effects on the Senate and Slavery," *American Journal of Political Science* 55, no. 2 (2011): 289–30; Iain McLean, "Adam Smith, James Wilson, and the U.S. Constitution," *Adam Smith Review* 8 (2015) 141–160; David Gelman, "Ideology and Participation: Examining the Constitutional Convention of 1787," *Political Research Quarterly* 71, no. 3 (2018): 546–559; Keith L. Dougherty and Jac C. Heckelman, "A Pivotal Voter from a Pivotal State: Roger Sherman at the Constitutional Convention," *American Political Science Review* 100 (2006): 297–302. Finally, for some of the arguments over ratification, see John P. Kaminski and Richard Leffler, eds., *Federalists and Antifederalists: The Debate over the Ratification of the Constitution* (Madison, WI: Madison House Publishers, 1998); Garry Wills, *Explaining America* (Garden City, NY: Doubleday, 1981); David Epstein, *The Political Theory of "The Federalist"* (Chicago: University of Chicago Press, 1984); and Robin Einhorn, "Patrick Henry's Case against the Constitution: The Structural Problem of Slavery," *Journal of the Early Republic* 22 (2002): 549–73.

Edinburgh, University of, x, 6, 9, 13, 33,
    47, 49, 68, 77, 124, 125, 161, 171–177,
    179–181, 189, 231, 240, 251–252, 256,
    275
Edwards, Jonathan, 12, 71, 72, 95, 96,
    106, 180, 187, 225, 228
Elementa Philosophica (Samuel Johnson),
    108, 195, 201, 210
Elitism, 257
    at the Convention, 1, 2, 11, 27, 218,
        251, 279, 282
    in colleges, 34–35, 210, 224–225
Elizabethtown Academy, ix, 20, 179,
    187–188, 213, 233
Ellsworth, Oliver, ix, 73, 107, 222, 283
    at the Convention, 7, 24, 26, 72, 76,
        157, 221, 247, 250, 252, 253, 255,
        258–260, 263–268, 270, 277, 280
    education of, 7, 21, 71, 72, 73, 94, 103,
        150, 153, 222, 227–229, 231, 236, 250,
        277
England, 46, 66, 68, 113, 120, 131, 135, 137,
    141, 142, 145, 167, 173, 174, 197, 214,
    224–225, 276
equal representation in Congress, 249,
    254, 256, 266. *See also* New Jersey
    Plan
equipoise. *See* overpoise
Essay on Human Understanding (John
    Locke), 46, 90, 129, 189, 240
ethics. *See* moral philosophy
Euripides, 129, 131
Evangelical Presbyterians, Scotland,
    164, 232, 242
Evangelical protestants (modern), 26, 242
executive. *See* president of the United
    States

faction, 1, 11, 49, 132, 162, 242, 244, 248,
    259–260, 276
Fagg's Manor school, 186, 225
Fairfax, Sarah (Sally), 63
F.H.C. *See* Flat Hat Club
Federal Convention of 1787. *See*
    Constitutional Convention

Federalist, The (Hamilton, Jay, and
    Madison), 24, 40, 44, 49, 132, 162,
    217, 218, 242, 243, 246, 249, 258,
    259, 274, 275
Ferguson, Adam, 11, 47, 108, 136, 154,
    162, 174, 176, 232, 240, 242, 252, 259,
    276
Few, William, xi, xiii, 20, 264
    education of, 6, 41, 55, 56, 59, 60, 150,
        156
    at the Convention, 27, 75, 270, 278
financial aid (at colleges), 35–36, 115, 164,
    209, 231
Finley, Samuel, 72, 171, 179, 180, 183–188,
    190, 225–226, 228, 230, 231
Fithian, Philip Vickers, 67, 235–238
Fitzsimons, Thomas, x, 132, 133
    at the Convention, 27, 278
    education of, 12, 133
Flat Hat Club, 36, 37, 93, 115, 116, 121
Flynt, Henry, 88, 90
France, 4, 62, 72, 76, 130, 131, 168, 172,
    174, 276
Franklin, Benjamin, ix, xiii, 5, 7, 20, 30,
    74, 75, 79, 104, 125, 130, 140, 164,
    172, 175, 176, 185, 194, 204, 221, 240,
    251, 283
    education of, 5, 6, 28, 41, 43, 55–58,
        60, 182
    and College and Academy of
        Philadelphia, 40–41, 46, 69, 195–200
    at the Convention, 18, 19, 20, 24, 27,
        59, 164, 205, 250–251, 253, 266, 271,
        278
Freneau, Philip, 237–238, 241
frequency of speaking at the
    Convention, 74–76, 82, 86, 108, 154,
    171, 205, 251, 255, 262, 263, 271
Friends, Society of, 67, 183, 197–199,
    201, 209
Friends' Public School, x, xiv, 83, 202

Garrick, David, 140, 148, 251
Gerry, Elbridge, ix, xiii, 19, 23, 86, 107,
    130, 248, 282, 283

Hopkins School, ix, 79, 107
Horace (Quintus Horatius Flaccus), 66, 73, 114, 129, 145, 163, 165, 186
Houdon, Jean-Antoine, 31
House of Representatives, 120, 234, 239, 256, 261
Houston, William Churchill, ix, xiv, 21, 82, 190–191, 193, 222, 245
  at the Convention, 19, 179
  education of, 5, 7, 152, 156, 179, 190, 222, 225, 231
Houstoun, John, 68, 142, 156
Houstoun, William, xi, xiv, 218, 283
  at the Convention, 266, 270
  education of, 4, 68, 137, 141–142, 144, 149, 156
Hume, David, 5, 8, 10, 11, 28, 38, 44, 47, 48, 49, 50, 58, 72, 91, 101, 151, 154, 164, 166–167, 172, 174, 176, 177, 216, 217, 232, 241, 242, 244, 250, 254, 257–259, 276, 278
Hutcheson, Francis, 3, 6, 10, 11, 12, 28, 33, 38, 42, 45, 47, 48, 49, 65, 72, 89, 91, 101, 108, 132, 133, 136, 162, 165–166, 181, 182, 183, 195, 198–199, 201, 202, 211, 215, 223, 232, 240–242, 244, 253, 254, 258, 259, 262, 271, 278

idealism. See immaterialism
immaterialism, 12, 48, 166, 196, 201, 232
Independent Reflector, 97, 207–209, 213, 219, 237
Independent Whig, 207
Indian Queen (Philadelphia inn), 24, 266, 267
Indian School (Harvard), 34
Indian School (William and Mary), 34, 112, 115, 120
Ingersoll, Jared (father of the Framer), 97, 103–104, 107, 140
Ingersoll, Jared (Framer), ix, 107, 130
  at the Convention, 87, 271
  education of, 21, 79, 87, 94, 103–105, 107, 137, 140, 144
Inner Temple, xi, 139, 141–142, 156

Inns of Court, 4, 12, 33, 67, 107, 125, 127, 137, 139–149, 157, 172–173, 251, 272, 276. See also Inner Temple; Middle Temple
Inquiry into the Original of the Ideas of Beauty and Virtue (Francis Hutcheson), 48, 65, 89, 163, 211, 212
Ireland, x, 4, 8, 12, 13, 68, 131–137, 161, 172, 177–179, 184, 224, 226, 228
Isocrates, 38, 39, 88, 211

Jackson, Cyril, 128, 298
Jay, John, 22, 24, 211, 218
Jefferson, Thomas, 7, 23, 30–31, 40, 42, 60, 66, 114, 115, 169, 172, 220, 228, 238
  attitude toward Convention, 30, 169, 282
  education of, 6, 45, 113, 153, 162, 188
  as legal mentor, 150, 155
Jenifer, Daniel, of St. Thomas, x, 20, 22, 65, 248, 259, 283
  at the Convention, 251, 270
  education of, 65, 83
Johnson, Samuel (educator), ix, xiii, 69, 95, 97, 101, 108, 195–196, 204–207, 209, 210, 218, 225
Johnson, Samuel (poet and lexicographer), xiii, 107, 129, 175
Johnson, William Samuel, ix, xiii, 21, 33, 108, 207, 218, 267
  at the Convention, 17, 24, 27, 87, 157, 251, 255, 270, 271, 278
  education of, 5, 20, 34, 43, 69, 87, 94, 95, 97–98, 101, 107, 154
Junto, 58, 75, 175
Juvenal (Decimus Junius Juvenalis), 145, 163, 211

Kames, Lord (Henry Home), 11, 47, 58, 101, 136, 154, 174, 176, 227, 232, 241, 242
Killen, William, x, 67
Kimber, Edward, 62, 86, 110, 122

King, Rufus, ix, 86, 107, 218, 248, 269, 283
  at the Convention, 17, 24, 80, 84, 92, 107, 108, 157, 247, 253, 256, 261–264, 266, 271, 272, 277, 278
  education of, xiv, 5, 8, 44, 70, 71, 78, 80, 87, 92, 93, 107, 150–151, 154
King's College (New York), ix, xiii, 4, 5, 6, 13, 24, 34, 69, 94, 121, 124, 179, 183, 193, 195, 200, 206–219, 245–246, 257, 271, 276, 277
  in American Revolution, 211, 213–215, 223
  controversy over founding of, 32, 197, 206–209
  curriculum, 29, 33, 38, 39, 45, 48, 163, 167, 199, 201, 210, 211, 252
  faculty, 210, 211, 212
  geographical make-up, 38, 210, 251
  regulations, 209, 210, 212
  student life, 36, 210, 212, 214
  students' family backgrounds, 38, 210, 211, 251
King William's School, x, 83
Knox, Hugh, 187–188, 224

lands, speculation in, 74, 88, 108, 121–122, 187, 221, 249, 268
Langdon, John, ix, 172
  at the Convention, 278
  education of, 5, 79
Lansing, John, ix, 248
  at the Convention, 20, 25, 81
  education of, 7, 21, 81, 82
"large" states, 28, 107, 108, 249, 266, 268, 270. See also Great Compromise
law
  civil, 144, 154, 165, 168–169, 200, 250
  common, 137, 154, 168169, 173
  education in, 4, 99, 106, 130, 138–157, 168, 216, 276
Lawson, Peter, 73, 74
Lectures on Moral Philosophy (John Witherspoon), 28, 44, 48, 183, 221, 232–233, 239–244, 246, 254, 261, 276

Lee, Arthur, 173, 175
Lee, Charles, 119–120
Leiden, University of, 125, 172, 245
Liberty Hall Academy, 192
libraries, 40
  academic, 40, 46, 47, 91–92, 95, 100–101, 112, 115, 127, 139, 143, 164, 165, 167–168, 192, 211, 215, 216, 223–224, 230
  private, 11, 40, 56, 59, 63, 64, 65, 73, 74, 75, 82, 112, 116, 133, 150, 153, 171, 190, 210, 211, 277, 278
Library Company. See Philadelphia Subscription Library
Lives of the Noble Greeks and Romans (Plutarch), 10, 39, 56, 65, 67, 135
Livingston, William, ix, 3, 5, 17, 21, 22, 28, 40, 85, 104, 172, 187–188, 217, 246, 275, 283
  and American Whig, 108, 237
  at the Convention, 2, 87, 251, 270, 271
  education of, 5, 20, 69, 73, 81, 82, 87, 94–98, 107, 139–141, 150–152, 154
  and King's College, 40, 207–209, 213
Livy (Titus Livius), 4, 39, 88, 114, 122, 129, 211, 226
Locke, John, 30, 41, 42, 45–47, 58, 65, 79, 89, 90, 93, 95, 105, 106, 114, 122, 129, 186, 199, 201, 216, 217, 242, 250, 253, 255, 258
Log College, 179, 180, 186. See also Tennent, William
logic, 9, 33, 69, 89, 96, 99, 112, 114, 129, 146, 154, 164, 182, 186, 195, 197, 200, 201, 205, 223, 228, 229
London, 57, 99, 104, 107, 113, 137, 140–142, 144–147, 157, 171–174, 185, 225, 232, 252
loyalists, 93–94, 210, 214, 215, 223, 240

Machiavelli, Niccolò, 47, 65, 155, 187, 242, 257
MacPherson, John, 151–152, 154, 204, 227
Madison, James, Jr. (Framer), x, xiii, xiv, 21, 22, 44, 47, 49, 50, 51, 114,

Westminster School, xi, 4, 123, 125, 126, 129, 130, 192, 252, 275
Whitefield, George, 98–99
Whittelsey, Chauncey, 97, 98, 107
Wilkes, John, 225, 251
William and Mary, College of, x, xi, xiii, 4, 6, 8, 9, 12, 28, 36, 62, 66, 86, 106, 109–123, 124, 132, 182, 214, 245, 246, 255, 256, 259, 272, 275, 277, 278
   in American Revolution, 94, 121, 122, 223
   curriculum, 38, 44, 46, 112–114, 120, 227, 244
   faculty, 6, 113–116, 118, 171, 189
   founding, 11–112
   geographical make-up, 7, 38, 68, 83, 222, 251, 252
   regulations, 112, 114
   student life, 33, 36, 37, 38, 41, 115, 126
   students' family backgrounds, 38, 111, 222, 251
Williams, Henry, x, 61, 62, 64
Williamson, Hugh, x, 20, 23, 173, 175, 185, 231, 264, 283
   at the Convention, 24, 171, 179, 184, 205, 256, 262, 264, 267–269, 271
   education of, 5, 7, 20, 49, 161, 171–173, 175, 177, 179, 181, 183–185, 192, 199, 201, 275
Wilson, James, x, 172, 283
   at the Convention, 10, 20, 24, 28, 49, 68, 74, 134, 157, 163, 169–171, 202, 203, 205, 243, 249, 253, 255–261, 263, 264, 266, 269, 271, 272, 277, 278, 280, 303
   education of, 4, 6, 36, 47, 49, 136, 154, 161–162, 164–165, 167–170, 250, 252, 263, 275
Wilson, Woodrow, 221, 226
Winthrop, John, 42, 87, 90
Witherspoon, John, 6, 39, 68, 201, 220–221, 240–242, 254, 258, 321

   as educator, 10, 28, 42, 47, 48, 72, 121, 162, 163, 166, 171, 177, 183, 186, 188, 189, 210, 214, 223, 226, 231–235, 238, 240–246, 252, 257, 259, 262, 275, 276, 321
   as patriot, 152, 214, 220, 221, 239, 240, 244–245
   and Scottish Enlightenment, 163, 166, 240–244
Wollaston, William, 58, 99, 100, 105, 106
Wordsworth, William, 78
Wren, Christopher, 32, 186
Wythe, George, x, 21, 30, 73, 111, 114, 118, 155–156
   at the Convention, 19, 61, 157
   education of, 60, 84, 150

Xenophon, 88, 129, 132, 199, 201, 210, 228

Yale College, ix, xi, 6, 8, 9, 12, 20, 28, 34, 47, 60, 79, 84, 85, 86, 88, 94–109, 110, 111, 124, 139, 150, 157, 180, 182, 204, 207, 222, 245, 246, 250, 251, 255, 259, 270, 271, 275, 278
   curriculum, 11, 38, 44, 46, 47, 58, 87, 89, 96, 97, 99, 100, 105, 106, 199, 201, 223, 227, 229, 244, 250, 252, 263
   faculty, 97, 99, 103, 105, 194
   founding, 94–95
   geographical make-up, 7, 38, 222, 252
   regulations, 33, 70, 96–97, 99–100, 102–105, 227, 230, 235
   religious controversy, 32, 69, 71, 72, 87, 94, 95, 98, 104
   student life, 5, 12, 36, 37, 96–100, 102–104, 229
   students' family backgrounds, 35–36, 38, 235
Yates, Robert, ix, 20, 248, 255
   at the Convention, 24, 25, 253, 266
   education of, 7, 21, 81